Rick Steves®

NAPLES & THE AMALFI COAST

I DECUMANI
PIZZERIA
61

CONTENTS

Welcome to Rick Steves' Europe

Travel is intensified living—maximum thrills per minute and one of the last great sources of legal adventure. Travel is freedom. It's recess, and we need it.

I discovered a passion for European travel as a teen and have been sharing it ever since—through my bus tours, public television and radio shows, and travel guidebooks. Over the years, I've taught millions of travelers how to best enjoy Europe's blockbuster sights—and experience "Back Door" discoveries that most tourists miss.

This book offers a balanced mix: the gritty, urban intensity of Naples; the best-in-Europe ancient cityscapes at the foot of Mount Vesuvius (Pompeii and Herculaneum); the sublime coastal beauty of Sorrento and the Amalfi Coast; and dreamy castaway islands in the Bay of Naples. It's selective: Rather than covering every island or coastal village, I recommend only the best. And it's in-depth: My self-guided museum tours and town walks provide insight into this region's vibrant history and today's living, breathing culture.

I advocate traveling simply and smartly. Take advantage of my money- and time-saving tips on sightseeing, transportation, and more. Try local, characteristic alternatives to expensive hotels and restaurants. In many ways, spending more money only builds a thicker wall between you and what you traveled so far to see.

We visit Italy to experience it—to become temporary locals. Thoughtful travel engages us with the world, as we learn to appreciate other cultures and new ways to measure quality of life.

Judging by readers' positive feedback, I believe this book will help you enjoy a fun, affordable, and rewarding vacation—whether it's your first trip or your tenth.

Buon viaggio! Happy travels!

Rick Steves

NAPLES & THE AMALFI COAST

Gritty Naples, serene Sorrento, poignant Pompeii, and the sumptuous Amalfi Coast. Few places combine intense yet entertaining urban chaos with sublime natural beauty—all within a short train, bus, car, or boat ride—like this unforgettable slice of Italy.

If you like Italy as far south as Rome, go farther south—it gets better. Italy intensifies as you plunge deeper. And Naples is Italy in the extreme—its best (birthplace of pizza) and its worst (home of the Camorra, Naples' "family" of organized crime).

Naples is southern Italy's leading city; the second-biggest metro area in Italy, after Milan; one of Italy's poorest corners; and one of the most densely populated places in all of Europe. Its more than one million people live in a metropolis with few open spaces or parks. While in many ways it feels like an urban jungle, Naples surprises the observant traveler with its impressive knack for living, eating, and raising children with good humor and decency. Overcome your fear of being run down or ripped off long enough to talk with

people. Focus not on the graffiti but on the song merchants sing in the markets. Enjoy a few smiles and jokes with the man running the neighborhood tripe shop, or the woman taking her day-care class on a walk along traffic-clogged streets.

Naples is not just a city; it's an entire region. The Bay of Naples, slopes of Mount Vesuvius, and nearby coastline and islands are bursting with sightseeing options. Vesuvius is the (currently) slumbering volcano that looms, Mount Doom-like, over the entire Naples region. It famously erupted in AD 79, burying in hot ash the busy hive of humanity that lived between its caldera and the bay.

Two of those towns have been excavated by modern archaeologists and are among Europe's most compelling ancient sites: Pompeii, once a busy commercial port of 20,000 souls; and Herculaneum, a smaller community of 5,000. There's no better place to get a glimpse of Roman life, two millennia ago, than right here.

Across the Bay of Naples from the big city, perching on its cliff, is Sorrento—the sleepy, pristine yin to Naples' busy, chaotic yang. This charming resort town is a handy transit hub and a fine home base for exploring the region.

Sorrento is also the natural springboard for the stunning Amalfi Coast, just south of the Bay of Naples. This breathtaking shoreline is renowned for its sheer cliffs, crazy cantilevered houses, shimmering seaside beauty, and

Limoncello captures Italy's sunshine in a delicious form; Mount Vesuvius looms over the Bay of Naples

Naples: Birthplace of Pizza

Pizza—Naples' great culinary creation—has been exported around the world. And yet, it still tastes best in its birthplace. If this sounds like hyperbole...come to Naples and find out for yourself.

The origins of pizza date back 2,500 years, to when flatbreads were dressed with oil, salt, herbs, and sometimes cheese. Tomatoes arrived in Campania only after Columbus' journeys to the Americas, and were not routinely used with flatbread until the early 19th century. But once Italians figured out this recipe, the Neapolitans perfected it.

An ideal Neapolitan-style pizza must have a light crust—more chewy than crispy. To keep the pizza delicate, Neapolitan pizzerias often make the crust the day before, using very little yeast, and then they let it rise for 12 to 15 hours. They brag it takes several years of practice to get the dough just right. (Lesser pizzerias—especially outside of Naples—use ample yeast to effect a quicker rise, but this toughens the crust and gives it a yeasty flavor.) The *pizzaiolo* (pizza maker) makes an individual pie for each diner and bakes it in a very hot wood-burning oven for about three minutes.

Local *pizzaioli* use very few toppings, and the ones they use are of the best possible quality. For example, a classic pizza margherita, named after the first Italian queen, uses just three in the colors of the Italian flag. First comes the fresh white *mozzarella di bufala* (made from the milk of water buffaloes—or, in a pinch, absolutely fresh mozzarella made of cow's milk). To this are added red San Marzano tomatoes, a green basil leaf, and a few drops of good olive oil. A pizza ▶▶▶

Naples' pizza is known for its delicate crust and simple ingredients, baked in a wood-fired oven to delicious perfection.

▶▶▶ marinara contains tomato sauce, garlic, and oregano, but no cheese. What matters is not the quantity of ingredients but the quality.

Around the Naples region, there are a few famous pizza places, which can be fun to try. But a neighborhood dive can be just as good—look for a happy commotion of locals eating there. Most pizzerias offer both takeout and eat-in, and pizza is often the only thing on the menu. Neapolitans typically drink beer or mineral water with pizza, rarely wine.

Another kind of pizza is the calzone, in which the crust is folded over to enclose the ingredients, which can include cheese, veggies, and meats. This originated as a cheap and filling alternative to real pizza during the postwar years, and remains a beloved street food.

No taste of Naples is complete without a pizza. Head to a humble Neapolitan pizzeria for an evening of delicious, inexpensive indulgence. ■

A pizza margherita is topped with mozzarella made from the milk of water buffaloes.

postcard-pretty towns—including posh Positano, exotic Amalfi, cliff-capping Ravello, and the untouristy flip side of the coast, Maiori and Minori. It's all tied together by a scenic, precipitous road where white-knuckled drivers hug the curves between viewpoints.

Paestum, even farther south and worth a side trip for those interested in the ancient world, is a collection of 2,500-year-old temples...built not by ancient Romans but by the Greek traders who established Magna Graecia (Greater Greece).

And there are several holiday islands off the coast of Naples. Capri, favored by the jet set, is an upscale choice—and has been for a very long time (it was a favorite getaway for Roman emperors). This gorgeous place, with its stark limestone cliffs and sea stacks, lush gardens, elaborate villas, and famous Blue Grotto aquatic cave, continues to entice visitors. Across the bay, pastel Procida is the Back Door alternative island—less popular, less glitzy, less expensive, but just as beautiful.

Seaside Naples anchors the otherwise rugged and mountainous region of Campania, which is home to about five million people. Taken together, the Naples area is a congested, complicated knot of humanity. That Neapolitan sprawl comes with its own distinct culture and personality, which can feel foreign even to fellow Italians. Naples is more brazen and disorderly—but also more intensely devoted to the delicately crafted Nativity scenes called *presepi.*

Many of Campania's hallmarks are edible. This region is famous for the sweet, delicious San Marzano tomatoes (long, skinny, and pointy at one end); for *mozzarella di bufala,* made from the milk of water buffaloes; for a variety of deep-fried street foods; for large, sweet lemons used for making *limoncello* and other drinks and treats; and for delectable pastries, including the delightfully crunchy *sfogliatelle,* delicate phyllo layers filled with ricotta. And, of

Sorrento's main drag, Corso Italia; Positano's scenery and sand

course, this region—and Naples specifically—is famous for its pizza (see sidebar).

Visitors to this area face one important decision: How much Naples do you want to include? This big city is not to everyone's taste, so be realistic about its pros and cons. Travelers who enjoy a city crammed with chaos settle in here as a home base for seeing everything in this book and beyond. Others use it strictly as a transit hub to reach its surrounding towns, ancient sites, coastline, and islands.

For me, the mark of a good traveler is how much they enjoy Naples. I make time to embrace the intensity of the city, which deserves at least a full day to tour its museums and churches, stroll its hectic and entertaining streets, and sample its famous pizza—before (if you choose) relaxing in the more genteel resorts to the south.

This region of Italy offers an *antipasto misto* of travel thrills: From the urban intensity of Naples to the serenity of Sorrento, from glamorous Capri to sparkling Amalfi towns, from ancient Pompeii to even more ancient Paestum—this is Italy's coast with the most.

Naples & the Amalfi Coast's Top Destinations

Mamma mia! There's a lot to see in and around Naples and the Amalfi Coast. This overview categorizes the region's top destinations into must-see places (to help first-time travelers plan their trip) and worth-it places (for those with extra time or special interests). I've also suggested a minimum number of days to allow per destination.

MUST-SEE DESTINATIONS

▲▲▲Amalfi Coast (allow 1-2 days)

Traveling the Amalfi Coast's cliff-hanging road ranks among Italy's top experiences, whether as a day trip or with an overnight at a coastal town. Positano, with its big beauty and bigger prices, lures travelers with Sophia Loren dreams for an overnight. The historic maritime town of Amalfi and the romantic clifftop town of Ravello are popular stops, worth an hour or two each. And the beach towns of Minori and Maiori somehow stay under the mass-tourism radar in spite of delightful Riviera charm.

WORTH-IT DESTINATIONS

▲▲Naples (allow 0.5-3 days)

This massive city—sprawling between Mount Vesuvius and the Bay of Naples—feels like a world unto itself. It's a once-genteel transit hub with some excellent sightseeing (most notably its Archaeological Museum, with the finest treasures from Pompeii); a gritty, intense port city; a culinary center justifiably famous for its pizza; and perhaps Europe's best and most vibrant destination for thriving street life. You'll likely pass through Naples on your visit to this region; it's worth at least a half-day, but more adventurous travelers will crave more time—and may choose to home-base here for their entire trip.

▲Procida (1 day)

Pretty and pastel Procida is your ideal destination for a peaceful island break from Naples. This tiny island, with its humble fishing port and sleepy beaches, is just a short ferry ride across the bay.

Welcome to Positano; medieval watchtower near Maiori; budget-friendly street food in Naples; Naples' Capodimonte art museum; a quiet Procida street

Frescoes in Pompeii; sampling limoncello in Sorrento; Capri's soul-nourishing scenery; Greek temple in Paestum

▲▲Pompeii and Nearby (half-day)

South of Naples are the ruins of famous Pompeii (worth ▲▲▲) and smaller Herculaneum, both thriving ancient cities that were smothered by Mount Vesuvius in AD 79. The sites are an easy stop between Naples and Sorrento; of the two, Pompeii is better, while Herculaneum is more compact and easier to see. Visitors can also ascend the still-steaming Vesuvius itself.

▲Sorrento (1.5 days with 2-4 nights)

Sorrento is both a busy port and a pleasant resort town. It features lemon-scented lanes, grand views over the Bay of Naples, a good selection of hotels and restaurants, and convenient connections to nearby sights by train, bus, or boat. While it offers no big-league sights, Sorrento is the most appealing choice for home-basing in this region. Several nights here with day trips to Capri, Pompeii, and the Amalfi Coast can make a lot of sense.

▲▲Capri (1 day)

Known for its stunning views and tourist hordes, this tiny island is home to the fabled Blue Grotto, with its otherworldly azure water (and often long waits).

▲Paestum (1 day)

South of the Amalfi Coast, this site predates most of the great Roman landmarks by centuries. Paestum is crowned with well-preserved Greek temples from a time this storied land was Magna Graecia, or Greater Greece.

Planning Your Trip

To plan your trip, you'll need to design your itinerary—choosing where and when to go, how you'll travel, and how many days to spend at each destination. For my best general advice on sightseeing, accommodations, restaurants, and more, see the Practicalities chapter.

DESIGNING AN ITINERARY

As you read this book and learn your options...

Choose your top destinations.

My recommended itinerary (see the sidebar on page 19) gives you an idea of how much you can reasonably see in a week, but you can adapt it to fit your own interests and time frame. A key choice is how much—or how little—time you want to spend in Naples itself, and whether you want to overnight there or in a lower-impact resort town nearby.

Decide when to go.

Southern Italy's best travel months are May, June, September, and October. They're also the busiest and most expensive times to visit. Crowds aside, these months combine the convenience of peak season with pleasant weather.

The heat in July and August can be brutal; temperatures frequently hit the 90s. Fortunately, most accommodations come with air-conditioning. August is also when many Italians take their summer vacations; big cities like Naples tend to be relatively quiet, but beach resorts—like most of the other towns in this book—are jammed (with higher hotel prices).

Winter offers cooler temperatures and fewer tourists, except on major holidays. Expect shorter hours for sights, fewer activities, and many accommodations closed for the season.

Connect the dots.

My recommended itinerary starts and ends in Naples, making it simple to arrive and depart on a round-trip flight. Begin your search for transatlantic flights at Google Flights.

Once in Italy, trains, buses, and boats connect the destinations in this book with relative ease (even if sorting through your options can feel a bit daunting). A simple Google search will give you a general idea, while the "Connections" sections in each chapter provide typical schedules, advice, and official websites.

I would never rent a car for travel in this region. Traffic, parking, and car-free destinations make driving a regrettable choice. (That's why, for the benefit of your trip, I'll give you no more info about driving!)

To maximize efficiency and minimize stress, some travelers hire a private driver for key Amalfi Coast journeys or join a shared tour (described in that chapter).

If you're continuing beyond Naples, slick trains connect Naples and Rome (several per hour, in about 1.5 hours). From there, you'll be impressed by Italy's impressive train system (www.trenitalia.com). For connections elsewhere in Europe (or longer-distance trips within Italy), budget flights can be

Naples' Galleria Umberto I shopping mall (left); Toledo Metro station (below); and Castle Nuovo (next page)

an alternative to long train rides. Check Skyscanner.com for intra-European flights (but keep in mind air travel's larger carbon footprint).

Write out a day-by-day itinerary.

Figure out how many destinations you can comfortably fit in your time frame. Don't overdo it—few travelers wish they'd hurried more. Allow enough days per stop (see estimates on pages 12-15). Minimize one-night stands. It can be worth taking a late-afternoon train or boat to settle into a town for two consecutive nights—and gain a full uninterrupted day for sightseeing.

Staying in a home base (most likely Naples or Sorrento) and making day trips can be more time-efficient than changing locations and hotels. Pompeii, Capri, and Paestum work better as side trips than as overnights.

Take sight closures into account. Avoid visiting a town on the one day a week its must-see sights are closed. Check if any holidays or festivals fall during your trip—these attract crowds and can close sights (for the latest, visit Italy's tourist website, www.italia.it). Note major sights where advance tickets are smart or a free Rick Steves audio tour is available.

Give yourself some slack. Every trip, and every traveler, needs downtime for doing laundry, picnic shopping, people-watching, and so on. Pace yourself. Assume you will return.

Naples and the Amalfi Coast's Best One-Week Trip by Public Transportation

Day	Plan	Sleep
1	Arrive in Naples	Naples
2	Naples	Naples
3	See more of Naples, or day-trip to Paestum (1.5 hours each way)	Naples
4	Morning train to Sorrento (or more time in Naples, then train)	Sorrento
5	Day-trip to Pompeii; enjoy Sorrento with the rest of your day	Sorrento
6	Scenic Amalfi Coast drive (by bus, shared tour, or private driver); return to Sorrento or settle in to Minori or Maiori	Sorrento or Minori/Maiori (Amalfi Coast)
7	From Sorrento, side-trip to Capri; or enjoy a beach day in Minori or Maiori	Sorrento or Minori/Maiori
8	Return to Naples (2 hours) and fly home...or link to your next European destination	

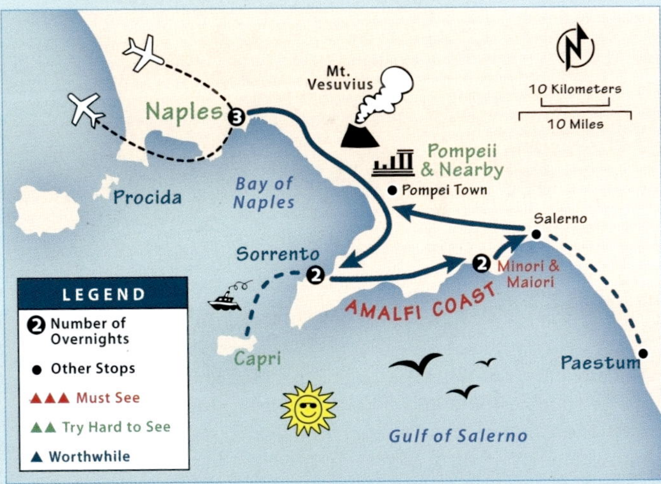

Notes: This plan offers roughly equal tastes of Naples and Sorrento. Depending on your interests, you could instead home-base in Sorrento and see Naples as a day trip; or settle in to Naples and day-trip to Sorrento and the Amalfi Coast (long but doable). Efficient sightseers squeeze Pompeii into Day 4 and see Capri on Day 5, leaving Day 7 free for the beach. Farther afield, Paestum is skippable for those uninterested in ancient sites.

Trip Costs per Person

Run a reality check on your dream trip. You'll have major transportation costs in addition to daily expenses.

Flight: A round-trip flight from the US to Italy costs about $900-1,500, depending on where you fly from and when.

Public Transportation: Once in this region, fares are cheap. You can see everything in my suggested itinerary by train or bus for a total of well under $100, including some short taxi rides within the towns and cities.

AVERAGE DAILY EXPENSES PER PERSON

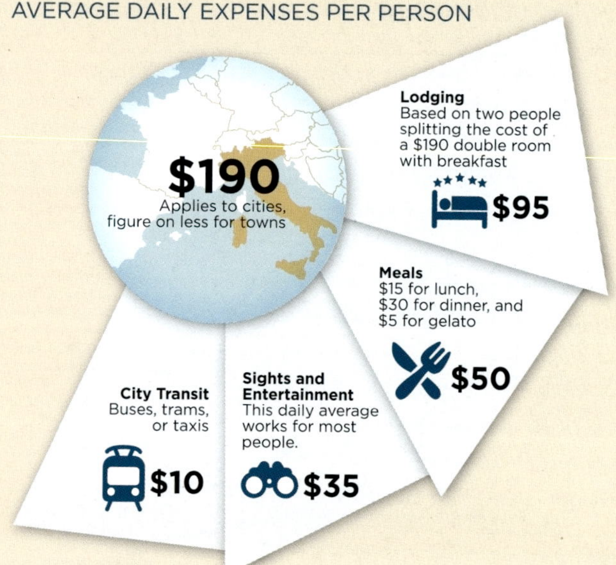

Budget Tips

To cut your daily expenses, take advantage of the deals you'll find throughout Italy and mentioned in this book. Public transit rather than taxis, picnics rather than restaurants, and alternatives to fancy hotels all save plenty. When you splurge, keep in mind that experiences you'll always remember (hiring a private guide, taking a food tour, scaling that volcano) are the lasting value. Rather than spending time and money souvenir shopping, focus on collecting memories. And good travelers find that many favorite moments are the free ones.

Some hotels, restaurants, and tour companies offer discounts to my readers. Look for the RS% symbol in the listings in this book.

BEFORE YOU GO

You'll have a smoother trip if you tackle a few things ahead of time. For more details on these topics, see the Practicalities chapter and RickSteves.com, which has helpful travel-tip articles and videos.

Make sure your travel documents are in order. If your passport expires within six months of your return date, you need to renew it (allow eight weeks). Get passport and country-specific travel info at Travel.State.gov. Be aware of entry requirements; you may need to register with the European Travel Info and Authorization System (ETIAS, quick and easy process, https://travel-europe.europa.eu/etias), and if traveling through the United Kingdom, the Electronic Travel Authorization (ETA, www.gov.uk/visas-immigration).

Arrange your transportation. Book your international flights (start your search online at Google Flights or Kayak). Figure out your transportation options. It's worth thinking about buying essential train tickets online in advance, getting a rail pass, renting a car, or booking cheap European flights. (You can wing it once you're there, but it may cost more.) Drivers: Consider bringing an International Driving Permit (sold at AAA offices in the US, www.aaa.com) along with your license.

Book rooms well in advance, especially if your trip falls during peak season or any major holidays or festivals.

Reserve ahead for key sights and experiences. Make reservations or buy tickets in advance for major sights. In Naples, you must reserve a time slot for the Cappella Sansevero, and you'll avoid long lines for the underground tours by purchasing your ticket online. A timed-entry ticket is required to hike to the summit of Mount Vesuvius, and you may need one to guarantee entry to Pompeii.

It's also smart to book ahead for experiences such as a food tour or hiring a local guide.

Consider travel insurance. Compare the cost of insurance to the cost of your potential loss. Understand what protections your credit card might offer and whether your existing insurance (health, homeowners, or renters) covers you and your possessions overseas.

Manage your money. "Tap-to-pay" or "contactless" cards are widely accepted and simple to use. You may need your credit card's PIN for some purchases—request it if you don't have one. Alert your bank that you'll be using your debit and credit cards in Europe. Don't bring euros from home; you can withdraw euros from ATMs in Europe.

Use your smartphone smartly. Sign up for an international service plan, or plan to rely on Wi-Fi. Download any useful apps you'll want on the road, such as maps, translators, and Rick Steves Audio Europe (see sidebar).

Pack light. You'll walk with your luggage more than you think. I travel for weeks with a single carry-on bag and a day pack. Use the packing checklist in the appendix as a guide.

Rick's Free Audio Tours and Video Clips

Rick Steves Audio Europe, a free app, makes it easy to download my audio tours and radio interviews and listen to them offline as you travel. For this book, the app includes audio tours of my City Walk and Archaeological Museum tour in Naples, and Pompeii tour (look for the ∩), plus many interviews relating to Naples and the Amalfi Coast from my public radio show. Scan the QR code to find it in your app store or visit RickSteves.com/AudioEurope.

Rick Steves Classroom Europe, a powerful tool for teachers, is also useful for travelers. This video library contains about 600 short clips excerpted from my public television series. Enjoy these videos as you sort through options for your trip and to better understand what you'll see in Europe. Check it out at Classroom.RickSteves.com.

Travel Smart

Italy, which seems as orderly as spilled spaghetti, actually functions quite well. If you have a positive attitude, equip yourself with good information (this book), and expect to travel smart, you will.

Read—and reread—this book. To have an "A" trip, be an "A" student. Note opening hours of sights, closed days, crowd-beating tips, and whether reservations are required or advisable. Check the latest at RickSteves.com/update.

Be your own tour guide. As you travel, get up-to-date info on sights, reserve tickets and tours, reconfirm hotels, and check transit connections. Upon arrival in a new town, lay the groundwork for a smooth departure; confirm the train, bus, or road you'll take when you leave.

Outsmart thieves. Pickpockets abound in crowded places—especially places where tourists congregate. Treat commotions as smokescreens for theft. Take commonsense precautions with your valuables, especially credit cards and cash (store them securely). Don't set phones or other important items down on counters or café tabletops, where they can be quickly stolen or easily forgotten (and don't hang day packs on the backs of chairs).

Minimize potential loss. Keep expensive gear to a minimum. Bring copies or take photos of important documents to aid in replacement if they're lost or stolen. Back up devices to the cloud as you travel.

Beat the summer heat. If it's hot, start your day early, take a midday siesta, and resume your sightseeing later. Wear sunscreen and drink lots of water. Do what you can to avoid long lines in the sun. Churches offer a cool haven (but dress modestly—no bare shoulders or shorts). Join the *passeggiata*, when locals stroll in the cool of the evening.

Guard your time and energy. Taking a taxi or Uber can be a good value if it saves you a long wait for a cheap bus or an exhausting walk across town. To avoid long lines, follow my crowd-beating tips, such as buying tickets in advance or sight-seeing early or late.

Be flexible. Even if you have a well-planned itinerary, expect changes, strikes, closures, sore feet, bad weather, and so on. Your Plan B could turn out to be even better.

Attempt the language. Many Italians speak English—especially young people and those in the tourist trade. And apps such as Google Translate work for on-the-go translation help. But if you memorize and use some Italian, even just a few pleasantries, you'll get more smiles and make more friends. The survival phrases near the end of this book are a good starting point.

Connect with the culture. Interacting with locals carbonates your experience. Enjoy the friendliness of the Italian people. Ask questions; most locals are happy to point you in their idea of the right direction. Set up your own quest for the best piazza, scenic view, or pizza. When an opportunity pops up, make it a habit to say "yes."

Your next stop: Naples and the Amalfi Coast!

NAPLES

Napoli

The pulse of Italy throbs in Naples. Like Cairo or Mumbai, it's shocking and captivating at the same time, the closest thing to "reality travel" that you'll find in western Europe. But this tangled mess still somehow manages to breathe, laugh, and sing—with a joyful Italian accent.

Before Italy unified in the late 1800s, Naples was the richest city in Italy's southern Campania region and one of Europe's most vibrant. But Naples' fortunes nosedived when modern Italy chose Rome as its capital in 1871. Things got so bad that many of its residents emigrated. The Italy America knows—pizza, spaghetti, and "O Sole Mio"/"Santa Lucia"—came from 19th-century Naples, brought to the US by all those immigrants.

Today, Naples impresses visitors with one of Europe's top archaeological museums (showcasing the artistic treasures of Pompeii), fascinating churches that convey the city's unique personality and powerful devotion, an underground warren of Greek and Roman ruins, fine works of art (including pieces by Caravaggio, who lived here for a time), and evocative Nativity scenes (called *presepi*). Of course, Neapolitans make great pizza and tasty pastries (try the crispy, ricotta-stuffed *sfogliatella*). But more than anything, Naples has a brash and vibrant street life—it's "Italy in your face" in ways both good and bad. Walking through

its colorful old town is one of my favorite experiences anywhere in Europe. For a grand overlook, head to the hilltop San Martino viewpoint for sweeping views of the city and its bay.

PLANNING YOUR TIME

Yes, Naples is huge and a barrage to the senses. But if you stick to my suggestions and grab a cab when you're lost or tired, it's fun. With three nights and two days in Naples, you could plan your time this way:

Day 1

9:00 Start your day at the Archaeological Museum (closed Tue)
11:00 Take my self-guided Naples Walk, visiting the sights along Spaccanapoli (Church of Gesú Nuovo, Church of Santa Chiara, the Duomo, and Cappella Sansevero—reservation needed)
16:00 Detour from the walk to explore the Napoli Sotterranea (Underground Naples) archaeological site
18:00 Dinner in the fun-loving Spanish Quarter
20:00 Join the *passeggiata* along the Lungomare harborside promenade, capping it off with a drink in lively Chiaia

Day 2

9:00 Wander the Via Pignasecca street market (best in the morning)
10:00 Ascend the Montesanto funicular for views and to tour the San Martino Carthusian Monastery and Museum
14:00 Descend on the Centrale funicular, then take in Via Toledo and sights near the port (Piazza del Plebiscito, Royal Palace, and more)
17:00 Take my Sanità District Stroll, enjoying the colorful neighborhood scene and hole-in-the-wall dining options

Day 3

Choose from an array of day trips (ranging from 30 minutes to two hours away by public transit): Procida, Pompeii, Capri, or Paestum.

Orientation to Naples

Naples sprawls around the large, curving Bay of Naples, and stretches from the sea to the slopes of Mount Vesuvius, whose broken cone looms just 15 miles away. Though the city is vast, its compact center contains the most interesting sights. The tourist's

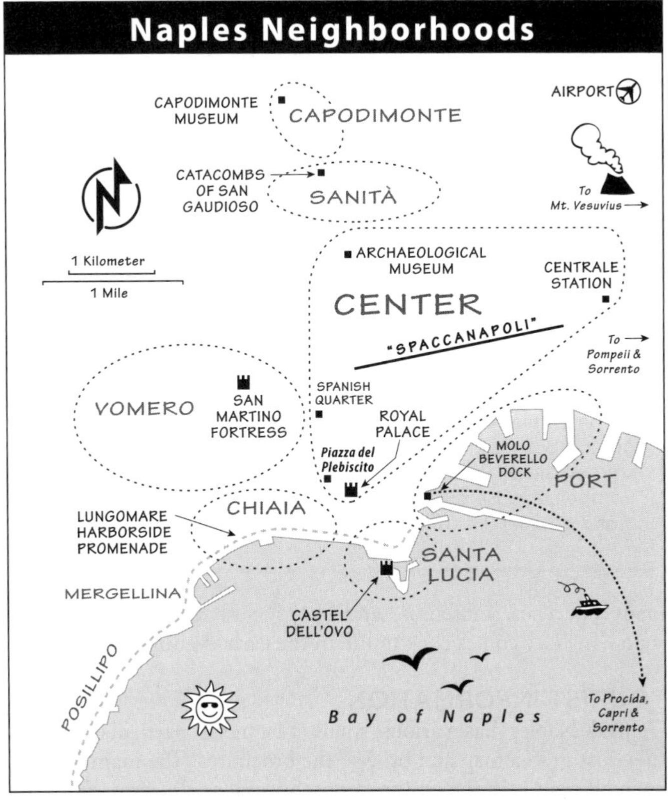

Naples is a triangle, with its points at Centrale train station, the Archaeological Museum, and Piazza del Plebiscito (with the Royal Palace). The lively Spanish Quarter is north of the palace. A series of linked streets known as **Spaccanapoli** bisects the center in a straight line.

The port area bustles, with the Molo Beverello dock (passenger boats to islands), cruise terminal, and car ferry terminal. Steep hills rise above the historic core. North of the core is the gritty Sanità neighborhood and the hill of Capodimonte, with Naples' top art museum. To the west, funiculars climb to the leafy Vomero district and the hill of San Martino, capped with a mighty fortress.

To the southwest a harborside promenade hugs the bay, passing through the colorful districts of Santa Lucia, Chiaia, and Mergellina, and ending at the distant Posillipo hillside. Captivating islands beckon on the blue horizon.

Treat yourself well in Naples; the city is cheap by Italian standards. Splurging on a sane and comfortable hotel is a worthwhile investment. On summer afternoons, Naples' street life slows and

Campania ArteCard Regional Pass

The **Campania ArteCard** regional pass may save you a few euros, but it also saves the time and hassle of buying tickets. Consider it if you'll be here for two or three days, use public transportation, and visit multiple major sights (such as Pompeii, Herculaneum, Naples' Archaeological Museum, and several other museums in Naples). The **three-day Campania** version (€41) is good if you'll be visiting both Naples and its surrounding sights; it includes free entry to two sights, a discount on others, and transportation within Naples and on the Circumvesuviana train (but not the Campania Express). The **seven-day Campania** version (€34) covers five sights and discounts on others, but no transportation. If you're focusing on Naples, the **three-day Napoli** version (€27) covers transportation within Naples and three city sights, plus discounts on others, but doesn't cover outlying ancient sites. The card is sold online or in the ArteCard app, or at some TIs in Naples, Pompeii, and Herculaneum (cards activate on first use, expire 3 or 7 days later at midnight, www.campaniartecard.it).

many churches, museums, and shops close as the temperature soars. The city comes back to life in the early evening.

TOURIST INFORMATION

Central Naples has various small TIs, none particularly helpful—just grab a map and browse the brochures. The main branch, open all year, is in the city center on Spaccanapoli, across from the **Church of Gesù Nuovo** (daily 9:00-18:00, +39 081 551 2701). Seasonally, you may also find TI branches at **Centrale train station** and the **airport**—look around when you arrive.

ARRIVAL IN NAPLES

No matter how you arrive, expect some chaos. Instead of getting frustrated, consider it part of the charm of Naples—as most locals do. If you're connecting to another destination from Naples, see the "Getting Around the Bay of Naples" sidebar on page 96.

By Train

Naples has several train stations, but all trains coming into town stop at either Napoli Centrale or its underground partner Garibaldi (they are essentially the same place, with Centrale on top of Garibaldi). Stretching in front of this station complex is the vast Piazza Garibaldi, with Galleria Garibaldi (an underground shopping mall) and a Metro entrance.

Centrale station, on the ground floor, is the slick, modern main station, with intercity connections across Italy. Baggage check (*deposito bagagli,* run by Kibag) is near track 2; pay WCs are down the stairs across from track 13. A nice Food Hall Napoli is located near tracks 2-8; other shops and eateries are mainly concentrated on the underground level. In high season, a TI may be set up somewhere in the station; the inStazione desk is a private agency but can be helpful in a pinch. Out the front door to the left, you'll find a big bookstore (La Feltrinelli) and a good supermarket (Sapori & Dintorni).

Garibaldi station, on the lower level, is used by the narrow-gauge Circumvesuviana commuter train and the Campania Express train (both serving Pompeii, Herculaneum, and Sorrento; to get to these tracks, follow signs to *Circumvesuviana* and *Linee Vesuviane*). Note that the Circumvesuviana terminates one stop closer to downtown, at the station called **Porta Nolana**—a good place to board the Circumvesuviana to beat the crowds. For details on riding either train, see the "Getting Around the Bay of Naples" sidebar at the end of this chapter.

"Stazione Piazza Garibaldi," or "Napoli S.G." for short, is a stop on Naples' Metro line 2 (operated by Trenitalia—see next); these tracks are downstairs near the middle of Centrale station (follow signs for *M Linea 2*). In addition to stops in Naples, some of these trains go all the way out to Pompei (the modern town) and Salerno.

Getting Downtown: Arriving at either Centrale or Garibaldi, you can reach most Naples sights and hotels by Metro, taxi, or Uber (which works well here; it summons an official taxi). **Metro** lines 1 and 2 are both downstairs—in separate areas because they are operated by separate companies with separate tickets—and signposted throughout the Centrale and Garibaldi stations. Line 1 (direction: Piscinola) is handy for city-center stops, including the port (Municipio), the main shopping drag (Toledo and Dante), and the Archaeological Museum (Museo). Line 2 is slightly quicker for reaching the Archaeological Museum (direction: Pozzuoli, go one stop to Piazza Cavour, then walk 5 minutes). For tips on navigating the Metro, see "Getting Around Naples," later.

Long rows of white **taxis** line up in front of the station complex, ready to gouge tourists. To avoid hustlers, hike to the far side of the piazza, where there's a taxi stand with more honest and less aggressive cabbies (or use Uber). Ask the driver to charge you the fixed rate *(tariffa predeterminata),* which varies from €10 for the old center to €15 for the most distant hotel I list.

By Plane or Cruise Ship

For information on Naples' airport, cruise ship terminal, and ferry docks, see the end of this chapter.

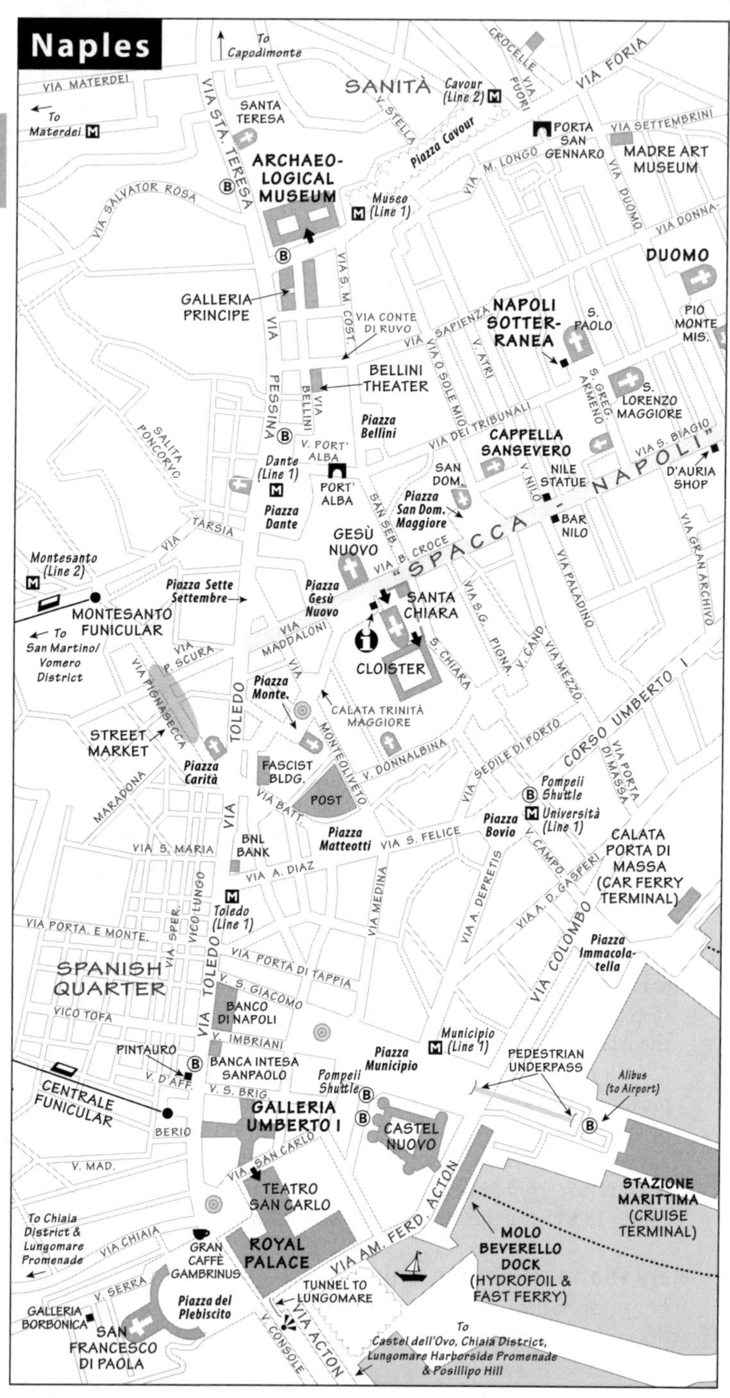
Naples
To Capodimonte
SANITÀ
Cavour (Line 2)
VIA MATERDEI
To Materdei
SANTA TERESA
VIA STA. TERESA
Piazza Cavour
PORTA SAN GENNARO
VIA SETTEMBRINI
MADRE ART MUSEUM
VIA FORIA
ARCHAEOLOGICAL MUSEUM
VIA SALVATOR ROSA
Museo (Line 1)
VIA M. LONGO
VIA DUOMO
VIA DONNA-
DUOMO
GALLERIA PRINCIPE
VIA S. M. COST.
VIA CONTE DI RUVO
NAPOLI SOTTERRANEA
S. PAOLO
PIO MONTE MIS.
VIA SAPIENZA
BELLINI THEATER
VIA BELLINI
VIA PESSINA
Piazza Bellini
S. GREG. ARMENO
S. LORENZO MAGGIORE
SALITA PONCORVO
VIA DEI TRIBUNALI
CAPPELLA SANSEVERO
VIA S. BIAGIO
D'AURIA SHOP
V. PORT' ALBA
Dante (Line 1)
PORT' ALBA
SAN DOM.
NILE STATUE
Piazza San Dom. Maggiore
BAR NILO
Piazza Dante
VIA TARSIA
GESÙ NUOVO
"SPACCA NAPOLI"
VIA B. CROCE
VIA GRAN ARCHIVIO
VIA PALADINO
Montesanto (Line 2)
Piazza Sette Settembre
Piazza Gesù Nuovo
SANTA CHIARA
MONTESANTO FUNICULAR
To San Martino/ Vomero District
VIA MADDALONI
CLOISTER
S. CHIARA
VIA S.G. PIGNA.
VIA MEZZO.
VIA P. SCURA
VIA PIGNASECCA
Piazza Monte.
CALATA TRINITÀ MAGGIORE
CORSO UMBERTO I
STREET MARKET
VIA TOLEDO
Piazza Carità
FASCIST BLDG.
V. DONNALBINA
VIA SEDILE DI PORTO
VIA PORTA DI MASSA
POST
VIA BATT.
MONTEOLIVETO
Pompeii Shuttle
Università (Line 1)
MARADONA
Piazza Matteotti
VIA S. FELICE
Piazza Bovio
V. CAMPO
CALATA PORTA DI MASSA (CAR FERRY TERMINAL)
VIA S. MARIA
BNL BANK
VIA A. DIAZ
VIA A. DEPRETIS
VIA A. D. GASPERI
Toledo (Line 1)
VIA MEDINA
VIA PORTA. E MONTE.
VIA SPER.
VICO LUNGO
VIA PORTA DI TAPPIA
Piazza Immacolatella
VIA COLOMBO
SPANISH QUARTER
V. S. GIACOMO
BANCO DI NAPOLI
VICO TOFA
V. IMBRIANI
Municipio (Line 1)
PINTAURO
V. D'AFF.
BANCA INTESA SANPAOLO
Piazza Municipio
PEDESTRIAN UNDERPASS
Alibus (to Airport)
V. S. BRIG.
CENTRALE FUNICULAR
GALLERIA UMBERTO I
CASTEL NUOVO
BERIO
V. MAD.
VIA SAN CARLO
TEATRO SAN CARLO
VIA AM. FERD. ACTON
STAZIONE MARITTIMA (CRUISE TERMINAL)
To Chiaia District & Lungomare Promenade
VIA CHIAIA
GRAN CAFFÈ GAMBRINUS
ROYAL PALACE
MOLO BEVERELLO DOCK (HYDROFOIL & FAST FERRY)
V. SERRA
Piazza del Plebiscito
TUNNEL TO LUNGOMARE
GALLERIA BORBONICA
SAN FRANCESCO DI PAOLA
V. CONSOLE
VIA ACTON
To Castel dell'Ovo, Chiaia District, Lungomare Harborside Promenade & Posillipo Hill

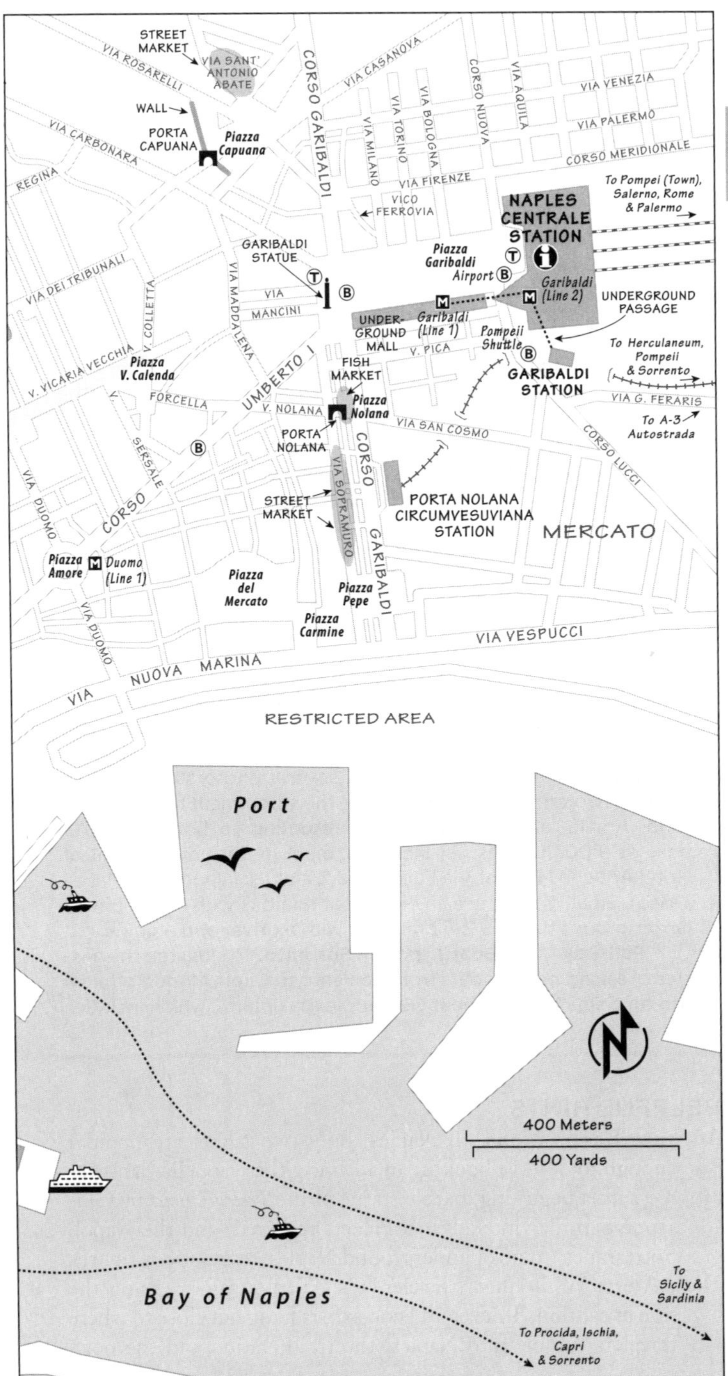

STREET MARKET
VIA SANT' ANTONIO ABATE
VIA ROSARELLI
WALL
PORTA CAPUANA
Piazza Capuana
VIA CARBONARA
REGINA
CORSO GARIBALDI
VIA CASANOVA
VIA MILANO
VIA TORINO
VIA BOLOGNA
CORSO NUOVA
VIA AQUILA
VIA VENEZIA
VIA PALERMO
CORSO MERIDIONALE
VIA FIRENZE
VICO FERROVIA
To Pompei (Town), Salerno, Rome & Palermo
NAPLES CENTRALE STATION
Piazza Garibaldi
Airport
Garibaldi (Line 2)
UNDERGROUND PASSAGE
GARIBALDI STATUE
VIA MANCINI
VIA DEI TRIBUNALI
VIA MADDALENA
V. COLLETTA
UNDER-GROUND MALL
Garibaldi (Line 1)
V. PICA
Pompeii Shuttle
GARIBALDI STATION
To Herculaneum, Pompeii & Sorrento
VIA G. FERARIS
To A-3 Autostrada
V. VICARIA VECCHIA
Piazza V. Calenda
UMBERTO I
FISH MARKET
Piazza Nolana
V. NOLANA
FORCELLA
PORTA NOLANA
VIA SAN COSMO
CORSO LUCCI
SERSALE
VIA DUOMO
CORSO
VIA SOPRAMURO
STREET MARKET
PORTA NOLANA CIRCUMVESUVIANA STATION
MERCATO
Piazza Amore
Duomo (Line 1)
Piazza del Mercato
Piazza Pepe
Piazza Carmine
VIA VESPUCCI
VIA NUOVA MARINA
RESTRICTED AREA
Port
400 Meters
400 Yards
Bay of Naples
To Sicily & Sardinia
To Procida, Ischia, Capri & Sorrento

Mondo Guide Tours for My Readers

Mondo Guide, a Naples-based company, offers "shared tours" for Rick Steves readers. These allow you the luxury of a private professional guide, at a fraction of the usual cost, because you'll be sharing the expense with other travelers using this book. I don't receive a cut from the tours; I set this up with Mondo Guide to help my readers have the most economical experience in this region.

Tours run from April through October and include a walking tour of **Naples,** a **Pompeii** tour, and two longer-distance trips from Sorrento: an **Amalfi Coast** van tour and a private boat to the **isle of Capri.** The Pompeii and Naples tours are timed so you can do both on the same day. Mondo also offers shore excursions for cruise passengers arriving in Naples or Salerno. Here are the details:

Historic Naples Walk: On this three-hour walk, a local Neapolitan guide helps you uncover the true character of the city (€30, daily at 15:30, meet at the steps of the Naples Archaeological Museum—you can do the museum on your own before joining your guide, generally 6-8 people).

Pompeii Tour: This two-hour guided walk brings to life the ruins of the excavated city (€20, Pompeii entry extra—your guide will collect money and buy tickets, daily at 11:15; meet in Pompeii at Hotel/Ristorante Suisse, a 5-minute walk from the train station—exiting the station, turn right, pass the Porta Marina entrance, and continue down the hill to the restaurant, on the right).

Full-Day Amalfi Coast Minibus Tour from Sorrento: This nine-hour trip begins in Sorrento and heads south for the breathtaking (and lightly narrated) drive, several photo stops, and an hour or two on your own in each of the three main towns—Positano, Amalfi, and Ravello—before returning to Sorrento (€70, daily at 9:00, lunch is not included; meet in Sorrento in front of Hotel Antiche Mura, at Via Fuorimura 7, a block inland from Piazza Tasso). Small groups use an eight-seat minibus with only a driver; larger groups use a 19-seat minibus with a driver and a guide.

Full-Day Capri Boat Trip from Sorrento: To sidestep the hassles of taking public boats from Sorrento to Capri, Mondo offers a trip on a small private boat (12 people maximum), which includes

HELPFUL HINTS

Advance Reservations: In Naples, only two sights are popular enough to deserve booking in advance: the Cappella Sansevero (with a beguiling marble statue of the *Veiled Christ* by Giuseppe Sammartino; advance tickets required) and the Napoli Sotterranea (tours of underground Naples; reservations smart).

Theft Alert: While most travelers visit Naples safely, err on the side of caution. Thieves and con artists hang out close to where travelers tumble into Naples: the train station and the port.

an early visit to the Blue Grotto sea cave (when conditions allow) and about four hours of free time to explore Capri on your own. After your time on land, the boat takes you on a lightly narrated trip around the island with drinks, snacks, and a chance to swim—if the weather cooperates. Note that tours meet at Sorrento's Marina Grande—specifically Bar Nonna Emilia at #21—not at Marina Piccola, where the ferries are (€140, extra €20 for optional Blue Grotto visit; daily at 8:00, may be canceled in bad weather).

Shore Excursions from Naples or Salerno: For cruise-ship passengers, Mondo Guide offers all-day itineraries in a shared minivan or bus from the port of Naples or the port of Salerno that combine a guided visit to Pompeii with free time in towns along the scenic Amalfi Coast. From Naples, it's an hour of free time each in Sorrento and Positano; from Salerno, it's an hour of free time each in Sorrento and Amalfi town (€90, daily at 8:00 from the main exit of the Naples cruise terminal building or from your ship in Salerno).

Additional itineraries can be found at SharedTrips.com; Rick Steves readers receive a 10 percent discount.

How to Book

Reservations are required. For specifics and to sign up, go to SharedTours.com (Mondo +39 081 751 3290, mobile +39 340 460 5254, www.mondoguide.it, sharedtours@mondoguide.com). On the website, use your credit-card number to reserve a spot. You'll then pay cash for the tour (directly to the guide). If you must cancel, email more than three days in advance or you'll be billed.

Each tour requires a minimum of six participants. You'll be sent an email confirmation as soon as they're sure your tour will run. If there's not enough demand to justify the trip, they'll notify you three days before the departure date (giving you time to come up with alternative plans). Confirmed departures are continually updated on the website. Thousands of Rick Steves travelers use this service each year, and Mondo and I want this to be a great experience for all: Please email rick@ricksteves.com if you have any frustrations.

Although the train station itself has been nicely spruced up, its glow doesn't extend far. And even in its nicest areas, Naples can strike many visitors as a bit scruffy. Remember that poor and chaotic does not necessarily mean dangerous, and don't let your first impressions get in your way of enjoying Naples. Touristy Spaccanapoli, Capodimonte, and the Via Toledo shopping boulevard are more upscale.

As in most big cities, consider any jostle or commotion a possible thief-team smokescreen. Walk with confidence, as if you know where you're going and what you're doing. Thieves on scooters have been known to snatch bags as they swoop by. Keep valuables buttoned up and out of sight (or leave them at your hotel).

Safety on the Circumvesuviana: Perhaps your biggest risk of theft is while catching or riding the often crowded and sometimes run-down Circumvesuviana commuter train. While I ride the Circumvesuviana comfortably and safely, each year I hear of travelers who get ripped off on this train. You won't be mugged—but you may be conned or pickpocketed. At the train station, carry your own bags—there are no official porters. Be ready for this very common trick: A team of thieves blocks the door at a stop, pretending it's stuck. While everyone rushes to try to open it, an accomplice picks their pockets.

Traffic Safety: In Naples, pedestrians need to be wary, particularly of motor scooters that zip among the cars. Even on "pedestrian" streets, stay alert to avoid being sideswiped by scooters (or even cars) that nudge their way through the crowds. Residents suggest that you jaywalk in the shadow of bold locals, who generally ignore crosswalks. They wait for a break in traffic, cross with confidence, and make eye contact with approaching drivers and motor scooters.

Bookstore: La Feltrinelli, conveniently located at Centrale station, carries a small selection of English-language books (daily 8:00-20:00, near track 24, also accessible from outside the station).

Laundry: Lav@Sciuga, a block from the Università Metro stop, is convenient but has just a few washing machines (Mon-Fri 9:00-17:00, closed Sat-Sun, Via Sedile di Porto 54—see map on page 82, +39 327 754 6639).

GETTING AROUND NAPLES

Sightsee Naples with help from its subway (Metro), funiculars, and taxis/Uber. Public buses are generally useful only for reaching Capodimonte. For an overview, see the color "Naples Transportation" map at the back of this book. For general transit information, maps, and fares, visit UnicoCampania.it. For schedules, your best option is Google Maps, which suggests public transit connections and works as well as anything for journey planning. Italian-only ANM.it also has schedules.

Tickets and Passes: Naples' Metro line 1 and funicular system accept contactless payment at turnstiles—simply tap in and out using a contactless credit card or payment app.

As of this writing, a physical ticket is still required for buses, Metro day passes, and Metro line 2. You can purchase physical tickets at tobacco stores, some newsstands, and clunky machines at Metro stations (these accept coins, small bills, and sometimes

Daily Reminder

Monday: Everything is open except Naples' fish market.

Tuesday: The Archaeological Museum, Capella Sansevero, and MADRE museum are closed, as is the art museum inside Castel Sant'Elmo.

Wednesday: Many sights are closed today, including the Royal Palace, Capodimonte Museum, the Catacombs of San Gennaro and San Gaudioso, and the San Martino Carthusian Monastery and Museum.

Thursday: All sights are open today.

Friday: All sights are open today. The Jago Museum has extended hours.

Saturday: All sights are open today. The Jago Museum has extended hours.

Sunday: Castel Nuovo has shorter hours while the Jago Museum has extended hours.

credit cards, but can be tricky to operate). Basically, anywhere you see a frustrated queue near the station, people are trying to buy paper tickets. (The system is notoriously fraught.) Buses and funiculars have the same price (€1.30) while Metro line 1 and line 2 each require a separate ticket (see next).

A €1.50 single ticket covers Metro line 1, with no transfers. For Metro line 2 you need the €1.60 version (this ticket is a long, printed receipt with a QR code that needs to be punched at the machine—fold your ticket in half and insert; contactless payment may be possible by the time you visit). A *giornaliero* day pass costs €4.50 and pays for itself quickly (but doesn't work on line 2).

By Metro: Naples' subway has two main lines *(linea).* Station entrances and signs to the Metro are marked by a red square with a white M. Stations often come with both archaeological exhibits (artifacts unearthed during construction) and entertaining modern art, reminding riders that Naples—both very old and very new—is built upon layers.

Line 1 (Metropolitana) is very useful for tourists. Starting from Centrale train station (stop: Garibaldi), it heads to Duomo (Via Duomo at Piazza Amore), Università (the university), Municipio (at Piazza Municipio, just above the harbor and cruise terminal), Toledo (south end of Via Toledo, near Piazza del Plebiscito), Dante (Piazza Dante), and Museo (Archaeological Museum). Four stops beyond Museo is the Vanvitelli stop, near the hilltop San Martino sights; the end of the line is Piscinola. By the time you visit, line 1 may extend from Garibaldi to the airport.

Line 2 (part of Trenitalia) is most useful for getting quickly from Centrale train station to Piazza Cavour (a 5-minute walk from the Archaeological Museum) or Montesanto (near Piazza Dante and the base of the funicular up to San Martino). Note that the stop on this line for the main train station is called "Napoli S.G." (for Stazione Piazza Garibaldi). Some trains on this line run out into the suburbs to Pompei (the modern town) and all the way to Salerno. (Combined with the Circumvesuviana and the Campania Express, Metro line 2 is a good way to return from the excavations at Pompeii, as explained in the next chapter and in the "Getting Around the Bay of Naples" sidebar, later.)

A third line, **line 6,** connects Piazza Municipio with waterfront neighborhoods such as Chiaia and Mergellina.

By Funicular: Three funiculars *(funicolare)* carry commuters and sightseers into the hilly San Martino neighborhood just west of downtown. All three converge near Piazza Fuga, a short walk from the hilltop fortress and monastery/museum. The Centrale line runs from the Spanish Quarter, just near Piazza del Plebiscito and the Toledo Metro stop; the Montesanto line from the Montesanto Metro stop and Via Pignasecca market zone; and the Chiaia line (likely closed for renovation) from near the Piazza Amadeo Metro stop. A fourth funicular connects the harborfront Mergellina district to the hilltop Posillipo neighborhood.

By Taxi: A **taxi** lets you experience Naples traffic without actually driving in it—an experience worth at least ▲. A short ride in town should cost €6-12 (the drop change is €3.50). While the reputation is that cabbies will rip you off, except for at the train station and the cruise port, you can expect the meter. Just get in and act confident...you're no fool. If the meter's not running, say *"Tassametro, per favore"* (taxi meter, please). For some rides the driver will expect a fixed rate *(tariffa predeterminata).* You'll see these rates plus the latest prices and extras posted prominently inside any legitimate taxi (with fares for sightseeing excursions by cab on the back side). Look for a taxi stand (they are common) or simply hail a cab.

Uber also works in Naples—the app connects you with a standard white taxi. If you like ride-booking services at home, this can be an easy way to hail a cab without the rigamarole.

Tours in Naples

🎧 To sightsee on your own, download my free Rick Steves **audio tours,** which cover my Naples Walk and the Naples Archaeological Museum.

Local Guides

Pina Esposito has a PhD in ancient archaeology and art; she does fine private walking and driving tours of her native Naples and the region (Pompeii, Herculaneum, Capri, the Amalfi Coast), including Naples' Archaeological Museum (tours from €60/hour, 2-hour minimum, RS%—10 percent off with this book, up to 20 percent off for full-day tours, +39 338 763 4224, annamariaesposito1@virgilio.it).

The team at **Mondo Guide** offers private tours of the Archaeological Museum (€120/2 hours) and city (€240/4 hours) and can provide guides or drivers throughout the region. They can also arrange kayaking trips, boat trips, and whatever else you need (+39 081 751 3290, www.mondoguide.it, info@mondoguide.com).

Walking Tours

Napoli That's Amore is a hardworking little company run by Raffaele Terracciano and four guiding colleagues, offering daily tip-based walks of the city they love. Their Old Town walk covers sights on and near Spaccanapoli (leaves from Piazza Dante); Best of Naples explores the monumental neighborhood around the Royal Palace (leaves from Piazza Municipio). The two-hour guided walks (7-25 people) leave at 10:30 and at 16:30 on selected days—confirm times on website. A tip of €10 per person (or more) is fair, and you must book in advance (www.napolithatsamore.org).

Hop-On, Hop-Off Bus Tours

CitySightseeing tour buses make two different hop-on, hop-off loops through the city. Only the red line, which loops around the historical center, is particularly helpful, but the blue line takes you out along the seafront pedestrian promenade to the Posillipo area—a more upscale part of the city that Neapolitans love (€26, ticket valid 24 hours, 2/hour, buy from some drivers, scant recorded narration, +39 081 551 7279, www.city-sightseeing.it/naples).

CitySightseeing and the similar Tramvia Napoli bus (www.tramvianapoli.it) also offer **shuttles to Pompeii,** leaving from various locations, including Piazza Municipio, Piazza Bovio, and Piazza Garibaldi near the train station (€20 round-trip or €10 one way, 2-3/day in each direction, confirm schedules/stops at websites).

Shore Excursions

Convenient for cruise-ship passengers, the **Can't Be Missed** tour company takes you from the port of Naples along the Amalfi Coast on an all-day coach trip for up to 20 passengers. The tour includes a stop in Sorrento and a guided tour of Pompeii (€99, RS%—10 percent off when you use promo code "RS2024" on their website; meets in front of port—usually 30 minutes after ship docks, allow 7 hours, Pompeii ticket extra; +1 607 542 7981, www.cantbemissedtours.com).

Mondo Tours also offers shore excursions from Naples and Salerno (see sidebar).

Naples at a Glance

▲▲▲Naples Walk Independent or guided walk from the Archaeological Museum through the heart of the city, with distinctive piazzas, grand architecture, and colorful neighborhoods. See page 38. 🎧

▲▲▲Archaeological Museum One of the world's great collections of ancient art, featuring statues, mosaics, and other artifacts from Pompeii and Herculaneum. **Hours:** Wed-Mon 9:00-19:30, closed Tue. See page 51. 🎧

▲▲Cappella Sansevero Baroque chapel known for the marble *Veiled Christ* statue and Enlightenment-era creations. **Hours:** Wed-Mon 9:30-19:00, closed Tue. See page 61.

▲▲Lungomare *Passeggiata* Waterfront promenade with plenty of people-watching and views. **Hours:** Best after 19:00. See page 69.

▲▲Sanità District Stroll Walk through a vibrant and gritty historic neighborhood north of the Archaeological Museum. See page 71.

▲▲Catacombs of San Gennaro More than a thousand burial niches dating as far back as the second century. **Hours:** Thu-Tue 10:00-17:00, closed Wed. See page 78.

Naples Walk

This self-guided walk, worth ▲▲▲, takes you from the Archaeological Museum through the heart of town. (For efficiency, tour the Archaeological Museum before starting this walk.) Allow at least two hours for the full two-part walk, plus time for pizza and sightseeing stops. (If you're day-tripping and time is short, from Piazza Carità—near the middle of the walk—head down Via Toledo to the Toledo Metro stop to zip back to the train station.)

🎧 Download my free Naples City Walk **audio tour** and I'll personally give you this tour. If you'd like a live guide, Mondo Guides offers a daily walking tour that's similar to this route (see sidebar, earlier).

A SLICE OF NEAPOLITAN LIFE

Naples—perhaps Italy's most vibrant and least cosmopolitan city and certainly one of its most historic—is its own best sight. Cou-

▲▲San Martino Carthusian Monastery and Museum 14th-century monastery exploding with art, from ceremonial gondolas to life-size Nativity scenes. **Hours:** Thu-Tue 8:30-19:30, closed Wed. See page 80.

▲Church of Gesù Nuovo Honors the first modern doctor to be canonized, with hundreds of plaques of gratitude for prayers answered. **Hours:** Daily 8:00-13:00 & 16:00-20:00. See page 59.

▲Church and Cloister of Santa Chiara A peaceful stroll through a nun's world, an art gallery, and the excavation site of an ancient Greek bath. **Hours:** Church—daily 7:30-13:00 & 16:30-20:00; cloister—daily 9:30-17:00. See page 60.

▲Napoli Sotterranea Subterranean passageways and ruins, including portions of a 6,000-seat Greco-Roman theater. **Hours:** Daily 10:00-18:00. See page 62.

▲Naples Duomo Centuries-old cathedral with a mix of architectural and decorative styles. **Hours:** Mon-Sat 8:30-13:30 & 14:30-20:00, Sun 8:30-13:30 & 16:30-19:30. See page 63.

▲Capodimonte Museum Summer palace of the Bourbon dynasty set in a hilltop park, now a museum with works by Renaissance masters (Michelangelo, Raphael, Caravaggio). **Hours:** Thu-Tue 8:30-19:30, closed Wed. See page 74.

ples artfully make love on Vespas surrounded by more smiles per cobblestone than anywhere else in Italy. Sure, Naples has its important sights. But to capture its essence, take this walk through the core of the city.

Part 1: Archaeological Museum to Piazza Carità

Start at the Archaeological Museum, at the top of Piazza Cavour (Metro: Cavour or Museo; for directions on getting here and a tour of the interior, see page 51). From here, we'll ramble down a fine boulevard before cutting into the medieval heart of the city.

❶ **Archaeological Museum:** The palatial building, built in the mid-1700s, captures the glory of Naples at its peak and is a great introduction to the Naples we'll see. Back then, the city was rich from sea trade and home to erudite nobles from abroad. They built a magnificent capital of buildings like this one. On this walk we'll see that grand city they built...and its remnants following centuries of decline.

• *From the door of the Archaeological Museum, cross the street, veer*

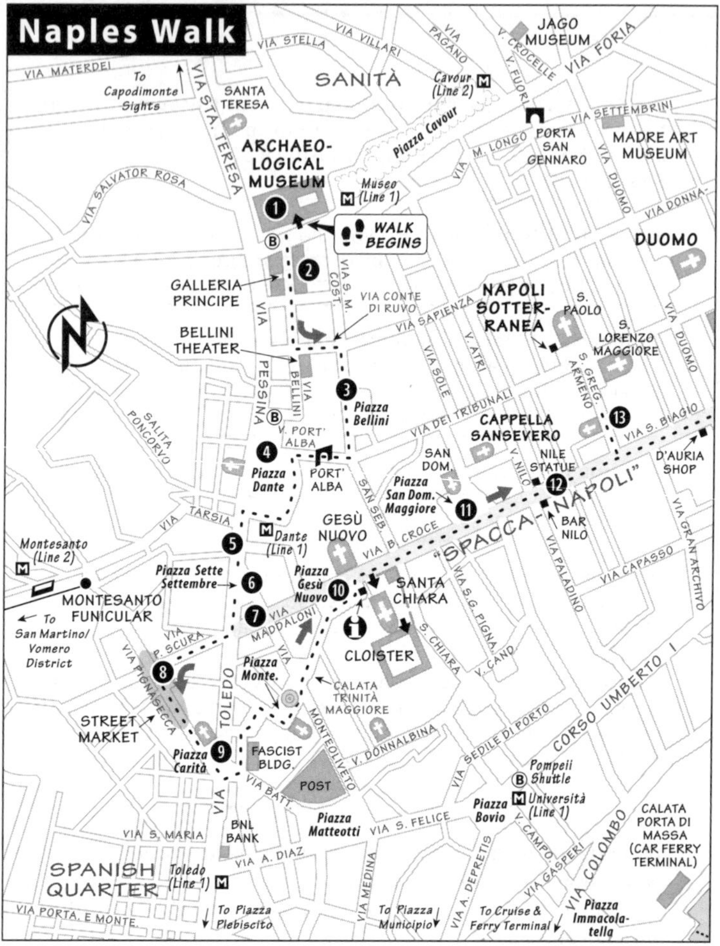

Naples Walk

right, and enter the arched doorway of the beige Galleria Principe di Napoli mall.

❷ **Galleria Principe di Napoli:** There's no better example of Naples' grandeur—and decline—than this elegant 19th-century shopping mall, patterned after popular arcades of the time in Paris and London. You'll enjoy a soaring skylight, carved woodwork, ironwork lanterns, playful cupids, an elegant atmosphere...and empty shops. Built with great expectations, the *galleria* was named for the first male child of the royal Savoy family, the prince of Naples. In the US, we call its decorative style Art Nouveau; in Italy

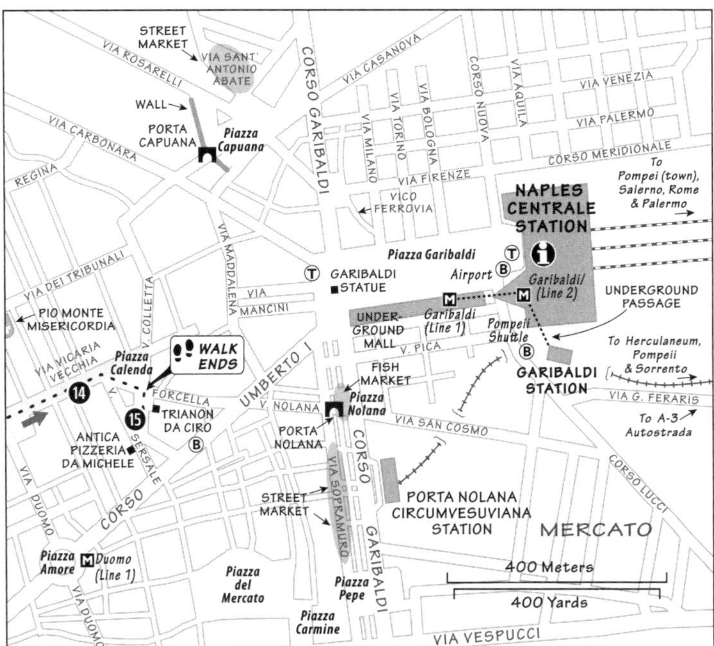

Part 1

1. Archaeological Museum
2. Galleria Principe di Napoli
3. Piazza Bellini
4. Piazza Dante
5. Via Toledo
6. Piazza Sette Settembre
7. Spaccanapoli
8. Via Pignasecca
9. Piazza Carità

Part 2

10. Piazza Gesù Nuovo
11. Piazza San Domenico Maggiore
12. Statue of the Nile & Chapel of Maradona
13. Via San Gregorio Armeno
14. Via Vicaria Vecchia
15. Pizza!

it's Liberty Style, named for a British department store that was in vogue at a time when Naples was nicknamed the "Paris of the South." (Parisian artist Edgar Degas even left Paris to adopt Naples—which he considered more cosmopolitan and sophisticated—as his hometown.) The Tesoreria cocktail bar (in the center) fits the time period well. Despite its grandeur, the mall never took off. Ambitious renovations have failed to attract much business, leaving the mall in a state of disrepair. Falling debris occasionally closes the entire structure.

• *Leaving the gallery through the opposite end, walk one block downhill on a pedestrian street.*

You'll pass alongside the palatial golden facade of the **Academy of Fine Arts,** fronted by tropical plants and (usually) busy with students at its outdoor cafés. (Wherever you find students in

Naples, it seems you'll smell marijuana. While not legal yet, it is tolerated.)

• *At Via Conte di Ruvo, turn left.*

Notice the entrance to the fine **Bellini Theater,** also in Liberty Style. All along our walk, be sure to enjoy the architecture of the late 19th century, when Naples was the last stop on Romantic Age travelers' Grand Tour of Europe.

• *After one block, turn right on Via Santa Maria di Costantinopoli.*

Walking between two grand yet empty **churches,** consider how today the Roman Catholic Church is Italy's biggest landowner. But with fewer practicing Catholics, much of the church's real estate sits unused. Rather than selling the surplus, the Vatican is developing it, turning vacant buildings into luxury hotels to be managed by outside contractors (and generating fabulous wealth for the Vatican).

• *Continue directly downhill to a small park with a statue in the center called...*

❸ **Piazza Bellini:** Suddenly you're in neighborhood Napoli. The statue honors the opera composer Vincenzo Bellini, whose career was launched in Naples in the early 1800s. Just past the statue, peer down into the sunken area to see Naples' ancient origins as a fifth-century BC Greek colony called Neapolis—literally, "the new city." These tuff blocks without mortar were part of a tower in the city wall. (And you're standing on land that, back then, was outside the town.) You can see how the street level has risen over the rubble of centuries.

Now look around at the city of today. Survey the many balconies—and the people who use them as a "backyard" in this densely packed city. The apartment blocks were originally the palaces of noble families, as indicated by the stately family crests above grand doorways. For centuries, laundry has blown in the breeze right here.

Piazza Bellini has become a happening gathering place after dark. On the far side of the square is the **Caffé Letterario Intra Moenia** (the "literary café inside the walls" of the ancient city). Known as the "just between you and me" café, it was the first gay bar in town and is now popular for its cocktails. The entire square has a good-time vibe with bars offering generous *apericena* (snack plates) with drinks; hundreds of spritzes shine like golden good-time lanterns.

• *Continue 30 yards downhill on Via Santa Maria di Costantinopoli.*

Stop at the horseshoe-shaped **Port'Alba gate** (just beyond the bottom of the square, on the right). Spin slowly 360 degrees and take in the scene. The proud tile across the street (upstairs, between the two balconies) shows Piazza Bellini circa 1890. Don't ignore the graffiti; try to figure out the issues that artists are calling attention to.

• *Pass through the gate, down Via Port'Alba, and stroll through this pleasant passage lined with book stalls. You emerge into a big square called...*

❹ **Piazza Dante:** This square is marked by a statue of Dante, the medieval poet. Fittingly, half the square is devoted to bookstores. Old Dante looks out over an urban area that was once grand, then chaotic, and is now slowly becoming grand again.

Along one side is a grandiose, orange-and-gray **pseudo-facade** of columns and statues from the late 1700s, representing the power of the Bourbon monarchy when Naples was at its peak. Originally, a statue of the king stood in the square. But in 1799, when Napoleon invaded, the Bourbon monarchy was toppled. The king's statue was removed and replaced with the generic figure of Dante. Later, the name of Victor Emmanuel II (Vittorio Emanuele)—the first king of a united Italy—was added to the facade. These suggest the next phase of Naples' history—its decline—which we'll see in just a bit.

The Neapolitan people are survivors. A long history of corrupt and greedy colonial overlords (German, Norman, French, Austrian, Spanish, Napoleon, etc.) has taught Neapolitans to deal creatively with authority. Many credit this aspect of Naples' past for the strength of organized crime here.

• *Before moving on, note the red* "M" *that Dante seems to gesture toward; this marks the* ***Dante Metro station.*** *Then, exit Piazza Dante at the far (bottom) end, walking downhill on...*

❺ **Via Toledo:** The long, straight street heading downhill from Piazza Dante is one of Naples' principal shopping drags. Named after the city that was the capital of Spain until the mid-1500s, it originated as a military road built by the Spanish viceroys who made Naples great in the 16th century. Back then, Via Toledo skirted the old town wall to connect the Spanish military headquarters (now the museum where you started this walk) with the Royal Palace (down by the bay). As you stroll, peek into the many lovely atriums, which provide a break from the big street.

• *After a couple hundred yards, you'll reach the triangular...*

❻ **Piazza Sette Settembre:** This public space recalls the event that precipitated Naples' swift decline. On September 7, 1860, from the white marble balcony of the Neoclassical building over-

Maradona—More Than a Soccer Star

Diego Maradona (1960-2020), the Argentinian soccer star who played for Naples in the 1980s and 1990s, is revered like a god in Naples. Even though he handled his fame and fortune poorly, had gambling and alcohol problems, and died young, Maradona is right up there with Naples' favorite (other) saint, St. Gennaro. Many *napolitano* men of a certain age are named Diego. And as you stroll around the old (and poor) quarters of town, you'll see plenty of Maradona murals, graffiti, and photographs—more than of the pope. There are even shrines to Maradona that, at first glance, may seem like jokes, but then you realize...maybe not.

To understand Maradona's popularity you must understand Naples' past. Naples was arguably Europe's second city for generations. But with Italian unification in the 1870s, Italy's north essentially beat the south. Perhaps a bit like the American South after the Civil War, the south never fully surrendered or recovered from the loss. Southern Italy remains hardscrabble and downtrodden compared to the affluent north. For Naples' working class, soccer is a welcome distraction from more real issues (much like bread and circuses in ancient Rome).

Locals told me winning at soccer is "social revenge"... it's the big "screw you." It's Naples telling Rome and Milan, "You've got more money, we've got more nerve. On the soccer field, it's 11 versus 11. And with Maradona, we win."

looking the square, the famous revolutionary Giuseppe Garibaldi celebrated his conquest of Naples. He declared Italy united and Victor Emmanuel II its first king. And a decade later, that declaration became reality when Rome also fell to unification forces. It was the start of a glorious new era for Italy, Rome, and the Italian people. But not for Naples.

Naples' treasury was confiscated to subsidize the industrial expansion of the north, and its bureaucrats were transferred to the new capital in Rome. Within a few decades, Naples went from being a thriving cultural and political capital to a provincial town, with its economy in shambles and its dialect considered backward.

• *Continue straight on Via Toledo. A block past Piazza Sette Settembre you'll come to Via Maddaloni, which marks the start of the long, straight, narrow street nicknamed...*

❼ **Spaccanapoli:** Via Maddaloni is the modern name for the beginning of this thin street that, since ancient times, has bisected the city. The name Spaccanapoli translates as "split Naples." Look left down the street (toward the train station), and right (toward San Martino hill), and you get a sense of how Spaccanapoli divides this urban jungle of buildings. From here, our walk loops to the right, through the edge of the intense residential Spanish Quarter neighborhood to Piazza Carità before cutting over to the Spaccanapoli district.

• *At the Spaccanapoli intersection, go right (toward the church facade on the hill), heading up Via Pasquale Scura. After about 100 yards, you hit a busy intersection where the street begins to climb steeply uphill. Stop. You're on one of Naples' most colorful open-air market streets...*

❽ **Via Pignasecca:** Take in the colorful scene at the intersection. Then, turn left down Via Pignasecca and stroll this colorful market strip. You'll pass fish stalls, tripe vendors, butchers, produce stands, cheap clothes stores, street-food vendors, and much more. There's more activity during the morning, but afternoon offers better light for photography.

This is a taste of Naples' famous **Spanish Quarter** (Quartieri Spagnoli; its center is farther down Via Toledo, but this area provides a good sampling). While it is becoming gentrified, the Spanish Quarter has long been a classic world of *basso* (low) living. The streets—which were laid out in the 16th century for the Spanish military barracks outside the city walls—are unbelievably narrow (and cool in summer), and the buildings rise five stories high. In such tight quarters, life—flirting, fighting, playing, and loving—plays out in the streets. While just a few years ago you'd avoid this area after dark, these days it's a fun, safe, and thriving scene for an unforgettable dinner out.

• *Follow Via Pignasecca as it leads back to Via Toledo at the square called...*

❾ **Piazza Carità:** This square, built for an official visit by Hitler to Mussolini in 1938, is full of stern, straight, obedient lines.

The big building belonged to an insurance company. (For the best example of fascist architecture in town, take a slight detour from here: With your back to Via Toledo, leave Piazza Carità downhill on the right-hand corner and walk a block to the Poste e Telegrafi building. There you'll see several government buildings with stirring reliefs singing the praises of lobotomized workers and a totalitarian society.)

In Naples—long a poor and rough city—rather than being heroic, people learn from the cradle the art of survival. The modern memorial statue in the center of this square celebrates Salvo D'Acquisto, a rare hometown hero. In 1943, he was executed after falsely confessing to sabotage...saving 22 fellow Italian soldiers from a Nazi revenge massacre.

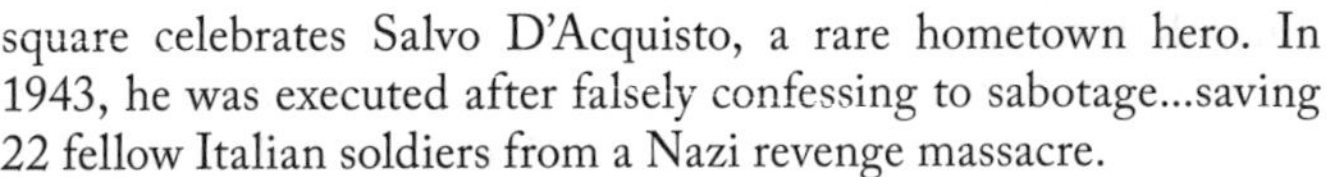

• *We're at the midpoint of this walk. Need a WC? Pop into the Burger King. Running out of time and energy? If you end the walk here, you'll find many cafés and wine bars nearby, and it's a short stroll down Via Toledo to the Toledo Metro station.*

To continue, we'll loop back to Spaccanapoli. Face the fascist-style building and take the street on its left side. Angle through a downhill square called Piazza Monteoliveto. At the bottom of the square, cross the busy street, then follow Calata Trinità Maggiore up to the fancy column in the piazza at the top of the hill.

Part 2: Piazza Gesù Nuovo to Via Pietro Colletta

• *You're back on the straight-as-a-Greek-arrow Spaccanapoli, formerly the main thoroughfare of the Greek city of Neapolis. (Spaccanapoli changes names several times: Via Maddaloni, Via B. Croce, Via S. Biagio dei Librai, and Via Vicaria Vecchia.) Linger for a moment on...*

⑩ **Piazza Gesù Nuovo:** This square is marked by a towering 18th-century Baroque monument to the Counter-Reformation. Although the Jesuit order was powerful in Naples because of its Spanish heritage, locals never attacked Protestants here with the full fury of the Spanish Inquisition.

From this piazza you can pop into two bulky old churches, starting with the dark, fortress-like, 17th-century **Church of Gesù Nuovo,** followed by the simpler **Church of Santa Chiara** (in the courtyard across the street; both are free and described under

"Sights in Naples," later). There's also a **TI** on this square (and a WC next to it).

• *Continue along the main drag for another 200 yards. Since this is a university district, you may see students and bookstores. As this neighborhood is also famously superstitious, look for incense-burning women with carts full of good-luck charms for sale.*

Passing Palazzo Venezia—the embassy of Venice to Naples when both were independent powers—you'll emerge into the next square...

⓫ **Piazza San Domenico Maggiore:** This square is marked by another ornate 17th-century monument, this one built to thank God for ending the plague. (From this square, you could detour left along the right side of the castle-like church, then follow yellow signs, taking the first right and walking one short block to the remarkable Baroque **Cappella Sansevero**—but you'll need a timed-entry ticket; see "Sights in Naples.")

• *Proceed down the long, straight Spaccanapoli (called Via B. Croce at this point) and continue your cultural scavenger hunt. At the intersection with Via Nilo, opposite one another, are two landmarks.*

⓬ **Statue of the Nile and "Chapel of Maradona":** First, on your left, the ancient Greek **statue of the Nile** stands in what was once the Egyptian quarter...a reminder that, even centuries before Christ, ancient Naples was an important and multiethnic trading port. Today locals like to call this statue *The Body of Naples,* with the overflowing cornucopia symbolizing the abundance of their fine city. (I once asked a Neapolitan man to describe the local women, who are famous for their beauty, in one word. He replied, simply, "Abundant.") This intersection is considered the center of old Naples.

Directly opposite the statue, head inside **Bar Nilo** to find the **"Chapel of Maradona."** This small "chapel" on the right wall of the café/bar is dedicated to Diego Maradona, an Argentinian soccer star who played for Naples in the 1980s and early 1990s—pushing the team to its greatest success. Locals consider soccer almost a religion, and this guy was practically a deity. You can even see a "hair of Diego" and a teardrop (spinning slowly in a veil above) from the city when, in 1991, he went to another team for more money.

Maradona's reputation was later sullied by problems with organized crime, drugs, and police. However, when he died in 2020 (at age 60), Naples was overwhelmed with grief. Street-art murals of Maradona popped up all over the city—

Still Naples After All These Years

For three centuries (1500-1800), Naples was one of the world's richest and most sophisticated cities. The remnants we see today are an elegant reminder of those glory days and a fascinating case study in what went wrong.

500 BC-AD 500—Greek-Speaking Romans: Naples got its start as Neapolis ("new city"), a thriving Greek colony. Even when conquered by the Romans, the city never fully adopted the Latin language and Roman ways. Actually, those sophisticated Hellenist traditions were exactly what the Romans admired about Naples and induced them to vacation there. For the next 2,000 years, this pattern would repeat itself: The city, living under foreign rule, would evolve independently from the rest of the Italian peninsula.

500-1500—Independence Despite Foreign Rule: The city powered on relatively unchanged after the fall of Rome, ruled as the independent duchy of Naples under Ostrogoths, Byzantines, and Lombards. Next, in late medieval times, it was the Germans and French (the "Angevins") who possessed it as the kingdom of Naples. As sea trade became more important to the European economy, Naples was suddenly smack-dab in the geographical heart of commerce—the Mediterranean.

1500-1800—Flourishing Under Foreign Rule: In 1502, Spain took control of Naples from the French, and their combined wealth made Naples one of the great cities on earth. With a population of 300,000, Naples was eclipsed only by Paris. Deputies of the Spanish king called viceroys presided over the city and proceeded to use Spain's New World wealth to beautify Naples.

As Spain's monarchy passed through the Austrian Habsburgs to the Spanish Bourbons (1734), the cosmopolitan nature of Naples was only enhanced. During this golden age, Naples was home to nobles and royalty from across Europe. Baroque culture thrived, with artists like Caravaggio and Bernini, thinkers like Giordano Bruno, composers like Scarlatti, and a new art form called

in many cases, alongside a portrait of a bishop. The bishop is St. Gennaro, the city's third-century patron saint—and his juxtaposition with Maradona indicates where the soccer star still ranks in the hearts of Neapolitans. (For more on Maradona, see the sidebar on page 44.)

Meanwhile, the coffee bar has posted a quadrilingual sign (though, strangely, not in English) threatening that those who take a picture of the shrine without first buying a cup of coffee may find their camera exploded...*Capisce?*

• *Continue another 100 yards. You may pass gold and silver shops. Some say stolen jewelry ends up here, is melted down immediately, and gets resold in some other form as soon as it cools. Look for* compro oro ("I buy opera. Naples took on the "look" it retains today, with palatial Neoclassical buildings in pastel colors and lavishly ornamented churches.

Despite its veneer of sophistication, trouble was brewing. In 1656, a vicious bubonic plague (Europe's last) killed off half the population. Trade routes shifted west as Europe industrialized, but Naples languished, remaining feudal and agricultural, with the church owning much of the land. The gap between rich foreign elites and homegrown poor grew.

1800-2000—Nationhood: Napoleon conquered the city. Then the monarchy was restored under a medieval-era political arrangement called the Kingdom of the Two Sicilies (uniting Naples and Sicily). The city was still rich, thanks to its Spanish Bourbon rulers, but it was increasingly backward, left behind by a more industrialized and democratic Europe.

Meanwhile, sweeping down from the north, there was a movement for Italian nationhood. Naples—with its legacy of independence from the rest of the peninsula—resisted. In 1860, Naples was forcefully united with the new nation-state of Italy. Its vast wealth was confiscated and taken to the capital in Rome. This began a century-plus of decline. There was no foreign wealth and no local economy. An estimated 4 million southern Italians fled, emigrating to northern Italy and the US. During World War II, Naples suffered Italy's worst bombings. The postwar economic recovery in northern Italy never trickled to the south, which remained under the thumb of the Camorra organized-crime syndicate (the Naples-based Mafia).

Today: The lack of a postwar economic recovery is a boon to tourists. It preserved an independent way of life that dates back centuries. Visitors today enjoy a rare sight—a city that has been continuously inhabited, independent minded, and self-sustaining for over 2,000 years.

gold") *signs—a sign of Naples' perpetual economic woes. Continue to a tiny square at the intersection with...*

⓭ Via San Gregorio Armeno: Stroll up this tiny lane toward the fanciful tower that arches over the street. The street is lined with stalls selling lots of souvenir kitsch, as well as some of Naples' most distinctive local crafts. Among the many figurines on sale, find ***presepi*** (Nativity scenes). Just as many Americans keep an eye out year-round for Christmas-

tree ornaments, Italians regularly add pieces to the family *presepe,* the centerpiece of their holiday decorations. You'll see elaborate manger scenes made of bark and moss, with niches to hold Baby Jesus or Mother Mary. You'll also see lots of jokey figurines caricaturing local politicians, soccer stars, and other celebrities.

Another popular Naples souvenir sold here—and all over—is the ***corno,*** a skinny, twisted, red horn that resembles a chili pepper. The *corno* comes with a double symbolism for fertility: It's a horn of plenty, and it's also a phallic symbol turned upside-down. Neapolitans explain that fertility isn't sexual; it is the greatest gift a person can give—life—and it ensures that one's soul will live on through the next generation. In today's Naples, just as in yesterday's Pompeii (where bulging erections greeted visitors at the entrance to a home), fertility is equated with good luck.

By the way, a bit farther up Via San Gregorio Armeno, you'll find the underground **Napoli Sotterranea archaeological site,** along Via dei Tribunali, which also has some of the city's famous pizzerias. (For more on Napoli Sotterranea, see the listing under "Sights in Naples," later.) Back on Spaccanapoli, some of the highest-quality *presepe* pieces are sold at the **D'Auria shop,** a little farther down on the right opposite #46. Expressive figures are made from terra-cotta, wood, and cloth, often fetching over €250. They even sell the classy *campane* version, under a glass bell.

• *Next you hit busy Via Duomo. Consider detouring five minutes north (left) up Via Duomo to visit Naples'* ***Duomo;*** *just around the corner from that is the* ***Pio Monte della Misericordia Church,*** *with a fine Caravaggio painting (both described later). But for now, continue straight, crossing Via Duomo. Here, Spaccanapoli is named...*

⓮ **Via Vicaria Vecchia:** Here along Via Vicaria Vecchia, the main "sight" is the vibrant street life. It's grittier and less touristy, but just as atmospheric as what we've been seeing. The street and side-street scenes intensify. The area is said to be a center of the Camorra (the Naples-based Mafia-like criminal organization), but as a tourist, you won't notice. Paint a picture with these thoughts: Naples has the most intact street plan of any surviving ancient Greek or Roman city. Imagine this city during those times (and retain these images as you visit Pompeii), with streetside shop fronts that close up after dark, and private homes on upper floors. What you see today is just one more page in a 2,000-year-old story of a city: all kinds of meetings, beatings, and cheatings; kisses; near misses; and little-boy pisses.

You name it, and it occurs right on the streets today, as it has since ancient times. People ooze from crusty corners. Black-and-white death announcements add to the clutter on the walls. Widows sell individual cigarettes. For a peek behind the scenes in the shade of wet laundry, venture down a few side streets. Buy two carrots as a gift for the woman on the fifth floor, if she'll lower her bucket to pick them up. The neighborhood action seems best at about 18:00.

At the tiny fenced-in triangle of greenery, hang out for a few minutes to just observe the crazy motorbike action and teen scene.

• *From here, veer right onto Via Forcella. You emerge into Piazza Vincenzo Calenda, where there's a round fence protecting another chunk of that ancient* ***Greek wall*** *of Neapolis. Hungry? Turn right here, on Via Pietro Colletta, and close out the walk with two typical Neapolitan pizzerias.*

⓯ **Pizza!:** Two of Napoli's most competitive pizzerias are nearby. **Trianon da Ciro** has been serving up pies hot and fast for almost a century. A block farther, on the right (where Via Pietro Colletta hits Via Cesare Sersale; just look for the crowd) is the place where some say pizza was born—at **Antica Pizzeria da Michele.** Michele is for pizza purists. It famously served just two varieties, margherita (tomato sauce and mozzarella) and marinara (tomato sauce, oregano, and garlic, no cheese), but has added two more: *marita* (half margherita and half marinara), and *cosacca* (tomato and pecorino romano). For more on both, see "Eating in Naples," later. Enjoy the classic Neapolitan scene.

Continuing to Centrale Station: If you're catching a train, it's easy to get to Centrale station. Continue downhill on Via Pietro Colletta until you hit the grand boulevard, Corso Umberto I (with a taxi stand). Turn left and walk 15 minutes to the station. Or cross the street and hop on any bus; they all go to the station.

Sights in Naples

Naples' best sights are the Archaeological Museum (next) and my self-guided Naples Walk (earlier). For extra credit, consider the many churches along Spaccanapoli, the gritty Sanità district (north of the Archaeological Museum), Piazza del Plebiscito and other sights near the port, and, farther out, a harborside promenade, the Capodimonte Museum, and the monastery on San Martino—all described in this section.

ARCHAEOLOGICAL MUSEUM (MUSEO ARCHEOLOGICO)

Naples' Archaeological Museum, worth ▲▲▲, is one of the world's great museums of ancient art. It boasts supersized statues as well as art and decorations from Pompeii and Herculaneum, the two ancient burgs that were buried in ash by the eruption of Mount Vesuvius in AD 79. For lovers of antiquity, this museum alone makes Naples a worthwhile stop. When Pompeii was excavated in the late 1700s, Naples' Bourbon king bellowed, "Bring me the best of what you find!" The finest art and artifacts ended up here, leaving the ancient sites themselves barren (though still impressive). It's here at the Archaeological Museum that you can get up close and personal with the ancient world.

Cost and Hours: €22; Wed-Mon 9:00-19:30, last entry at 18:00, closed Tue. While it's rarely a problem, you can avoid lines by purchasing your ticket online. Early and temporary closures are noted on a board near the ticket office: The Secret Room tends to have shorter hours (sometimes closing in the early afternoon), and additional rooms can be closed in July and August.

Information: +39 081 442 2149, www.museoarcheologiconapoli.it.

Getting There: From Centrale station, you can reach the museum by Metro (line 1 to the Museo stop) or taxi (figure about €15 from the train station to the museum).

Tours: The self-guided tour in this chapter covers all the basics. For more detail, the decent **audioguide** (€5, leave ID at ticket desk) focuses largely on the provenance of the artifacts and how they ended up here. For a **guided tour,** book Pina Esposito (see "Tours in Naples," earlier).

🎧 Download my free Archaeological Museum **audio tour**.

Visitor Services: Bag check is obligatory and free. WCs are behind the main staircase on the ground floor.

Eating: The museum's **€ Mann Caffè** has both a counter and table service, and a full menu. The recommended **€ Pizzeria Starita** is a 10-minute walk up Via Santa Teresa degli Scalzi (at Via Materdei 27). For more suggestions, see page 88.

➲ Self-Guided Tour

Entering the museum, cross the atrium and stand at the base of the grand staircase. To your right, on the ground floor, are the larger-than-life statues of the Farnese Collection, starring the *Toro Farnese* and the *Farnese Hercules.* Up the stairs on the mezzanine level are mosaics and frescoes from Pompeii, including the Secret Room of erotic art. On the top floor are more artifacts from Pompeii, a scale model of the doomed city, and bronze statues from Herculaneum.

NAPLES

Naples Archaeological Museum

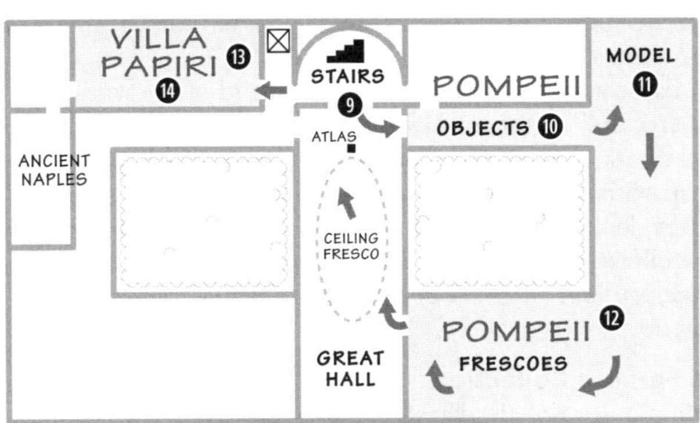

Second Floor (2)

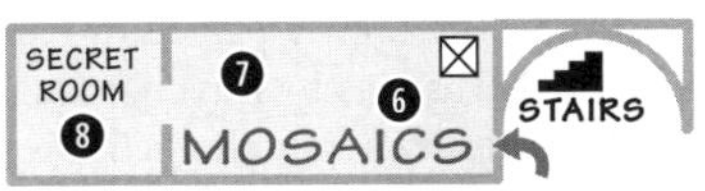

Mezzanine (1)

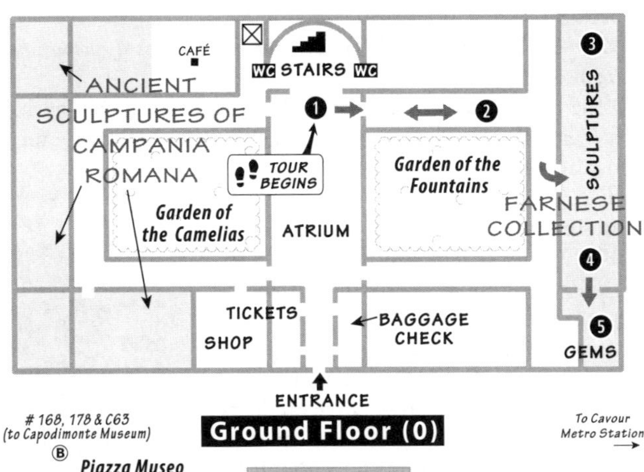

Ground Floor (0)

168, 178 & C63 (to Capodimonte Museum)

B Piazza Museo

To Cavour Metro Station →

GALLERIA PRINCIPE

1. Grand Staircase
2. Hall of the Busts
3. Toro Farnese
4. Farnese Hercules
5. Farnese Cup
6. Various Mosaics
7. Dancing Faun & Battle of Alexander
8. Secret Room
9. Great Hall
10. Metal, Ivory & Glass Objects
11. Model of Pompeii
12. Frescoes
13. Papyrus Scrolls
14. Bronze Statues

Ground Floor

• *From the base of the* ❶ ***grand staircase,*** *turn right through the door marked* Collezione Farnese *and head for the far end, walking through a rich collection of ancient portrait* ❷ ***busts.***

Pause at the busts of **Caracalla** (a third of the way down, on the left), and marvel at how he evolved from idealistic youth to cruel tyrant. Admire the **seated Agrippina** (two-thirds of the way down) with her typical hairstyle, realistic face, and pensive look. Nearby, look in **Vespasian**'s right ear and see how the huge head was hollowed out in medieval times.

• *Now, continue to the end of the hall and jog right, then left, entering Room 13.*

The Farnese Collection

The antiquities of the Farnese Collection are not from Pompeii, but from Rome. Peruse the larger-than-life, wonderfully restored statues filling the hall. They were dug up from Rome's Baths of Caracalla in the 1540s at the behest of Alessandro Farnese (by then Pope Paul III) while he was building the family palace in Rome. His main purpose in excavating the baths was to scavenge quality building stone. The sculptures were a nice extra and helped the palace come in under budget on decorations. In the 1700s, the collection ended up in the hands of Charles, the Bourbon king of Naples (whose mother was a Farnese). His son, the next king, had the lot brought to Naples.

• *Quick—look down to the left end of the hall. There's a woman being tied to a snorting bull.*

The tangled ❸ ***Toro Farnese*** tells a thrilling Greek myth. At 13 feet, it's the tallest ancient marble group ever found, and the largest intact statue from antiquity. A third-century AD copy of a lost bronze Hellenistic original, it was carved out of one piece of marble. Michelangelo and others "restored" it at the pope's request—meaning that they integrated surviving bits into a new work. Some pieces were actually carved by Michelangelo: the head of the woman in back, the torso of the enchantress Dirce (under the bull), and the dog. (Imagine how the statue would stand out if it weren't surrounded by white walls.)

Here's the tragic story behind the statue: Once upon an ancient Greek time, King Lycus was bewitched by Dirce. He abandoned his pregnant wife, Antiope (standing regally in the background). The single mom gave birth to twin boys. When they grew up, they killed their deadbeat dad and tied Dirce to the horns of a bull to be bashed against a mountain. Captured in marble, the action is thrilling: cape flailing, dog snarling, hooves in the air. You can almost hear the bull snorting. And in the back, Antiope oversees this harsh ancient justice with satisfaction.

At the opposite end of the hall stands the ❹ ***Farnese Hercules.*** The great Greek hero is exhausted. He leans wearily on his club (draped with his lion skin) and bows his head. He's just finished the daunting Eleventh Labor, having traveled the world, fought men and gods, freed Prometheus from his rock, and carried Atlas' weight of the world on his shoulders. Now he's returned with the prize: the golden apples of the gods, which he cups behind his back. But, after all that, he's just been told he has to return the apples and do one final labor: descend into hell itself. Oh, man.

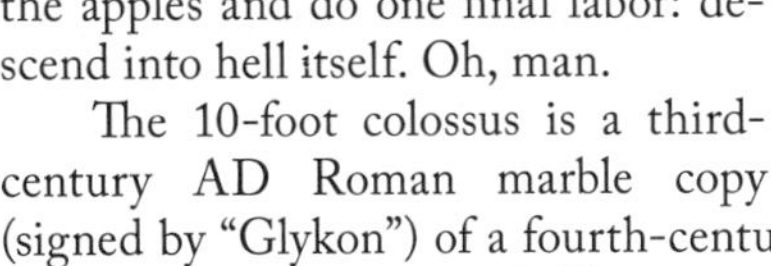

The 10-foot colossus is a third-century AD Roman marble copy (signed by "Glykon") of a fourth-century BC Greek bronze original (probably by Lysippos). The statue was enormously famous in its day. Dozens of copies—some marble, some bronze—have been found in Roman villas and baths. This version was unearthed, along with the *Toro Farnese,* in Rome's Baths of Caracalla.

The *Farnese Hercules* was equally famous in the 16th through 18th century. Tourists flocked first to Rome (then to Naples) to admire it, art students studied it from afar in prints, Louis XIV made a copy for Versailles, and petty nobles everywhere put small-scale knockoffs in their gardens. This curly-haired version of Hercules became the modern world's image of the Greek hero.

• *Behind Hercules is a doorway into the impressive Farnese gem collection (*Gemme Farnese, *Rooms 9 and 10, may be closed for restoration). If open, you'll see cameos and the ancient cereal-bowl-shaped* ❺ **Farnese Cup,** *which features a portrait thought to be of Cleopatra.*

Mezzanine

• *When you're ready to move on, backtrack to the main entry hall with its grand staircase—perhaps stopping briefly to admire the magnificent sarcophagi in adjacent rooms—then head up to the mezzanine level (turn left at the lion and go under the* Mosaici *sign), and enter Room 57.*

Pompeiian Mosaics and the Secret Room

These ❻ **mosaics**—mostly of animals, battle scenes, and geometric designs—were excavated from the walls and floors of Pompeii's ritzy villas. The *Chained Dog* once graced a home's entryway. The colorful mosaic columns (to your right in adjoining Room 58) shaded a courtyard, part of an ensemble of wall mosaics and bubbling fountains. In Room 59, admire the realism of the tambourine-playing musicians, the drinking doves, and the skull—a reminder of the inevitability of death.

Continue a few steps into Room 63, with objects taken from one of Pompeii's greatest villas, the House of the Faun. The 20-inch-high ❼ ***Dancing Faun*** statue was the house's delightful centerpiece. This rare surviving Greek bronze (from the fourth century BC) is surrounded by some of the best mosaics of that age. (Find the wild-eyed little cat, who's caught a bird.)

A museum highlight, just beyond the statue, is the grand ***Battle of Alexander,*** a second-century BC copy of the now-lost original Greek fresco, done a century earlier (may be out for restoration). It decorated a floor in the House of the Faun and was found intact. (The damage you see occurred as this treasure was moved from Pompeii to the king's collection here.) Alexander (left side of the scene, with curly hair and sideburns) is about to defeat the Persians under Darius (central figure, in chariot with turban and beard). This pivotal victory (331 BC) allowed Alexander to quickly overrun much of Asia. Alexander is the only one without a helmet...a confident master of the battlefield while everyone else is fighting for their lives, eyes bulging with fear. Notice how the horses, already in retreat, add to the scene's propaganda value. Notice also the shading and perspective, which Renaissance artists would later work so hard to accomplish. (A modern reproduction of the mosaic is now back in Pompeii, at the House of the Faun.)

Farther on, the ❽ **Secret Room** (*Gabinetto Segreto,* Room 65) contains a sizable assortment of erotic frescoes, well-hung pottery, and perky statues that once decorated bedrooms, meeting rooms, brothels, and even shops at Pompeii and Herculaneum. These bawdy statues and frescoes—many of them once displayed in Pompeii's grandest houses—were entertainment for guests. (By the time they made it to this museum, in 1819, the frescoes could be viewed only with permission from the king—

see the letters in the glass case just outside the door.) The Roman nobles commissioned the wildest scenes imaginable. Think of them as ancient dirty jokes. If you're easily offended, or find scatological humor juvenile, skip this room.

At the entrance, you're enthusiastically greeted by big stone penises that once projected over Pompeii's doorways. A massive phallus was not necessarily a sexual symbol, but a magical amulet used against the "evil eye." It symbolized fertility, happiness, good luck, riches, straight A's, and general well-being.

Circulating counterclockwise through this section, look for the following: the fresco—high up—of a faun playfully pulling the sheet off a woman (#12), only to be surprised to find both sets of genitalia. A few steps farther, see horny "pygmies" from Africa in action (#27). There's a toga with an embarrassing bulge (#34). A particularly high-quality statue depicts a goat and a satyr engaging in a sex act (#36). And, watching over it all with remarkable aplomb, is Venus, the patron goddess of Pompeii (#39).

The back room is furnished and decorated the way an ancient brothel might have been. The 10 frescoes on the wall functioned as both a menu of services offered and as a kind of *Kama Sutra* of sex positions. The glass cases contain more phallic art, including dangling mobiles used as party favors at rowdy banquets.

Top Floor

• *So, now that your travel buddy is finally showing a little interest in art...finish up your visit by climbing the stairs to the top floor.*

At the top of the stairs, pause and get oriented to our final sights. Directly ahead is a doorway (marked Salone Meridiana*) that leads into a big, empty hall. To the left of this grand hall is a series of rooms with more artifacts from Pompeii. To the right are rooms of statues from Herculaneum. Keep this general layout in mind, because occasionally doorways and routes are altered, and you may have to improvise a bit to find your way.*

Frescoes, Statues, Artifacts, and a Model of Pompeii

First, step into the Salone Meridiana. This was the ❾ **great hall** of the university (17th and 18th centuries) until the building became the royal museum in 1777. Walk to the center. The sundial in the floor (angling off to the right, from 1791) still works. Look up to the far-right corner of the hall and find the tiny pinhole. At noon (13:00 in summer), a ray of sun enters the hall and strikes the sundial, showing the time of the year...if you know your zodiac.

Now, back where you entered, go into the series of rooms to the left of the grand hall, with ❿ **metal, ivory, and glass objects** found in Pompeii. You enter through a doorway marked *Oggetti di Vita Quotidiana* (Objects of Daily Life), which leads into Room 89. Browse your way to the far end (Room 85), with a stunning blue vase, decorated with cameo Bacchuses harvesting grapes. Turn left, then right, to find the huge, room-filling ⓫ **model of Pompeii,** a 1:100 scale model of the ruins (Room 96). Face the model from the side labeled *plastico di Pompei*. This is how tourists enter today, up the street, and spilling into the large rectangular forum with the Temple of Jupiter at one end. Farther up in the model are the city's two amphitheater-shaped theaters. This was all that had been excavated when the model was made in 1879. Another model (displayed on the wall) shows the site in 2004, after more excavations, when they'd dug up as far as the huge oval-shaped arena. Video screens capture images from the 1879 model and reconstruct buildings in 3-D as they would have appeared before the eruption.

Continue on (through Rooms 83-80) and enter Room 80 (marked *Affreschi*) to see the museum's impressive collection of (nonerotic) ⓬ **frescoes** taken from the walls of Pompeii villas. Pompeiians loved to decorate their homes with scenes from mythology (Hercules' labors, Venus and Mars in love), landscapes, everyday market scenes, and faux architecture. To the left (in Room 78), find the famous dual portrait of baker Terentius Neo and his wife—possibly two of the 2,000 victims when Vesuvius erupted.

• *Browse through more frescoes and objects from Pompeii in this labyrinth of rooms until, eventually, you end up back at the great hall. From here, exit the hall at the top of stairs: Turn left, and go down and up a dozen stairs and straight into the wing labeled* La Villa dei Papiri.

The artifacts displayed here came from the Herculaneum holiday home of Julius Caesar's father-in-law. Apparently he was an educated man who appreciated everything from Greek philosophy to Latin history and accumulated a robust collection of ⓭ **papyrus scrolls** as well as ⓮ **bronze sculptures** (Room 116).

Look into the lifelike blue eyes of the intense *Corridore* (runners), bent on doing their best. The *Five Dancers,* with their inlaid-ivory eyes and graceful poses, decorated a portico. The next room (117) has more fine works: *Resting Hermes* (with his tired little heel wings) is taking a break. Nearby, the *Drunken Faun* (singing and snapping his fingers to the beat, a wineskin at his side) is clearly living for today. This statue epitomizes the *carpe diem* lifestyle of the Epicurean philosophy followed by Caesar's father-in-law and so many other Romans living in Herculaneum and Pompeii on that fateful morning of August 24, AD 79, when Vesuvius changed everything.

• *Head back down to the ground floor and enjoy the series of rooms cir-*

cling the courtyard, featuring the finest ancient statuary from southern Italy.

Courtyard Rooms: The Art of Campania Romana
While Rome has its famed statue galleries, Naples has its own world-class collection of great art from antiquity. The west half of this museum's ground floor, around its garden courtyard, is filled with sculptures and paintings created for public buildings and excavated from Pompeii, Herculaneum, and beyond in southern Italy, all showing the splendor of ancient Campania. Before leaving the museum, enjoy this finale (well described in English).
• Ka-pow. *Your visit to this mighty museum and its explosion of art is now over.*

SIGHTS ON OR NEAR SPACCANAPOLI

These sights are linked—in this order—on the second half of my Naples Walk, earlier.

▲Church of Gesù Nuovo
This church's unique pyramid-grill facade survives from a fortified 15th-century noble palace. Step inside and appreciate a brilliant Neapolitan Baroque 17th-century interior. The altar celebrates Mary, the art is textbook Counter-Reformation, and the dome is nicely restored after being bombed in 1943.

Cost and Hours: Free, daily 8:00-13:00 & 16:00-20:00, Piazza del Gesù Nuovo.

Visiting the Church: The second chapel on the right features a much-adored statue of St. Giuseppe Moscati (1880-1927), a Christian doctor famous for helping the poor. In 1987, Moscati became the first modern doctor to be canonized. Sit and watch a steady stream of Neapolitans taking turns to pay their respects.

Continue to the third chapel (past Moscati's vertical tombstone) and enter the **Sale Moscati.** Look high on the walls of this long room to see hundreds of ex-votos—tiny red-and-silver plaques of thanksgiving for prayers answered with the help of St. Moscati (each has a symbol of the ailment cured). Naples' practice of using ex-votos, while incorporated into its Catholic rituals, goes back to its pagan Greek roots. Rooms from Moscati's nearby apartment are on display, and a glass case shows possessions and photos of the great doctor.

Just before leaving the Sale Moscati, notice the big bomb casing that hangs high in the left corner. It fell on the church's nave in 1943, but didn't explode...yet another miracle.

▲Church and Cloister of Santa Chiara (Complesso Conventuale di Santa Chiara)

Dating from the 14th century, this church and its ▲ cloister are from a period of French royal rule under the Angevin dynasty. During their two centuries in power (1266-1435), the Angevins (or Anjou) built some of Naples' most recognizable fortresses: Castel Nuovo and Castel Sant'Elmo. Their patronage attracted artists from around Italy who helped create the city's take on Gothic style. Consider the stark contrast between this church (Gothic) and the Gesù Nuovo (Baroque) across the street.

Cost and Hours: Church—free, daily 7:30-13:00 & 16:30-20:00; cloister—€7 includes QR code tour, daily 9:30-17:00, Via Benedetto Croce, www.monasterodisantachiara.it.

Visiting the Church and Cloister: Process up the single **nave,** marveling at the wide-angle view. What you see is a 20th-century reconstruction in Gothic style of the original church, which was extensively damaged by WWII Allied bombs. Stop in the center at the huge inlaid-marble Angevin coat of arms on the floor. Notice the ceiling, rebuilt from reinforced concrete painted to look like wood. Only a few faded bits of medieval frescoes survive of those that once wallpapered the place. Most were stuccoed over during Baroque times or destroyed in the bombing. Turn a slow 360 degrees and notice the lavish **burial chapels**—each a gift from the church to a leading family for their generous and ongoing financial support.

Walk to the right and slowly circle counterclockwise around the perimeter. The chapels (many with multiple tombs) are well described. To the right of the main altar is the densely populated **Bourbon family chapel.** The complexity of their family coat of arms is the result of their "make love, not war" approach to gaining power (expanding by marrying into other blue-blooded families).

The **high altar** is adorned with four finely carved Gothic tombs of 13th-century Angevin kings. Finish your circuit in the rear with a look at an elaborate **manger scene** *(presepe)* peopled with a folkloric Neapolitan crowd from the 1700s. And finally, on the back wall, look for the faded Trinity **fresco** peeking out from the Baroque-era stucco (under the stone canopy). Dating from 1414, it shows a dove representing the Holy Spirit between the heads of God the Father and Christ.

For more art, loop around to the back of the church to the tranquil **cloister** of the attached Franciscan convent. Frescoed religious scenes, including the lives of St. Francis and St. Clare, line the cloister's arcade. A 15-minute video (with English subtitles) gives context. The garden is a touching reminder that daughters of the wealthy (those with a big enough dowry to be accepted) were cloistered here. The lanes of this tranquil garden are lined with majolica-tiled benches and pillars (from about 1600) that show sweet scenes—not religious, but memories of life outside the convent.

The church museum filling the nuns' **dormitory** includes Gothic and Baroque art treasures plus photos of the 1943 destruction. An ongoing excavation site gives a peek at the scant remains of an ancient Greek bath complex. Before leaving, find the grand *presepe* from about 1700.

▲▲Cappella Sansevero

This small chapel is a Baroque explosion mourning a marble-carved body of Christ, who lies on a soft pillow under an incredibly realistic veil. It's also the personal chapel of Raimondo de Sangro, an eccentric Freemason, containing his tomb and the tombs of his family. Like other 18th-century Enlightenment figures, Raimondo was a wealthy man of letters, scientist and inventor, and patron of the arts—and he was also a grand master of the lodge of the Freemasons in Naples. His chapel—filled with Masonic symbolism—is a complex ensemble, with statues representing virtues such as self-control, religious zeal, and the Masonic philosophy of freedom through enlightenment.

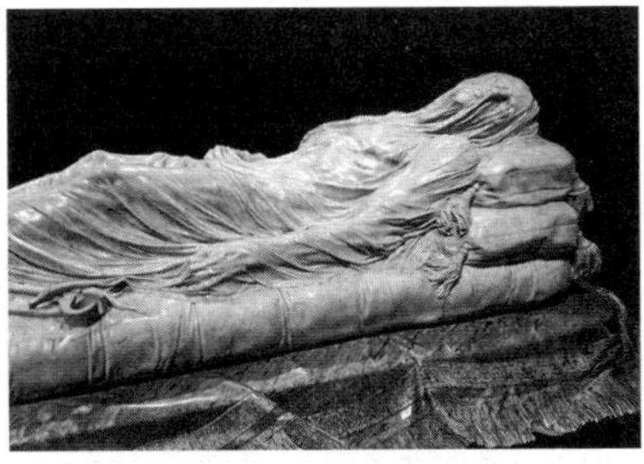

Cost and Hours: €10, online reservations required; open Wed-Mon 9:30-19:00, closed Tue; Via de Sanctis 19, +39 081 551 8470, www.museosansevero.it.

Visiting the Chapel: Pick up the free floor plan, which identifies each of the statues lining the nave. Once inside, study the incredible ***Veiled Christ*** in the center. Carved from marble, it's like no other statue I've seen (by Giuseppe "Howdeedoodat" Sammartino, 1753). The Christian message (Jesus died for our salvation) is accompanied by a Masonic message (the veil represents how the body and ego are obstacles to real spiritual freedom). As you walk from Christ's feet to his head, notice how the expression on Jesus' face goes from suffering to peace.

Raimondo's mom and dad are buried on either side of the **main altar.** To the right of the altar, marking his father's tomb, a statue representing *Despair* or *Disillusion* struggles with a marble rope net (carved from a single piece of stone), symbolic of a troubled mind. The flames on the head of the winged boy represent human intellect—more Masonic symbolism, showing how knowledge frees the human mind. To the left of the main altar is a statue of *Modesty,* marking the tomb of Raimondo's mother (who died after his birth, and was only 20). The veiled woman fingers a broken tablet, symbolizing an interrupted life.

Raimondo de Sangro himself lies buried in a side altar (on the right). Among his inventions was the deep-green pigment used on the ceiling fresco. The inlaid M. C. Escher-esque maze on the floor around de Sangro's tomb is another Masonic reminder of how the quest for knowledge gets you out of the maze of life. This tilework once covered the floor of the entire chapel.

Your Sansevero finale is downstairs: two mysterious, skeleton-like **"anatomical machines."** Perhaps this was another of the mad inventor's fancies: Inject a corpse with a fluid to fossilize the veins so that they'll survive the body's decomposition. While that's the legend, investigations have shown that the veins were artificial, and the models were created to illustrate how the circulatory system works.

▲Napoli Sotterranea (Underground Naples)

This archaeological site, a man-made underground maze of passageways and ruins from Greek and Roman times, can only be toured with a guide. You'll descend 121 steps under the modern city to explore two underground areas. One is the old Greek tuff quarry used to build the city of Neapolis, which was later converted into an immense cistern by the Romans. The other is an excavated portion of a Greco-Roman theater that once seated 6,000 people. Modern development has encroached on the space—some current residents' windows literally look down into the theater ruins.

The tour involves a lot of stairs, as well as one section on a long, narrow, 20-inch-wide walkway—lit only by candlelight—that uses an ancient water channel (claustrophobes will be miserable—it's easy to just skip that part and wait 10 minutes for the group to return). Although there's not much to see, the experience is fascinating and includes a little history from World War II, when the quarry/cistern was turned into a shelter to protect locals from American bombs.

Cost and Hours: €15 for 1.5-hour tour, tours in English run every two hours daily 10:00-18:00, may add tours at busy times, about 40 people/departure; +39 081 296 944, www.napolisotterranea.org. Avoid the very long lines by booking a timed entry online in advance. If stuck in the line without a ticket, talk to an attendant: They *might* be able to move you into the next English-language tour. Bring a light sweater.

Getting There: The site is at Piazza San Gaetano 68, along the lively Via dei Tribunali pizza zone, and just a couple of blocks uphill from Spaccanapoli's statue of the Nile. The entrance is immediately to the left of the Church of San Paolo Maggiore (look for the *Sotterranea* signs or the crowds).

▲Naples Duomo (Duomo di Napoli)

Naples' historic cathedral, built by imported French Anjou kings in the 14th century, boasts a breathtaking Neo-Gothic facade added in the 19th century. Step into the vast interior to see the mix of styles along the side chapels—from pointy Gothic arches to rounded Renaissance ones to gilded Baroque decor.

Cost and Hours: Free, Mon-Sat 8:30-13:30 & 14:30-20:00, Sun 8:30-13:30 & 16:30-19:30, Via Duomo. A handy WC is inside on the left.

Visiting the Church: The cathedral honors St. Gennaro, Naples' patron saint. The **main altar** at the front is ringed by carved wooden seats, filled three times a year by clergy to witness the Miracle of the Blood. Thousands of Neapolitans cram into this church for a peek at two tiny vials with the dried blood of St. Gennaro. As the clergy roots for the miracle to occur, the blood temporarily liquefies. Neapolitans take this ritual with deadly seriousness, and believe that if the blood remains solid, it's terrible luck for the city. Sure enough, on the rare occasion that the miracle fails, locals can point to a terrible event soon after—such as an earthquake, an eruption of Mount Vesuvius, a global pandemic, or an especially disappointing soccer loss.

The stairs beneath the altar take you to a circa-1500 Renaissance **crypt** with the relics of St. Gennaro and a statue of the bishop who rescued them from a rival town. These relics are said to have stopped lava from a 1631 Vesuvius eruption from destroying the city.

The cathedral has two large side chapels (flanking the nave, about halfway to the transept)—each practically a church in its own right. The **Chapel of Santa Restituta** (on the left) stands on the site of the original, early Christian church that predated the cathedral. You'll find some 14th-century golden mosaics in a chapel within the chapel, up at the front left.

The **Chapel of San Gennaro** (on the right) is Baroque with a Greek cross plan and plenty of Counter-Reformation art, dating from around 1650, and a dome filled with a vivid portrayal of Paradise. The vials of St. Gennaro's blood are kept behind the main altar. Read the prayer posted (in English) at the altar to better understand the spirit of the faithful here.

Finally, the **Treasury of San Gennaro** is filled with impressive church art for those who just can't get enough of it (steep €12 admission includes audioguide, daily 9:30-18:00, use external entry under the arcades when the church is closed).

Pio Monte della Misericordia

This small church (near the Duomo, and run by a charitable foundation) displays one of the best works by Caravaggio, *The Seven Works of Mercy*. Upstairs is a ho-hum art gallery. The price is high, but it may be worth it for Caravaggio fans.

Cost and Hours: €10 (ticket booth across the street), Mon-Sat 10:00-18:00, Sun 9:00-14:30, Via dei Tribunali 253, +39 081 446 944, www.piomontedellamisericordia.it.

Visiting the Church: Caravaggio's *Seven Works of Mercy* hangs over the main altar in a darkened gray chapel. The painting is well lit, allowing Caravaggio's characteristically dark canvas to really pop. In one crowded scene, the great early Baroque artist illustrates seven virtues: burying the dead (the man holding a corpse by the ankles), visiting the imprisoned and feeding the hungry (Pero breastfeeding her starving father—a scene from a famous Roman story), sheltering the homeless (a pilgrim on the Camino de Santiago, with his floppy hat, negotiates with an innkeeper), caring for the sick and clothing the naked (St. Martin offers part of his cloak to the injured man in the foreground), and giving drink to the thirsty (Samson chugs from a jawbone in the background). The figures are gathered in a dark Neapolitan alley and watched over by Mary, Jesus, and a pair of angels.

Caravaggio painted this work in Naples in 1607 while in exile from Rome, where he had been sentenced to death for killing a man in a duel. Three years later Caravaggio died from an unknown illness on his way back to Rome to receive a pardon from the pope.

MADRE

MADRE, a museum of contemporary art, displays works by Jeff Koons, Anish Kapoor, Francesco Clemente, and other big names in the art world. Aficionados of modern art consider it one of the better collections in Italy. Some descriptions are in English—you'll need them.

Cost and Hours: €8; Wed-Mon 10:00-19:30—Sun until 20:00, closed Tue, last entry one hour before closing; Via Settembrini 79, +39 081 1973 7254, www.madrenapoli.it.

NEAR THE PORT

This cluster of important sights can be found between the big ceremonial square, Piazza del Plebiscito, and the cruise ship terminal.

For those touring the entire neighborhood, I've linked the piazza to Galleria Borbonica with walking directions. For locations, see the map on page 30.

Getting There from Spaccanapoli: Head down Via Toledo (it's pedestrianized from Piazza Carità to Piazza del Plebiscito). You'll pass the **Banca Intesa Sanpaolo** (filling an older palace); it hosts Caravaggio's blood-spurting *Martyrdom of Saint Ursula* in a small art gallery. Also along here, on a parklike little piazza on your right, is the easy-to-miss **Centrale funicular** up to the San Martino mountaintop. As you near Piazza del Plebiscito, you'll go through a congested area with popular bars, pizza windows, and gelato shops. Push on until you reach the gigantic, semicircular square facing the orange-ish palace.

▲Piazza del Plebiscito

This square celebrates the 1860 vote (*plebiscito,* plebiscite) in which Naples became a part of a unified Italy. Dominating the top of the square is the **Church of San Francesco di Paola,** with its Pantheon-inspired dome and broad, arcing colonnades. If it's open, step inside to ogle the vast interior—a Neoclassical re-creation of one of ancient Rome's finest buildings.

• *Opposite is the...*

Royal Palace (Palazzo Reale)

The exterior of this building displays statues of all those who stayed here: Spanish, French, and even Italian royalty. From the square in front of the palace, look for eight kings in the niches, each from a different dynasty (left to right): Norman, German, French, Spanish, Spanish, Spanish, French (Napoleon's brother-in-law), and, finally, Italian—Victor Emmanuel II, king of Savoy. The statues were done at the request of V. E. II's son, so his dad is the most dashing of the group. As far as palaces go, the interior is relatively unimpressive.

Cost and Hours: €15, skip the dry audioguide (each room has excellent panel descriptions in English); Thu-Tue 9:00-20:00, closed Wed, last entry one hour before closing; +39 848 082 408, www.palazzorealedinapoli.org.

Visiting the Palace: The palace's grand Neoclassical staircase leads up to a floor with 30 plush rooms (visit is all on one floor). You'll follow a one-way route featuring the palace theater, paintings by "the Caravaggio Imitators," Neapolitan tapestries, and furnishings from the 1800s—fine inlaid-stone tabletops, chandeliers, gilded woodwork, and more. As a less-visited sight, wandering through the rooms at leisure makes you feel like royalty yourself. Don't miss the huge, tapestry-laden Hercules Hall or the chance to dance on the wooden floor of this wide-open ballroom. Out the window you'll see the terrace garden with sweeping views of the Bay of Naples. On the way out, peek into the royal chapel, with an altar made entirely of precious stones and (in the next room, behind a curtain) a fantastic Nativity scene—a commotion of 18th-century ceramic figurines.

Hanging Gardens: This beautiful garden terrace, overlooking the Bay of Naples, costs extra (book online) and can be seen only a few times a day (with an attendant). If your visit happens to coincide with one of these times—and the weather's fine—it's worth adding on.

• *Continue 50 yards past the Royal Palace (toward the trees) to enjoy a...*

Fine Harbor View

While boats busily serve Procida, Capri, and Sorrento, Mount Vesuvius smolders ominously in the distance. Look back to see the vast "Bourbon red" palace. The hilltop above Piazza del Plebiscito is San Martino, with its Carthusian monastery-turned-museum and the fortress called Castel Sant'Elmo (the Centrale funicular to the top is just across the square and up Via Toledo). The promenade you're on continues to Naples' romantic harborfront—the fisherman's quarter (Borgo Marinaro)—a fortified island connected to the mainland by a stout causeway, with its fanciful, ancient Castel dell'Ovo (Egg Castle) and trendy harborside restaurants. From there, the Lungomare harborside promenade—described later—continues past the Santa Lucia district, stretching out along the Bay of Naples. This long promenade, running along Via Francesco Caracciolo to the Mergellina district and beyond, is a delightful people-watching scene on balmy nights.

• *Head back through the piazza and pop into (on the left)...*

Gran Caffè Gambrinus

This coffeehouse, facing the piazza, takes you back to the elegance of 1860. It's a classic place to sample a crispy *sfogliatella* pastry, or perhaps the mushroom-shaped, rum-soaked bread-like cakes called *babà,* which come in a huge variety. Stand at the bar *(banco),* pay double to sit *(tavola),* or just wander around as you imagine the café buzzing with the ritzy intellectuals, journalists, and artsy bohemian types who munched on *babà* here during Naples' 19th-century heyday (long hours daily, Piazza del Plebiscito 1).

• *A block away, tucked behind the palace, you can peek inside the Neoclassical...*

Teatro di San Carlo

Built in 1737, 41 years before Milan's La Scala, this is Europe's oldest opera house and Italy's second most respected (after La Scala). The original theater burned down in 1816 and was rebuilt within the year. Guided 35-minute visits in English basically just show you the fine auditorium with its 184 boxes—each with a big mirror to reflect the candlelight (€9; 30-minute tours in English usually run daily at 12:30 and 15:30, additional departures in Italian; schedule can change so check online or email visiteguidate@teatrosancarlo.it to confirm; theater box office +39 081 797 2331, tour info +39 081 7972 412, www.teatrosancarlo.it).

• *Beyond Teatro di San Carlo and the Royal Palace is the huge, harborfront...*

Castel Nuovo

This imposing castle now houses government bureaucrats and the **Civic Museum,** as well as tourable underground areas, archaeological excavations, and a rooftop terrace (all but the museum require a pricey tour). The castle feels like a mostly empty shell, with a couple of dusty halls of Neapolitan art, but the views over the bay from the upper terraces are impressive (museum-€6, Mon-Sat 9:00-18:00, Sun until 13:00, last entry one hour before closing; €16 tours run at the top of each hour, +39 081 795 7722). The castle also hosts frequent special events and exhibits.

• *Head back to Teatro di San Carlo, cross the street, and go through the tall yellow arch into...*

▲Galleria Umberto I

This Victorian iron-and-glass shopping mall opened in 1890 to reinvigorate the district after a devastating cholera epidemic occurred here. Gawk up, then down—it's traditional to get a photo standing on your zodiac sign. Exiting through the left wing (with a possible stop at La Sfogliatella Mary—famous for their still-warm namesake pastries) brings you back out on Via Toledo.

• *Just up the street and behind Piazza del Plebiscito is an interesting subterranean experience.*

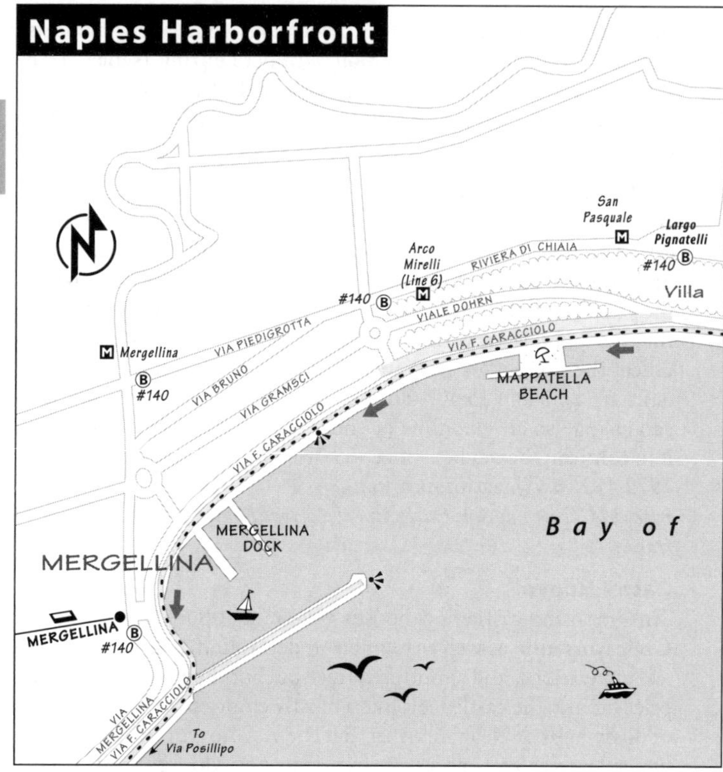

▲Galleria Borbonica

Beneath Naples' Royal Palace was a vast underground network of caves, aqueducts, and cisterns that originated as a quarry in the 15th century. In the mid-1800s, when popular revolutions were threatening royalty across Europe, the understandably nervous king of Naples, Ferdinand II, had this underground world expanded to create an escape tunnel from the palace to his military barracks nearby. In World War II, it was used as an air-raid shelter; after the war, the police used it to store impounded cars and motorcycles. Today, enthusiastic guides take the curious on a fascinating 70-minute, 500-yard-long guided walk through this many-layered world littered with disintegrating 60-year-old vehicles upon which Naples sits.

Cost and Hours: €11 English-language tours leave Fri-Sun at 10:00, 12:00, 15:00, and 17:00; +39 081 764 5808, www.galleriaborbonica.com. The most convenient entry is just behind Piazza del Plebiscito—up Via Gennaro Serra and left on Vico del Grottone to #4.

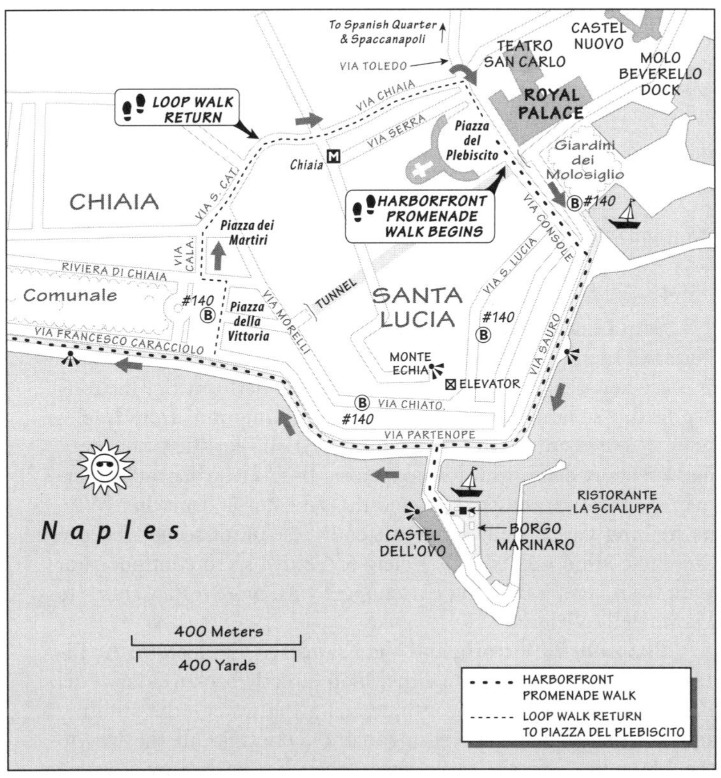

WEST ALONG THE BAY

▲▲Lungomare *Passeggiata* (Harborside Promenade)

Each evening, relaxed and romantic Neapolitans in the mood for a scenic harborside stroll do their *vasche* (laps) along the inviting Lungomare harborside promenade and beyond. To join in (best after 19:00), stroll down to the waterfront from Piazza del Plebiscito and then along Via Nazario Sauro to the beginning of a delightful series of harborside promenades that stretch romantically all the way out of the city. Along the way, you'll enjoy views of Mount Vesuvius and the Bay of Naples. Crowded on weekends and lively on any good-weather evening, the entire route attracts families, amorous couples, and friends hanging out. For a bonus vista, ride the elevator (corner of Via Chiatamone and Via Santa Lucia, €1.30) to the Monte Echia viewpoint.

***Passeggiata* Options:** The simplest approach is to simply walk as far as you like away from the city center and, when you're ready to return, hop on a bus, ride Metro line 6, or grab a cab. Convenient bus #140 mirrors much of this walk, running to the end point at Via Posillipo (note that the first part of its route is a block off the water, on Riviera di Chiaia; see the "Naples Harborfront" map). Metro line 6 gets you back to Piazza Municipio.

Or, to turn your walk into a **good loop** full of people-watching action, consider this route (which can easily be done in reverse order): Stroll from Piazza del Plebiscito down Via Nazario Sauro and Via Partenope to Piazza della Vittoria; from there head inland through Piazza dei Martiri and down Via Chiaia to return to Piazza del Plebiscito.

Here's a brief rundown of the promenade's three sections:

Santa Lucia and Borgo Marinaro: The first stretch, along Via Nazario Sauro, passes the Santa Lucia district, so called because this is where the song "Santa Lucia" was first performed. (The song is probably so famous in America because immigrants from Naples sang it to remember the old country.) At the fortified causeway, make a short detour out to the historic Borgo Marinaro ("Fisherman's Quarter"), and poke around this fabled island-marina. With its striking Castel dell'Ovo and trendy restaurant scene, you can dine here amid yachts with a view of Vesuvius. To continue your walk from here, follow Via Partenope—with more restaurants—to Piazza della Vittoria.

Piazza della Vittoria and Via Francesco Caracciolo: At Piazza della Vittoria, you can either loop directly back to Piazza del Plebiscito (see earlier) or continue along the water—the strolling action stretches along the Lungomare Caracciolo all the way to the Mergellina district. Tree-shaded benches backed by a waterfront park invite you to pause and enjoy the views. (Or you can skip ahead to Mergellina by hopping on bus #140 at Piazza della Vittoria.)

Mergellina and Via Posillipo: The promenade continues past yacht harbors and rocks popular for swimming and sunbathing, under lavish Liberty Style villas, to tiny coves and inviting fish restaurants. Perched on the hillside at Posillipo (about 30 minutes beyond Lungomare Mergellina) awaits the delightful **€€€ Ristorante Reginella,** with majestic views (closed Tue, Via Posillipo 45a, +39 081 240 3220, www.ristorantereginella.com)—and a #140 bus stop is right there for your quick return.

Posillipo Hill

More a very long, tree-covered, villa-slathered peninsula than a "hill," this promontory helps define the southern boundary of the Bay of Naples. Only conquered by road-building engineers in the early 19th century, Posillipo is best known for its many waterfront villas. While they come in a dizzying array of architectural styles, most Posillipo villas share these features: huge cellars (for protection against both sea storms and invaders), decorative fringes on top (often castle-like crenellations), and watchtowers. This area is perhaps best appreciated from the water—giving a look at a spacious, green, and colorful side of Naples in contrast to the congested, tight lanes of the historical center. (If you go by bus, the best option is #C21 from Lungomare Mergellina—avoid bus #140, as it stops beneath the overpass into the park and there's no easy way up.) Italians, who romanticize Posillipo, recognize many of these villas from their favorite movies and TV shows. Out at the tip of Posillipo is the fine, sprawling Parco Virgiliano, which locals call "Lovers' Park" for its restful trails and gorgeous views over the Bay of Naples, with Vesuvius looming on the horizon.

SANITÀ DISTRICT

While the characteristic Spaccanapoli and Spanish Quarter are being tamed, today's clear winner for wild-and-crazy Neapolitan life in the streets is the colorful Sanità district, north of the Archaeological Museum.

▲▲Sanità District Stroll

A big part of the attraction of Naples is its *basso* living (life in the streets). Many locals with enough money to move to the sanity of the suburbs choose instead to keep living where the action is—in a cauldron of flapping laundry, police sirens, broken cobblestone lanes, singing merchants, sidewalks clogged with makeshift markets, and walls crusted with ancient posters and graffiti.

One of Naples' most historic zones, Sanità is sometimes called "the living *presepe*" for the way people live stacked on top of each other in rustic conditions, as if in an elaborate manger scene. (Because organized crime is still strong in this quarter, development is slow.) Literally "the healthy place" (named for the freshness of the air, originally so high above the dense city), this is *the* place for a photo safari.

The reason to visit Sanità is simply to swim through its amazing river of life. From near the **Porta San Gennaro** gate (three blocks east of the Archaeological Museum and a block downhill from Metro: Cavour), head up **Via Fuori,** the pedestrian lane directly opposite the gate (across Via Foria), and then along Via dei Vergini, diving deep into a thriving daily market scene.

Pop into the courtyard of the **Palazzo dello Spagnolo** (#19 on the left) to peek at an extravagant 18th-century staircase. While originally the palatial residence of one noble family, with a courtyard for the horse carriages, today it accommodates many families.

Then dogleg onto **Via Arena della Sanità** and continue uphill (past a massive staircase in the courtyard of Palazzo San Felice at #6). Ahead, you'll see the big graffiti **wall mural** of movie stars

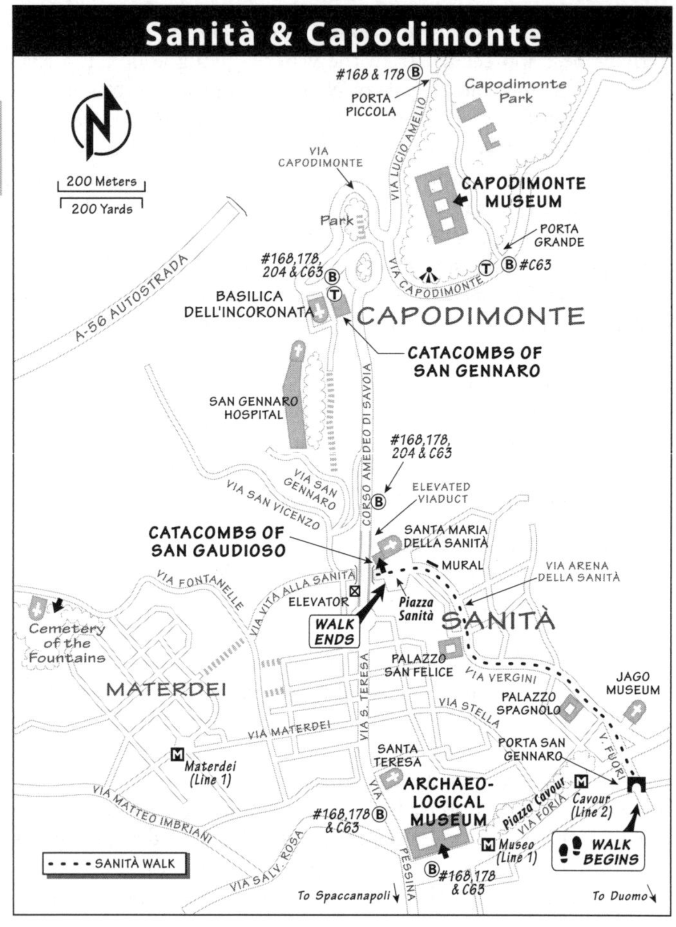

Totò and Peppino, an Italian Laurel and Hardy-type 1950s duo who played up the cliché of Naples for all Italy.

You then reach Piazza Sanità, where you'll stand before the Basilica Santa Maria della Sanità, which sits atop the **Catacombs of San Gaudioso.** Because this area was just outside the old city walls, the dead were buried here in the fifth and sixth centuries (catacomb entrance farther left of the church, just before the viaduct, €13 ticket includes Catacombs of San Gennaro—described later, hourly English tours run Thu-Tue 10:00-17:00, closed Wed, www.catacombedinapoli.it).

From here you have three options: Browse back down the way you just came, continue 10 minutes up Via Sanità and Via Fontanelle to the Cemetery of the Fountains (may be closed—ask at the Catacombs ticket office before you go; described next), or ride a free elevator (just past the church, under the viaduct) up to Capodimonte and the Catacombs of San Gennaro.

Cemetery of the Fountains (Cimitero delle Fontanelle)

These quirky caves—stacked with human bones and dotted with chapels—closed during the Covid-19 pandemic and may still be closed when you visit. Ask locally before venturing out.

A thousand years ago, a quarry was cut into the hills at the high end of Napoli. Then, in the 16th century, churches with crowded cemeteries began moving the bones of their long dead here to make room for the newly dead. Later these caves housed the bones of plague victims and the city's paupers. In the 19th century, many churches again emptied their cemeteries and added even more skulls to this vast ossuary. Then a cult of people appeared whose members adopted the skulls. They named the skulls, put them in little houses, brought them flowers, and asked them to intervene with God for favors from the next life.

Getting There: It's at Via Fontanelle 77, a 15-minute walk through a slightly sketchy neighborhood from the Catacombs of San Gaudioso. You can also get here by hopping in a taxi or by riding the Metro to the Materdei stop and following the brown signs for 10 minutes.

Jago Museum

This museum, which opened in 2023 at the base of the Sanità district, features the work of "Neapolitan Michelangelo" Jacopo Cardillo (a.k.a. Jago), a modern sculptor who is all the buzz for his ability to channel the magic of Giuseppe Sammartino in his statues. You could say he's the Enya of marble. Jago's workshop/exhibition space is in the 17th-century Baroque Church of Sant'Aspreno ai Crociferi, which had been abandoned for nearly 40 years until a mission-driven cooperative—run by a group of young Sanità residents—came together during the pandemic to breathe life into this previously neglected neighborhood.

Jago's sculptures are notable for his progressive take on classics such as Michelangelo's *Pieta;* Jago's interpretation was inspired by a famous image of a Turkish police officer carrying the body of a young Syrian refugee who washed ashore in 2016. Meanwhile, at the back of the church, *Aiace and Cassandra* depicts the Greek myth of Cassandra's rape at the hands of Ajax during the Trojan War—only this time she fights back. By the time you visit, Jago may have finished his greatest work yet: a

15-foot answer to Michelangelo's *David*...but his version will be a woman.

Cost and Hours: €10; daily 10:00-14:00, Fri-Sun also 15:00-19:00, ask about tours in English; show ticket at Catacombs of San Gennaro and San Gaudioso for discount: near the Cavour Metro station at the Church of Sant'Aspreno ai Crociferi, https://jago.art/en/museum.

ON CAPODIMONTE

Capodimonte, beyond Sanità and about a mile due north from the Archaeological Museum, is one of Naples' three hills. It's home to an excellent art museum, its surrounding park, and, not far away, tourable catacombs.

Getting There: Reaching Capodimonte is easiest by taxi or Uber (figure €15 from the city center). Various public buses run from near Piazza Dante and the Archaeological Museum up to Capodimonte, including #168, #178, #204, and #C63—these stop near the catacombs (hop off when you get to the huge, domed church) before continuing up to the museum and park. Note that the walled Capodimonte Park has two entrances—Porta Piccola and Porta Grande—near the museum.

Linking Capodimonte and Sanità: Start at the Capodimonte Museum, walk through its park 15 minutes to the Catacombs of San Gennaro, then taxi to Porto San Gennaro for the start of my Sanità district stroll, finishing at the Catacombs of San Gaudioso (included with your San Gennaro ticket). Alternatively, it's a 15-minute walk between the San Gennaro and San Gaudioso catacombs, from where you can reverse my Sanità district stroll and finish with a meal in this funky neighborhood.

▲Capodimonte Museum (Museo di Capodimonte)

This hilltop is home to Naples' lesser-known but outstanding art museum. It fills a cavernous summer palace from the city's golden age—from the 1750s until unification in the 1870s. Built by the Bourbon kings, the palace seems to say, "We're as powerful as our French rivals." The palace and the art that fills it are the legacy of several ruling dynasties—including the Farnese, Bourbons, and Savoys. The collection bursts with masterful works by Michelangelo, Raphael, Titian, Caravaggio, and other big names. Along with its art, the museum—set in the midst of a sprawling hilltop park overlooking Naples—showcases the palace's history

and its splendid furnishings. Most visitors to Naples understandably prefer to focus on the city's vibrant street life, characteristic churches, and ancient artifacts. But for art lovers and royalty buffs, Capodimonte rates ▲▲.

Cost and Hours: €15, Thu-Tue 8:30-19:30, closed Wed, last entry one hour before closing, café, Via Miano 2, +39 081 749 9111, http://capodimonte.cultura.gov.it.

Nearby: Don't overlook the expansive **Capodimonte Park.** Once a hunting ground for royalty, the park is now a pleasure garden—beloved by Neapolitans—with elegant paths and lovely gardens sprouting trees and exotic plants from around the world. If you've planned ahead, this is a lovely spot for a picnic.

Visiting the Museum: The gigantic collection sprawls through the massive building. Thanks to a curator who enjoys rearranging things and loaning and borrowing works, it's hard to get a handle on exactly what's on view, and where. Room numbers are hard to follow (they're sometimes faint and high up on door frames). Still, here's a hit list of highlights that you may see on your visit.

• *After buying your ticket, head up several flights of stairs (or ride the elevator) to the...*

First Floor: One of the first rooms you encounter may be dark, until you step in and the lights pop on to reveal large charcoal drawings by Raphael (Moses shields his eyes from the burning bush, 1514) and Michelangelo (a group of soldiers, 1546; and *Venus and Love,* 1534).

As you work your way through the next set of rooms, you may see works by Titian (1488-1576). Look for ***Portrait of Pope Paul III.*** It depicts Alessandro Farnese, the local bigwig whose family married into Bourbon royalty; later, as Pope Paul III, he was responsible for bringing great art to Naples. Also look for one of many versions of Titian's ***Danaë,*** where—as told in the Greek myth—the sensuous central character looks up at a cloud containing the essence of Zeus (a shower of coins), about to impregnate her. Enjoy the cupid's surprised look at the action as the courtesan awaits her union. Finally, find Titian's poignant portrait of a penitent **Mary Magdalene,** with finely detailed tears running down her cheeks (1565).

You may also see works by the Renaissance pioneer Masaccio; Mantegna's medallion-like *Portrait of Ludovico Gonzaga,* c. 1461, a very small but finely executed profile portrait; and Giovanni Bellini's *Circumcision of Christ.* (Bellini was Titian's master.)

Collezione Farnese: The core of the museum's collection sprawls through several rooms. These highlights may appear in roughly this order:

Several works by Raphael, including a portrait of the man who will become Pope Paul III, back when he was "just" Alessandro Farnese; and some pieces by El Greco, too.

Parmigianino's ***Antea*** (1531-1535)—one of the collection's highlights—addresses us with an unblinking, dilated gaze. She wears a mink stole (astonishingly lifelike, with disgusting little teeth), gold chain, and hair brooch—items commonly presented by a lover. By wearing the gifts, Antea signals her acceptance of her suitor's advances.

The Misanthrope (1568) is a remarkable work by Pieter Bruegel the Elder. The painting suggests the pointlessness of giving up on life and becoming a hermit; cut off from the world and lost in thought, the title figure doesn't even notice that he's about to step on a trail of thorns. Behind him, a wild-eyed young man is stealing the misanthrope's money pouch (Hey! I saw that guy on the Circumvesuviana!).

Annibale Carracci's ***Hercules at the Crossroads*** (1596) presents the hero with a choice: virtue (on the left, nature and letters, but a steep uphill climb) or vice (on the right, scantily clad women, music, theater masks, and an easy, flat path). While his foot points one way, he looks the other...his mind not yet made up.

• *At the end of the Collezione Farnese, turn left to enter the...*

Royal Apartments: It's easy to forget that this museum is set in a royal palace. Originally a simple hunting lodge, in the 18th century the king decided it could be a grand palace. Several dynasties enjoyed its regal ballrooms and imposing reception rooms while amassing their impressive collections of art. The **grand hall** comes with a massive bronze chandelier hanging over an ancient Roman inlaid-marble floor, which originally decorated the palace of Roman Emperor Tiberius on Capri (installed here in 1877). The rooms that follow tell the stories of three Bourbon kings with portraits and objects from their reign. At the opposite corner of this wing, imagine attending a regal ball in the opulent **Salone delle Feste.**

Collezione delle Ciccio: Branching off from the royal apartments, this section is filled with royal porcelain—considered white gold—from all corners of Europe: Naples, Vienna, Paris (Sèvres), and Meissen (Germany).

• *From here, depending on which areas are open, you may circle through even more apartments (perhaps seeing rooms decorated in the Napoleon-pleasing Neoclassical style—a reminder that Napoleon's older brother once ruled the kingdom of Napoli). Or you may be routed back to the Collezione Farnese.*

Either way, when done on this level, head back to where you entered and continue up the stairs (or take the elevator) to the...

Second Floor: First you may see a cycle of Flemish **tapestries** (depicting the Battle of Pavia). Then, as you pass through a few halls of Gothic altarpieces, watch out for a few highlights:

Near the end of the altarpiece corridor, on the right is a fine **altarpiece** from Nottingham, England. Carved from alabaster in the 15th century, it shows expressive scenes from the Passion of Christ. At the far end of this corridor is a darkened room with Simone Martini's lavish and delicate 1317 painting of ***St. Louis of Toulouse*** crowning his brother, Robert, the Anjou king of Naples.

Proceeding down a long line of adjoining rooms, look for Colantonio's painting ***San Girolamo nello Studio*** (c. 1445), in which the astonishing level of detail—from the words on the page of the open book, to the balled-up pages tucked away at the bottom of the frame—drives home the message: Only through complete devotion and meticulous dedication can you hope to accomplish great things...like pulling a thorn out of a lion's paw.

Finally, near the end of this wing, watch for one of the museum's top pieces, Caravaggio's ***The Flagellation.*** Typical of his *chiaroscuro* (light/dark) style, Caravaggio uses a ribbon of light to show us only what he wants us to see: a broken Christ about to be whipped, and the manic fury of the man (on his left) who will do the whipping. This scene could be set in a Naples alley. Compare this with most of the paintings we've seen so far—of popes, saints, and aristocrats. Caravaggio was given refuge in Naples while fleeing a murder trial in Rome. (They put him to work painting. Of the eight canvases he painted during this period, three remain in Naples.) Caravaggio was revolutionary in showing real life rather than idealized scenes—helping common people to better relate to these stories.

The rest of this floor is a maze of rooms, all with 17th-century works by artists who were inspired by Caravaggio and the lesser-known **Jusepe de Ribera,** a Spaniard who came to Naples in 1616 just after Caravaggio's death.

▲▲Catacombs of San Gennaro

Behind the towering modern church of Madre del Buon Consiglio (Mother of Good Counsel) are tucked the most impressive ancient catacombs south of Rome. It started as a pagan tomb of little consequence, but then St. Agrippino, the local bishop, was buried here in the third century. Later, in the fifth century, the bones of St. Gennaro (patron of Naples) were moved here. Suddenly a site of special reverence—complete with miracles—it became a place where Neapolitans wanted to be buried as well. Today, the catacombs are run by a nonprofit organization of earnest young people who conduct walking tours. These half-mile walks survey more than a thousand burial niches on two levels that date from the second to sixth century (many with frescoes and mosaics surviving...barely). You won't see any bones here; they were moved to the Cemetery of the Fountains (see listing, earlier).

Cost and Hours: €13 ticket includes Catacombs of San Gaudioso—described earlier, at busy times it's wise to book online, included English-language tours depart on the hour Thu-Tue 10:00-17:00, closed Wed, café; bus #168, #178, #204, or #C63 to Via di Capodimonte 13, +39 081 744 3714, www.catacombedinapoli.it.

ON SAN MARTINO

The ultimate view overlooking Naples, its bay, and the volcano is from San Martino hill, just above (and west of) the city center. Up top you'll find a mighty fortress, Castel Sant'Elmo, and the adjacent Baroque San Martino monastery-turned-museum. While the castle requires a lot of walking for little payoff, the monastery/museum is a city highlight and comes with less hiking and the best views. The surrounding neighborhood (especially Piazza Fuga) has a classy uptown vibe compared to the gritty city-center streets below. Cheapskates can enjoy the views for free from the benches on the square in front of the monastery.

Getting There: From Via Toledo, the Spanish Quarter gradually climbs up San Martino's lower slopes, before steep paths take you up the rest of the way. While three different funiculars make climbing the hill easy and memorable, I'd catch the **Montesanto funicular,** which leaves just a few steps below the Metro stop of the same name (three blocks above Via Toledo, near the wonder-

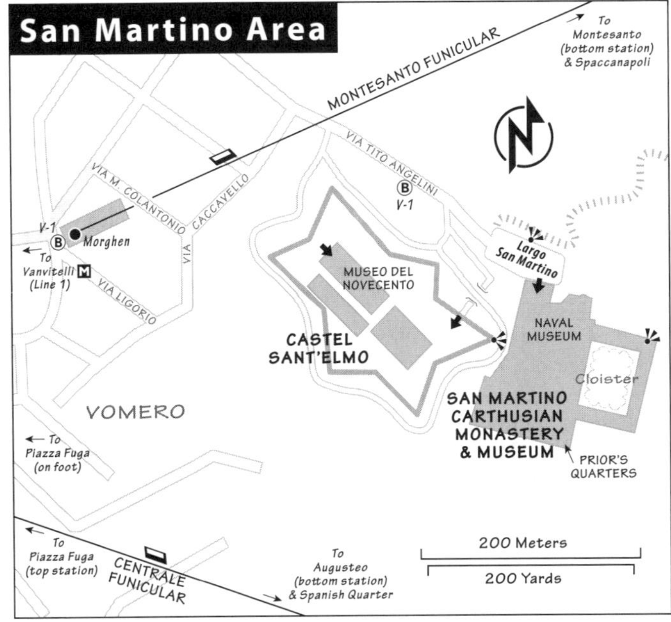

ful Via Pignasecca street market). Ride to the Morghen station, which puts you just under the sights and above the elegant Vomero neighborhood.

Leaving the funicular, look right and follow the brown signs for *Castel S. Elmo* and *Museo di San Martino,* heading uphill; in about five minutes you'll reach the castle, with its bronze plaque, and then the monastery/museum.

Another convenient—if less scenic—approach is via **Metro line 1** to the Vanvitelli stop, at Piazza Vanvitelli in the center of the Vomero neighborhood. From there it's a straight shot up Via Alessandro Scarlatti via stairs (and escalators) to the Morghen funicular station and the sights.

Castel Sant'Elmo

This massive castle, built in the 16th century by the Spanish, must have been effective at asserting their rule. Notice how much of it was cut right from the *tufo*-stone hilltop. While little more than an empty husk today, the star-shaped fortress boasts commanding views over the city and the entire Bay of Naples. From the ticket booth, you'll hike a long ramp to the upper courtyard and climb up to the ramparts to enjoy the 360-degree views.

In the middle of the yard (entry at the far side) is the likeable little Museo del Novecento, a gallery of works by 20th-century Neapolitan artists displayed in chronological order from 1910 to 1980 (covered by same ticket).

Cost and Hours: €5; open daily 8:30-19:30, art museum closes at 17:00 and on Tue; Via Tito Angelini 22, +39 081 229 4401, www.museicampania.cultura.gov.it (under "Luoghi della Cultura").

▲▲San Martino Carthusian Monastery and Museum (Certosa e Museo di San Martino)

The San Martino monastery, founded in 1325 and dissolved in the early 1800s, is now a sprawling museum with perhaps the most beautiful church in Italy south of Rome; this sight gets my vote for the best grand views of Naples. The square out front offers fine city views for free and a few cafés angling for your business.

Cost and Hours: €6, Thu-Tue 8:30-19:30, closed Wed, never crowded, €5 audioguide brings meaning to the art and palatial rooms, Largo San Martino 5, +39 081 229 4502, www.museicampania.cultura.gov.it (under "Luoghi della Cultura").

Visiting the Monastery and Museum: After purchasing your ticket, step into the **church** across the courtyard. First built in the Gothic style in the mid-1300s, this church (as well as the entire complex) received an extreme Baroque makeover centuries later. But notice how even with all the gorgeous Baroque statues, paintings, and gilding, the Gothic lines still pop. To protect the inlaid marble floor, you're not allowed into the nave. (The space behind the altar is accessible later in your visit.)

A variety of museum exhibits, art, and sculpture are housed throughout the complex. The **Naval Museum** has nautical paintings, model boats, and giant ceremonial gondolas that were used by various royalty.

Beyond the Naval Museum is a view terrace. Then turn right into the **Prior's Quarters**—a former palace (appreciate the ceilings as you wander) that's now an art gallery with fine paintings, including romantic views of 19th-century Naples. A series of rooms leads to a corner terrace with the ultimate dramatic Bay of Naples view. Enjoy an excellent collection of ***presepi*** (Nativity scenes), both life-size and miniature, including a spectacular one (the size of a pickleball court) by Michele Cucinello—the best I've seen in this *presepe*-crazy city.

Beyond the *presepi* is the large **garden cloister,** where monks would eventually rest in peace. Circle the cloister counterclockwise. It's ringed by cells. The tiny wooden windows were for feeding monks when in solitude. On the far side a 1465 painting shows Naples—already with its most historic buildings and serious harbor. The route then leads through the historic map gallery, the church's apse and choir, and to the sacristy with a Renaissance celebration of perspective in its inlaid wooden cupboards. You leave thinking the prior and his monastery must have been very wealthy.

Sleeping in Naples

As an alternative to intense Naples, some travelers prefer to sleep in mellow Sorrento, just over an hour away. But to really get a feel for the Neapolitan way of life, stay in the city. High season in Naples is spring and fall. Prices are soft during the hot, slow summer months (July-Sept) and plunge during the pleasantly cool winters. You can assume all hotels have air-con and elevators.

Many places in the center are on the higher floors of old buildings and can be hard to find; get detailed instructions from your hotel before you arrive. You may also need to ring a buzzer to open a gate (or a small door set into larger doors).

AROUND SPACCANAPOLI

To see the city's best face, stay in the area above and below Spaccanapoli stretching between Piazza Gesu Nuovo and Piazza Vincenzo Calenda.

South of Spaccanapoli

€€€€ Decumani Hotel de Charme is a classy oasis tucked away on a residential lane in the very heart of the city, just off Spaccanapoli. While the street is Naples-dingy, the hotel is an inviting retreat, filling an elegant 17th-century palace with 39 rooms and a stunning breakfast room (family rooms, Via San Giovanni Maggiore Pignatelli 15, Metro: Università; if coming from Spaccanapoli, this lane is one street toward the train station from Via Santa Chiara, +39 081 551 8188, www.decumani.com, info@decumani.com).

€€€ Artemisia Domus has a luxurious feel without luxury prices. This peaceful oasis on the fourth floor of a historic building has a warm, inviting lobby. Its eight rooms, some with views and some with jacuzzis, blend a timeworn elegance with artsy touches (elevator to top floor but some stairs, spa, Via dei Carrozzieri a Monteoliveto 13, Metro: Dante, +39 081 304 6280, www.artemisiadomus.com, info@artemisiadomus.com).

€€ B&B l'Alloggio dei Vassalli is an unexpected rustic gem hidden down a graffitied side street. The former palazzo has wood-beam ceilings, tiled floors, and cozy common areas. While it's part of a chain, it has a personal bed-and-breakfast vibe (no elevator, family rooms, self-service laundry across the street, Via Donnal-

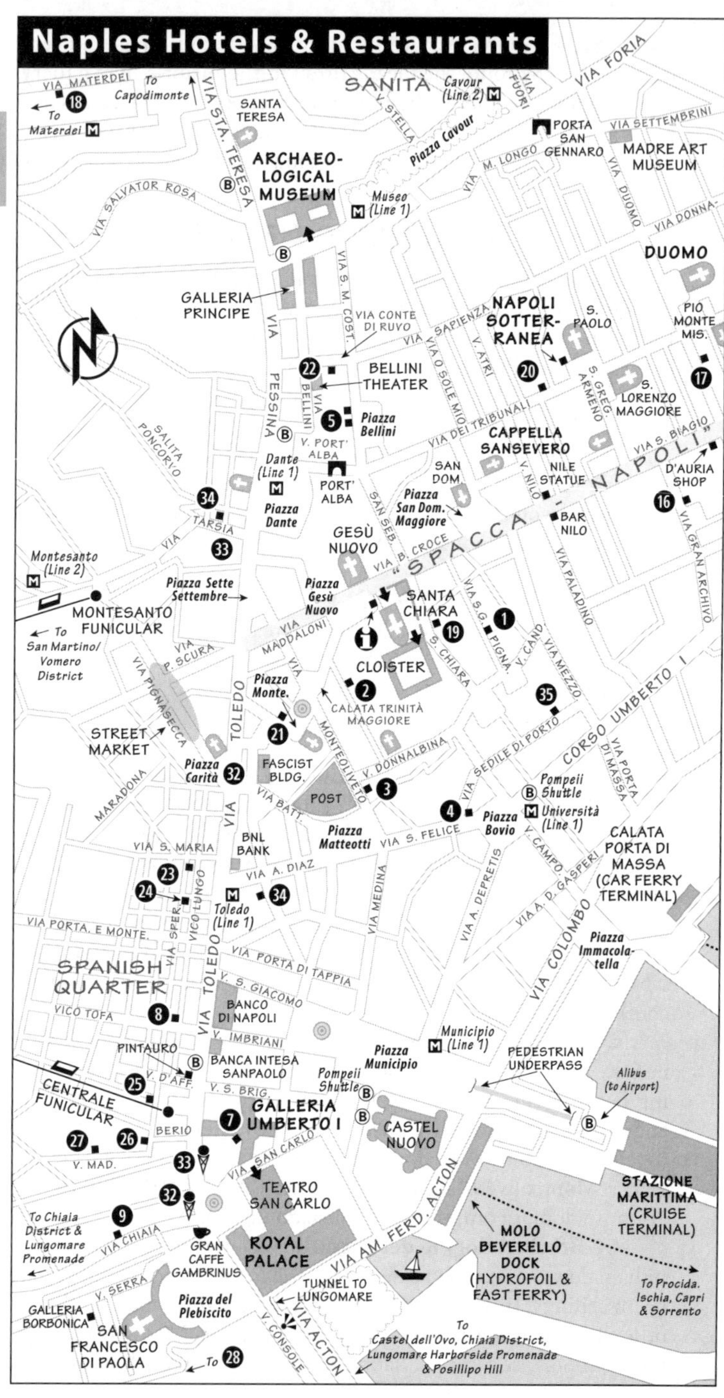

Naples Hotels & Restaurants
SANITÀ
ARCHAEOLOGICAL MUSEUM
GALLERIA PRINCIPE
BELLINI THEATER
Piazza Bellini
NAPOLI SOTTERRANEA
DUOMO
PIO MONTE MIS.
S. LORENZO MAGGIORE
CAPPELLA SANSEVERO
NILE STATUE
BAR NILO
D'AURIA SHOP
PORTA SAN GENNARO
MADRE ART MUSEUM
Piazza Cavour
Cavour (Line 2)
Museo (Line 1)
Dante (Line 1)
Piazza Dante
PORT' ALBA
GESÙ NUOVO
Piazza Gesù Nuovo
SANTA CHIARA
CLOISTER
"SPACCA - NAPOLI"
Piazza San Dom. Maggiore
MONTESANTO FUNICULAR
Montesanto (Line 2)
To San Martino/ Vomero District
Piazza Sette Settembre
STREET MARKET
Piazza Carità
FASCIST BLDG.
POST
CALATA TRINITÀ MAGGIORE
Piazza Monte.
Piazza Matteotti
Piazza Bovio
Pompeii Shuttle
Università (Line 1)
CALATA PORTA DI MASSA (CAR FERRY TERMINAL)
Piazza Immacolatella
BNL BANK
Toledo (Line 1)
SPANISH QUARTER
BANCO DI NAPOLI
PINTAURO
BANCA INTESA SANPAOLO
CENTRALE FUNICULAR
GALLERIA UMBERTO I
CASTEL NUOVO
Municipio (Line 1)
Piazza Municipio
PEDESTRIAN UNDERPASS
Alibus (to Airport)
STAZIONE MARITTIMA (CRUISE TERMINAL)
TEATRO SAN CARLO
ROYAL PALACE
MOLO BEVERELLO DOCK (HYDROFOIL & FAST FERRY)
To Procida, Ischia, Capri & Sorrento
GRAN CAFFÈ GAMBRINUS
TUNNEL TO LUNGOMARE
Piazza del Plebiscito
GALLERIA BORBONICA
SAN FRANCESCO DI PAOLA
To Chiaia District & Lungomare Promenade
To Castel dell'Ovo, Chiaia District, Lungomare Harborside Promenade & Posillipo Hill
To Capodimonte
To Materdei
SANTA TERESA
VIA FORIA
VIA TOLEDO
CORSO UMBERTO I
VIA COLOMBO
VIA AM. FERD. ACTON
VIA CHIAIA
VIA DUOMO
VIA S. BIAGIO
VIA DEI TRIBUNALI
VIA B. CROCE
VIA MEDINA
VIA S. FELICE
VIA A. DIAZ
VIA PORTA DI TAPPIA
VIA S. MARIA
VICO TOFA
VIA PESSINA
VIA SALVATOR ROSA
VIA PIGNASECCA
VIA MADDALONI
VIA MONTEOLIVETO
V. DONNALBINA
VIA SEDILE DI PORTO
VIA SAN CARLO
To 28

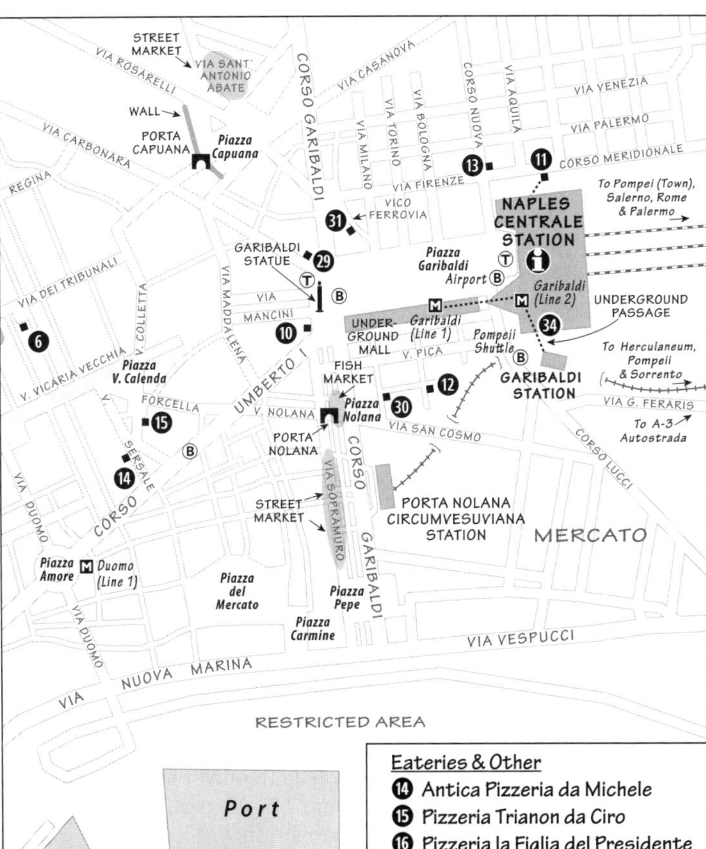

Port

To Sicily & Sardinia

400 Meters

400 Yards

Accommodations

1. Decumani Hotel de Charme
2. Artemisia Domus
3. B&B l'Alloggio dei Vassalli
4. B&B Dimora San Felice
5. Hotel Piazza Bellini & L'Etto
6. Sotto le Stelle ai Decumani
7. Art Resort Galleria Umberto
8. Hotel il Convento
9. Chiaja Hotel de Charme
10. Unahotel Napoli
11. Hotel Stelle
12. Ibis Styles Napoli Garibaldi
13. Grand Hotel Europa

Eateries & Other

14. Antica Pizzeria da Michele
15. Pizzeria Trianon da Ciro
16. Pizzeria la Figlia del Presidente
17. Pizzeria il Figlio del Presidente
18. Pizzeria Starita
19. Taverna a Santa Chiara
20. Trattoria Campagnola
21. Osteria il Garum
22. Osteria da Carmela
23. Trattoria a Pignata
24. Trattoria da Concetta
25. Trattoria Antica Capri
26. Trattoria Scialapopolo
27. Pizzeria con Cucina 'Ntrella
28. To Ristorante la Scialuppa
29. Mimì alla Ferrovia
30. Ristorante da Donato
31. Fratelli Attanasio Bakery
32. Mennella Il Gelato (2)
33. Gay-Odin (2)
34. Groceries (3)
35. Laundry

bina 56, Metro: Università +39 081 551 5118, https://hotelself.it/it/alloggiodeivassalli, hotelanapoli@gmail.com).

€€ B&B Dimora San Felice is just around the corner from L'Alloggio dei Vassalli and owned by the same company but less personally run. With simple, modern rooms, its main draw is the location—it's just off the busy Piazza Giovanni Bovio and steps from the Università Metro (some street noise, Via Cardinale Guglielmo Sanfelice 8, +39 081 551 5118, www.hotelself.it/en/dimorasanfelice, hotelanapoli@gmail.com).

North of Spaccanapoli

€€€ Hotel Piazza Bellini is an artistically decorated hotel with 48 minimalist but solid and comfortable rooms and seven apartments surrounding a peaceful, inviting courtyard. This bright, clean, and fun place has a boutique feel despite its size. Two blocks below the Archaeological Museum, just off the lively Piazza Bellini, and close to the great pizzerias and restaurants on Via dei Tribunali, it offers modern sanity in a strategic city-center location (Via Santa Maria di Costantinopoli 101, Metro: Dante, +39 081 451 732, www.hotelpiazzabellini.com, info@hotelpiazzabellini.com).

€ Sotto le Stelle ai Decumani, a block from the Duomo, has just four simple rooms but tons of charm. On the fourth floor of a building believed to be the site of a Spanish Inquisition tribunal, you'll never feel the weight of history in this bright, breezy space. There's no elevator—you'll need to haul yourself (and your bags) up 84 steps, though kind Fabio can likely help (family room, communal kitchenette, Piazzetta Sedil Capuano 243, Metro: Duomo, +39 081 060 8166, www.sottolestelleaidecumani.it).

IN AND NEAR THE SPANISH QUARTER

These places are in the heart of the Via Toledo and Spanish Quarter action. All have thick windows and provide ear plugs, but if you're sensitive to noise, ask for a quieter room—or stay elsewhere, especially on weekends.

€€€ Art Resort Galleria Umberto has 25 rooms in two buildings inside the Umberto I shopping gallery at the bottom of Via Toledo, just off Piazza del Plebiscito. This genteel-feeling place gilds the lily, with an aristocratic setting and decor. Consider paying extra for a room overlooking the gallery (Galleria Umberto 83, fourth floor, Metro: Municipio, +39 081 497 6224, www.artresortgalleriaumberto.com, booking@hotelgalleriaumberto.com).

€€ Hotel il Convento is a good choice for those who want to sleep in the tight tangle of lanes in the Spanish Quarter. You're only a couple of short blocks off the main Via Toledo drag, and heavy-duty windows help block out some (if not all) of the scooter noise and church bells. A rare haven of calm in this sometimes chaotic corner of town, it has 14 small but comfortable rooms—all with teensy balconies—as well as top-floor rooms with a private garden terrace (family rooms; Via Speranzella 137A, Metro: Toledo—from just below Banco di Napoli entrance on Via Toledo, walk two blocks up Vico Tre Re a Toledo; +39 081 403 977, www.hotelilconvento.com, info@hotelilconvento.com).

€€ Chiaja Hotel de Charme, with the same owner as the Decumani Hotel de Charme (listed earlier), rents 33 rooms on the Via Chiaia pedestrian shopping drag near Piazza del Plebiscito. The building has a fascinating history: Part of it was the residence of a marquis, and the rest was one of Naples' most famous brothels. To enter, ring the bell, then duck and squeeze through a small rectangle cut into the large wooden doors—don't worry, you'll fit (some view rooms, Via Chiaia 216, first floor, +39 081 415 555, www.hotelchiaia.it, info@hotelchiaia.it).

NEAR THE TRAIN STATION

These hotels are less convenient for sightseeing and dining, and the neighborhood gets dodgy as you move away from the station. But they're handy for train travelers, practical for a quick stay, and (for the most part) less expensive. All are handy to Metro: Garibaldi.

€€€€ Unahotel Napoli is a sleek escape from the station-area grit. The 89 rooms are business-hotel classy and its rooftop restaurant/bar (which doubles as the breakfast room) has nearly 360-degree city views (family rooms, gym, Piazza Giuseppe Garibaldi 9, +39 02 6982 6982—press 1, www.gruppouna.it/unahotels, hotel.napoli@unahotels.it).

€€ Hotel Stelle has 38 sterile, identical, newly remodeled rooms with modern furnishings. It feels sane compared to its hectic surroundings, and a back entrance leads directly into the train station (Corso Meridionale 60, exit station near track 5, +39 081 1889 3090, www.stellehotel.com, info@stellehotel.com).

€ Ibis Styles Napoli Garibaldi, with 88 rooms, offers chain predictability and a bright, youthful color scheme a five-minute walk from the station (pay parking; Via Giuseppe Ricciardi 33, exit station onto Piazza Garibaldi, then take second left onto Via G. Ricciardi; +39 081 690 8111, www.ibis.com, h3243@accor.com).

€ Grand Hotel Europa, across the seedy street right next to the station, has 89 decent rooms and hallways whimsically decorated with not-quite-right reproductions of famous paintings. It's a decent value, and its retro-feeling bar/restaurant is a classy place to relax (family rooms, restaurant—dinner only, Corso Meridionale 14, across street from station's north exit near track 5, +39 081 267 511, www.grandhoteleuropa.com, info@grandhoteleuropa.com).

Eating in Naples

Yes, Naples is justifiably famous for pizza. But the Campania region has other delicious tastes as well. The abundant sunshine and volcanic soil produce excellent fruits and vegetables, the famous San Marzano tomatoes come from just outside Naples, and Italy's best mozzarella (*di bufala,* from water buffalo milk) also originates in Campania. Pastas with bright, flavorful tomato and other sauces are a highlight here. And don't miss the classic dessert, the delicate, super-crunchy, ricotta-filled *sfogliatella.*

If craving a good pizza but wanting a more refined dining experience, remember that top-end restaurants seem determined to offer a variety of good pizzas at reasonable prices. People who want to dine elegantly—but otherwise couldn't—can enjoy the finer scene affordably.

FAMOUS PIZZA

Naples is the birthplace of pizza. Using traditional wood-burning ovens, its pizzerias bake just the right combination of fresh dough (soft and chewy, as opposed to thin and crispy Roman-style), mozzarella, and tomatoes. You can head for the famous, venerable places, but these can have long lines stretching out the door and hour-long waits for a table. To skip the hassle, just ask your hotel for directions to the neighborhood pizzeria. An average one-person pie (usually the only size available) costs €8-12; most places offer both takeout and eat-in, and pizza is often the only thing on the menu.

Near the Station

These two pizzerias—the most famous—are both a few long blocks from the train station, and near the end of my self-guided Naples Walk. Michele is insanely crowded; Trianon da Ciro could be your fallback.

€ Antica Pizzeria da Michele has been around since the late 19th century and claims to make Naples' most authentic pizza. They focus primarily on the classics: margherita and marinara. Come early to sit and watch the pizza artists in action. A pizza with beer costs around €8. As this place is often jammed with a long line, arrive early or late to get a seat. If there's a mob, head inside to get a number. If it's just too crowded to wait, try the less exceptional Pizzeria Trianon (described next), which often has room (daily; look for the vertical red *Antica Pizzeria* sign—and the crowd—at the intersection of Via Pietro Colletta and Via Cesare Sersale at #1; +39 081 553 9204).

€ Pizzeria Trianon da Ciro, across the street and left a few doors, has been Michele's archrival since 1923—and these days, as if beaten in the game, it survives mainly on their overflow. It offers more choices, higher prices, and a cozier atmosphere; for less chaos, head upstairs (daily 11:00-15:30 & 19:00-23:00, Via Pietro Colletta 42, +39 081 553 9426 to reserve).

On and near Via dei Tribunali

This street, which runs a couple of blocks north of Spaccanapoli, is legendary for its pizzerias and fun eateries. It's packed with hungry strollers and long lines marking the most popular places—especially Pizzeria dal Presidente at #120 and Gino Sorbillo at #32 (with an insane queue snaking down the street). The peak-time crowds are too much for me.

Nearby: Within a five-minute walk of the famous and overcrowded original Presidente are two great alternatives, both with wonderful pizza, more comfortable seating, and none of the "most famous" intensity. While totally separate businesses, they are run by the daughter *(figlia)* and son *(figlio)* of the founder of the famous Presidente.

€ Pizzeria la Figlia del Presidente, a short walk south from the legendary joints on Via dei Tribunali, is quickly establishing its own loyal clientele. Push your way through the locals gathered around the door and get a number, then patiently wait for a slice of heaven. Or you can dine in the big, plain, high-ceilinged cellar (craft beer, no outside seating, Tue-Sat, Mon lunch only, closed Sun, Via Grande Archivio 24, +39 081 286 738).

€ Pizzeria il Figlio del Presidente, the bastard son of the famous branch, has the wonderful vibe of a hardworking local neighborhood pizzeria with great pies and a fun-loving, attentive waitstaff. Sit inside to enjoy the action or on the street to be immersed in the scene. It's an honest, good pizzeria without the silliness of an Instagram mob (closed Mon, Via Duomo 181, +39 081 210 903).

Near the Archaeological Museum

Walk just 10 minutes behind the museum to create an edible memory.

€ Pizzeria Starita is a neighborhood fixture buried deep in the back lanes of Naples, with a local following that fills their sprawling dining rooms. In business for over 100 years (first as a cantina), this bustling, friendly eatery is just off the normal tourist circuit. For Neapolitans less is more for pizza, but Starita offers both modern and traditional toppings (closed Mon, no reservations—just show up and add your name to the wait list, from the museum walk 10 minutes up Via Santa Teresa degli Scalzi to the intersection with Via Materdei—the pizzeria is two blocks down on the left at #27, +39 081 557 3682).

SIT-DOWN RESTAURANTS

If you want a full meal rather than a pizza, consider these options.

Between Spaccanapoli and Via Toledo

€€ Taverna a Santa Chiara is your classic little eatery buried deep in the old center of Naples. With her menu including the names of farmers and pointing to her slow-food ethic, Nives is proudly mission-driven. Her convivial, warmly run, and simple, happy place is 100 yards from the tourist commotion of Spaccanapoli and provides a fun, easygoing break (closed Sun, Via Santa Chiara 6, +39 081 048 4908).

€€ Trattoria Campagnola is a classic family place with a home-cooking-style chalkboard menu on the back wall, mamma busy cooking in the back, and a passion for wine. Here you can venture away from pastas, be experimental with a series of local dishes, and not go wrong (daily, opposite a pizzeria at Via Tribunali 47, +39 081 459 034 but no reservations).

€€ Osteria il Garum is great if you'd like to eat fresh fish on a classic Neapolitan square. It's named for the ancient fish sauce that Roman cooks used. These days, mild-mannered, helpful Luigi and his staff inject their local cuisine with centuries of tradition, served in a cozy split-level cellar or outside on a covered terrace facing a neighborhood church. It's just between Via Toledo and Spaccanapoli, a short walk from the Church of Gesù Nuovo (closed Tue, Piazza Monteoliveto 2A, +39 081 542 3228).

Near the Archaeological Museum

€€ Osteria da Carmela serves up traditional Neapolitan classics in an elegant, old-fashioned dining room. They serve plates only mamma could make—like *ragù, polpetti,* and tasty fried fish—with a dash of Old World charm and a sprinkle of modern class. Affordable house wine and fine cheeses complete the meal. Tables are limited, so reservations are smart (closed Sun, Via Conte di Ruvo 11, +39 081 549 9738, www.osteriadacarmela.it).

€€ L'Etto is *not* the place to go for traditional Neapolitan cooking. This stylish little restaurant—with a white, minimalist interior, a long row of stay-awhile tables lining the sidewalk, and a smart clientele—focuses on creatively assembled, nutritious bowls (meat, fish, and vegetables) that are as healthy as a salad but more filling. Trendy cocktails are also on offer (daily, facing Piazza Bellini at Via S. Maria di Costantinopoli 102, +39 081 1932 0967).

In the Spanish Quarter

The Spanish Quarter—just a few years ago dark, dangerous, and where tourists went not to eat, but to be eaten—is now a festival of low-end happy dining in the streets. You'll encounter a fun-loving mix of locals, tourists, cobbles, scooters, restaurant tables, graffiti, and twinkling lights, all inviting exploration. My recommended places all serve the same Neapolitan classics, are inexpensive (**€-€€**; don't come here for elegant dining), generally take no reservations, close one day a week, and serve lunch from noon and dinner from 18:30 or 19:00 to around 23:00. Countless little eateries line two long lanes (Vico Lungo del Gelso and Via Speranzella) running parallel to Via Toledo, starting just uphill from the Toledo Metro stop (these places are listed in walking order from the Metro).

Trattoria a Pignata is convivial and serves classic dishes in a bright, happy dining room and at a few outside tables. Their "mixed appetizer of the house" *(antipasta misto)*—10 plates for €26—can be a meal for two (closed Mon, Vico Lungo del Gelso 110, +39 081 413 526).

Trattoria da Concetta has a fun vibe and a seafood focus along with *ragù* and *genovese* pastas (the Neapolitan beef-and-onion *genovese* differs from the pesto version served in the north). I like their outside seating best (closed Mon, Via Speranzella 19, +39 081 402 208).

Trattoria Antica Capri is a family-run winner. The humble dining room has a Capri theme and the charming outside seating on the tiny square is immersed in the quarter's charm. Their specialties are a bean-and-seafood pasta with a *"cappello,"* or pizza-crust hat (closed Thu, lunch only on Sun, Via Speranzella 110, +39 081 038 3486).

Trattoria Scialapopolo is the biggest place on the lane, with high energy inside and out. Their mixed seafood pasta, *scialatielli scialapopolo,* is the signature dish (closed Thu, Via Speranzella 98, +39 081 1811 2988).

Pizzeria con Cucina 'Ntrella, a half-block off the busy street on a quiet stepped lane, has a plain vibe with a fun list of creative and classic pizzas that locals appreciate. Rather than the sprawling, characterless interior, I sit outdoors under the trees (closed Wed, near end of Via Speranzella on the right at Vico Maddalenella degli Spagnoli 19, +39 081 427 970).

Dining with Locals in Sanità

Sanità still has the rough edges that the Spanish Quarter has lost. Wander up this colorful district's main drag, Via Vergini, to Piazza Sanità and survey the scene. The neighborhood doesn't really have a market for fine or romantic dining. But there's an abundance of characteristic dives, tiny osterias, and busy little pizzerias. Avoid the bright new places capitalizing on the 'hood's rising popularity and seek a traditional place with local roots. Explore and then eat once you spot the hole-in-the-wall that rolls your gnocchi. (For more on this district, see page 71; see also "The Panini Challenge" sidebar, opposite.)

A Romantic Splurge on the Harbor

For a yacht-clubby meal and a different view of Naples, stroll out to the harborfront and the historic island fisherman's quarter, Borgo Marinaro (see page 69 for more about the waterfront).

€€€€ Ristorante la Scialuppa ("The Rowboat") is a great bet for a romantic local meal on the harbor in the fabled Santa Lucia district. You'll walk from the harborfront across a causeway to Castel dell'Ovo into the little island-marina (just off Via Partenope). They boast fine indoor and outdoor seating facing the marina, attentive formal waitstaff, white-tablecloth elegance, a wonderful assortment of *antipasti,* and great seafood. While main plates can run to splurge levels, good pizzas are still affordable. Reservations are smart (closed Mon, Piazzetta Marinari 5, +39 081 764 5333, www.ristorantelascialuppa.net).

Near the Station

€€€ Mimì alla Ferrovia is a classic neighborhood *trattoria;* stepping inside, surrounded by well-dressed, in-the-know locals, it's clear you're in for a good meal of well-executed Neapolitan classics. The chef combines a passion for tradition (and fish) with a willingness to innovate. Their ricotta is heavenly. I prefer the energy on the ground floor to the quieter dining upstairs (closed Sun, Via Alfonso d'Aragona 19, +39 081 553 8525).

€€ Ristorante da Donato is a traditional, family-run *trattoria* on a glum street near the station. But hiding inside is a festival of good eating, where Ciro, Marilena, and son Francesco serve delicious food in an unpretentious atmosphere. Their inviting menu is heavy on seafood; their *ragùs* (both white and red) and pizza are hits (closed Mon, two blocks from Piazza Garibaldi—turn down Via Silvio Spaventa to #39, +39 081 287 828).

SWEET TREATS

To get the full overview of Neapolitan pastries at good prices, visit the bakery outlet of **Fratelli Attanasio** on a small alley near the train station—with your back to the station building, it's off the far-right corner of the big square. Come early for the best selec-

The Panini Challenge

For an unforgettable lunch in Naples, find a corner grocery store that looks like it's never seen a tourist (maybe one named "Nonna's"—Grandma's). Step up to the counter showing off various meats and cheeses (with a bin of fresh buns behind), and ask for a panini made to order.

Here's how the sandwich typically comes together: Grandma springs into action, making me not only a sandwich... but also a lifelong memory. Step by step, she demonstrates her art with joy and pride: confirming the freshness of her rolls with a tender squeeze, laying down a careful pavement of salami, gently bringing over a fragile mozzarella ball as if performing a kidney transplant, slicing a tomato with rapid-fire precision, and lovingly pitting the olives by hand before hanging them like little green paintings on a tasty wall. Nonna finishes it all off with a celebratory drizzle of what she promises is Italy's finest olive oil. One sandwich feeds two easily (Nonna can slice it for you). Add a little fruit, a carrot, and a drink, and you're on your way to what I consider the best budget meal in Naples.

tion—they open at 6:30 (closed Mon, Vico Ferrovia 1, +39 081 285 675).

Neapolitans' favorite gelato, made from all organic ingredients, is **Mennella Il Gelato.** There are two on either end of Via Toledo, among many throughout the city (Via Toledo 110 and Piazza Trieste e Trento 57). Also on Via Toledo are two outposts of **Gay-Odin,** a venerable chocolatier and *gelateria* (Via Toledo 214 and 427).

PICNICS

A good supermarket for picnic supplies is **Sapori & Dintorni,** in the train-station complex (daily, enter from outside, to the right of bookstore). By Piazza Dante is a small **Superò** that's convenient to hotels near this stretch of Via Toledo (daily, at corner of Via Tarsia and Vico San Domenico Soriano). By the Toledo Metro station, a small **Conad** is handy to hotels near Galleria Umberto I and the Spanish Quarter (daily, Via Roberto Bracco 4). Little neighborhood groceries often make sandwiches to-go (see "The Panini Challenge" sidebar, above).

Shopping in Naples

Naples' most traditional souvenirs can be found on Via San Gregorio Armeno, just off Via Tribunali. You'll find the treasured ***presepi*** (Nativity scenes, both classy and tacky), as well as the ubiquitous ***corno,*** the pepper-like horn that supposedly offers good luck. For more on this area, see page 49 of my Naples Walk.

SHOPPING *PASSEGGIATA*

To get a good overview of Naples' top shopping areas, do this shopping *passeggiata* in the early evening; most shops stay open until 20:00 (except on Sundays, when many close either early or completely).

Start on Via Toledo at the Toledo Metro station. Diving into the Spanish Quarter, head a half-block up Vico due Porte a Toledo and look on the left for **Mario Talarico Ombrelli,** an umbrella maker in business since 1860. Check out the photos outside of some famous clients, and see whose likeness ended up on an umbrella handle. Their most famous client: King Charles III, who shelled out £20,000 for a bamboo-handled umbrella (go inside to see the thank-you letter he penned and say hello to the friendly staff).

Back on Via Toledo, walk five minutes toward Piazza del Plebescito to **Ditta Leonardo Gaito** (#278, on the right), a maker of unique jewelry. Notice its classic facade, one of just a few of its kind left on the street, which has been taken over by modern chains. You'll see another similar storefront a little farther down, at the women's clothing store on the right (#291).

Another classic facade—and a classic treat—is on the left at #214: **Gay-Odin** gelato and chocolates, in business since 1894. Take a break from Via Toledo by turning right up **Via Chiaia** for more upscale clothing...and upscale people. Notice the sudden difference in the age and style of those who take their *passeggiata* here compared to Via Toledo (not to mention the relative lack of trash and noise).

When you reach the top of the hill, admire the elegant offerings at **Mariano Rubinacci** men's clothing store (on the right at #149, next to the Metropolitan movie theater).

Another block ahead, at the end of the tree-lined street, you emerge at the main intersection of the Chiaia neighborhood. Head right down **Via Gaetano Filangieri** for more high(er)-end places and glamorous people. At the end of the block, when you reach the Louis Vuitton store, look right to see an impressive staircase leading up to some of Naples' most expensive real estate.

You could keep strolling for blocks, but if you've had enough luxury, go one more block (checking out the Art Deco stained glass on the left at #25 and the extravagant Spanish consulate on the right at #40), then take a left down **Via Nicolo Nisco.** Another left puts you in the heart of Chiaia's trendy nightlife district.

MARKETS

Porta Nolana Open-Air Fish Market

Naples' fish market squirts and stinks as it has for centuries under the darkened Porta Nolana (gate in the city wall), four long blocks down from Centrale station. Of the town's many boisterous outdoor markets, this one will net you the most images and memories. From Piazza Nolana, wander under the medieval gate and take your first left down Via Sopramuro, enjoying this wild and entirely edible cultural scavenger hunt (Tue-Sun 8:00-14:00, closed Mon). Stalls display the best catch of the day as water jets caress mounds of mussels and clams.

Street Markets

Two other street markets, with more clothing and fewer fish, are at Piazza Capuana (several blocks northwest of Centrale station and tumbling down Via Sant'Antonio Abate, Mon-Sat 8:00-18:00, Sun 9:00-13:00) and a similar cobbled shopping zone along Via Pignasecca (just off Via Toledo, west of Piazza Carità, described on page 45).

Nightlife in Naples

If you're looking for a good time in the evening, take it from one local: All of Naples is nightlife (and every night is Friday night). This youthful, vibrant city has something going on seemingly around every corner. If you want fun, just follow your ears. Friday and Saturday evenings can be particularly rowdy, especially in the Spanish Quarter.

In the **Spanish Quarter,** escape the crowds on Via Toledo and head up any of the characteristic side streets with string lights that climb up the hill. You'll find two quieter wine bars serving drinks and nibbles on and near tiny Vico Berio. **Apoteca** (#10, closed Mon) sprawls halfway up the lane with inviting outdoor tables, while **Cu.Qu.** (at tiny Vicoletto Berio #12, closed Sun-Mon) has indoor and outdoor seating. All around this area, you'll hear occasional live bands, tableside accordions, and locals breaking into impromptu sing-alongs.

For a slightly more laid-back atmosphere, join the *spritz*-sipping crowd on **Piazza Bellini.** Overlooking a bit of ruined Neapolis, you'll be joined by university students and sophisticated locals. Nearby, **Piazza San Domenico Maggiore,** just off Via Tribunali and a few minutes from Piazza Bellini, has inviting outdoor tables with a church view.

A nice way to spend an evening is to link up the *passeggiata* along the Lungomare harborside promenade with drinks in **Chiaia** (see page 69 for details on the full *passeggiata*). From Piazza della Vittoria, walk away from the water through the park and carefully cross the busy street, then head up one block to Piazza dei Matiri. Cross to the top left corner and turn down Via Alabardieri. Wander the surrounding grid of streets for an eclectic mix of wine bars, cocktail dens, clubs, and eateries. For a faster and less scenic route, from Piazza del Plebiscito, take Via Chiaia up and over the hill until it drops down into Piazza dei Matiri.

Naples Connections

See the "Getting Around the Bay of Naples" sidebar for more tips on traveling this region by train, bus, taxi, and boat, as well as the color map "Naples Transportation" at the back of this book.

BY TRAIN

Any train listed on the schedule as leaving from "Napoli S.G." or "Napoli Piazza Garibaldi" departs from Garibaldi station below Napoli Centrale.

See the "Getting Around the Bay of Naples" sidebar for information on getting to **Herculaneum,** the ruins at **Pompeii, Pompei town,** and **Sorrento** by train.

By Train to: Rome (Trenitalia: 1-5/hour, 70 minutes on Frecciarossa, 2 hours on Intercity, 3 hours and much cheaper on regional trains; Italo: at least hourly, 70 minutes), **Civitavecchia** (at least hourly, 3 hours, most change in Rome), **Florence** (Trenitalia: at least 2/hour, 3 hours, some change in Rome; Italo: hourly, 3 hours), **Salerno** (Trenitalia: at least hourly, 35-45 minutes, change in Salerno for bus or boat to Amalfi; avoid slower Metro line 2 trains; Italo: 6/day, 45 minutes), **Paestum** (12/day, 1.5 hours, direction: Sapri or Reggio), **Brindisi** (6/day, 5-6 hours, change in Caserta; from Brindisi, ferries sail to Greece), **Milan** (Trenitalia: 2/hour, 5 hours; Italo: 1-2/hour), **Venice** (Trenitalia: almost hourly, 5.5 hours, some change in Bologna or Rome; Italo: 5/day, 5.5 hours), **Palermo** (2/day direct, 9.5 hours, also an overnight train).

BY BOAT

Fast ferries and cruise ships dock next to each other in the shadow of the old Castel Nuovo fortress, a short walk from the old town sightseeing action. Naples has great ferry connections to Procida, Capri, Sorrento, and other nearby destinations. Cruise ships use the giant Stazione Marittima cruise terminal; hydrofoils and faster ferries use the adjacent Molo Beverello dock. Slower car/passenger ferries leave from Calata Porta di Massa, east of the cruise terminal. If you're prone to seasickness, consider taking a car ferry (bigger boat, smoother ride) over a hydrofoil (smaller boat, bumpier ride). Car ferries are also more likely to run in bad weather.

Whether arriving by ferry or cruise ship, you can get to the city center by taxi, Metro, or on foot; the Alibus shuttle bus runs from the port to the airport (see "By Plane," later). A **taxi** stand is in the center of the port area. Expect to pay around €15 to connect the port to the train station or the Archaeological Museum.

Straight ahead from the cruise terminal (past the scrum of rip-off cabbies), a modern underpass leads beneath the traffic to the handy Municipio **Metro** stop. From here, line 1 zips you right to the Archaeological Museum (Museo stop) or, in the opposite direction, to the train station (Garibaldi stop). See page 34 for details on using the Metro.

On foot, it's a 10-minute **walk**—past the gigantic Castel Nuovo, then to the left—from the port to Piazza del Plebiscito and the old city center.

Buying Boat Tickets

For **Capri and Procida,** don't get caught up in the many potentially confusing options. Boats start running basically at daylight and stop running around 19:00. There's no need to book online or even a day in advance. You can look up schedules online (see "Getting Around the Bay of Naples" sidebar for various companies) or go to the Molo Beverello dock the day before to choose your departure for the next day (schedules posted at each company's ticket window). Arrive 30 minutes prior to departure.

Or just show up on the day of your departure: The big, handy electronic info board shows all the upcoming departures, and because the various companies stagger their trips, you won't wait long. The port has baggage storage, a WC, and cafés.

Boats to **Sorrento** run less frequently, but you can still buy tickets the day of your journey. Seasonal boats sometimes go to Positano and Amalfi—ask. For a map showing boat routes, see page 137.

Getting Around the Bay of Naples

For specifics, check the "Connections" sections of each chapter. Confirm times and prices locally.

By Circumvesuviana Commuter Train: The dingy, crowded Circumvesuviana is popular with locals, tourists, and pickpockets, and links Naples, Herculaneum, the Pompeii ruins, and Sorrento. The most important Circumvesuviana station in Naples is Garbaldi, located on the lower levels of Centrale station; follow signs downstairs to *Stazione Garibaldi* and then *Circumvesuviana* and/or *Linee Vesuviane* signs to the Circumvesuviana turnstiles (contactless payment accepted; ticket windows also nearby). After tapping your card or scanning your ticket, confirm the time and track on the electronic board, and head down another level to the platforms.

On the Naples platform, double-check with a local that the train goes to Sorrento (avoid lines that branch out to other destinations). Any Circumvesuviana train marked *Sorrento* stops at Pompeii, but for Herculaneum beware of express trains marked *DD*—many skip the Ercolano Scavi station for the ruins (check schedule online or ask at train station). Sorrento-bound trains (€2.60) depart twice hourly, typically from track 1, and take about 15 minutes to reach Ercolano, 30 minutes to reach Pompei Scavi Villa dei Misteri (for the ruins), and 75 minutes to reach Sorrento, the end of the line. Express DD trains (6/day) reach Sorrento 15 minutes sooner. For schedules, see EAVSRL.it. The Circumvesuviana is covered by most versions of the Campania ArteCard (see page 28).

To avoid the Circumvesuviana crush at Centrale/Garibaldi, consider boarding at the Porta Nolana station, just a five-minute walk from Centrale station. It's the terminus for the Circumvesuviana; boarding here gives you a better chance at snaring a seat.

By Campania Express Train: These higher-end trains link Naples, Herculaneum, the Pompeii ruins, and Sorrento and use the same tracks and stops as the Circumvesuviana train. They run only four times a day (starting around 8:20 from Naples' Garibaldi station) and are pricier, but they're less crowded and have air-conditioning. Campania Express trains typically depart from track 3 (€15 one-way in high season to any destination: Herculaneum, 10 minutes; Pompei Scavi Villa dei Misteri, 30 minutes; Sorrento, 75 minutes; mid-March-Oct only, not covered by Campania ArteCard, buy tickets in advance at http://ots.eavsrl.it or at station ticket windows).

By Metro Line 2: Operated by Trenitalia, Naples' Metro line 2 connects the city center with Pompei town, a short taxi ride or 10-to-15-minute walk from the ruins (trains run 1-2/hour, 45 minutes, connection works best *from* Pompei to Naples; see details on page 109). In Naples, line 2 stops at Garibaldi station (lower level of Centrale station, near the center of the station—look for *Metro linea 2*) and conveniently also links to the Naples Archaeological Museum (Piazza Cavour stop). Note that Metro line 2 is

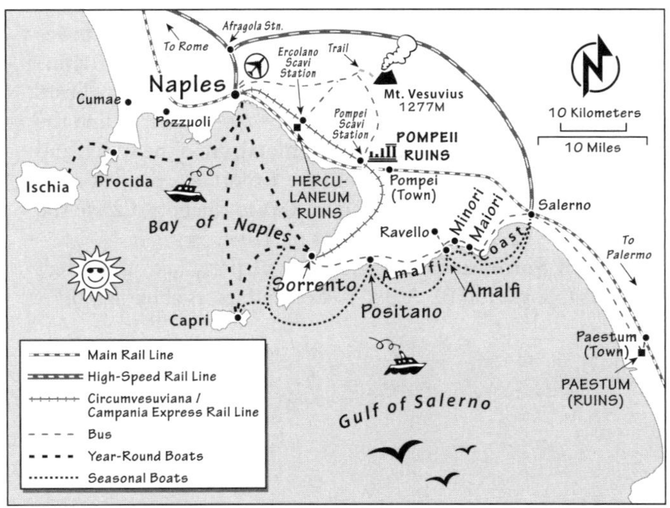

not convenient for reaching Herculaneum or Sorrento, but a slow extension does go to Salerno.

By Bus: CitySightseeing's fleet of bright red buses with audio commentary fights traffic from Naples to the ruins at Pompeii (see page 37); Tramvia Napoli runs similar routes (www.tramvianapoli.it). Crowded SITA buses also traverse the Amalfi Coast; see page 181.

By Taxi: A taxi or Uber from Naples to Pompeii can be affordable for a group of four. The 30-mile taxi ride directly to your Sorrento hotel costs about €150 (ask the driver for the nonmetered *tariffa predeterminata*). Taxis on the Amalfi Coast are expensive but can be convenient, especially for groups. See "Getting Around the Amalfi Coast" on page 180.

By Boat: Major companies connecting Naples with Procida, Capri, and Sorrento include Caremar (www.caremar.it), SNAV (www.snav.it), NLG (www.nlg.it), and Alilauro (www.alilauro.it); on the Amalfi Coast the major companies are Alilauro and Travelmar (www.travelmar.it). Each company has different destinations and prices; some compete for the same trips. Some lines (like Sorrento-Capri) run all year; others (on the Amalfi Coast, for example) run only in summer. Trips can be canceled in bad weather. A pricey but scenic and swift hydrofoil skims between Naples and Sorrento.

For any route, it's unnecessary to book tickets in advance. Scout schedules at the port or online the day before, then arrive 30 minutes before your desired boat. Before embarking, note the return times—the last boat usually leaves around 19:00. For more on boats from Naples, see page 95.

BY PLANE

Naples International Airport (Aeroporto Internazionale di Napoli, a.k.a. Capodichino, code: NAP, www.aeroportodinapoli.it) is close to town. In summer, you may find a TI here. Alibus **shuttle buses** zip from the airport to Naples' Centrale train station in 10 minutes and then continue another 10-15 minutes to the port (buses run daily 6:00-23:00, 4/hour, €5 on board—tap-to-pay; to find the outbound stop at the airport, exit the terminal, cross the street, and bear left). If you take a **taxi** to or from the airport, ask the driver for the fixed price (€18 to the train station, €21 to the port, €25 to the Chiaia district near the waterfront), or try Uber.

To reach **Sorrento** from the Naples airport, take the direct Curreri bus (see page 160). A taxi to Sorrento costs about €130.

PROCIDA

To escape the hustle and bustle of Naples, many tourists visit one of two islands—Ischia and Procida—that huddle just a short ferry ride away from the mainland. Jet-set Ischia, with its hot springs and high-end hotels, is bigger and more famous. I prefer Ischia's little sister, the tiny isle of Procida. With its humble fishing port, Procida offers pastel village charm. It's also a fine off-the-beaten-path island-life alternative to crowded Capri.

GETTING THERE

From Naples, you have two options for getting to Procida: high-speed hydrofoil or slow ferry. Hydrofoils depart from Naples' Molo Beverello terminal (45 minutes to Procida), while slower ferries use the Calata Porta di Massa car-ferry terminal (over an hour to Procida). I'd avoid chaotic Calata Porta di Massa and take the faster boat from Molo Beverello.

Several companies run boats, with various departure times and routes, including SNAV (www.snav.it), Alilauro (www.alilaurogruson.com), and Caremar (https://shop.caremar.it). It's easy enough to just show up at Naples' port and buy your ticket for the next departure, but if you're day-tripping, make sure to verify the last return boat time.

PLANNING YOUR TIME

It's easy to see Procida (PRO-chee-dah) as a day trip from Naples. But to have a proper island experience and a real break from the big city—especially if you're looking for a vacation from your vacation—I'd give it two nights and a full day.

While I haven't covered Ischia here, hopping between the two

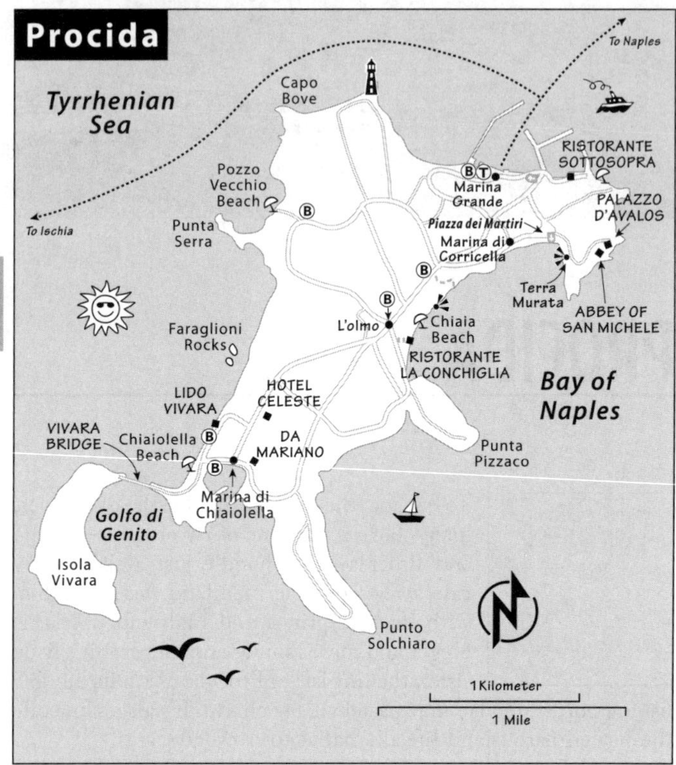

islands is easy. Many ferries to Procida are just stopping off on their way to Ischia (they're each about an hour from Naples and 30 minutes from one another).

Orientation to Procida

Just 1.5 square miles, tiny Procida (pop. 10,000) is a perfect place for strolling, taking photos, and licking a gelato while you marvel at the perfectly pastel townscape that hides behind its main port. This picture-perfect backdrop has inspired writers, poets, and filmmakers, many of whom have set their stories here (*The Talented Mr. Ripley* and *Il Postino* were both filmed on Procida).

While the island can feel sleepy most of the year, July and August are popular with vacationing Neapolitans. Book rooms well in advance (or stick with a day trip).

ARRIVAL IN PROCIDA

Boats arrive at Marina Grande, the island's main port/village. At the far end to the right is the boat ticket office (with pay WCs), the bus stop (sometimes behind the ticket office), and a taxi stand. Nearby, you'll see the E-Movete shop, which rents e-bikes (popular on this hilly island) and has a luggage-storage service (Via Roma 120, +39 081 353 5291, www.emovete.it).

GETTING AROUND PROCIDA

Only resident Procidanos are allowed to have cars, but Procida is small enough for you to walk nearly everywhere (and buses and taxis work well too).

Frequent buses make exploring the isle easy. Just check before you board a bus that it's going to your desired destination. Buy tickets (cash only) from the boat-ticket office or from the driver and remember to validate your ticket onboard. If you're headed to one of the beaches, tell the driver when you board where you want to get off. (You can also follow the route on Google maps, which shows all the bus stops).

Procida Walk

Do this quick orientation walk and then get down to the *dolce far niente* (sweetness of doing nothing) tempo of island life.

Boats from Naples land at **Marina Grande.** Facing the docks is a line of scrappy tourist services: places to check your bag, rent an e-bike or scooter, book boat trips around the island, and so on. Now is a good time, if you're day-tripping, to check when the last boat back leaves.

Turning left, walk toward the yellow church along the **harborfront.** You won't be competing with much traffic on the road, since the only cars here belong to residents. Stroll the harborfront (perhaps scouting a place you'll return to for a meal). A few hardy commercial fishing boats still moor here when not harvesting the sea to help stock the island restaurants (and those in Naples).

This harborfront lane, **Via Roma,** is the scene of the evening ritual of the *passeggiata* (staying overnight allows you to join in). As you pass pastry shops, look for the island's favorite sweet treat: *Linque di Procida* (tongues of Procida), made with cream and the island's homegrown lemons. Locals brag that these lemons, grown in volcanic soil, are sweeter than Amalfi Coast lemons. (Ischia and Procida are volcanic, while their island rival, Capri, is just a big rock. Procida's many harbors echo the craters of long-ago eruptions.)

Up ahead, the yellow church—**Santa Maria della Pietà,** the historic church of the mariners, built in 1624—gave fishermen a convenient point to aim for when returning home. Today the harbor is filled with the vacation dreams of Italian mainlanders and yachts available to charter. Veer right on Via Roma as it hugs the church, reaching the entrance on your left. If it's open, peek inside at its Baroque interior.

Exiting the church, you can either continue past the square in front of the church for more harborfront strolling (passing the recommended Ristorante Sottosopra) or head away from the coast along **Via Vittorio Emanuele** across from the church (walking beneath the colorful metalwork) and climb uphill past tourist shops and steep, steep lanes leading to old homes.

If you opt for the second route, turn left at the first intersection onto Via P. Umberto, and do the long slog straight up the hill. You'll eventually come to **Piazza dei Martiri** (Square of the Martyrs) with its fine little church, Santa Maria delle Grazie, and a memorial to the heroes of the 1799 uprising (inspired by the French Revolution 10 years earlier). Twelve patriots were hung on this square by the Bourbons, the Spanish ruling family.

From this intersection, we'll eventually continue downhill to the delightful pastel port of Marina Corricella below. But first continue uphill to the island's top sightseeing attractions: Palazzo d'Avalos, the Abbey of San Michele Arcangelo, and the grand viewpoint of Marina Corricella.

En route, at the **Terra Murata terrace,** enjoy the best commanding view of Procida's colorful harbor and the peaks of Ischia beyond, which makes all the huffing and puffing worthwhile.

After catching your breath, keep venturing up the curving road Salita Castello to the town's 16th-century **Palazzo d'Avalos,** the former Bourbon palace turned military school turned prison (closed in 1988), which is now being transformed into a museum (limited opening hours, check locally).

Then stroll a little farther (and higher) to the **Abbey of San Michele Arcangelo** (free, donations accepted, daily 10:00-12:45 but hours can change).

Use the English handout for a self-guided tour of this impressive 11th-century church that operated as a Benedictine monastery for hundreds of years. It contains several impressive chapels, most notably the Blessed Sacrament Chapel, with its unique horizontal (and asymmetrical) triptych. It's thought that these three unrelated panels were joined together after one of three major fires that destroyed much of the church's art.

Before working your way back down the hill, exit the abbey and turn right, wandering to the very end of this hill (following signs to *Terrazzo Bar*), where you'll find a **terrace** overlooking the Bay of Naples.

Back at the Piazza dei Martiri, descend left downhill on Via San Rocco. After about 200 meters (following the sign to *Marina Corricella*), take the steps steeply down on the left to reach the **Marina di Corriccella.**

This tiny pedestrian-only fishing village of colorful cottages crowded together like a child's building blocks is the most iconic sight on Procida. It's also a great place to stop for lunch, with tables set directly on the pier where you can sample local seafood specialties (see my recommendations on page 105). Across the way is **Chiaia Beach.** You'll see boat companies advertising water taxis to the beach as well as tours around the island. Take some time to walk to both ends of the pier, enjoying the colorful houses up close. As tour guides love to say, the Corricella houses were historically painted in different colors so local fishermen would be able to recognize their own homes from out at sea.

Procida Beaches

As if to demonstrate Procida's compact size, these beaches can all be reached within a 40-minute walk of Marina di Corricella, though Chiaia is the closest and most walkable (also accessible by water taxi). It's easiest to reach Chiaiolella and Pozzo Vecchio by bus or taxi (or a "minitaxi" tuk tuk).

Chiaia Beach (Spiaggia Chiaia)

This long beach, visible from Marina di Corricella, is just a 15- or

20-minute walk from the center, depending on which entrance you use (buses L1 and L2 also stop near either entrance on Piazza Olmo). The farther entrance, down Via Pizzaco (follow *Spiaggia Chiaia* signs), requires descending almost 200 stairs to the water's edge (think about whether you want to take those back up; otherwise keep walking across the beach to the much easier, mostly ramped entrance on the other side). Once at Chiaia, you can choose between free public areas or rent chairs and an umbrella. At the base of the 200 steps is a beach club that also has a good restaurant, **La Conchiglia,** with excellent views of Corricella.

Chiaiolella Beach

The sleepy southwestern part of the island has a long, spacious beach, a busy harbor, and a handful of restaurants that specialize in local seafood dishes. From here you'll also get views of Procida's Faraglioni Rocks (sea stacks) and the Vivara island nature preserve (likely only accessible with an Italian-only tour). The town also has a few streets worth exploring and a recommended restaurant and hotel (see later).

Pozzo Vecchio

Also known as "*Il Postino* beach" after appearing in several scenes from the 1994 movie, this beach is located on the island's northwestern coast. The horseshoe-shaped beach, with dark volcanic sand, is generally quieter than the others. You can reach it by bus—just ask the driver to drop you at the nearest stop.

Sleeping on Procida

At Marina di Corricella

€€€ San Michele Procida is the top choice on the island, with 12 fresh, modern rooms right in the heart of Corricella village, just a few steps down from Piazza dei Martiri. The rooms—all with view balconies—cascade down nearly to the marina. The hotel also owns the recommended Il Pescatore restaurant below, where guests are offered breakfast (Via San Rocco 61, +39 081 810 1564, www.sanmicheleprocida.com, info@sanmicheleprocida.com).

€€ La Casa sul Mare, just a short walk up from Piazza dei Martiri, is another top choice for unwinding. The 10 tastefully decorated rooms over two floors all have terraces with a view of the pastel town below. Breakfast is served in the garden overlooking the marina (family rooms, closed in winter, Via Salita Castell 13, +39 081 896 8799, www.lacasasulmare.it, info@lacasasulmare.it).

€€ Hotel la Corricella is small and family-run, with nine basic but spacious rooms, each with a view and some with balconies. At the far end of Corricella's pastel village, it offers stunning views and a convenient location. It's also just above the recommended La Lampara restaurant (some rooms require 3-night minimum in summer, no elevator—lots of stairs, Via Marina Corricella 88, +39 081 896 7575, www.hotelcorricella.it, info@hotelcorricella.it).

Above Marina di Chiaiolella

€ Hotel Celeste is a cheery place with a terrace and a lemon-tree-filled patio. In a quiet neighborhood a few blocks up from the marina, its blue-and-white motif, classy bar, and vast outdoor spaces inspire relaxation (some view rooms, family rooms, Via Rivoli 6, +39 081 896 7488, www.hotelceleste.it, info@hotelceleste.it).

Eating on Procida

At Marina Grande

Of the many places to choose from within a stone's throw of the boat dock, I like **Ristorante Sottosopra,** which offers an inventive take on the typical seafood and pasta dishes (daily 12:00-15:30 & 18:30-22:30, Via Roma 11, +39 081 810 1013).

At Marina di Corricella

€€€ Il Pescatore serves up seafood classics. It's a bit pricier than other places in town, but their dishes are higher quality. The unique lemon salad—sweet rather than tart—is a must-try; manager Celeste calls it "the island on a plate" (closed Wed, Via Marina di Corricella 63, +39 081 1972 1905).

€€ Caracalè, next to Il Pescatore, has fine seating inside and out and is respected for its fresh seafood (long hours daily, Via Marina di Corricella 62, +39 081 896 9192).

€€€ La Lampara owns the best view in town, with tables overlooking the pastel village and excellent food to match (daily, Via Marina di Corricella 88, +39 081 896 0609).

€ Blu, at the opposite end of the marina, is a cozy, casual place with fun outdoor tables serving drinks and light bites (long hours daily, Via Marina di Corricella 93).

At Marina Chiaiolella

€€€ Da Mariano is a family-run place, where Mariano welcomes you and cooks up some inventive dishes (daily 12:00-15:00, Fri-

Sun also 19:30-22:00, Via Marina Chiaiolella 32, +39 081 896 7350, www.facebook.com/DaMarianoristorante).

At Chiaiolella Beach

€€ Lido Vivara is the perfect place for a beachside lunch or, if you're staying overnight, a romantic sunset dinner (daily 12:30-16:00 & 19:30-23:00, Lungomare Cristoforo Colombo 4, +39 081 896 0594, www.lidovivara.com).

POMPEII & NEARBY

Pompeii • Herculaneum • Vesuvius

Stopped in their tracks by the eruption of Mount Vesuvius in AD 79, Pompeii and Herculaneum offer the best look anywhere at what life in Italy must have been like around 2,000 years ago. These two cities of well-preserved ruins are yours to explore. Of the two sites, Pompeii is grander, more famous, and more crowded, while Herculaneum is smaller, more intimate, and has better surviving art. (But the best Pompeiian art of all is at the National Museum of Archaeology in Naples.) Both Pompeii and Herculaneum are easily reached from Naples or Sorrento by train.

Beyond Pompeii and Herculaneum, Vesuvius rises up on the horizon, still smoldering ominously. It last erupted in 1944 and is still an active volcano. Buses connect travelers from the train stations at Herculaneum or Pompeii to drop you a half-hour hike below its crater rim (you must reserve a timed entry for the hike in advance).

Pompeii

A once-thriving commercial port of 10,000 to 20,000 people, Pompeii (worth ▲▲▲) grew from Greek and Etruscan roots to become an important Roman city. Then, on August 24, AD 79, everything changed. Vesuvius erupted and buried the city under 20 feet of hot volcanic ash. Pompeii was accidentally rediscovered in 1599; excavations began in 1748. For the archaeologists who excavated it, this was a shake-and-bake windfall, teaching them volumes about daily life in Roman times.

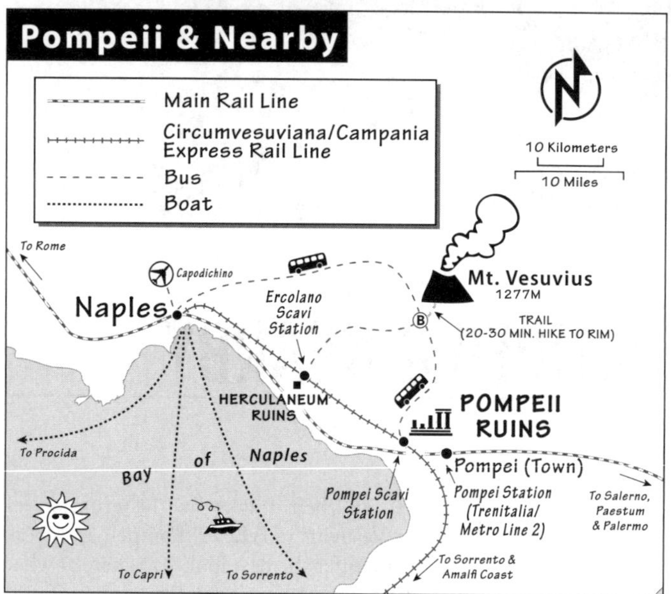

GETTING THERE

Getting to Pompeii involves enduring what can be horrible traffic from Naples or Sorrento or enduring a run-down, crowded, and sometimes creepy (between Naples and Pompeii) commuter train. But there are nicer train alternatives. The train from Naples or Sorrento is cheaper and generally faster than the bus.

By Train from Naples or Sorrento: Pompeii is roughly midway between Naples and Sorrento (about 30 minutes from either) on both the Circumvesuviana commuter line and the Campania Express train; both trains use the same tracks.

The **Circumvesuviana** is much cheaper and runs more frequently but can be unbearably crowded, is not air-conditioned, and can be prone to pickpocketing—hang onto your bag and see page 34 for tips (2/hour, €2.60 one-way, contactless pay accepted, Italian-only but readable website: www.eavsrl.it; at busy times, consider boarding the Circumvesuviana at Naples' Porta Nolana station, a 5-minute walk from Centrale/Garibaldi station).

The **Campania Express** is pricey and much less frequent but also less crowded and air-conditioned (4/day, €15 one-way, book online or at station ticket window, mid-March-Oct only, http://ots.eavsrl.it). For more train details, see page 96.

From Naples, both trains leave from the same area of Garibaldi station: Follow signs for *Circumvesuviana* as well as for *Linee Vesuviane.* Circumvesuviana trains to Pompeii typically leave from track 1, Campania Express from track 3. From Sorrento, it's an enjoyable ride to Pompeii since the line originates here. You may even get a seat!

To reach the ruins, from either train get off at the **Pompei Scavi Villa dei Misteri** stop (from Naples, it's the stop after Villa Regina). From the Pompei Scavi train station, it's a two-minute walk to the ruins' Porta Marina entrance: Leaving the station, just power past the hustlers and follow the crowds.

By Shuttle Bus from Naples or Sorrento: Various bus companies offer shuttle services to Pompeii, but schedules are limited and traffic can be maddening. Try **CitySightseeing** (www.city-sightseeing.it/naples), **Tramvia Napoli** (www.tramvianapoli.it), or **SITA** (www.sitasudtrasporti.it).

By Taxi from Naples: Groups of four who don't want to ride the crowded Circumvesuviana can consider hiring a taxi or Uber from Naples to Pompeii. Ask locally about pricing and see if it makes economical sense. (There's no reason to take a taxi from Sorrento, as the Circumvesuviana from there is easy, cheap, and uncrowded).

By Car: Although I don't recommend driving in this region, if you do have a car you can park at Camping Zeus, next to the Pompei Scavi train station; several other campgrounds/parking lots are nearby.

PLANNING YOUR TIME

To visit Pompeii from either Naples or Sorrento, allow at least a half-day—an hour each way for transit, then two hours at the site (three if you visit the theater and amphitheater).

Linking Pompeii and Naples' Archaeological Museum: A visit to Pompeii pairs well with Naples' excellent Archaeological Museum, which contains the greatest artifacts uncovered from Pompeii and Herculaneum. Here's a convenient way to connect Pompeii and the museum (if you're staying in Naples):

Take an early Circumvesuviana or Campania Express train from Naples' Garibaldi station and plan to be at Pompeii right when it opens at 9:00. Tour the ruins and exit at Piazza Anfiteatro. To return to Naples, walk 10 to 15 pleasant minutes to the Pompei city train station (for directions, see the end of this self-guided tour), and purchase a Metro line 2 ticket (operated by Trenitalia, €3.30, 2/hour, 45 minutes, ask for a ticket to Naples' Piazza Ca-

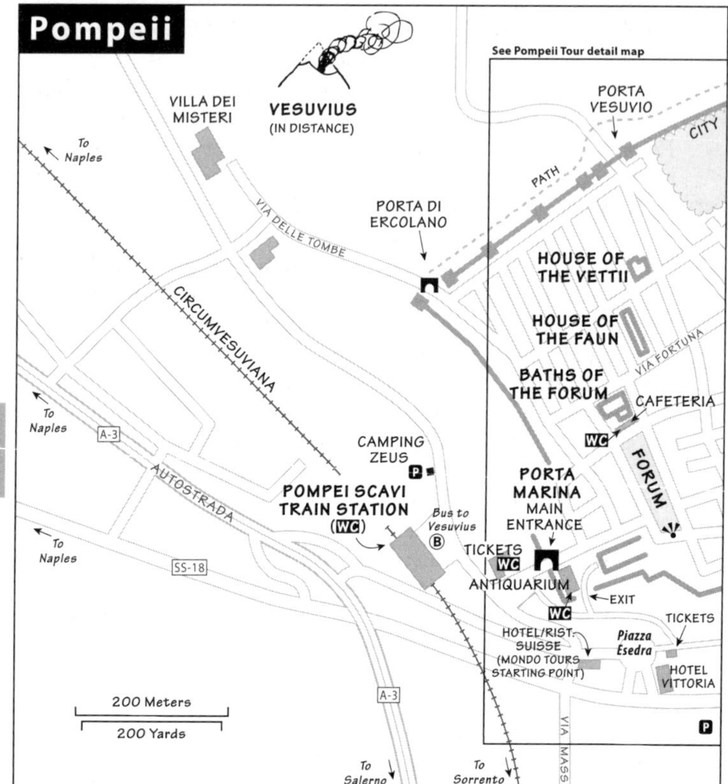

vour). Back in Naples, from Piazza Cavour, it's a five-minute walk to the museum.

POMPEII TOUR OPTIONS

Here are several ways to enjoy an organized and educational visit to Pompeii.

Self-Guided Tour: Simply follow the self-guided tour in this chapter or, better, 🎧 download and enjoy my free Pompeii **audio tour.** Both cover the basics and provide plenty of information for do-it-yourselfers.

Group Tours: The **Mondo Guide shared tour** for Rick Steves readers is your best budget bet for a tour with an actual guide (2 hours, €20, Pompeii entry extra, daily at 11:15, reservations required, don't be late as they start punctually; meet at Hotel/Ristorante Suisse, just down the hill from the Porta Marina entrance; for details, see page 32). Otherwise, when you step off the train, you'll likely be accosted by touts for the "info point" kiosk, which sells €15 **group tours** that depart whenever enough people sign up.

Local Guides (Booked in Advance): Guides lead two-hour

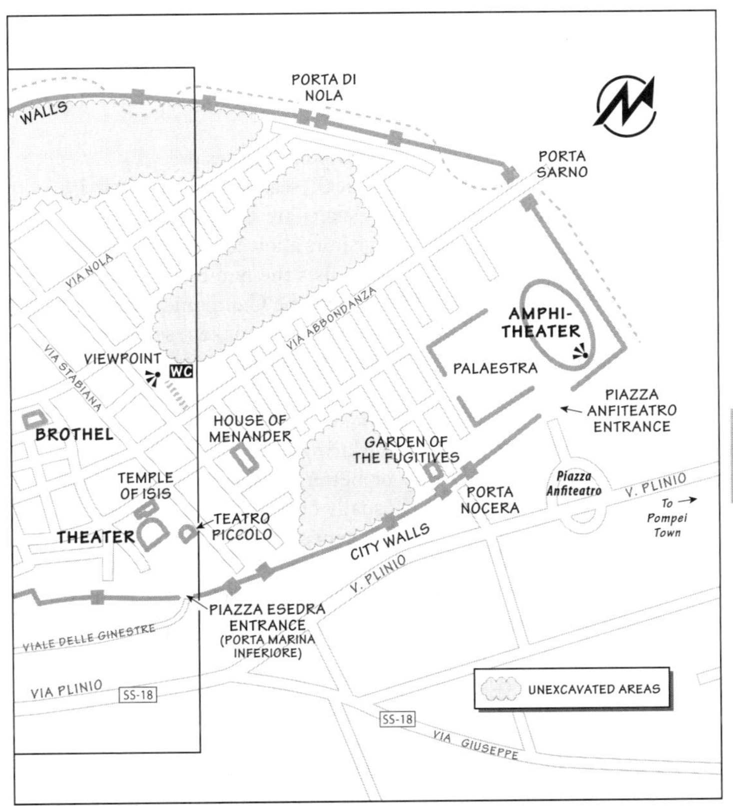

tours of the excavation site for individuals and small groups, helping you skip the lines and get the most out of your visit. **Paolo Damiano** and his wife **Giovanna De Gennaro** lead private tours of Pompeii (€160) and destinations throughout the Amalfi Coast (+39 340 318 9339, www.albireotravels.com, info@albireotravel.it). **Antonio Somma** and his team of guides offer tours of Pompeii for €180 (+39 393 406 3824 or +39 081 850 1992, www.tourspompeiiguide.com, info@pompeitour.com).

Local Guides (Booked On-Site): Random local licensed guides hang out at the turnstile looking for work. They charge around €150 for two hours. Establish a firm price. If on a budget, get others to join you and share the cost. If more people join your group, insist on the basic price being shared and not multiplied. It's unethical for a guide to double charge by combining two groups into one tour. Instead, tourists should enjoy the savings and tip higher.

Audioguides: Audioguides are available from a kiosk near the ticket booth at the Porta Marina entrance (€8, €13 for 2, ID required).

ORIENTATION TO POMPEII

Cost: €19, book in advance in peak season (see below).

Hours: Daily 9:00-19:00, Nov-March until 17:00, last entry 1.5 hours before closing.

Information: +39 081 857 5347, www.pompeiisites.org.

Reservations Recommended: In peak season (April-Oct), it's smart to book in advance, as tickets are by timed entry and there's a cap on the number of visitors allowed in per day (book at www.ticketone.it). Each ticket lists the name of the visitor, and ID may be required. If you have the Campania ArteCard (described on page 28) you do not need to make reservations.

Crowd-Beating Tips: If you're buying tickets on-site and there's a very long ticket line at the main Porta Marina entrance, you can walk three minutes to the ticket booth near Hotel Vittoria (called Piazza Esedra or Porta Marina Inferiore; see the "Pompeii" map) where lines may be better. Avoid visiting Pompeii on crowded free entry days (usually once a month on Sun).

Within Pompeii, tourists generally crowd into a tight corner of the otherwise vast and empty site. The most popular ruins have attendants that control the crowds. The brothel (Lupanare) is the most crowded single stop. (To skip that mob scene, remember there's more and better erotic Pompeiian art in Naples at the Archaeological Museum.)

Visitor Information: Pick up the very handy map with your ticket before entering. Some buildings and streets are bound to be closed for restoration when you visit. Use your map to find your way. Street names and building numbers are marked throughout the site.

The bookshop sells books with plastic overlays that allow you to re-create Pompeii from the ruins (€20). Another good book is the €6 *Pompeii (Brief) Guide,* with excellent photos and additional walking routes.

Bypass the "info point" kiosk at the train station: It's an aggressive private agency selling tours. They purport to be a nonprofit, which is deceptive.

Inside the site, there are so many guides working, you can often just cock your ear to overhear the rundown in English.

Rated Risqué: Note that the ancient brothel and its sexually explicit frescoes are included on tours; let your guide know if you'd rather skip that stop (or spend a little extra time there). There is also erotic art at the House of the Vettii.

Baggage Check: Use the free baggage check near the turnstiles at the site entry (desk at the turnstiles, lockers around the corner). The train station also offers pay luggage storage (downstairs, by the WC).

Services: There's a pay WC at the train station. The Pompeii site has four free WCs—at the entrance, in the cafeteria, in the Antiquarium museum, and at the "viewpoint" (near the end of this tour, uphill from the theaters).

Eating: These **€** eateries offer reasonably priced meals (though your cheapest bet may be to bring your own food for a discreet picnic).

The **Chora cafeteria,** within the site, sells overpriced sandwiches at a counter. You're welcome to picnic here if you buy a drink.

A strip of simple restaurants and snack bars lines the road between the station and the entrance: **Bar Sgambati,** the café/restaurant at the train station, has air-conditioning, sandwiches to go, and pastas and pizzas. **Marius Juice Shop,** run by local guide Antonio Somma's family, sells good salads, pastas, and sandwiches to go.

A second cluster of eateries around the ticket booth near Hotel Vittoria dishes out handy slices of pizza, salads, and pasta.

Starring: Roofless (collapsed) but otherwise intact Roman buildings, plaster casts of hapless victims, some erotic frescoes, and the dawning realization that these ancient people were not that different from us.

OVERVIEW

Pompeii, founded in 600 BC, eventually became a booming Roman trading city. Not rich, not poor, it was middle class—a perfect example of typical Roman life. Most streets would have been lined with stalls and jammed with customers from sunup to sundown. Chariots vied with shoppers for street space. Two thousand years ago, Rome controlled the entire Mediterranean—making it a kind of free-trade zone—and Pompeii was a central and bustling port.

There were no posh neighborhoods in Pompeii. Rich and poor mixed it up as elegant houses existed side by side with simple homes. While nearby Herculaneum would have been a classier place to live (a smaller, seaside resort with traffic-free streets, fancier houses, and far better drainage), Pompeii was the place for action and shopping. It served an estimated 10,000 to 20,000 residents with more than 40 bakeries; 130 bars, restaurants, and hotels; and

30 brothels. With most of its buildings covered by brilliant white ground-marble stucco, Pompeii in AD 79 was an impressive town.

Today's ruin is a vast site, and my suggested tour is guilty of contributing to the main problem: Everyone does the same crowded route, lacing together the five or so most famous stops. Guides observe that tourists are most excited to see two things: sexy frescoes and the casts of human victims. The image that's most impactful? The cast of the dead dog.

As you tour Pompeii, remember that its best art is safeguarded in the Archaeological Museum in Naples (described in the Naples chapter). Visiting the museum before or after going to Pompeii will help put this fascinating place into context.

SELF-GUIDED TOUR

• *Just past the ticket-taker, start your approach up to the...*

1 Porta Marina

The city of Pompeii was born on the hill ahead of you. This was the original town gate. Before Vesuvius blew and filled in the harbor, the sea came nearly to here. Notice the two openings in the gate (ahead, up the ramp). Both were left open by day to admit major traffic. At night, the larger one was closed for better security.

• *Pass through the Porta Marina and continue up to the top of the street, pausing at the three large stepping stones in the middle.*

2 Pompeii's Streets

Every day, Pompeiians flooded the streets with gushing water to clean them. These stepping stones let pedestrians cross without getting their sandals wet. Chariots traveling in either direction could straddle the stones (all had standard-size axles). A single stepping stone in a road means it was a one-way street, a pair indicates an ordinary two-way, and three (like this) signifies a major thoroughfare. The basalt stones are the original Roman pavement. The sidewalks (elevated to hide the plumbing—you'll see ancient metal piping revealed throughout the site) were paved with bits of broken pots (an ancient form of recycling) and studded with

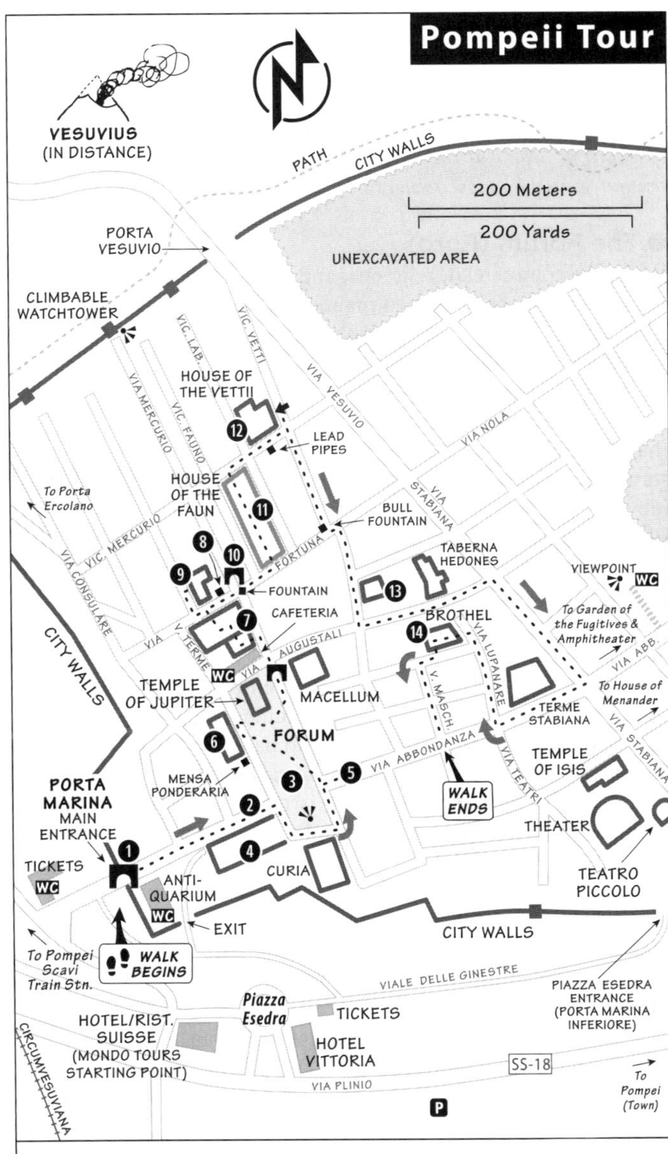

1 Porta Marina
2 Pompeii's Streets
3 Forum
4 Basilica
5 Via Abbondanza
6 Forum Granary; Plaster Casts of Victims
7 Baths of the Forum
8 Fast-Food Joint
9 House of the Tragic Poet
10 Aqueduct Arch
11 House of the Faun
12 House of the Vettii
13 Bakery & Mill
14 Brothel

reflective bits of white marble. These "cats' eyes" helped people get around after dark, either by moonlight or with the help of lamps.

• *Continue straight ahead, don your mental toga, and enter the city as the Romans once did. The road opens up into the spacious main square: the Forum. Stand at the right end of this rectangular space (near the centaur statue) and look toward Mount Vesuvius.*

❸ The Forum (Foro)

Pompeii's commercial, religious, and political center stands at the intersection of the city's two main streets. While it's the most ruined part of Pompeii, it's grand nonetheless. Imagine the piazza surrounded by two-story buildings on all sides. The pedestals that line the square once held statues of VIPs and various gods (now safely displayed in the museum in Naples). In Pompeii's heyday, its citizens gathered here in the main square to shop, talk politics, and socialize. Business took place in the important buildings that lined the piazza.

The Forum was dominated by the **Temple of Jupiter,** at the far end (marked by a half-dozen ruined columns atop a stair-step base). Jupiter was the supreme god of the Roman pantheon—you might be able to make out his little white marble head at the center-rear of the temple. To the left of the temple is a fenced-off area, the **Forum granary,** where many artifacts from Pompeii are stored (and which we'll visit later).

At the near end of the Forum (behind where you're standing) is the **curia,** or City Hall. Like many Roman buildings, it was built with brick and mortar, then covered with marble walls and floors. To your left (as you face Vesuvius and the Temple of Jupiter) is the **basilica,** or courthouse.

Since Pompeii was a pretty typical Roman town, it has the same layout and components that you'll find in any Roman city—main square, curia, basilica, temples, axis of roads, and so on. All power converged at the Forum: religious (the temple), political (the curia), judicial (the basilica), and commercial (this piazza was the main marketplace). Even the power of the people was expressed here, since this is where they gathered to vote. Imagine the hubbub of this town square in its heyday.

Look beyond the Temple of Jupiter. Five miles to the north looms the ominous backstory to this site: **Mount Vesuvius.** Mentally draw a triangle up from the two remaining peaks to reconstruct the mountain before the eruption. When it blew, Pompeiians had no idea that they were living under a volcano, as Vesuvius hadn't erupted for centuries. Imagine the wonder—then the horror—as a column of pulverized rock roared upward, and then ash began to fall. The weight of the ash and small rocks collapsed Pompeii's roofs later that day, crushing people who had taken refuge inside buildings instead of fleeing the city.

• *Step inside the basilica (to your left, as you face Vesuvius), lined with stumps of columns.*

❹ Basilica

Pompeii's basilica was a first-century palace of justice. This ancient law court has the same floor plan later adopted by many Christian churches (which are also called basilicas). The big central hall (or nave) is flanked by rows of columns marking off narrower side aisles. Along the side walls are traces of the original stucco imitating marble.

The columns—now stumps all about the same height—were not ruined by the volcano. Rather, they were left unfinished when Vesuvius blew. Pompeii had been devastated by an earthquake in AD 62, and was just in the process of rebuilding the basilica when Vesuvius erupted, 17 years later. The half-built columns show off the technology of the day. There were no marble columns at Pompeii, just brick columns stuccoed to look like marble—an economical construction method found throughout Pompeii (and the Roman Empire). Uniform bricks were stacked around a cylindrical core. Once finished, they were coated with marble-dust stucco to simulate marble.

Besides the earthquake and the eruption, Pompeii's buildings have suffered other ravages over the years, including Spanish plunderers (c. 1800), 19th-century souvenir hunters, WWII bombs, creeping and destructive vegetation, another earthquake in 1980, and modern neglect. The fact that the entire city was covered by the eruption of AD 79 actually helped preserve it, saving it from the sixth-century barbarians who plundered many other towns into oblivion.

• *Exit the basilica and cross the short side of the square to where the city's main street hits the Forum. Stop at the three white stones that stick up from the cobbles.*

The Eruption of Vesuvius

At about 1:00 in the afternoon on August 24, AD 79, Mount Vesuvius erupted, sending a mushroom cloud of ash, dust, and rocks 12 miles into the air. It spewed for 18 hours straight, as winds blew the cloud southward. The white-gray ash settled like a heavy snow on Pompeii, its weight eventually collapsing roofs and floors, but leaving the walls intact. And though most of Pompeii's residents fled that day, a couple thousand stayed behind.

Although the city of Herculaneum was closer to the volcano—about four miles away—at first it largely escaped the rain of ash, due to the direction of the wind. However, 12 hours after Vesuvius awoke, the type of eruption suddenly changed. The mountain let loose a superheated avalanche of ash, pumice, and gas. This red-hot "pyroclastic flow" sped down the side of the mountain at nearly 100 miles per hour, engulfing Herculaneum and cooking its residents alive. Several more flows over the next few hours further entombed Herculaneum, burying it in nearly 60 feet of hot material that later cooled into rock, freezing the city in time. Then, at around 7:30 in the morning, another pyroclastic flow headed south and struck Pompeii, dealing a fatal blow to those who'd remained behind.

❺ Via Abbondanza

Glance down Via Abbondanza, Pompeii's main street. Lined with shops, bars, and restaurants, it was a lively, pedestrian-only zone. The three "beaver-teeth" stones are traffic barriers that kept chariots out. On the corner at the start of the street (just to the left), take a close look at the dark travertine column standing next to the white one. Notice that the marble drums of the white column are not chiseled entirely round—another construction project left unfinished when Vesuvius erupted.

• *Our tour will eventually end a few blocks down Via Abbondanza after making a big loop. But now, head toward Vesuvius, cutting across the Forum. To the left of the Temple of Jupiter is the...*

❻ Forum Granary

A substantial stretch of the west side of the Forum was the granary and ancient produce market. Today, it houses thousands of artifacts excavated from Pompeii. You'll see lots of crockery, pots, pans, jugs, and containers used for transporting oil and wine.

You'll also see casts of a couple of eruption victims (and possibly a dog). These casts show Pompeiians eerily captured in their last moments, hands covering their mouths as they gasped for air. They were quickly suffocated by a superheated avalanche of gas and ash, and their bodies were encased in volcanic debris. While excavating, modern archaeologists detected hollow spaces underfoot, created when the victims' bodies decomposed. By gently filling the holes with plaster, the archaeologists created molds of the Pompeiians who were caught in the disaster. (Note: If the Forum Granary is closed, you can see casts across the square at the Macellum—see below.)

A few steps to the left of the granary is a tiny alcove that contained the **Mensa Ponderaria,** a counter where standard units (such as today's liter or gallon) were used to measure the quantities of liquid and solid food that were sold. And just to the right of the granary is the remains of a public toilet. You can imagine the many seats, lack of privacy, and constantly flushing stream running through the room.

• *Exit the Forum by crossing it again in front of the Temple of Jupiter. For the* **Macellum,** *angle left and step into the courtyard on the far side, where you'll see a commotion of people standing around three casts of bodies in three glass cases.*

Continuing on, walk under the arch. In the road are more "beaver-teeth" traffic blocks. On the pillar to the right, look for what could be a pedestrian-only road sign or an indication that here was a porter service (two guys carrying an amphora, or ancient jug; it's above the REG VII INS IV *sign).*

The modern **cafeteria** *(on the left) fills a piece of real estate that was bombed in World War II. Today it's the only eatery inside the archaeological site (and the only place with air-conditioning; there's also a WC inside). Twenty yards past the cafeteria, on the left-hand side at #24, is the entrance to the...*

❼ Baths of the Forum (Terme del Foro)

Pompeii had six public baths, each with a men's and a women's section. You're in the men's zone. The leafy courtyard at the entrance was the gymnasium. After working out, clients could relax with a hot bath *(caldarium)*, warm bath *(tepidarium)*, or cold plunge *(frigidarium)*.

The first big, plain room you enter served as the **dressing**

room. Holes on the walls were likely for wooden lockers (all of the wood here is long gone) or pegs to hang clothing. High up, the window (with a faded water god underneath) was originally covered with a less translucent Roman glass. Peek into the small cold-water pool *(frigidarium)* under the window. Walk over the nonslip mosaics into the next room.

The ***tepidarium*** is ringed by mini statues, or *telamones* (male caryatids, figures used as supporting pillars), which divided the lockers. Clients would undress and warm up here, perhaps relaxing on one of the bronze cow-footed benches near the bronze heater while waiting for a massage. Look at the ceiling—half crushed by the eruption and half intact, with its fine blue-and-white stucco work.

Next, admire the engineering in the steam-bath room, or ***caldarium.*** The double floor was heated from below—so it was nice for bare feet (look down into the grate across from where you entered to see the brick support towers). The double walls with brown terra-cotta tiles held the heat. Romans soaked in the big tub, which was filled with hot water. Opposite the big tub is a fountain, which spouted water onto the hot floor, creating steam. The lettering on the fountain reminded those enjoying the room which two politicians paid for it...and how much it cost them. (On the far right, the Roman numerals indicate the price: 5,250 *sestertii*). To keep condensation from dripping annoyingly from the ceiling, fluting (ribbing) was added to carry water down the walls.

• *Today's visitors exit the baths through the original entry (at the far end of the dressing room). Hungry? Immediately across the street (at #8) is an ancient...*

❽ Fast-Food Joint

After a bath, it was only natural to want a little snack. So, just across the street is a fast-food joint, marked by a series of rectangular marble counters. Most ancient Romans didn't cook for themselves in their tiny apartments, so to-go places like this were commonplace. The holes in the counters held the pots for food. Each container was like a thermos, with a wooden lid to keep the soup hot, the wine

cool, and so on. You could dine in the back or get your food to go. Notice the groove in the front doorstep and the holes out on the curb. The holes likely accommodated cords for stretching awnings over the sidewalk to shield the clientele from the hot sun, while the grooves were for the shop's folding accordion doors. Look at the wheel grooves in the pavement, worn down through centuries of use. Nearby are more stepping stones for pedestrians to cross the flooded streets.

• *Just a few steps uphill from the fast-food joint, at #5 (behind a glass wall), is the...*

❾ House of the Tragic Poet (Casa del Poeta Tragico)

This house is typical Roman style. The front door is flanked by two family-owned shops (each with a track in the threshold for a collapsing accordion door). The home is a series of rooms running straight away from the street: atrium (with skylight and pool to catch the rain), den (where deals were made by the shopkeeper), and garden (with rooms facing it and a shrine to remember both the gods and family ancestors). In the entryway is the famous "Beware of Dog" *(Cave Canem)* mosaic.

When it's open (rarely), today's visitors enter the home by the back door (circle around to the left). But even when it's locked, you can look through the door to see the richly frescoed dining room that's off the garden. Diners lounged on their couches (the Roman custom) and enjoyed frescoes with fake "windows," giving the illusion of a bigger and airier room. Next to the dining room is a humble BBQ-style kitchen with a little closet for the toilet (the kitchen and bathroom shared the same plumbing).

• *Return to the fast-food place and continue about 10 yards downhill to the big intersection. From the center of the intersection, look left to see a giant arch, framing a nice view of Mount Vesuvius. In the foreground notice one of 12 watchtowers on the city wall—climbable for a commanding view.*

❿ Aqueduct Arch—Running Water

Water was critical for this city, and this arch was part of Pompeii's water-delivery system. A 100-mile-long aqueduct carried fresh water down from the hillsides to a big reservoir perched at the highest point of the city wall. Since overall water pressure was disappointing, Pompeiians built arches like the brick one you see here (originally covered in marble) with hidden water tanks at the top. Located just below the altitude of the main tank, these smaller tanks were filled by gravity and provided each neighborhood with reliable pressure. Embedded in the arch are 2,000-year-old pipes (made of lead imported all the way from Cornwall in Britannia).

If there was a water shortage, democratic priorities prevailed: First the baths were cut off, then the private homes. The last to go were the public fountains, where all citizens could get drinking and cooking water.

• *If you're thirsty, fill your water bottle from the modern fountain—as thirsty people have done on this spot for 2,000 years. Then continue straight downhill one block (50 yards), to #2 on the left.*

⓫ House of the Faun (Casa del Fauno)

Stand across the street and marvel at the grand entry with "*HAVE*" (hail to you) as a welcome mat. Go in. Notice the two shrines facing each other above the entryway—one dedicated to the gods, the other to this wealthy family's ancestors. (Contemporary Neapolitans still carry on this practice; you'll notice little shrines embedded in walls all over Naples.)

You are standing in Pompeii's largest home, where you're greeted by the delightful small bronze **statue of the *Dancing Faun*,** famed for its realistic movement and fine proportion. (The original is in Naples' Archaeological Museum.) With 40 rooms and 27,000 square feet, the House of the Faun covers an entire city block. Just think of how vibrant and luxurious this house would have seemed before the eruption.

At the back end of the first garden is the famous floor mosaic of the ***Battle of Alexander.*** (The original is also at the museum in Naples.) In 333 BC, Alexander the Great beat Darius and the Persians. Romans had much respect for Alexander, the first great emperor before Rome's. While most of Pompeii's nouveau riche had notoriously bad taste and stuffed their palaces with over-the-top, mismatched decor, this guy had class. Both the faun (an ancient copy of a famous Greek statue) and the Alexander mosaic show an appreciation for history and art.

The house's back courtyard is lined with pillars rebuilt after the AD 62 earthquake. Take a close look at the brick, mortar, and fake-marble stucco veneer.

• *Leave the House of the Faun through its back door in the far-right corner, past a tiny guard's station. (If closed, exit out the front and walk around to the back.) Turn right and walk about a block until you see two-foot-tall metal cages over the sidewalk protecting exposed stretches of ancient lead water pipes. Continue east and take your first left, walking about 20 yards to the entrance (on your left) to the...*

⓬ House of the Vettii

This is Pompeii's best-preserved home, retaining many of its mosaics and frescoes. The House of the Vettii was the bachelor pad of two wealthy merchant brothers. In the entryway (on the right), it's hard to miss the huge erection. This was not pornography. This was a symbol of success: The penis and sack of money balance each other on the goldsmith scale above a fine bowl of fruit. Translation? Only with a balance of fertility and money can you enjoy true abundance.

Step into the atrium with its replica wooden ceiling open to the sky. The pool was flanked by two large moneyboxes (one survives, the footprint of the other shows how it was secured to the ground). To the immediate right of the entryway, venture into the slaves' quarter: kitchen, bedrooms, and a room in the back for sex (with an explicit fresco surviving on the wall).

Now go to the central courtyard of the *domus* (with a surviving lead pipe circling the garden, which fed the fountains and daily life). The brothers wanted all who entered to know how successful they were. A variety of rooms face the interior courtyard. The scenes portrayed in the frescoes in each room give an intimate peek at elegant Pompeiian life.

Notice more white "cat's eye" stones embedded in the floor. Imagine these glinting like little eyes as the brothers and their friends wandered around by oil lamp late at night, with their sacks of gold, bowls of fruit, and enormous...egos.

• *Our next stop, the bakery, is located about 150 yards south (downhill) from here. To get there, return to the street in front of the House of the Vettii. Walk downhill along Vicolo dei Vetti. Go one block, to where you dead-end at a T-intersection with Via della Fortuna. The intersection is marked by a* ***fountain*** *decorated by the head of a bull (one of more than 40 such fountains at major intersections in Pompeii). Go 10 steps left and then right at the first corner. Continue down this gently curving road to #22 (on the left).*

⓭ Bakery and Mill

The stubby stone towers are flour grinders. Grain was poured into the top and donkeys or slaves, treading in a circle, pushed wooden bars that turned the stones that ground the grain. The powdered grain dropped out the bottom as flour—flavored with tiny bits of rock. Nearby, the thing that looks like a modern-day pizza oven was...a brick oven. Each neighborhood had a bakery just like this.

• *Continue down the curvy road to the next intersection. At the intersec-*

tion with Via degli Augustali, turn left. As you walk, notice the chariot grooves worn into the pavement. Also notice how there must have been some "road work" going on when Vesuvius blew its top—the grooves are replaced by a stretch of new pavement.

Ahead, in 50 yards, at #44 (on the left), is the ***Taberna Hedones,*** *an ancient tavern. While likely closed, you can look through its two doors to see its original floor mosaic still intact.*

Our last stop on this tour is the site's most popular attraction. Consequently, even though it's just 50 yards from here (just past Taberna Hedones—look down the lane on the right for the horny mob), we'll have to circle all the way around to reach it from the other side. Proceed beyond Taberna Hedones and turn right at the next big street. Follow it downhill, turning right when you reach the wide Via Abbondanza. (This is the "main drag" we looked down earlier. In the distance, dead ahead, is the main square and the exit.) Walk along here, passing the entrance to #8 (Terme Stabiane). Eventually you'll come to a narrow lane on the right where there's usually a big commotion of visitors. If you'd like to visit one of Pompeii's many brothels, head up here (to #18) and get in line.

⑭ Brothel (Lupanare)

You'll find the biggest crowds in Pompeii at a place that was likely also quite popular 2,000 years ago—the brothel. Prostitutes were nicknamed *lupe* (she-wolves), alluding to the call they made when attracting business. The brothel was a simple place, with beds and pillows made of stone and then covered with mattresses. The ancient graffiti includes tallies and exotic names of the sex workers, indicating how they came from all corners of the Mediterranean (it also served as feedback from satisfied customers). The faded frescoes above the cells may have been a kind of menu for services offered. Note the idealized women (white, which was considered beautiful; one wears an early bra) and the rougher men (dark, considered horny). The bed legs came with little disk-like barriers to keep critters from crawling up, the tiny rooms had curtains for doors, and the prostitutes provided sheepskin condoms.

• *On that note, we conclude this walk. Leaving the brothel, go back downhill two blocks to return to Via Abbondanza.*

To ***exit,*** *go right on Via Abbondanza, cross the forum, and walk back down the street you arrived on. On your way out, you'll be routed through the shop and the* ***Antiquarium****—a fine museum with a variety of slice-of-life artifacts, on three floors, from ancient Pompeii. While all the best stuff is in Naples' Archaeological Museum, here you can see a few frescoes, pottery, statues, other decor, and more casts of Pompeiians frozen in time.*

But to see more, go left on Via Abbondanza to explore the...

Rest of the Archaeological Site

While you've seen the most famous points in the excavation, there is much, much more. These extra stops are worth the time and energy (if you have any left). To locate them, refer to your map. You can weave them together easily. But perhaps the most enjoyable bonus would be to take what you've learned so far and simply wander the back lanes of the once-thriving city.

Temple of Isis

This temple, located near the theater, served Pompeii's Egyptian community. The little white stucco shrine with the modern plastic roof housed holy water from the Nile. Isis, from Egyptian myth, was one of many foreign gods adopted by the eclectic Romans. Pompeii must have had a synagogue, too, but it has yet to be excavated.

Theater

Originally a Greek theater (Greeks built theirs with the help of a hillside), this was the birthplace of the Greek port here in 470 BC. During Roman times, the theater sat 5,000 people in three sets of seats, all with different prices: the five marble terraces up close (filled with romantic wooden seats for two), the main section, and the cheap nosebleed section (surviving only on the high end, near the trees). The square stones above the cheap seats once supported a canvas rooftop. The high-profile boxes, flanking the stage, were for guests of honor. From this perch, you can see the gladiator barracks—the colonnaded courtyard beyond the theater. They lived in tiny rooms, trained in the courtyard, and fought in the nearby amphitheater. Check out the adjacent and well-preserved smaller Teatro Piccolo.

House of Menander (Casa di Menandro)

Once owned by a wealthy Pompeiian, this house takes its current name from a fresco of the Greek playwright Menander on one of the walls. Admire the grand atrium (with frescoes depicting scenes from Homer's *Iliad* and *Odyssey,* and an altar to the family gods), the wall frescoes, and the mosaics. The cloister-like back courtyard leads to a room with skeletons (not plaster casts) of eruption victims from this house. Farther back, a passage leads to the servants' quarters.

Viewpoint

In the very center of the excavation site is a viewpoint. It's high above because it's at ground level—post eruption (and pre-excavation). This was the center for the excavation work back in the 19th century (with the only WC in the neighborhood). Surveying the view from up here, you can see farmland showing how locals lived on top of the ruins for centuries without knowing what was underneath. And you can see the entire ancient city of Pompeii spread out in front of you and appreciate the magnitude of the excavations.

Garden of the Fugitives

There's no better reminder in Pompeii of the horror caused by a volcanic eruption (and how we all might act given the same circumstances) than this "garden." Archaeologists identified this house as belonging to a middle-class merchant family. Plaster casts of this fleeing ("fugitive") family are placed exactly as the bodies were found after the eruption: lined up in single file as they attempted to escape several cubic feet of already fallen ash. Their exit was stopped by a sudden wave of hot gas and volcanic material, likely traveling over 100 miles per hour. Frozen in time, servants cannot be distinguished from their masters.

Amphitheater

If you can, climb to the upper level of the amphitheater (though the stairs are often blocked). With Vesuvius looming in the background, mentally replace the tourists below with gladiators and wild animals locked in combat. Walk along the top of the amphitheater and look down into the grassy rectangular area surrounded by columns. This is the **Palaestra,** an area once used for athletic training. (If you can't get to the top of the amphitheater, you can see the Palaestra from outside—in fact, you can't miss it, as it's right next door.) Facing the other way, look for the bell tower that tops the roofline of the modern city of Pompei, where locals go about their daily lives in the shadow of the volcano, just as their ancestors did 2,000 years ago. If Vesuvius blew again as it did back in the first century (as some geologists worry could happen), the death toll could be far greater, thanks to today's denser population.

• *Make your way back to the* ***main entrance.*** *If it's too crowded to bear hiking back along uneven lanes to the entrance, you can slip out the site's "back door," next to the amphitheater (at Piazza Anfiteatro). Exiting, turn right and follow the site's wall all the way back to the entrance (about 15 minutes).*

Or, if heading directly to the ***Archaeological Museum*** *in Naples (as described under "Planning Your Time," earlier), exit here and walk to the Pompei town train station. From the exit, turn left on Via Roma (on lava-rock pavement, with lots of eateries along the way), walk to the big church tower marking the tidy main piazza of modern Pompei, turn right, and continue down to the train station to find Metro line 2.*

Herculaneum

Smaller, less crowded, and not as ruined as its famous big sister, the buried city of Herculaneum (Ercolano in Italian—also the name of the modern town) is worth ▲▲ and offers an even more intimate peek into ancient Roman life. It lacks the grandeur and fame of Pompeii (there's barely a colonnade), but is a refreshingly uncrowded Back Door alternative.

GETTING THERE

Ercolano Scavi, the nearest train station to Herculaneum, is about 20 minutes from Naples and 50 minutes from Sorrento on the same **Circumvesuviana train line** as Pompeii (roughly 2/hour but check schedule at www.eavsrl.it or ask at the station; confirm that your train will stop at the Herculaneum stop—Ercolano Scavi; typically trains marked *DD* are express trains and skip Ercolano). You can also get there on the **Campania Express** (4/day). Note that Trenitalia trains stop in Ercolano at a station that's farther from the site, and isn't recommended.

From the station, it's about a 10-minute **walk** to the ruins. Leave the station and turn right, then left down the main drag; continue straight several blocks gradually downhill to the end of the road, where you'll run right into the grand arch that marks the entrance to the ruins. (Skip Museo MAV.) Pass through the arch and continue 200 yards down the path—taking in the bird's-eye first impression of the site to your right—to the ticket office in the modern visitors center. **Taxis** make the trip for about €5; to return to the station by taxi, ask the staff to call one for you.

Combining Herculaneum and Vesuvius: It's easy to visit Herculaneum and Vesuvius in one day, since both require arriving at the Ercolano Scavi train station. My advice: Book the morning **Vesuvio Express combo entrance/bus ticket** (see page 133), which includes the transfer between Ercolano Scavi and Vesuvius, and includes your Vesuvius ticket (otherwise you have to buy it in advance on your own). In the afternoon, visit the Herculaneum ruins and head back to your home base from Ercolano Scavi.

ORIENTATION TO HERCULANEUM

Cost and Hours: €13; daily 8:30-19:30, off-season until 17:00, last entry 1.5 hours before closing; avoid crowded free entry days (usually once a month on a Sunday); +39 081 777 7008, http://ercolano.beniculturali.it.

Closures: As excavations and renovations are ongoing, expect changes to this tour.

Tours: The audioguide provides more information, but it's pricey (€10, €16 for 2, ID required); this book's tour covers the basics for a targeted visit.

Length of This Tour: Allow two hours, including time to visit the Antiquarium museum.

Baggage Storage: The Vesuvio Express bus company, which has an office just outside the Ercolano Scavi station, offers baggage storage. At the site, you can store bags for free in lockers just beyond the bookstore (get a key from the office across from the ticket window; bags must be picked up at least 30 minutes prior to site closing).

Services: A free WC is to the left of the ticket office entrance as you approach it; inside the site, a WC is near the Antiquarium.

Eating: There are several eateries between the site and the train station. Within the site, the "food court" near the Antiquarium is just a lineup of vending machines.

➲ SELF-GUIDED TOUR

Caked and baked by the same AD 79 eruption that pummeled Pompeii, Herculaneum is a small community of intact buildings with plenty of surviving detail. While Pompeii was initially smothered in ash, Herculaneum was spared at first but got slammed that night by a superheated avalanche of ash and hot gases roaring off the volcano (see "The Eruption of Vesuvius" sidebar, earlier). The city was eventually buried under nearly 60 feet of ash, which hardened into a volcanic rock called tuff, perfectly preserving the city until excavations began in 1748.

After leaving the visitors center, go through the turnstiles and walk the path to the entry point. Look seaward and note where the shoreline is today; before the eruption, it was where you are standing, a quarter-mile inland. This gives you a sense of how much volcanic material piled up. The present-day city of Ercolano hovers just above the ruins. The modern buildings don't look much different from their ancient counterparts. Vesuvius looms above it all.

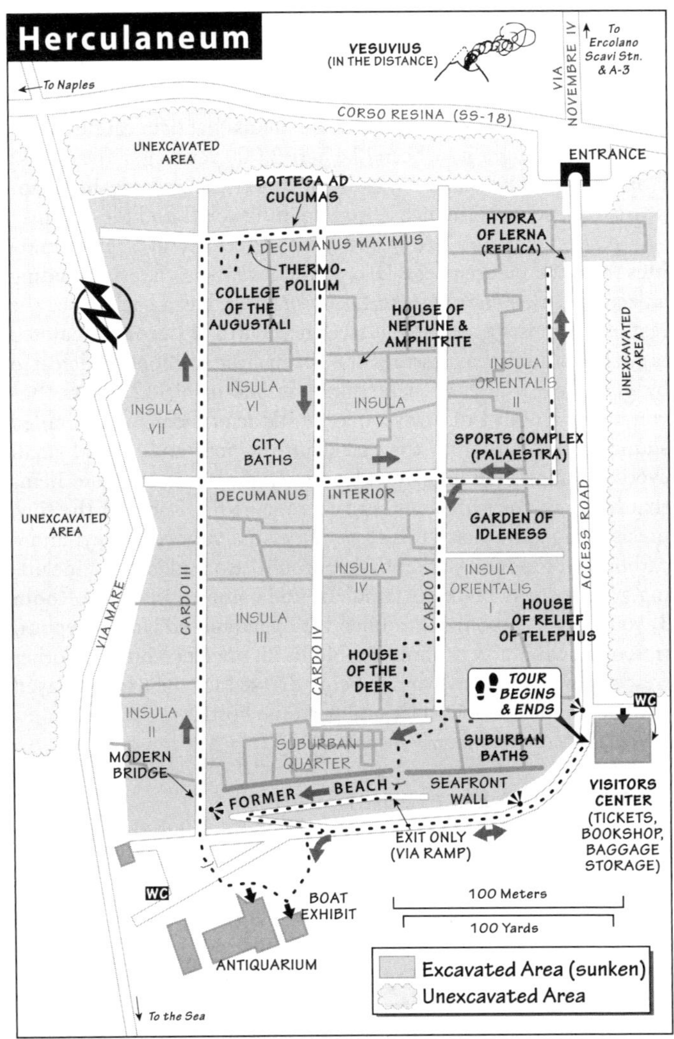

• *Before entering the site, watch on your left for two buildings that house worthwhile museums.*

Museums

• *Just before the Antiquarium, the small, red-brick building merits a quick look.*

Boat Exhibit (Padiglione Barca): In this space you'll find an ancient, 30-foot, wooden fishing boat (with three sets of oars on each side) that was found on the beach in front of Herculaneum in 1982.

• *The bigger building (farther along) is more worthwhile.*

Antiquarium: This houses some stunning original pieces from Herculaneum (you'll see replicas of some of these as we tour the site), as well as several slice-of-life items that help capture what ordinary life might have been like here 2,000 years ago. The exhibit ("Splendori da Ercolano") was intended to be temporary, but it appears to be semi-permanent—so hopefully you'll find these items:

As you enter, go left up the ramp to see several original **marbles** from the House of the Deer (which we'll visit later), including a deer, *Drunken Hercules,* and *Drunken Satyr.* Head back to see the rest of the museum. First you face the **Hydra of Lerna,** a sculpted bronze fountain that features the seven-headed monster defeated by Hercules—the city's namesake—as one of his 12 labors. Beyond that, **Room 1** displays a marble statue of Demeter, a detailed statue of Bacchus from the blacksmith's shop, and several small everyday items. Circling into **Room 2,** you see even more items that help resurrect life at ancient Herculaneum. Look for the tiny, precise surgeon's tools (a row of scalpels); a very rusty key; and a carbonized rope and wicker basket. You'll also find jewelry, including golden snake bracelets, amulets, and combs. Finally, in **Room 3,** you'll see a carbonized wooden table, juxtaposed with a (replica) fresco showing a very similar table in an ancient home. Another fresco shows a wealthy woman being dressed for the day, displayed with actual pieces of jewelry and perfume bottles.

• *Now let's head into Herculaneum itself.*

Herculaneum Excavation Site

Go down the stairs and cross the modern bridge into the site, looking down into the moat-like **ditch.** On one side, you see Herculaneum's seafront wall. On the other is the wall that you just walked on, a solidified ash layer from the volcano that shows how deeply the town was buried.

After crossing the bridge, stroll straight up the **street.** As at Pompeii, Herculaneum's streets were ruts that sat well below the sidewalk level, so they could be flushed easily with water for quick cleaning. You can duck into any number of houses along here, but I've called out some of the more interesting ones.

At the far end of the street find the **College of the Augustali** (Sede degli Augustali, #24). Decorated with frescoes of Hercules (for whom this city was named), it belonged to an association of freed slaves working together to climb their way up the ladder of Roman society. Here and farther on, look around doorways and ceilings to spot ancient wood charred by the pyroclastic flows. Most buildings were made of stone, with wooden floors and beams (which were preserved here by the ash but rarely survive at ancient sites).

Leave the building and head right, down the lane. The adjacent ***thermopolium*** (#19) was the Roman equivalent of a lunch counter or fast-food joint, with giant jars for wine, oil, and snacks. Most of the buildings along here were shops, with apartments above.

A few steps on, the **Bottega ad Cucumas** wine shop (#14, on the right) still has charred remains of beams, and its drink list remains frescoed on the outside wall (under glass).

Just past a courtyard entrance, take the next right and walk halfway down the street to find the **House of Neptune and Amphitrite** (Casa di Nettuno e Anfitrite, on the left at #7). Outside, notice the intact upper floor and imagine it going even higher. Inside, you'll see vivid, intact mosaics and a unique "frame" made of shells.

Back outside, continue downhill to the intersection, then head left for a block and proceed straight across the street into the don't-miss-it **sports complex** (*palaestra;* #4). First you'll see a row of "marble" columns, which (look closer) are actually made of rounded bricks covered with a thick layer of plaster, shaped to look like carved marble. While important buildings in Rome itself had solid marble columns, these imitations are typical of ordinary buildings outside the capital.

Continuing deeper into the complex, look for the hole in the hillside and walk through the triangular-shaped entrance to find a replica of the **Hydra of Lerna** statue (the original is in the Antiquarium).

Backtrack through the sports complex. As you exit, turn left, heading downhill. On the left, look for **Il Giardino dell'Ozio** ("The Garden of Idleness"), where you can take a break in one of the lounge chairs set up under a pomegranate orchard planted here following a 1934-1936 excavation.

Continuing along the lane, just before the path goes underground, on the right is the **House of the Deer** (Casa dei Cervi, #21). It's named for the statues of deer being attacked by dogs found in the garden courtyard (these are copies; the originals are in the Antiquarium). As you wander through the rooms, notice the colorfully frescoed walls. Ancient Herculaneum, like all Roman cities of that age, was filled with color, rather than the stark white we often imagine (even the statues were painted).

You can see more of these colors, this time bright orange, across the street in the **House of the Relief of Telephus** (Casa del Rilievo del Telefo, #2). The largest (and most luxurious) house in Hercula-

neum is named for a marble bas-relief of Achilles healing Telephus with rust from his spear (this is a replica; the original is in the National Archaeological Museum in Naples).

Continue downhill through the archway. The **Suburban Baths** illustrate the city's devastation (Terme Suburbane, #3; enter near the side of the statue on the terrace, often closed). After you descend into the baths, look back at the steps. You'll see the original wood charred in the disaster, protected by the wooden planks you just walked on. At the bottom of the stairs, in the waiting room to the right, notice where the floor collapsed under the sheer weight of the volcanic debris. (The sunken pavement reveals the baths' heating system: hot air generated by wood-burning furnaces and circulated between the different levels of the floor.) A doorway in front of the stairs is still filled with solidified ash. Despite the damage, elements of refinement remain intact, such as the delicate stuccoes in the *caldarium* (hot bath).

Back outside, make your way down the steps to the sunken area just below. As you descend, you're walking across what was formerly Herculaneum's beach. Look for the **arches** that were part of boat storage areas (you may even see some human remains). Archaeologists used to wonder why so few victims were found in Herculaneum. But during excavations in 1981, hundreds of skeletons were discovered here, between the wall of volcanic stone behind you and the city in front of you. Some of Herculaneum's 4,000 citizens tried to escape by sea, but were overtaken by the pyroclastic flows.

• *Our tour is over, and thankfully, your escape is easier—just exit the way you came in.*

Vesuvius

The 4,000-foot-high Vesuvius, mainland Europe's only active volcano, has been sleeping restlessly since 1944. While Europe has other dangerous volcanoes, only Vesuvius sits in the middle of a three-million-person metropolitan area that would be impossible to evacuate quickly.

Many tourists don't know that you can easily visit the summit. Up top, it's desolate and lunar-like, and the rocks are newly born. Walk the entire accessible part of the crater lip for the most interesting views. Be still. Listen to the wind and the occasional cascades of rocks tumbling into the crater. Any steam? Vesuvius could blow again. (Don't worry—there'd likely be at least a few hours or days of warning.)

GETTING THERE

Don't even think about driving to Vesuvius. Buses clog the road, and there's almost no parking. Leave it to the experts.

By Bus from Herculaneum: The easiest way to visit is to buy a combo entrance/bus ticket from **Vesuvio Express,** which makes the 30-minute drive from Ercolano Scavi (the train station serving Herculaneum) to the Vesuvius entrance; from there you get two hours to explore before being driven back to Ercolano (€30 round-trip for transfer and summit admission, daily from 9:00, 9/day, 30 minutes each way—about 3 hours total, office on square in front of train station, pay WC and baggage storage, +39 081 777 76 52, www.vesuvioexpress.it). You'll need to get to Herculaneum's Ercolano Scavi station on your own (for details, see the Herculaneum "Getting There" section, earlier).

If you arrive in Herculaneum without a reservation, ask at the Vesuvio Express office about a last-minute ticket (ticket office opens at 8:30). While there's no guarantee, if they do have tickets for later in the day, you can easily spend your wait time visiting Herculaneum and having lunch in town.

By Bus from Pompeii: It's about 40 minutes each way between Pompeii and the drop-off point for the Vesuvius hike. From near the Pompei Scavi train station on the Circumvesuviana line (just outside the main entrance to the Pompeii ruins), you can take an EAV **public bus** to Vesuvius (about hourly, €3.80 each way, pay on board). For this option, you must book your Vesuvius ticket in advance online (see "Orientation to Vesuvius," later).

By Bus from Naples: Tramvia offers trips either directly to Vesuvius or as a combined Vesuvius-Pompeii trip (Vesuvius only—€20 transit only, €45 also covers Vesuvius entry fee, 4/day; Vesuvius and Pompeii—€35 transit only, €85 includes entry fees, 3/day; buses depart from several points in Naples starting at the Molo Beverello port, +39 081 777 3247, www.tramvianapoli.com). Vesuvio Express (described earlier) also offers transfers from Naples (€40, 2/day).

By Taxi: A taxi costs about €110 round-trip from Naples and €100 from Pompeii, and includes two hours at the site.

ORIENTATION TO VESUVIUS

Cost and Hours: You must book a €12 timed-entry ticket in advance (see below); ticket covers national park entry and the park guide's orientation; first entry 9:00 year-round, last entry 18:00 in July-Aug, earlier throughout remainder of the year; must arrive within 30 minutes before or after your appointed time or you won't be let in; bad weather can occasionally close the trail; +39 081 865 3911, www.vesuviopark.it.

Advance Tickets Required: You must reserve a time slot online in advance, either at www.vivaticket.it (search for "Vesuvio" and select "Gran Cono del Vesuvio," must create an account), or with one of the bus companies listed earlier under "Getting There." Tickets are released on the website 30 days in advance (but are available further in advance through bus companies). A few tickets may be released same-day, but you must still book online: There's no ticket office at Vesuvius.

When to Go: Early-morning visitors enjoy the freshest air. The mountain is open all year, but spring and fall are the most comfortable times to visit. Wildflowers blossom in May and June.

Be Prepared: Bring sunscreen, water, a hat, and a light jacket in summer, and a warm hat and coat in winter.

VISITING VESUVIUS

To reach the volcano crater, the bus or taxi takes you up a good but windy road from Torre del Greco (between Herculaneum and Pompeii). As you drive up and up, you'll pass (on your left) what's now called Monte Somma (what looks like two separate mountains was actually one before the AD 79 eruption blew it apart). You'll also see lava flows from the most recent 1944 eruption.

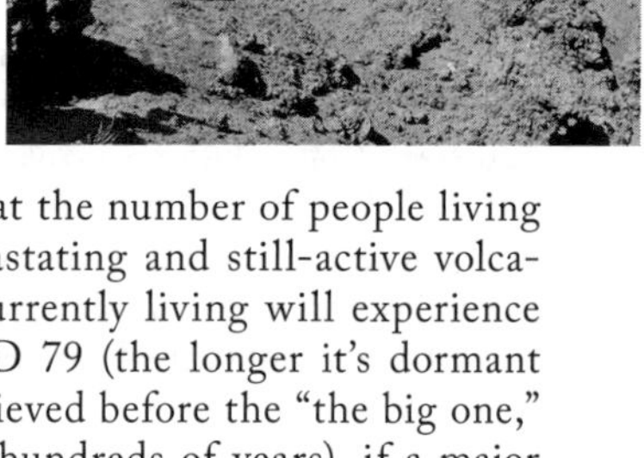

As you look back over the urban sprawl of Naples, marvel at the number of people living in the shadow of this once-devastating and still-active volcano. Though it's likely no one currently living will experience the type of eruption seen in AD 79 (the longer it's dormant the bigger the blast...and it's believed before the "the big one," Vesuvius had been dormant for hundreds of years), if a major eruption were to threaten, officials say they can evacuate the 100,000 people living in the six-mile *zona rossa* (red zone)... with three to seven days' notice. If you've seen the traffic in Naples, you—like many locals—might be skeptical.

When you reach the parking lot, use the WC, as there isn't one at the summit. From the entrance, it's a moderately steep half-mile hike (with a 600-foot elevation gain) up a dirt access road to the top. When you reach the summit, at the first snack bar/souvenir stand you can join a small group walk led by one of the excellent mountain guides (leaves every 10-15 minutes). The guide will orient you for several minutes before setting you free to peer into the crater and take in the sweeping views of the Bay of Naples.

SORRENTO

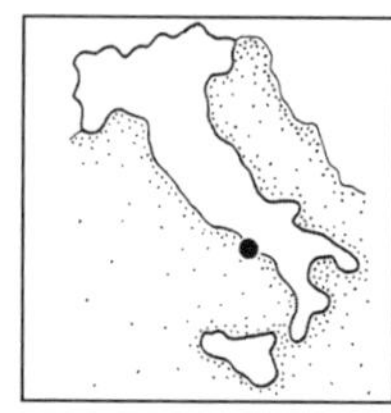

Just an hour south of Naples, serene Sorrento makes an ideal home base for exploring this fascinating region. From this easy-to-enjoy town, you can take day trips to Naples, Pompeii, the Amalfi Coast, the Greek temples at Paestum, and the romantic island of Capri. And every night you can return "home" to Sorrento, to enjoy its elegant strolling scene and sort through its many fine restaurant options.

Wedged on a ledge under the mountains and over the Mediterranean, spritzed by lemon and olive groves, Sorrento is an attractive resort of 16,000 residents and, in summer, just as many tourists. It's as well located for regional sightseeing as it is a fine place to stay and stroll. The Sorrentines have gone out of their way to create a relaxed place for tourists to come and spend money. As 90 percent of the town's economy is tourism, everyone seems to speak fluent English and work for the Chamber of Commerce. This gateway to the Amalfi Coast has a pedestrianized old quarter, lively shopping streets, and a spectacular cliffside setting. Residents are proud of the many world-class romantics who've vacationed here, such as famed tenor Enrico Caruso, who chose Sorrento as the place to spend his last months.

PLANNING YOUR TIME

Sorrento itself has no world-class sights, but can easily give you a few pleasant hours...or a home base for a pleasant few days. Using Sorrento as your sunny springboard, you can spend a day in Naples, a day exploring the Amalfi Coast, and a day split between Pompeii and the town of Sorrento. These nearby destinations are all reachable within an hour or so: Naples (by boat or train); Pompeii, Her-

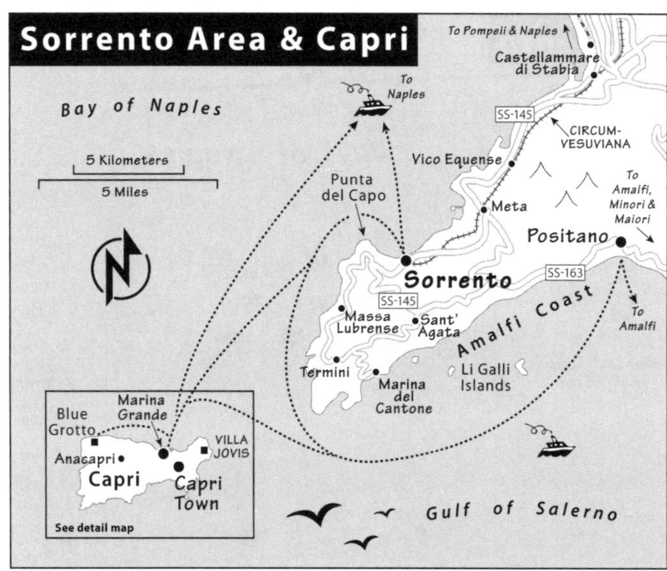

SORRENTO

culaneum, and Mount Vesuvius (by train, plus a bus for Vesuvius); the Amalfi Coast (by bus or boat); and the island of Capri (just 30 minutes by boat).

Sorrento hibernates in winter. Many places close down for two or three months until the town reawakens in March.

Orientation to Sorrento

Downtown Sorrento is long and narrow. Piazza Tasso marks the town's center. The main drag, Corso Italia, runs parallel to the sea through Piazza Tasso and then out toward the cape, where the road's name becomes Via Capo. Nearly everything mentioned here (except Marina Grande and the hotels on Via Capo) is within a 10-minute walk of the station. The town is perched on a cliff (some hotels have elevators down to sundecks on the water); the best real beaches are a couple of miles away.

Sorrento has three separate port areas. Marina Piccola is a functional harbor with boats to Naples and Capri, as well as cruise-ship tenders. Central Marina San Francesco has sunbathing piers and beaches. Despite its name, Marina Grande, below the other

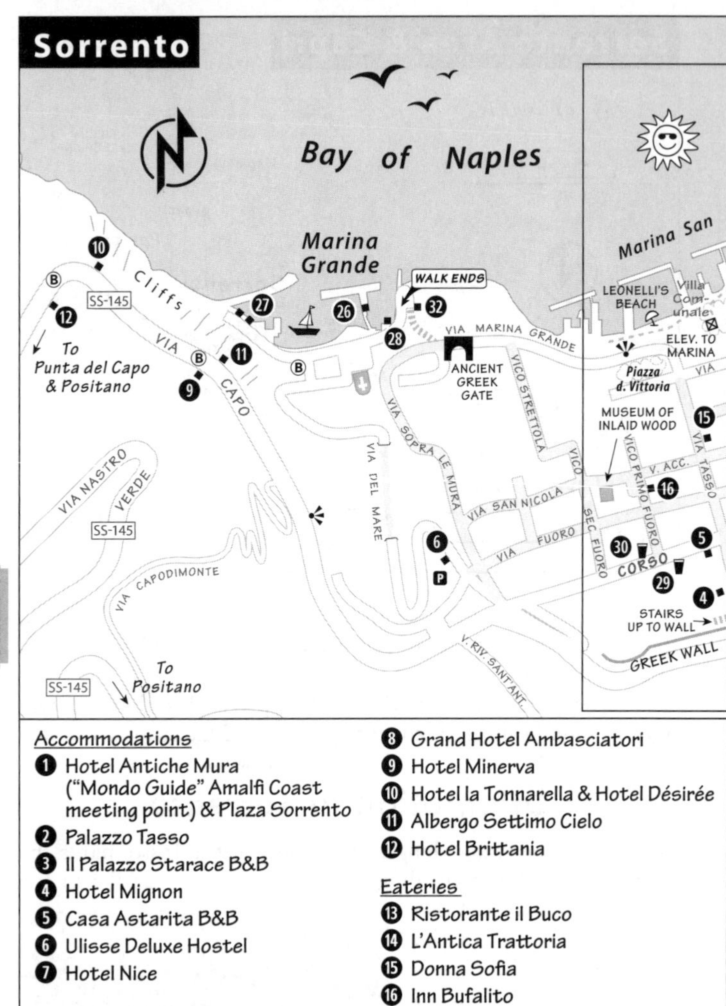

end of downtown, is a little fishing enclave, with recommended restaurants and more charm.

TOURIST INFORMATION

The challenge: to distinguish actual TI services from aggressive sales outlets masquerading as TIs. There are two legit InfoPoints: at the **train station** (flanked by pop-up tour sales desks, in the converted caboose out front; daily 10:00-15:00) and **Piazza Tasso** (at #25, under the clock tower).

The privately run website SorrentoInsider.com also has lots of good practical information.

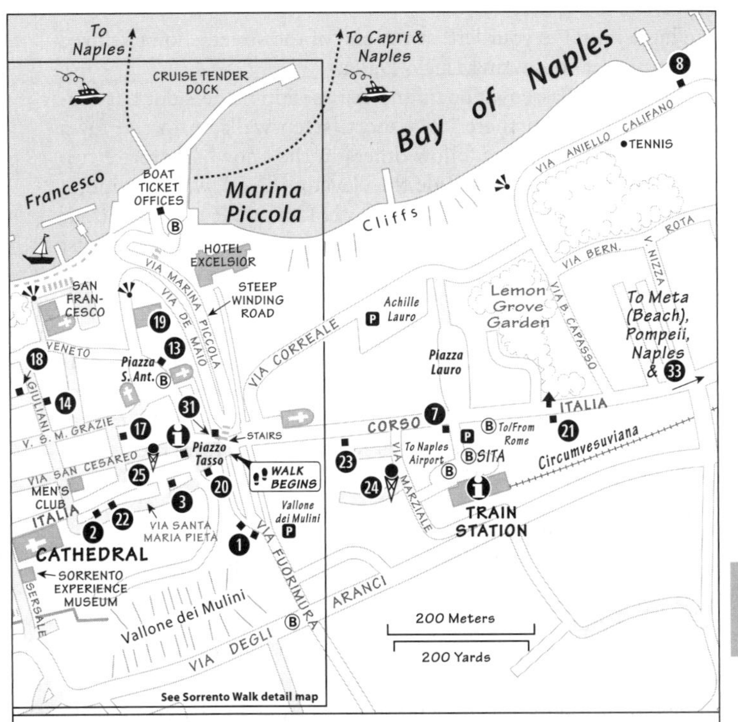

17 Ristorante Pizzeria da Gigino
18 Gnocchi Osteria di Famiglia
19 Terrazza delle Sirene
20 Fauno Bar
21 Pizzeria da Franco
22 Kebab Ciampa & Satisfhair Salon
23 Supermarket
24 Gelateria David
25 Gelateria Primavera
26 Ristorante Bagni Sant'Anna
27 Soul & Fish; Delfino
28 Trattoria da Emilia, Porta Marina & Bar Nonna Emilia ("Mondo Guide" Capri meeting point)

Nightlife & Other

29 The English Inn
30 Chaplin's Irish Bar
31 Daniele's Club
32 Bar da Giniello
33 To Launderette

SORRENTO

ARRIVAL IN SORRENTO

By Train or Bus: Sorrento is the last stop on the Circumvesuviana and Campania Express train lines from Naples (same tracks and stops). In front of the train station is the town's main bus stop, as well as taxis waiting to overcharge you (€20 minimum). You can buy bus and train tickets at the newsstand in the train station (daily from 7:00, helpful Ilaria and Gianluigi).

All recommended hotels—except those on Via Capo—are within a 10-minute walk. (For details on taking the bus to Via Capo, see "Sleeping in Sorrento," later.) As you exit the station, the huge mural to your left, at the end of the street, shows beloved Italian singer-songwriter Lucio Dalla.

By Boat: Passenger boats and cruise-ship tenders dock at Marina Piccola. From there it's a short, steep walk up to the town center (10 minutes, just follow others in the know). There are two alternatives to the climb: Ride the elevator (€1.20, walk 5 minutes along the harbor, see map) to the Villa Comunale city park (four blocks from Piazza Tasso) or catch the shuttle bus that parks just below the taxi stand (€2, buy ticket from driver, to Piazza Tasso and train station).

By Car: While I don't recommend driving here, if you do have a car, the public Achille Lauro underground parking garage is centrally located, just a couple of blocks in front of the train station, and good for a short stay (on Via Correale). Overnight rates are lower at the Autoparco Vallone dei Mulini, across from the recommended Hotel Antiche Mura.

HELPFUL HINTS

Church Services: At Santa Maria delle Grazie (perhaps the most beautiful Baroque church in town), cloistered nuns sing from above and out of sight during a Mass each morning at 7:30, except Sun when it starts at 7:45 (on Via Santa Maria delle Grazie just off Piazza Sant'Antonino).

Baggage Storage: The underground parking lot Parcheggio de Curtis, just downhill from the train station, moonlights as a convenient place to store luggage (daily 7:30-23:30, shorter hours off-season, Via E. de Curtis 5, just before Corsa Italia). Tempio Travel (see later), just to the left after you exit the station, also stores bags.

Laundry: A handy 24-hour self-service launderette, **Rosy Laundry,** is a 10-minute walk past the train station (daily, Corso Italia 321g, across from Esso gas station, +39 331 912 1122).

Haircuts: A fun hair salon for men, **Satisfhair,** is run by hairless Luca and Tony and makes for a happy memory (€20 for a good cut, closed Sun-Mon, Via S. Maria della Pieta 17, +39 081 878 3476).

Capri Funicular Tickets: Claudia at the *tabacchi* shop in Sorrento's Marina Piccola sells tickets for the funicular to Capri town, saving you a little time on the island (which often has long ticket-buying lines).

GETTING AROUND SORRENTO

Distances are short in Sorrento. If taking a bus seems too complicated, use the elevator, stairs, and your feet.

By Bus: Local EAV buses (the half-size buses) run from the train station to the **port** (Marina Piccola), the **fishing village** (Ma-

Lemons

Around here, *limoni* are ubiquitous: screaming yellow painted on ceramics, dainty bottles of *limoncello,* and lemons the size of softballs at the fruit stand.

The Amalfi Coast and Sorrento area produce several different kinds of lemons. The gigantic, bumpy "lemons" are actually citrons, called *cedri,* and are more for show—they're pulpier than they are juicy, and make a good marmalade. The juicy *sfusato sorrentino,* grown only in Sorrento, is shaped like an American football, while the *sfusato amalfitano,* with knobby points on both ends, is less juicy but equally aromatic. These two kinds of luscious lemons are used in sweets such as *granita* (shaved ice doused in lemonade), *limoncello* (a candy-like liqueur with a big kick, called *limoncino* in the Cinque Terre), *delizia al limone* (a dome of fluffy cake filled and slathered with a thick whipped lemon cream), *spremuta di limone* (fresh-squeezed lemon juice), and, of course, gelato or *sorbetto al limone.*

rina Grande), and **Meta beach** until at least 20:00 (€1.30, more expensive on board, about 2/hour). Stops are usually marked by a blue sign saying *Fermata a Richiesta* with a stylized *EAV.* Check the destination display on the front of the bus (*Porto* for Marina Piccola and *Stazione* for the train station), wave to flag down the driver, and let them know where you are going.

Buses to **Via Capo** leave from the main road behind the train station: Exit the station and head left toward the back until you see the little staircase on the right, then turn right on the main road and follow bus signs (€1.50, 3/hour, look for *Massa Lubrense* on bus display).

By Rental Car or Scooter: Places near the station and all over town rent motor scooters for about €35 per day. Tourists are notoriously bad drivers, dangerous on scooters on the coast and causing all kinds of trouble when driving rental cars. The best advice: Don't try to drive on the Amalfi Coast and don't rent scooters unless you are experienced on two wheels. In summertime, traffic jams (often caused by tourists driving) can mess up your day.

By Taxi: Taxis line up at the station and Piazza Tasso, but even short rides in town will cost at least €20. Thanks to traffic and one-way roads, you'll get to most central locations faster by walking.

Tours in Sorrento

Group Tours of Naples, Pompeii, the Amalfi Coast, and Capri

Naples-based **Mondo Guide** offers affordable shared tours of these destinations, including an Amalfi Coast drive that starts from Sorrento (meet in front of the Hotel Antiche Mura) and a Capri tour by boat from Sorrento (meet at Bar Nonna Emilia, facing Marina Grande at #21). You'll team up with fellow Rick Steves readers to split the cost. For details, see page 32 and page 163.

Tempio Travel, which markets very aggressively up and down the coast, offers convenient and fairly priced excursions: Amalfi by coach (€80, 7 hours with stops in Amalfi and Positano, departs Sorrento at 11:00); €140 eight-hour Capri trips; and €25 two-hour shared Pompeii walking tours (based at the Sorrento train station—look for the *i Ticket Office* sign, +39 081 878 2103, www.sorrentotickets.info).

Local Guides

For excursions around Sorrento, Capri, and Amalfi, **Giovanna Donadio** is a knowledgeable, upbeat guide (€200/day, same price for up to 8 people, +39 338 466 0114, giovanna_dona@hotmail.com). For this all-day fee Giovanna offers a well-organized full day of fun on Capri (plus public transport expenses and admissions).

Paolo Damiano is a Sorrento local, "born and raised under a lemon tree," who leads tours throughout the Amalfi Coast, including Pompeii (€160, 2 hours), and a Sorrento food walking tour (about €80/person—confirm, 3 hours, www.albireotravels.com, info@albireotravels.com).

Sorrento Food Tours

Tamara—a US expat with years of experience in Italian food and wine—and her colleagues dish up a fast-paced parade of local edibles interspersed with food history and shopping opportunities (with discount cards), stopping at eight places in three hours (€95, 15 percent discount for Rick Steves readers—use code "ricksteves"; departures at 10:30 and 16:00 with demand, maximum 14 people; +39 331 304 5666, www.sorrentofoodtours.com, info@sorrentofoodtours.com). You'll learn about the things the typical tourist would want to shop for and taste. (As you'll also get an orientation to the town it's best to do this early in your visit.)

Sorrento Walk

Get to know Sorrento with this lazy self-guided town stroll that ends down by the waterside at the small-boat harbor, Marina Grande.

• *Begin on the main square. Stand under the flags between the sea and the town's main square...*

❶ **Piazza Tasso:** As in any southern Italian town, this piazza is Sorrento's living room. It may be noisy and congested, but locals want to be where the action is...and be part of the scene. The most expensive apartments and top cafés are on or near this square.

Look out at the Bay of Naples. You can see the city of Naples in the distance. From here, it's a 10-minute walk—including 130 stairs—to Marina Piccola, the harbor for cruise-ship tenders and boats to Capri and Naples. On the right side of the gorge, overlooking the bay, is Hotel Excelsior Vittoria. This elegant, 19th-century Grand Tour hotel is where tenor Enrico Caruso (who died in 1921) spent his last months.

Turn to face the square. A statue of St. Anthony the Abbot, patron of Sorrento, is surrounded by traffic. He faces north as if greeting those coming from Naples (on festival days, he's equipped with an armload of fresh lemons and oranges).

This square bridges the gorge that divides downtown Sorrento. The newer section (to your left) was farm country just two centuries ago. The older part (to your right) retains its ancient Greek gridded street plan. (Like much of southern Italy, Sorrento was Greek-speaking for centuries before it was Romanized.)

For a better glimpse of the city's gorge-gouged landscape, take this quick detour: With the water to your back, cross through the square and walk straight ahead a block inland, under a canopy of trees and past a long taxi queue. Belly up to the railing in front of Hotel Antiche Mura and look down into the deep **Vallone dei Mulini** ("Valley of the Mills"). It's named after the sawmills and flour mills whose remains you see, next to the stream that powered them (along with a public laundry) until well into the 19th century. In fact, before about 1860 there was only a bridge over the gorge here and no Piazza Tasso at all.

The combination of the gorge and the seaside cliffs made Sorrento easy to defend. A small section of wall closed the landward gap in the city's defenses (you can still see a surviving piece of it a few blocks away, near Hotel Mignon).

Legend says Sorrento's name came from the Greek word for "siren," the mythical half-bird, half-woman that sang an intoxicating lullaby. According to Homer, the sirens lived on an island near here. All those who sailed by the sirens succumbed to their incred-

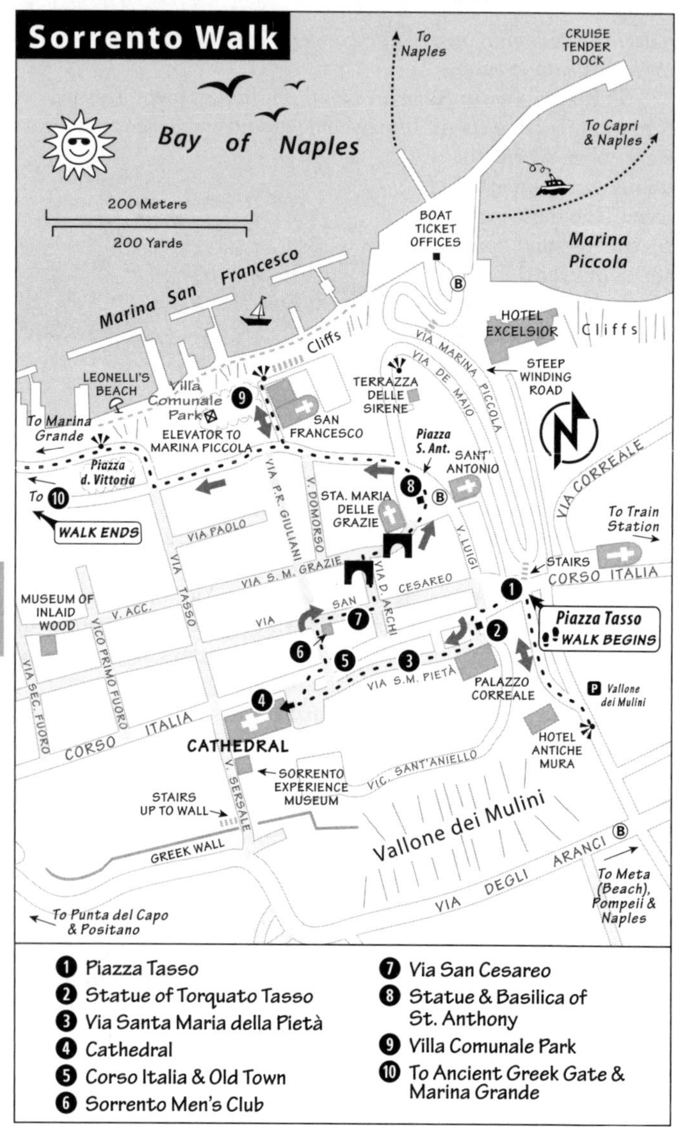

ible musical charms...and to death when they shipwrecked on the island. But Homer's hero Ulysses was determined to hear the song and restrain his manhood. He put wax in his oarsmen's ears and had himself lashed to the mast of his ship and survived their song. The sirens, thinking they had lost their powers, threw themselves into the sea, and the place became safe to inhabit. Ulysses' odyssey was all about the westward expansion of Greek culture, and to the ancient Greeks, places like Sorrento were the Wild West.

• *Back at Piazza Tasso, check out the scene at the recommended* ***Fauno Bar,*** *where locals have long sipped their drinks while surveying the square. Then head to the far-left inland corner of the piazza. You'll find a...*

❷ **Statue of Torquato Tasso:** The square's namesake, a Sorrento native, was a lively Renaissance poet—but today he seems only to wonder which restaurant to choose for dinner. Directly behind the statue, pop into the **Fattoria Terranova** shop, one of many fun, family-run, and touristy boutiques. They offer a friendly welcome, sell regional goodies, and offer free biscuits and tastes of liqueurs. The shop makes all of its organic products on an *agriturismo* outside the city. The gifty edibles spill into the courtyard of **Palazzo Correale,** at #18 next door. Duck in through the archway to get a feel for an 18th-century aristocratic palace's courtyard. Its patio walls are lined with characteristic tiles from 1772.

• *As you're leaving the courtyard, on your immediate left you'll see the narrow...*

❸ **Via Santa Maria della Pietà:** Here, just a few yards off the noisy main drag (Corso Italia), is a street that was Sorrento's main drag centuries before Christ. For hundreds of years this was the address for the town's big palazzos. About 100 yards down the lane, at #24 (on the left), find a 13th-century **palace** (no balconies back then...for security reasons), now an elementary school. Across the street (at #17) is a joyful **barbershop** where two bald men cut hair (pop in and say "*ciao*" to Luca and Tony). At #19, a church hosts the **Biagio Barile** inlaid wood exhibit. This is a town artform and they'd love to show you how it's done.

A few steps farther on, you'll see a tiny **shrine.** Typical of southern Italy, it's where the faithful pray to their saint, who contacts Mary, who contacts Jesus, who contacts God. This shrine is a bit more direct—it starts right with Mary.

• *Continue down the lane (passing a recommended kebab shop and trattoria) to reach the delightful...*

❹ **Cathedral:** Walk through the wrought-iron gate, which leads to the church patio. The church is free to enter (daily 8:00-12:30 & 16:30-20:30, except during Masses). Step inside the main door and examine the impressive *intarsio* (inlaid-wood) interior doors. They show religious scenes and depict this very church. Notice how the church's elegance matches the town's. Take a cool stroll down the right-hand side of the nave, checking out the intricate inlaid stations of the cross. You'll find even more inlaid wood on the side entrance doors. Open the door: The outer side features scenes of the town and its industry, as well as an old-town map (find Piazza Tasso before it was a piazza, trace the fortified walls, and notice the Greek grid street plan). These doors were made to celebrate Pope John Paul II's visit in 1992. At the altar, find the fine inlaid-marble seat of the bishop and then, before exiting, on the right rear corner find the *presepe* (manger scene) with its lovingly painted terra-cotta figures, each with an expressive face. This first Christmas is set in Sorrento, circa 1800—with pasta, salami, local lemons, and even Mount Vesuvius in the background.

• *From the church, step outside, and see the bell tower in need of weeding over the lane you walked. Return there and, directly under the tower, cross the street.*

❺ **Corso Italia and the Old Town:** In the evening, this traffic-free road hosts a wonderful *passeggiata.* Look up at the cathedral bell tower, then down to see the scavenged ancient Roman columns at its base. Now go left down Via Padre R. Giuliani, following the old Greek street plan. Locals claim the ancient Greeks laid out the streets east-west for the most sunlight and north-south for the prevailing and cooling breeze. Pause at the poster board on your right to see who's died lately. Traditionally, Italian women wore black when a relative died (1 year for an uncle, aunt, or sibling; 2-3 years for a husband or parent). Men got off easy, just wearing a black memorial button.

• *One block ahead, on your right, step into the 14th-century loggia (called Sedil Dominova). This is home to the...*

❻ **Sorrento Men's Club:** This building was once the meeting place of the town's nobles, then for generations a retreat for retired working-class men. Strictly no women—and no phones.

While times are changing and the club is looser these days (and fewer men hang out so far from their TVs), peek through the door window in the back to see a time warp. Here, men play cards and gossip under a finely frescoed, 16th-century domed ceiling, with marvelous 3-D scenes. Italian men venerate their mothers and often live at home if unmarried. (Italians joke that Jesus must have been a southern Italian because his mother believed her son was God, he believed his mom was a virgin, and he lived at home with her until he was 30.) But Italian men have also built into their culture ways to be on their own.

• *Turn right and continue along what I like to call "Via Airbnb"...*

❼ **Via San Cesareo:** This touristy pedestrian-only shopping street eventually leads back to Piazza Tasso. It's lined with competitive little shops where you can peruse (and sample) lemon products. While the typical tourist just thinks "*limoncello!,*" locals avoid this street. It makes them sad. This street is a perfect example of a dynamic that is changing (read: ruining) traditional neighborhoods all over Europe. Look up at the apartments overhead and imagine being a local living there. Very few actually do anymore, as skyrocketing rents have driven them away. Landlords can make more money with short-term rentals. Then look at the touristy shops: There's nothing useful for residents. While some locals profit from the tourist dollar, others have lost their neighborhoods.

After that buzzkill, perhaps you'll want to drop into **Nino & Friends** for a lemony and chocolaty world of gifty edibles and tasting opportunities (50 yards down the lane at Via San Cesareo 67).

• *After a block, take a left onto Via degli Archi, go under the arch, and then hang a right (under another arch) to the square with the...*

❽ **Statue and Basilica of St. Anthony** (Sant'Antonino): Sorrento's town saint humbly looms among the palms, facing the basilica dedicated to him (free to enter). Step inside the basilica and appreciate the dazzling baroque ensemble of painting, statues, and architecture. Then descend into the crypt (stairs beside main altar), where you'll find a chapel and reliquary containing a few of Anthony's bones surrounded by lots of votives.

Locals have long turned to St. Anthony when faced with challenges and hard times. Exploring the room, you'll find countless tokens of appreciation to the saint for his help. Before tourism, fishing was the big employer. The back walls feature paintings of storms with Anthony coming to the rescue. Circle behind the altar with Anthony's relics and study the shiny ex-votos (religious offerings) thanking the saint for healthy babies, good employment, surviving heart attacks and lung problems, and lots of strong legs.

• *Back outside, follow Via San Francesco, which skirts the piazza with St. Anthony's statue (don't go down the street with the line of trees and* Porto *signs). Soon after, on the right you'll see the trees in front of the Imperial Hotel Tramontano, and to their right a path leading to the...*

❾ **Villa Comunale Park:** This fine public park overlooks the harbor. Belly up to the banister to enjoy the view of Marina Piccola and the Bay of Naples (es-

SORRENTO

pecially popular at sunset). Notice Naples' skyline and the boats that commute from here to there in 40 minutes. Imagine the view in AD 79 when Vesuvius blew its top and molten mud flowed down the mountain, burying Pompeii. And look straight down to the piers of Marina San Francesco below, where lounge chairs, filled by vacationers working on tans, line the sundecks (the elevator across the square zips visitors up and down). The Franciscan church fronting this square faces a fine modern statue of Francis across the street.

Pop through the archway next to the church to see a dreamy little **cloister.** It's local Gothic—a 13th-century mix of Norman, Gothic, and Arabic styles, all around an old pepper tree. This is a popular spot for weddings and concerts.

At the left side of the cloister, stairs lead to a **photo exhibit:** *The Italians* shows off the work of local photographer Raffaele Celentano, who artfully captures classic Italian scenes from 1990 to 2016 in black and white.

• *From here, you can quit the walk and stay in the town center, or continue 10 minutes downhill to the waterfront at Marina Grande. If you take the elevator down here, the road to the right leads to Marina Piccola, where boats depart to Capri and other nearby towns. Be aware that piers and beaches to the left do not connect to the next stop on this walk.*

❿ To continue to **Marina Grande,** return to the road and keep going downhill (refer to the map on page 138). At the next square (Piazza Vittoria, with a dramatic WWI memorial and another grand view), cut over to the road closest to the water. After winding steeply down for a few minutes, it turns into a wide stairway, then makes a sharp and steep switchback (take the right fork to continue downhill). Farther down, just before reaching the waterfront, you pass under an...

Ancient Greek Gate: This gate fortified the city of Sorrento. Beyond it was Marina Grande, technically a separate town with its own proud residents—it's said that even their cats look different. Because Marina Grande dwellers lived outside the wall and were more susceptible to rape, pillage, and plunder, Sorrentines believe that they come from Saracen (pirate) stock. Sorrentines still scare their children by saying, "Behave—or the pirates will take you away."

• *Now go all the way down the steps into Marina Grande, Sorrento's "big" small-boat harbor.*

Marina Grande: Until recently, this little community was famously traditional, with its economy based on its fishing fleet. To this day, fathers pass their houses and fishing-boat stalls down to their sons and fishermen still go out at night to net a commotion of fish attracted to their *lampara,* or traditional lamp.

Several recommended restaurants are on the harbor. **Trattoria da Emilia** has an old newspaper clipping, tacked near the door, about Sophia Loren filming here.

• *From here, where the road hits the beach, a minibus returns to Piazza Tasso and the train station once an hour. Or you can walk back up (it's best to return the way you came).*

Sights in Sorrento

▲▲Strolling

On balmy evenings Sorrento offers one of Italy's most enchanting *passeggiata* scenes. The old-town stretch of Corso Italia is always traffic-free. Each night in summer and on weekends off-season, the police also close off the stretch east of Piazza Tasso to traffic, making Sorrento's whole main drag a thriving people scene. The *passeggiata* peaks at about 22:00 in the warmest months. Take time to enjoy the old-town streets between Corso Italia and the sea. The views from Villa Comunale, the public park next to Imperial Hotel Tramontano, are worth the detour. It's also worth walking to the end of Corso Italia and up the hill partway to Via Capo for views over the bay and back toward town (if you walk all the way up to Via Capo, you can catch the bus back to town).

Lemon Products Galore

Via San Cesareo is lined with hardworking rival shops selling a mind-boggling array of lemon products and offering samples of lots of sour goodies. You'll find *limoncello,* lemon biscuits, lemon pasta, lemon drops, lemon chocolate, lemon perfume, lemon soap, and on and on. Poke around for a pungent experience (and read the "Lemons" sidebar, earlier). A few produce stands are also mixed in. All over town (and all over the Amalfi Coast) you'll see the lemon-sorbet-served-in-a-lemon gimmick. It's ubiquitous and a bit pricey...but also brilliant.

Museum of Inlaid Wood (Museobottega della Tarsialignea)

Sorrento doesn't have much in the way of museums, but if you want to get out of the heat and crowds, this is a good place to do it. The life's work of an older couple, the museum is not only a collection of inlaid wood, but also a painting gallery featuring scenes of 19th-century Sorrento, antique maps, and portraits, and a fine decorative arts collection. The basement displays modern examples of inlaid wood. While pricey, it's serious, thoughtfully presented, and bursting with local pride.

Cost and Hours: €8, daily 10:00-18:30, Nov-March until 17:00, Via San Nicola 28, +39 081 877 1942.

Sorrento Experience Museum

This museum offers an earnest if overpriced 30-minute walk through a series of videos that tell (with no actual historic artifacts) the story of Sorrento (€13, Via Antonino Sersale 4). Nearby and next to Hotel Mignon, a bit of the **ancient Greek wall** may be open to climb on (free).

▲Swimming and Sunbathing

Sorrento's **Marina San Francesco** has several suntanning piers with tiny beaches. **Leonelli's Beach by Marina** (warmly run by Marina) is the most charming and family oriented, with the best restaurant and bar (€20 for your lounge chair and umbrella, daily 9:00-19:00, +39 081 878 1644). The other beaches feel trendier and offer more of a party scene. The elevator in Villa Comunale city park gets you down for about a euro. There's a tiny spot for public use here and at Marina Grande.

The Beach at Meta: The classic, sandy Italian beach two miles away at Meta can be overrun with families and teenagers from Naples. The local bus goes from the Sorrento station to Meta beach (last stop). At Meta, you'll find pizzerias, snack bars, and a little free section of beach, but the place is mostly dominated by several sprawling private-beach complexes—if you go, pay for a spot in one of these, such as Lido Metamare (manicured beach, lockable changing cabins, lounge chairs, +39 081 532 2505). It's a very Italian scene—some riffraff from Naples, loud pop music...and no international tourists.

Bagni Regina Giovanna at il Capo: More relaxing beaches are west of Sorrento. Jane might take Tarzan to the wild and stony beach at **Punta del Capo** (a.k.a. il Capo), a 15-minute bus ride from Sorrento (toward Massa Lubrense; 2/hour, get off at stop on Via Capo just after the Maxim Gorky house, then walk 10 minutes down Calata Punta del Capo, past ruined Roman Villa di Pollio).

Marina di Puolo, another good choice, is a tiny fishing town popular in the summer for its sandy beach, surfside restaurants, and beachfront disco (to get here, stay on the bus a bit farther beyond the Punta del Capo stop above—ask driver to let you off at Marina di Puolo—then follow signs and hike down about 20 minutes).

Nightlife in Sorrento

PUBS AND CLUBS

Sorrento is a fun place to enjoy a drink or some dancing after dinner. While the crowd here has traditionally skewed older, with British vacationers paving the way for you (many have holidayed here annually for decades), in recent years a younger crowd has discovered *la dolce vita* that this town inspires.

The **Fauno Bar,** which dominates Piazza Tasso with tables spilling onto the square, is a fine place to make the scene over a drink any time of day (see complete listing under "Eating in Sorrento," later). Live music sometimes takes over a Piazza Tasso bar, with impromptu dancing in the streets.

You can still find the Brits at several English-style pubs on Corso Italia, with big screens that show European soccer. **The English Inn** seems made for homesick Brits, with sloppy pub grub, English beer on tap, sports (British!), a beer garden out back, and lots of English vacationers (55 Corso Italia). Across the street and a few doors down at #18, **Chaplin's Irish Bar** is like the English Inn but with Guinness and Irish sports on the telly.

Terrazza delle Sirene (also known by its old name of **Foreigners' Club**) is a sprawling terrace below Piazza Sant'Antonino with a luxurious infinity view of the Bay of Naples. It offers live Neapolitan songs, Sinatra-style classics, and jazzy elevator music nightly at 20:00 throughout the summer. It's very British, with no locals—just right for old-timers feeling frisky (also serves food; see full listing under "Eating in Sorrento," later).

Daniele's Club is a tiny little dance club run by DJ Daniele, who tailors music to the audience (including karaoke, if you ask nicely). The scene, while sloppy, is generally comfortable for the 30-to-60-year-old crowd. If you're alone, there's a pole you can dance with (€10 drink purchase required, try their signature cocktail, "Come Back to Sorrento," a mojito made with *limoncello;* no food, nightly from 21:00, down the steps from the flags at Piazza Tasso 10, +39 081 877 3992).

In Marina Grande, **€ Bar da Giniello** is a basic little bar with drinks and no food. They've designed a cascade of small tables fitting into the stairs leading into the Marina Grande harbor, making a perfect spot for any romantic couple to oversee the harbor with a drink and a cuddle as the sun sinks below the horizon.

Sleeping in Sorrento

Given the location, hotels here often have beautiful views, and many offer balconies. At hotels that offer sea views, ask for a room *"con balcone, con vista sul mare"* (with a balcony, with a sea view).

Sorrento is a place to party, with live music and rowdy revelers. If you're staying in the center, hotels are not as equipped to handle the noise as some more notoriously loud places (like Naples). If noise is a problem for you, bring earplugs and request a quiet(er) room. *"Tranquillo"* is taken as a request for a quieter room off the street.

Hotels listed are either near the train station and city center (where balconies overlook city streets) or on cliffside Via Capo (with seaview balconies). Via Capo is a 20-minute walk—or short bus ride—from the station. Most hotels charge around €20-25/night to park a car.

You should have no trouble finding a room anytime except in August, when the town is jammed with Italians and prices often rise above the regular high-season rates. All rooms have air-con and an elevator unless otherwise noted.

IN THE TOWN CENTER

€€€€ Hotel Antiche Mura, with 50 rooms and four-star elegance, offers all the amenities, including an impressive breakfast buffet. Just a block off the main square, it's quieter than some central hotels because it's perched on the edge of a dramatic ravine. The pool and sundeck, surrounded by lemon trees, make a peaceful oasis (RS% when you book direct, some rooms with balconies, family rooms, pay parking, closed Jan-mid-March, a block inland from Piazza Tasso at Via Fuorimura 7, +39 081 807 3523, www.hotelantichemura.com, info@hotelantichemura.com, Luigi).

€€€€ Palazzo Tasso, nicely located near the center, has 12 small, sleek, fashionably designed modern rooms; there's no public space and breakfast is at a nearby bar on the square (some rooms with balconies, open all year, Via Santa Maria della Pietà 33, +39 081 807 1594, mobile +39 348 592 1019, www.palazzotasso.com, info@palazzotasso.com, Elena).

€€€€ Plaza Sorrento is a contemporary-feeling, upscale refuge in the very center of town (next door to Antiche Mura but with less expansive grounds). Its 65 rooms mix mod decor with wood grain, and the rooftop swimming pool is inviting (RS%, some rooms with balconies, closed Jan-mid-March, Via Fuorimura 3, +39 081 878 2831, www.plazasorrento.com, info@plazasorrento.com).

€€€ Il Palazzo Starace B&B, conscientiously run by Massimo and his friendly staff, offers seven tidy, modern rooms in a little alley off Corso Italia, one block from Piazza Tasso (RS% if paying in cash—use code "RSWEL," some rooms with balconies, family room, lots of stairs, luggage dumbwaiter but no elevator, extensive breakfast; ring bell around corner from Via Santa Maria della Pietà 9, +39 081 807 2633, mobile +39 349 290 7932, www.palazzostarace.com, info@palazzostarace.com).

€€€ Hotel Mignon rents 22 soothing blue rooms with beautiful, tiled public spaces, a rooftop sundeck, and a small garden surrounded by a lemon grove (RS%—use code "2022RSE" on their website, most rooms have balconies but no views, no elevator; from the cathedral, walk a block farther up Corso Italia and look for the hotel up a small gated lane to your left; Via Sersale 9, +39 081 807 3824, www.sorrentohotelmignon.com, info@sorrentohotelmignon.com, Paolo).

€€€ Casa Astarita B&B, hiding upstairs in a big building facing the main pedestrian street, has a crazy-quilt-tiled entryway and six bright, tranquil, creatively decorated rooms (three with little balconies). Noise from a nearby bar can spill over...bring earplugs (RS%—book direct and use code "RICK23," open year-round, 50 yards past the cathedral at Corso Italia 67, +39 081 877 4906, mobile +39 331 948 9738, www.casastarita.com, info@casastarita.com, Annamaria and Alfonso).

€€€ Ulisse Deluxe Hostel is basically a hotel, with 56 well-equipped, marble-tiled rooms and elegant public areas, but it also has two **€** single-sex dorm rooms with bunks—hence the name (RS%, family rooms, breakfast buffet extra, spa and pool use extra, pay parking, Via del Mare 22, +39 081 877 4753, www.ulissedeluxe.com, info@ulissedeluxe.com, Chiara). It's a five-minute walk from the old-town action: From Corso Italia, walk down the stairs just beyond the hospital *(ospedale)* to Via del Mare. Go downhill along the right side of the big parking lot to find the entrance.

€€€ Hotel Nice rents 24 simple, straightforward rooms 100 yards in front of the train station on the main drag. It's worth considering only for its very handy-to-the-train-station location. Alfonso promises a quiet room—double-paned windows help dim the hum from the busy street—request it when you book by email (RS%, family room, sundeck terrace, closed Jan-March, Corso Italia 257, +39 081 878 1650, www.hotelnice.it, info@hotelnice.it).

AT THE EAST END OF TOWN

€€€€ Grand Hotel Ambasciatori is a sumptuous five-star hotel with 80 rooms, a cliffside setting, a sprawling garden, a spa, and a pool. This is Humphrey Bogart land, with impressive public spaces, a relaxing stay-awhile ambience, and a free elevator to its "private beach"—actually a sundeck built out over the water (RS%, some view rooms, all rooms have balconies, pay parking, Via Califano 18,

+39 081 878 2025, www.ambasciatorisorrento.com, ambasciatori@manniellohotels.com). It's a short walk from the town center (10-15 minutes from the train station or Piazza Tasso).

WITH A VIEW, ON VIA CAPO

These cliffside hotels are outside of town, toward the cape of the peninsula (from the train station, go straight out Corso Italia, which turns into Via Capo). Once you're set up, commuting into town by bus or on foot is easy. Hotel Minerva is my favorite Sorrento splurge, while Hotel Désirée is a super budget bet with comparable views. If you're in Sorrento to stay put and luxuriate, especially with a car, these accommodations are perfect.

Getting to Via Capo: From the train station, it's a gradually uphill 25-minute walk (last part is a bit steeper), a €25 taxi ride, or a cheap bus ride (direction: Massa Lubrense). Either take the Sorrento city bus (about 3/hour) or look for one of the long-distance SITA buses that stop on Via Capo on their way to Massa Lubrense (about every 40 minutes; some buses heading for Positano/Amalfi also work—check with the driver; SITA day pass valid). Get off at the Hotel Belair stop (just up from the recommended Hotel Minerva) unless you're headed to Hotel Brittania, which has a stop right out front.

Getting from Via Capo into Town: Buses work great once you get the hang of them (and it's particularly gratifying to avoid the taxi racket). To reach downtown Sorrento from Via Capo, catch any bus heading downhill from Hotel Belair (buses run all day and evening). Or ask your hotel to call a taxi.

€€€€ Hotel Minerva is a sun-worshipper's temple. The road-level entrance (on a busy street) leads to an elevator that takes you to the fifth-floor reception. Getting off, you'll step onto a spectacular terrace with outrageous Mediterranean views. Bright common areas, a small rooftop swimming pool, and a cold-water Jacuzzi complement 63 large, tiled, colorful rooms with views, half with balconies (3-night peak-season minimum, pay parking, closed Dec-March, Via Capo 30, +39 081 878 1011, www.minervasorrento.com, info@minervasorrento.com).

€€€€ Hotel la Tonnarella is an old-time Sorrentine villa-turned-boutique-hotel, with several terraces, stylish tiles, and warm wood trim. Eighteen of its 24 rooms have views of the sea, and you can pay extra for a terrace (pay parking, small beach with private elevator access, closed Nov-March, Via Capo 31, +39 081 878 1153, www.latonnarella.it, info@latonnarella.it).

€€€ Albergo Settimo Cielo ("Seventh Heaven") is an old-fashioned, family-run cliffhanger sitting 300 steps above Marina Grande. The reception is just off the waterfront side of the road, and the elevator passes down through four floors with 46 clean but spartan rooms—all with grand views, and many with balconies. The rooms feel dated for the price—you're paying for the views (family rooms, parking, inviting pool, sun terrace, closed Nov-March, Via Capo 27, +39 081 878 1012, www.hotelsettimocielo.com, info@hotelsettimocielo.com; Giuseppe a.k.a. "Josef," son Massimo, and daughter Serena).

€€€ Hotel Brittania, up the road a little, has 30 crisp and cheery rooms. Take your pick relaxing on the fifth-floor view terrace with a jacuzzi or downstairs under the lemon trees in the garden. Charming Stefano, whose family also runs the Albergo Settimo Cielo down the road, is a welcoming host. The bus stops right outside the hotel, handy since the sidewalks end nearby and it can be treacherous to walk (some view rooms, family rooms, gym, pay parking, Via Capo 72, +39 081 878 2706, www.britanniasorrento.com, info@britanniasorrento.com).

€€ Hotel Désirée is more modest, with reasonable rates, humbler vistas, and no traffic noise. The 22 basic rooms have high, ravine-facing or partial sea views, and half come with balconies. There's a fine rooftop sunning terrace. Owner Corinna (a committed environmentalist), daughter Cassandra, and receptionist Antonio serve an organic breakfast and are helpful with tips on exploring the peninsula (family room, lots of stairs and no elevator, free parking, shares driveway and beach elevator with La Tonnarella, closed early Nov-Feb except open at Christmas, Via Capo 31, +39 081 878 1563, www.desireehotelsorrento.com, info@desireehotelsorrento.com).

Eating in Sorrento

GOURMET SPLURGES

In a town proud to have no McDonald's, consider eating well for a few extra bucks. These places are worthwhile splurges run by a hands-on boss with a passion for good food and exacting service. The first is gourmet and playful. The second is classic. And the third is more old-school. All are romantic. Be prepared to relax and stay awhile.

€€€€ Ristorante il Buco, once the cellar of an old monastery, is now a dressy restaurant with spacious seating in three zones: modern dining room, romantic under a medieval vault, and outside on the lane. Their delightfully presented and creative modern Mediterranean dishes have earned chef Peppe a Michelin star. He and his staff love to explain their sophisticated dishes (with an emphasis on seafood). They offer lots of fine wines by the glass. Reserve ahead (RS%—10 percent; extravagant five- and six-course fixed-price meals—sea or land, for €120-160; closed Wed and Jan;

just off Piazza Sant'Antonino at II Rampa Marina Piccola 5; +39 081 878 2354, www.ilbucoristorante.it).

€€€€ L'Antica Trattoria enjoys a *romantico,* candlelit ambience, tucked away in its own little world. The cuisine is traditional Italian but with modern flair. Run by the same family since 1930, the restaurant has a trellised garden outside and intimate nooks inside. Aldo and sons Luca and Tony will take care of you while Vincenzo—the Joe Cocker-esque resident mandolin player—entertains from 21:00. Reservations are smart (RS%—10 percent discount on a fixed-price meal, €50-90 fixed-price meals, good vegetarian and vegan; daily until late, closed Jan-Feb; Via Padre R. Giuliani 33, +39 081 807 1082, www.lanticatrattoria.it).

€€€€ At **Donna Sofia,** the six-course tasting menu is a meal you won't forget (€90, minimum 2 people). The à la carte options are strong on seafood and include affordable gourmet pizzas. Owners Mario (who lived in New York when young) and his wife Lina (who makes the desserts) serve in a comfy modern dining room and on an upstairs patio. Photos of Sophia Loren (the restaurant's namesake) decorate the walls, and diners watch the open kitchen at work. Reserve for dinner (closed Tue; Via Tasso 43, +39 081 877 3532, www.ristorantedonnasofia.com).

MIDPRICED RESTAURANTS

€€€ Inn Bufalito is where Franco and his team specialize in all things buffalo: *mozzarella di bufala* (and other buffalo-milk cheeses), steak, sausage, salami, carpaccio, and buffalo-meat ragu sauce on homemade pasta. The smartly designed space has a modern, borderline-trendy, casual atmosphere and a fun indoor-outdoor vibe (daily until late, Vico I Fuoro 21, +39 081 365 6975).

€€ Ristorante Pizzeria da Gigino, lively and congested with a sprawling interior and tables spilling onto the alley, makes huge, tasty, crunchy-crust pizzas in their wood-burning oven. Their *linguine gigino* is a favorite (good salads, closed Tue and Jan-mid-March, just off Piazza Sant'Antonino at Via degli Archi 15, +39 081 878 1927). Antonino and Greta offer a free *limoncello* after your meal with this book.

€€ Gnocchi Osteria di Famiglia, on a little lane just off busy Via Padre R. Giuliani, lays on the tomato theme thick, but their gnocchi is solid and the energetic staff works hard to keep you happy. To balance out all the red around you, try the pesto gnocchi (daily, Via San Paolo 9, +39 081 1755 7963).

With a Sea View: €€€ Terrazza delle Sirene (also known by its old name, the **Foreigners' Club**) has some of the best sea views in town (with a sprawling table-filled terrace under breezy palms), live music nightly at 20:00 (May-mid-Oct), and affordable—if uninspired—meals. It's a good spot for dessert or an after-dinner *limoncello.* You might see wedding banquets here ("snack" menu with light meals, good salads, daily, bar opens at 9:30, meals served 11:00-23:00, closed off-season, service can be gruff, Via Luigi de Maio 35, +39 081 877 3263). If you'd enjoy eating along the water (rather than just with a water view), see "Harborside in Marina Grande," later.

€€ Fauno Bar, with tables arranged like a theater overlooking Piazza Tasso, is Sorrento's venerable meeting place. Quite touristy but still a local hangout, it's well run with a professional waitstaff and a simple menu (Mediterranean plates, good salads, desserts and drinks, long hours daily, Piazza Tasso 13, +39 081 878 1135).

CHEAP EATS

€ Pizzeria da Franco is Sorrento's favorite place for basic, casual pizza in a fun atmosphere. Join locals and tourists on shared benches for great pizzas served on waxed paper in square tins. It's packed to the rafters with a youthful crowd that doesn't mind the plastic cups. Consider their *saltimbocca,* a baked sandwich with top-quality prosciutto and mozzarella on pizza bread—splitable and perfect to go (plenty of beers, daily until late, just across from the Lemon Grove Garden, Corso Italia 265, +39 081 877 2066).

€ Kebab Ciampa offers a good, cheap break from Italian cuisine. This little family-run hole-in-the-wall has a loyal following among eaters who appreciate Andrea's fresh bread and homemade sauces. The fun chart makes ordering easy (Thu-Tue 17:00-late, closed Wed, near the cathedral at Via Santa Maria della Pietà 23, enter around corner on small side street, +39 081 807 4595).

Picnics: Get groceries at the large **Dodeca** supermarket at Corso Italia 223 (daily 8:00-21:00).

Gelato: Near the train station, **Gelateria David** is Sorrento's long-time favorite gelato place, with about 30 flavors at any one time. Mario, who's clearly found his niche, makes his gelato on-site, like his grandfather Augusto Davide, who started the store in 1957. Before choosing a flavor, sample *Profumi di Sorrento* (an explosive sorbet of mixed fruits), "Sorrento moon" (white almond with lemon zest), or *brontolo*—salty pistachio (long hours daily, shorter hours off-season, closed Dec-Feb, near the train station at Via Marziale 19, +39 081 807 3649). Mario also offers gelato-making classes (€15/person, 7-person minimum, 1 hour, call or email ahead to reserve, www.gelateriadavidsorrento.itinfo@gelateriadavidsorrento.it).

Gelateria Primavera, more centrally located, is where Antonio and Alberta whip up 70 exotic flavors...and still have time to make pastries for the pope and other celebrities. Check out the nostalgic photos in their inviting back room, proving this also is a

Sorrento institution (long hours daily, just west of Piazza Tasso at Corso Italia 142, +39 081 807 3252).

HARBORSIDE IN MARINA GRANDE

For a decent lunch or dinner *con vista,* head down to any of these restaurants by Sorrento's small-boat harbor, Marina Grande. To get to Marina Grande, follow the directions from Villa Comunale on my self-guided Sorrento Walk, earlier. It's about a 15-minute stroll from downtown. You can also take the hourly minibus from Piazza Tasso or the station. Be prepared to walk back (last bus leaves at 20:00) or spring for a pricey taxi.

€€€€ Three **yacht-clubby pier restaurants,** sharing the Marina Grande harbor, offer more refined and expensive seafood literally out at sea: **Ristorante Bagni Sant'Anna** is in the center of the action on the harbor—and literally in the harbor on its own cozy pier (+39 081 807 4178); **Soul & Fish** (+39 081 878 2170) and **Delfino** (+39 081 878 2038) are the last two places at the end of the harbor and a bit quieter. Delfino might be the best of the bunch and offers stunning views through its floor-to-ceiling windows inside and has comfortable outside seating. Soul & Fish takes a more inventive approach and has good outdoor tables. At all three, the seafood is fresh, the service is attentive, and the views are out to sea. They're all open daily for lunch and dinner, reservations are smart, and their piers double as places to enjoy a little sunbathing.

€€ Trattoria da Emilia, at the city-side end of the Marina Grande waterfront, is good for straightforward, typical Sorrentine home cooking, including fresh fish, lots of fried seafood, and *gnocchi di mamma*—potato dumplings with meat sauce, basil, and mozzarella (daily, closed Nov-Feb, no reservations taken, indoor and outdoor seating, Via Marina Grande 62, +39 081 807 2720, free *limoncello* after your meal with this book).

€€ Porta Marina serves fresh-as-can-be seafood in a modest location next door to Trattoria da Emilia, with views every bit as good as more expensive places nearby. Servers will tell you the catch of the day—always the best option—but if grilled octopus is on the menu then think no more (daily, Via Marina Grande 64, +39 349 975 4761).

Sorrento Connections

It's impressively fast to zip by boat from Sorrento to many coastal towns and islands during the summer—in fact, it's quicker and easier than by train or car (see "By Boat," next, and the map on page 137).

BY BOAT

The number of boats that run per day varies; generally boats run more frequently in the peak of summer, with fewer departures off-season. Check all schedules locally at the port or online (use the individual boat-company websites—see below). Some ferry companies sell tickets online for an extra fee, but buying tickets at the port is easy (and keeps your departure options open—especially valuable if you're watching the weather). All boats take several hundred people each and (except for the busiest days) rarely fill up. The main companies are Caremar (www.caremar.it), SNAV (www.snav.it), NLG (www.nlg.it), and Alilauro (www.alilauro.it).

From Sorrento to Naples: Only a handful of ferries per day connect Sorrento and Naples, but you might consider the ferry over the train both for the more relaxed journey and because it puts you just a few minutes' walk away from some of the city's top sights, and a quick Metro ride from others. Most importantly, it allows you to avoid Naples' train station area, which can be a bit unseemly.

From Sorrento to Capri: Boats run at least hourly. Your options are a fast **ferry** (*traghetto* or *nave veloce,* takes cars, 30 minutes, smoother than hydrofoil) or a slightly faster and pricier **hydrofoil** (*aliscafo,* 25 minutes, bumpier ride). To visit Capri when it's least crowded, buy your ticket at 8:00 and take the 8:30 hydrofoil. These early boats can be jammed, but it's worth it once you reach the island.

Getting to and from Sorrento's Port (Marina Piccola): It's a five-minute walk from Piazza Tasso. Go down the steep stairs starting under the flags, then down the road. For fewer stairs, head to the Villa Comunale public park, where you can pay €1.20 to ride the elevator down (hang on to your ticket—you need it to exit; from the bottom, it's a five-minute walk to the port). Otherwise, catch the minibus from the station or Piazza Sant'Antonino (specify that you're going to the *porto;* buses run 3/hour). When you arrive at the port area, don't get distracted by the many tour offices selling package trips. Head toward the port and find the official boat companies' individual ticket offices.

To avoid the steep walk into town when arriving by ferry in Sorrento, look for the shuttle bus (stop marked *Fermata Riservata/EAV,* bus marked *Porto-Stazione*) waiting just below the taxi stand (€2 tickets, buy from driver, 3/hour), which stops at Piazza Tasso and the train station.

BY TRAIN AND BUS

At the newsstand in the train station, Ilaria and Gianluigi sell all these tickets and can explain your options (daily from 7:00).

From Sorrento to Pompeii, Herculaneum, or Naples by Train: The run-down **Circumvesuviana commuter train** runs twice hourly between Sorrento and Naples with crowds, pickpockets, and no air-conditioning (fares are cheap, schedules posted widely, www.eavsrl.it). Some trains marked *DD* skip Herculaneum (check online in advance or ask at the station) and make the journey about 15 minutes faster: Pompeii (30-45 minutes), Herculaneum (55 minutes), and Naples (60-75 minutes). Contactless payment is accepted. For physical tickets, if there's a line at the official ticket windows, go to the adjacent snack bar or downstairs to the newsstand.

Four **Campania Express** trains per day are no faster than the Circumvesuviana but have newer cars with air-conditioning, reserved seats, some luggage space, and prices seemingly designed to keep out the riffraff (€15 to Pompeii, Herculaneum, or Naples; online sales at http://ots.eavsrl.it or buy at the station). For more details, see "Getting Around the Bay of Naples" on page 96 of the Naples chapter.

From Sorrento to Naples Airport: Curreri buses make the trip in 1.5 hours (€13, online reservations wise, 8/day from 6:30-16:30, no service Dec 25 and Jan 1, departs from in front of train station, +39 081 801 5420, www.curreriviaggi.it). From Naples Airport to Sorrento, eight buses depart between 9:00 and 19:30 (ask the info desk in the arrivals hall to point you toward the bus departure lot).

From Sorrento to the Amalfi Coast: See page 180.

From Sorrento to Rome: Most people ride the train to Naples, then catch the Frecciarossa or Italo express train to Rome. Another option is the Sorrento-Rome bus: It's cheaper, although departure times can be inconvenient—confirm in advance (daily at 6:00, off-season Mon-Fri only with FlixBus, www.flixbus.com; daily at 16:00, off-season Sat-Sun only with Marozzi, www.marozzivt.it; 4 hours; departs Sorrento from Corso Italia 259B, by Bar Kontatto, a block from the train station, and runs to Tiburtina bus station in Rome; buy tickets at train station newsstand, on websites, or on board for a surcharge).

CAPRI

Capri was made famous as the vacation hideaway of Roman emperors Augustus and Tiberius. In the 19th century, it was the haunt of Romantic Age aristocrats on their Grand Tour of Europe. Later it was briefly a refuge for Europe's artsy gay community: Irish playwright Oscar Wilde, English poet D. H. Lawrence, and company hung out here back when being gay could land you in jail...or worse. And these days, the island is a world-class tourist trap, packed with gawky, nametag-wearing visitors searching for the rich and famous—and finding only their prices.

About 12,000 people live on Capri (although many Capreses winter in Naples); on any given day in high season, the island can host another 10,000 tourists—or more. The "Island of Dreams" can be a zoo from Easter to October, especially in July and August, when Capri is overrun with tacky group tourism at its worst. At other times of year, though still crowded, Capri can provide a relaxing and scenic break from the cultural gauntlet of Italy.

Even with its crowds, commercialism, fame, and glitz, Capri is a flat-out gorgeous and memorable place to visit: Limestone cliffs rocket boldly from the Mediterranean, and the famous Blue Grotto sea cave glows with reflected sunlight. Strategically positioned gardens, villas, and an easy-to-conquer little mountain all come with

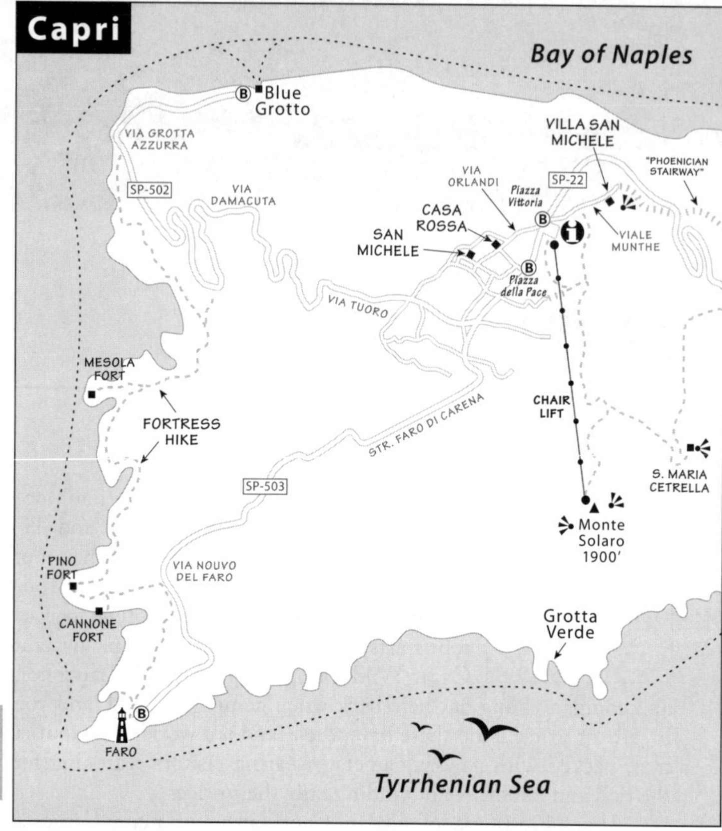

commanding views of the Sorrento Peninsula, Amalfi Coast, Vesuvius, and Capri itself.

Note: This chapter assumes you're doing Capri as a day trip and provides no fine dining or accommodations advice.

GETTING THERE

By Ferry

For instructions on getting to Capri by ferry, see the "Connections" sections of the Sorrento and Naples chapters, and the "Getting Around the Amalfi Coast" section of the Amalfi Coast chapter.

With a Tour from Sorrento

Private Tours with Giovanna Donadio: Giovanna is a knowledgeable, upbeat guide who can escort you from Sorrento on a well-organized full day of fun on Capri (€200 for up to 8 people, plus public transport expenses and admissions, +39 338 466 0114, giovanna_dona@hotmail.com). Giovanna's tours offer far more ac-

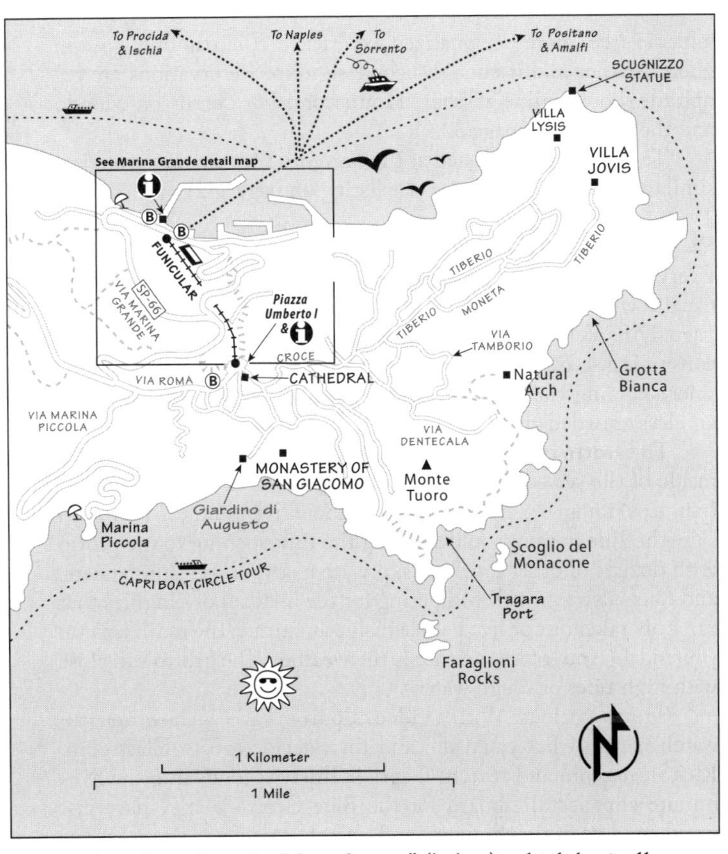

tual guiding than the "shared tours" (below), which basically organize the transfers and give you free time.

Shared Tours with Mondo Guide: Mondo Guide offers my readers a no-stress, all-day itinerary for €140: Board a small boat at Sorrento's Marina Grande (daily at 8:00, maximum 12 people, shared with other Rick Steves readers) and be taken across to Capri, anchoring by the Blue Grotto (extra €20 to hop in one of the little rowboats to go inside). Then you'll continue to Capri's Marina Grande for about four hours of free time on the island—just enough to head to Anacapri for sightseeing and the Monte Solaro chairlift (island transportation and admissions on your own). Finally, you'll reboard the boat for a lightly narrated circle around the island and pass by the iconic Faraglioni Rocks (includes drinks, a snack, and—conditions permitting—a chance to swim from the boat). Note that tours meet in Sorrento at Bar Nonna Emilia, facing Marina Grande at #21, not at Marina Piccola (the ferry port). For some travelers, the tour may be worth the approximately €45 extra (compared to the cost of doing everything on your own) for a hassle-free, more personalized experience. The trip only goes in good weather and if enough people sign up. Reservations are required—book online at SharedTours.com. For details on Mondo and their tours, see page 32.

Tempio Travel—based at the Sorrento train station—offers a similar trip at a similar price (see listing on page 142).

PLANNING YOUR TIME

Every day, thousands of people pile into boats and head for Capri, usually with the same idea: to see the Blue Grotto (described on page 170). While it's an unforgettable experience, it's also time-consuming, crowded, and overpriced. For a stress-free visit, consider skipping the grotto and focus instead on the island's easier and less crowded charms.

To Grotto or Not: Here's the Blue Grotto reality. To see the inside of the sea cave, you'll spend upwards of two hours and €43 (plus tips) for an experience that lasts about five minutes. There's no skip-the-line option; you'll arrive at the tiny opening to the grotto with dozens of other tour boats, private boats, cruise ship tenders, and tour bus groups all competing for the handful of dinghies that can only take four or five people inside at a time. The math isn't on your side. (And, often, neither is the weather: The grotto can close with high tides or rough water.)

Grotto-curious? With a **video clip** from my TV show, you can watch me do what you'd do, and then decide (go to Classroom.RickSteves.com and search "Capri"). Thirty seconds into the five-minute clip, it's all aboard for the Blue Grotto. I may have just saved you lots of time, money, and uncertainty.

Capri with the Blue Grotto

If you're determined to see the Blue Grotto, the smart plan is simply to beat the crowds. Here is the best-case-scenario, see-everything-in-a-day plan from Naples or Sorrento.

- **Early Morning:** Take an early boat to Capri (from Sorrento, buy ticket at 8:00, boat leaves around 8:30 and arrives around 9:00—smart). You'll land at Marina Grande; yes, Capri's port has the same name as the small-boat harbor at Sorrento.
- At the port, for a targeted strike, grab the next boat to the Blue Grotto. Early in the morning, spaces are generally available for departures every few minutes. If you're lucky, after the 15-minute ride to the entrance, you'll wait an hour to enter the grotto itself. Arrive after 10:00 and you risk waiting two hours or longer at the entrance.

  You can also see the grotto as part of a full circle-the-island tour (2-3 hours).
- **Post-Grotto Visit:** If you're only seeing the Blue Grotto, skip

the return trip to Marina Grande. Instead, have your boatman drop you at the stairway up to the grotto bus stop. From here you can catch a bus directly to Anacapri, which has two or three hours' worth of sightseeing.

If you're on a full circle-the-island tour, upon returning to Marina Grande, take a taxi from there to Anacapri. Alternatively, from the east end of Marina Grande, you can walk or take a bus to Capri town and reverse the next two stops. (Note that by midmorning, lines for buses to Anacapri from anywhere can be frustratingly long.)

- **Afternoon:** In Anacapri, see the town, ride the chairlift to Monte Solaro and back (or hike down), stroll out from the base of the chairlift to tour the fragrant and evocative beauty of Villa San Michele, and eat lunch.
- Afterward, catch a bus to Capri town, which is worth an hour of browsing.
- Finally, ride the funicular from Capri town down to the harbor and laze on the free beach or wander the yacht harbor while waiting for your boat back to Sorrento.

Capri Without the Blue Grotto

For the same amount of time and less money, you can enjoy a leisurely day on the island seeing the sights in Anacapri and Capri town. To get out on the water, cap your visit with a scenic one-hour circle-the-island tour by boat (an experience I find even more fun than the famed grotto).

Here's an enjoyable-even-in-peak-season day plan: Arrive on Capri on an early boat, as described above. Head straight from Marina Grande to Anacapri by taxi or bus and visit it, Monte Solaro, and Villa San Michele. Then bus to Capri town before the worst of the crowds and heat.

In the afternoon, return by funicular to Marina Grande, where you can catch the next boat for the circle-the-island tour (there are plenty of departures). Rested and relaxed, set sail back to Sorrento.

Planning Tips

If you're heading to Capri specifically to see the Blue Grotto, be sure to check weather and sea conditions for the day of your visit. If the tide is too high or the water too rough, the grotto can be closed. Ask the TI or your hotelier. Note that the grotto is also closed in winter. Stormy weather can also keep vessels in port. Take care not to get stranded on the island. Check the websites for the sturdy Caremar car ferries or the big SNAV ferries, which are the last to be canceled (www.caremar.it, www.snav.it).

Hyper-efficient travelers can see Capri on the way between destinations: Sail from Sorrento, check your bag at the harbor, see Capri, and take a boat directly from there to Naples or to the Amalfi Coast (or vice versa).

A one-way boat ticket to Capri (there's no round-trip discount) provides maximum schedule flexibility: You can take any convenient hydrofoil or ferry back. When you arrive on Capri, double-check the last return-trip time at the TI, boat company ticket windows, or CapriTourism.com. The last boats back to the mainland (generally big, reliable ones with virtually endless seating) usually leave around 18:30 (to Sorrento) and 20:00 (to Naples). In July and August, however, it's wise to get a round-trip ticket (ensuring you a spot). On busy days, be 20 minutes early for the return boat.

While tickets come with a timed entry and a guaranteed seat, they also work on other departures by the same company (but with no guarantee). For a steep, steep price, you can always hire a water taxi (about €100, weather permitting).

Those with extra time who can spend the night on Capri will experience a very different island. I haven't provided hotels, but the TI has a well-organized list at www.capritourism.com/en/hotels.

Orientation to Capri

First thing—pronounce it right: Italians say KAH-pree, not kah-PREE like the pants (or the old Sinatra song). The island is small—just four miles by two miles—and is separated from the Sorrentine Peninsula by a five-mile-wide strait. Capri has only two towns to speak of: Capri and Anacapri. The island also has some scant Roman ruins and a few interesting churches and villas. But its chief attraction is its famous Blue Grotto, and its best activity beyond the boat rides is the chairlift from Anacapri up the island's Monte Solaro ("the sunny mount").

TOURIST INFORMATION

Capri's English-speaking TI has three tiny offices, one each in Marina Grande, Capri town, and Anacapri. Their well-organized website has schedules and practical information in English (www.capritourism.com). All have free maps and are open daily in summer (generally 8:30-16:15; Mon-Fri only in winter).

The **Marina Grande TI** is in the port office building at the base of the breakwater (+39 081 837 0634).

The **Capri town TI** works out of a closet-like space under the bell tower on Piazza Umberto I and is less crowded than its sister at the port (+39 081 837 0686).

The **Anacapri TI** is at Piazza Vittoria 5, next to the WC near the chairlift entrance (+39 081 837 1524).

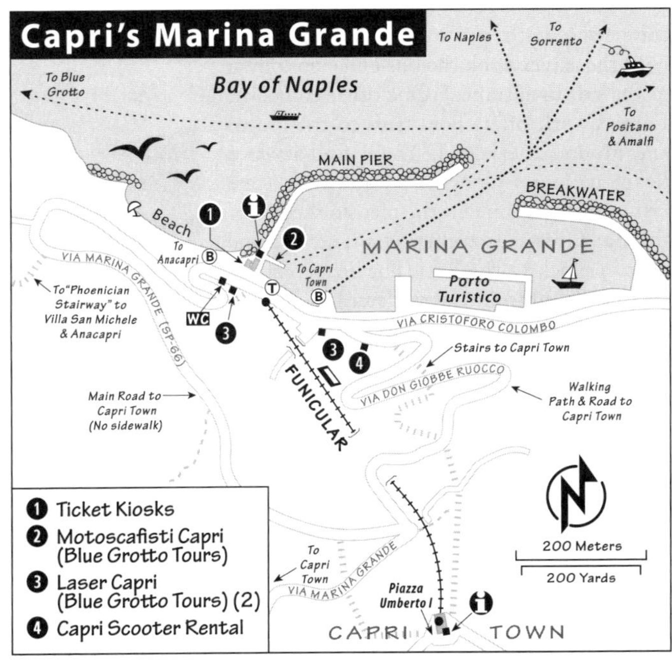

ARRIVAL IN CAPRI

Get oriented from the boat as you near the harbor with the island spread out before you. The port is a small community of its own, called **Marina Grande,** connected by a funicular and buses to the rest of the island. **Capri town** fills the ridge high above the harbor. The ruins of Emperor Tiberius' palace, **Villa Jovis,** cap the peak on the left. To the right, the dramatic *"Mamma mia!"* road arcs around the highest mountain on the island **(Monte Solaro),** leading up to **Anacapri** (the island's second town, just out of sight). Notice the old zigzag steps below the road. Until 1874, those steps were the only connection between Capri and Anacapri. (Though they're quite old, it's nowhere near as old as implied by their nickname, "The Phoenician Stairway.") The white house on the ridge above the zigzags is **Villa San Michele** (where you can go later for a grand view).

Arrival at Marina Grande: Remember that you're arriving with a boatload of other tourists with similar plans. You'll need a lot of patience as you get your bearings. After disembarking, you'll pass Dock Zero on your left, with little **ticket kiosks** and the dock for **Motoscafisti Capri** boat trips to the Blue Grotto and around the island. If you're heading to the grotto and there's barely a line, consider jumping in now, keeping in mind that a short line here doesn't mean there won't be a backup at the grotto entry (you're

competing with private boats, too, along with those who took the bus and steps down to the grotto entrance). One other company, **Laser Capri,** offers boat trips to the grotto and around the island. You'll find its two ticket windows along the waterfront—one just in front as you exit the pier, to the left of the Bar Grotta Azzurra restaurant, and the other a block to the left. (For boat-tour details, see "Sights on Capri," later.)

The **grotto dinghies** are the white rowboats beached on the shore. If there are no (or few) beached white rowboats facing Dock Zero, the grotto is open and they are hard at work.

If you're not heading straight for the Blue Grotto, keep walking to the main drag and find the base of the **funicular railway** (signed *funicolare*) that runs up to Capri town, and stand facing it, with your back to the water.

The fourth little clothing-and-souvenir shop to the right of the funicular provides **baggage storage** (€4/bag, look for the awning sign, daily 9:00-18:00, +39 081 837 4575, shorter hours or closed in winter).

Across from the Bar Grotta Azzurra are ticket windows for **funicular and bus tickets** (not always sold by drivers) and, a little farther along, for **boat tickets** to Naples and Sorrento. (Notice the grand electronic departure board on the terminal building listing all boats leaving in the next couple of hours.) Adjacent, just uphill, is the stop for **buses to Anacapri** and the rest of the island. (Another bus stop, only for **buses to Capri town,** is at the opposite end of Marina Grande.) Across the street is a pay **WC,** and a little farther on is Marina Grande's pebbly public beach.

To take the steep paved **footpath** up to Capri town, walk with the water on your left nearly to the end until you see the fountain, then head uphill and follow signs to *Capri centro;* allow 30 minutes to walk up.

HELPFUL HINTS

Cheap Tricks: A cheap day trip to Capri is tough, as you'll pay about €20 each way just to get there and about €45 to see the Blue Grotto. That's €85 already. But if you skip the grotto, and picnic and ride buses rather than enjoying restaurants and taxis, you'll find your time on the island itself to be relatively inexpensive. Many of Capri's greatest pleasures are free.

Tread Lightly: Be conscious of your personal impact on this island. More than 2.3 million annual visitors put a strain on local resources. Consider taking any trash out with you and carrying a reusable water bottle.

Best Real Hike: Serious hikers love the peaceful and scenic three-hour Fortress Hike, which takes you entirely away from the tourists. You'll walk under ruined forts along the rugged coast, from the Blue Grotto to the *faro* (lighthouse). From there, you can take a bus back to Anacapri (3/hour). The TI has a fine map/brochure. Hiking guru Giovanni Visetti has a great free map of the whole island on his website (www.giovis.com).

Free Beach: Marina Grande has a free pebbly beach (pay at the bar for a shower).

Local Guides: Sorrento-based **Giovanna Donadio** leads good Capri tours (see page 162).

GETTING AROUND CAPRI

By Bus and Funicular: Tickets for the island's buses and funicular cost €2.60 per ride (no transfers allowed). Think about how many tickets you'll need and save time by buying them all at once at the port kiosk. (Tickets are also available at the port office and throughout the island at newsstands, tobacco shops, and main bus stops.) The €8.20 all-day bus pass is available only at the port. Validate your ticket when you board.

The **funicular** runs about four times per hour (more when really crowded). If frustrated by long lines for the descent, you can walk down (stairs or ramp) in about 15 minutes.

Public **buses** are orange or red-and-gray, while blue-and-gray buses are for private tour groups. Schedules are clearly posted at all bus stations. Public buses from the port to Capri town, and from Capri town to Anacapri, are frequent (4/hour, 10 minutes). The direct bus between the port and Anacapri runs less often (2/hour, 25 minutes), and if you don't get there early in the day, lines can be painfully slow. From Anacapri, branch bus lines run north and south: to the parking lot above the Blue Grotto *(Grotta Azzurra)* and to the lighthouse (*faro;* 3/hour). Buses are teeny (because of the island's narrow roads) and often packed, the aisles filled with people standing. At most stops, you'll see ranks for passengers to line up in. Locals are allowed to cut the line. If the driver changes the bus's display to read *completo* (full), you'll need to wait for the next one.

By Taxi: Taxis have fixed rates (Marina Grande to Capri town-€20; Marina Grande to Anacapri-€25). You can hire a taxi for about €70 per hour—negotiate. If you're a group of three or fewer, don't be shy about linking up with another couple to fill a taxi and split the fare.

By Scooter: If you're an experienced scooter rider, this is the perfect way to have the run of the island. (For novice riders, Capri's steep and narrow roads aren't a good place to start.) **Capri Scooter** rents bright-yellow scooters with 50cc engines—strong enough to haul couples. Rentals come with a map and instructions with parking tips and other helpful information (€50/3 hours, €70/day, RS%—helpful Ciro offers a 10 percent discount with this book; includes helmet, gas, and insurance; daily April-Oct 9:30-18:00, may open in good weather off-season, at Via Don Giobbe Ruocco 55, Marina Grande, +39 338 360 6918).

Sights on Capri

ON THE WATER

▲▲▲Capri Boat Circle (Giro dell'Isola)

You have three boat-tour options: circle the island with a stop at the Blue Grotto, circle only, or Blue Grotto only. For me, the best experience on Capri is to take the scenic boat trip around the island. It's cheap, comes with good narration and lots of curiosities, and there are plenty of departures from Marina Grande.

Both **Laser Capri** and **Motoscafisti Capri** run trips that circle the island and pass stunning cliffs, caves, and views that most miss when they go only to the Blue Grotto (€23; about 80 passengers/boat; Motoscafisti Capri—+39 081 837 7714, www.motoscafisticapri.com; Laser Capri—+39 081 837 5208, www.lasercapri.com). The circular tour comes with a live guide and takes about an hour. You'll see quirky sights (a solar-powered lighthouse, tiny statues atop desolate rocks, holes in the cliffs with legends going back to Emperor Tiberius' times), pop into various caves and inlets, hear stories of celebrity-owned villas, and marvel at a nonstop parade of staggering cliffs.

With both companies, you can stop at the Blue Grotto at no extra charge (this adds at least an hour but usually more; check schedules to find out which departures allow a Blue Grotto stop).

You can also sail just to the grotto and back (15 minutes each way); this costs the same as circling the island.

All boats leave daily from 9:00 until at least 13:00 (or later, depending on when the Blue Grotto rowboats stop running—likely 14:00 in summer).

▲▲Blue Grotto (Grotta Azzurra)

Thousands of tourists a day visit Capri's Blue Grotto, a sea cave on the island's north shore that's accessible only by boat. I did—early (when the light is best) and with choppy waves making entrance nearly impossible...and it was great.

For many, this is a "must do" experience. It's also a greedy tourist trap. Going inside the cave is expensive, time-consuming, and unpredictable (it's often closed), and can clog up an otherwise great day. Before you decide, read "To Grotto or Not" and check out my video clip (see page 164).

The actual cave experience isn't much: a short dinghy ride through a three-foot-high entry hole to reach a 60-yard-long cave, where the sun reflects brilliantly blue on its limestone bottom. But the experience of getting there, getting in, and getting back is a scenic hoot. You get a fast ride and scant narration on a 30-foot boat partway around the gorgeous island; along the way, you see bird life and dramatic limestone cliffs. You'll understand why Roman emperors appreciated the invulnerability of the island—it's surrounded by cliffs, with only one good access point, and therefore easy to defend.

Just outside the grotto, your boat idles as you pile into eight-foot dinghies that hold four to five passengers each. Next, you'll be taken to a floating ticket counter to pay the grotto entry fee. From there, your ruffian rower will elbow his way to the tiny hole, then pull fast and hard on the cable at the low point of the swells to squeeze you into the grotto (keep your head down and hands in the boat). Then your man rows you around, spouting off a few descriptive lines and singing "O Sole Mio." Depending on the strength of the sunshine that day, the blue light inside can be brilliant.

The grotto was actually an ancient Roman *nymphaeum*—a retreat for romantic hanky-panky. Many believe that, in its day, a tunnel led here directly from the emperor's palace, and that the grotto experience was enlivened by statues of Poseidon and company, placed half-underwater as if emerging from the sea. It was ancient Romans who smoothed out the entry hole that's still used to this day.

When dropping you off, your boatman will fish for a €10 tip (read: he'll try to extort you). It's optional—don't let them bully you. Either €5/couple or €2/person is enough (you've already paid plenty). If you don't want to return by boat, ask to be let off at the little dock, where stairs lead up to a café and the Blue Grotto bus stop (see later).

Cost: On top of the €23 ride from Marina Grande and back, you pay a separate €20 entry fee at the grotto, which includes the rowboat service plus admission to the grotto. It's a bit of a racket: You decide if it's worth it.

Getting There: Most visitors arrive at the grotto by **boat** from Capri's Marina Grande (see the previous listing). It's also possible by **bus** via Anacapri, saving money but not time (roughly 3/hour, 10 minutes; buses depart from the Anacapri bus station at Piazza della Pace—not from the bus stop at Piazza Vittoria, direction: Grotta Azzurra).

Timing: When waves or high tide make entering dangerous, the boats don't go in—the grotto can close without notice, sending tourists (flush with anticipation) home without a chance to squeeze through the little hole. It's illegal and dangerous to try to swim here at any time.

Coming by boat from Capri's port (Marina Grande), allow at least two hours (or more if you arrive after 10:30) for the entire visit, depending on the chaos at the caves. Use the WC before you board, as there's nowhere to go once you get out there. Going with the first trip (around 9:00) will get you to the grotto at the same time as the boatmen in their dinghies—who hitch a ride behind your boat—resulting in less chaos and a shorter wait at the entry point.

If you arrive on the island later in the morning—when the Blue Grotto is already jammed—you could try waiting to visit until about 14:00, when most of the big tour groups have vacated. Any later, you'll risk getting out to the grotto entrance, waiting an hour or more, then finding out trips into the grotto have ended for the day.

Leaving the Blue Grotto by Bus: Even if you arrive at the grotto by sea, you can leave by bus. This is a smart option for getting to Anacapri (rather than going back to Marina Grande to catch a bus there). Ask your boat captain to have the dinghy row you over to the dock and drop you there (for a second small tip; you'll still have to pay the full boat fare). From the dock, climb up the stairs to the stop for the bus to Anacapri. Though the line at the grotto bus stop can be long, by late morning the line at the Marina Grande bus stop can be much longer.

ANACAPRI TOWN AND NEARBY

More interesting and less chaotic than the island's namesake town, Anacapri has two or three hours' worth of sights. Though Anacapri sits higher up on the island ("ana" means "upper" in Greek) than Capri town, there are no sea views at street level in the town center.

Tourist Information: Anacapri's TI is at Piazza Vittoria, next to the WC by the chairlift.

Arrival and Departure by Bus: Anacapri has two bus stops: at Piazza Vittoria, in the center of town at the base of the Monte Solaro chairlift; and 200 yards farther along at Piazza della Pace (pronounced "PAH-chay"), a larger bus station near the cemetery. Piazza Vittoria gets you closer to chairlift and Villa San Michele; Piazza della Pace is where you transfer to the Blue Grotto bus (marked *Grotta Azzurra*).

Buses leaving Anacapri for Marina Grande can be packed. For

better odds of getting on board, catch the bus from Piazza della Pace (where the bus starts). To find the actual stop, with your back to the covered bus terminal, walk right until you see the little bench under a map and bus schedule; the similarly unmarked stop across the street is for buses to Capri. (Another option is to catch a bus to Capri town, visit sights there, then take the funicular down to Marina Grande.) Bus tickets can be purchased at the minimarket just down from the bus stop in Piazza Vittoria.

Via Orlandi Stroll

Anacapri's pedestrianized old town is a delight to explore. The traffic-free main drag, Via Orlandi, takes you through the charming center of town. It's just a block or so from either bus stop. (From Piazza Vittoria, the street is right there—just go down the lane to the right of the Anacapri statue. From Piazza della Pace, cross the street and go down the small pedestrian lane called Via Filietto.)

To see the town, stroll along **Via Orlandi** for a few minutes. Signboards propose a quick circuit that links the Museo Casa Rossa, St. Michael's Church (both described later), and peaceful side streets, ending at Santa Sofia Church. You'll also find shops, hardworking little restaurants, and simple eateries, including good choices for quick, inexpensive pizza, *saltimbocca* (prosciutto and mozzarella on baked pizza bread—great for a filling picnic), *panini,* and other goodies.

Just past Casa Rossa and St. Michael's, at the corner with Via Trieste e Trento, you can stop for a made-to-order sandwich at **Alimentari Pollio Liberato.** Signore Liberato runs a tiny grocery store perfect for a picnic, as cheery Raffaella will make you a big, simple, splittable €5 *panino* (just the basics: fresh bread, mozzarella, and Parma ham; Mon-Sat 8:00-13:30 & 16:30-20:00, closed Sun; also sells bus tickets).

There are plenty of benches nearby on **Piazza Diaz,** fronting Santa Sofia Church. This piazza feels like Anacapri's main square—a soccer field for kids and the destination for people enjoying the evening *passeggiata.* The welcoming majolica benches have ceramic tile scenes from local winemaking, and **Santa Sofia Church** offers cool, meditative tranquility. The bone-room hatch labeled *1778* in the aisle floor likely marks a crypt below.

Sights in and near Anacapri

Of the sights below, the first two are in the heart of town (on or near Via Orlandi), while the next two are a short walk away.

Museo Casa Rossa (Red House Museum)

This "Pompeiian-red," eccentric home, a hodgepodge of architectural styles, is the former residence of John Clay MacKowen, a Louisiana doctor and ex-Confederate officer who moved to Capri in the 1870s and married a local woman. (MacKowen and the Villa San Michele's Axel Munthe—see later—loathed each other, and even tried to challenge each other to a duel.) Today the home hosts a museum working to promote social equity by providing opportunities on its staff for people with disabilities. Its small collection of 19th-century paintings of scenes from around the island recalls a time before mass tourism. There's also a good view from the rooftop.

Cost and Hours: €3.50; discounted to €1 with ticket stub from Blue Grotto, Villa San Michele, or Monte Solaro chairlift; Tue-Sun 10:00-13:30 & 18:30-20:00 in season; shorter hours off-season; closed Mon year-round; Via Orlandi 78, +39 081 838 7260, www.museocasarossa.it.

▲St. Michael's Church (Chiesa San Michele)

This Baroque church in the village center has a remarkable majolica floor showing paradise on earth in a classic 18th-century Neapolitan style. The precious tiles were made and fired in Naples in the late 1700s. The entire floor is ornately tiled, featuring an angel (with flaming sword) driving Adam and Eve from paradise. The devil is wrapped around the trunk of a beautiful tree. The animals—happily ignoring this momentous event—all have human expressions. Side chapels show off *presepe* figurines (painted terra-cotta and traditional costumes of silk). Notice that while the floor is exquisite and costly, the altars are done on the cheap with wood painted to look like marble. Cap your visit by climbing the spiral stairs from the postcard desk to the organ loft for a grand overview. Services are held only during the first two weeks of Advent, when the church is closed to visitors.

CAPRI

Cost and Hours: €2, daily 9:00-19:00; off-season mornings only, closed late Nov-mid-Dec; in town center just off Via Orlandi—look for *San Michele* signs, +39 081 837 2396, www.chiesa-sanmichele.com. On summer weekends, the small square just past the entrance hosts concerts.

▲▲Villa San Michele and Grand Capri View

This is the mansion of Axel Munthe, Capri's grand personality, an idealistic Swedish doctor who bought the property (then rundown) in 1887 and vacationed here until 1946. Munthe was the personal physician of Sweden's Queen Victoria, who often stayed here with him. Munthe enjoyed the avant-garde and permissive scene at Capri, during an era when Europe's leading artists and

creative figures gathered here and the island's many gay visitors could be honest about their sexual orientation.

At the very least, walk the path from Piazza Vittoria past the villa to a superb, free viewpoint (at the top of the dramatic Phoenician Stairway) over Capri town, Marina Grande, and—in the distance—Mount Vesuvius and Sorrento. Paying to enter the villa lets you see a few rooms with period furnishings and antiquities, as well as an exhibit on Munthe (follow the one-way route, good English descriptions). Then savor the sculpture-filled loggia and stroll through one of this region's most delightful gardens, with a chapel, the Olivetum (a tiny museum of native birds and bugs), and a view that's even better than the free one outside the complex. Throughout the gardens and the house, you'll see a smattering of original ancient objects unearthed here—and lots and lots of copies. Billy's Bar (named for Munthe's pet baboon) is perfect for a quiet drink—or how about a caprese salad—with a grand view.

Cost and Hours: €10, daily 9:00-18:00, closes earlier Oct-April, +39 081 837 1401, www.villasanmichele.eu.

Getting There: From Piazza Vittoria, walk up the grand staircase and turn left onto Via Capodimonte. At the start of the shopping street, on your right, pass the deluxe Capri Palace Hotel—venture in if you can get past the treacherously eye-catching swimming pool windows (behind the pillars). After squeezing past a long line of overpriced shops, just before the villa, notice the Swedish consulate. In honor of Munthe, Swedes get into the villa for free.

▲▲Chairlift up to Monte Solaro

From Anacapri, you can ride the chairlift *(seggiovia)* to the 1,900-foot summit of Monte Solaro for a commanding view of the Bay of Naples. Work on your tan as you float over hazelnut, walnut, chestnut, apricot, peach, kiwi, and fig trees, past a montage of tourists (mostly from cruise ships; when the grotto is closed, they bring passengers here instead). Prospective smoochers should know that the lift seats are all single. As you ascend, consider how

Capri's real estate has been priced out of the locals' reach. The ride takes 13 minutes each way, and you'll want at least 30 minutes at the top, where there are picnic benches and a café with WCs.

Cost and Hours: €11 one-way, €14 round-trip, daily 9:30-17:00, last run down at 17:30; March-April until 16:00, Nov-Feb until 15:30, +39 081 837 1438, www.capriseggiovia.it. Note that the lift gets more crowded with tour groups in the afternoon.

Getting There: From the Piazza Vittoria bus stop, just climb the steps and look right.

At the Summit: You'll enjoy the best panorama possible: lush cliffs busy with seagulls enjoying the ideal nesting spot. Even if skies aren't clear, the views are spectacular, with clouds surfing over the cliffs. Find the Faraglioni Rocks—with tour boats squeezing through every few minutes—which are an icon of the island. The pink building nearest the rocks was an American R&R base during World War II. Eisenhower and Churchill met here. On the peak closest to Cape Sorrento, you can see the distant ruins of Emperor Tiberius' palace, Villa Jovis. Pipes from the Sorrento Peninsula bring water to Capri (demand for fresh water here long ago exceeded the supply provided by the island's three natural springs). The Li Galli Islands mark the Amalfi Coast in the distance. Cross the bar terrace for views of Mount Vesuvius and Naples.

Hiking Down: A highlight for hardy walkers (provided you have strong knees and good shoes) is the one-hour downhill hike from the top of Monte Solaro, through lush vegetation and ever-changing views, past the 14th-century Chapel of Santa Maria Cetrella (at the trail's only intersection, it's a 10-minute detour to the right), and back into Anacapri. The trail starts downstairs, past the WCs (last chance). Down two more flights of stairs, look for the sign to *Anacapri e Cetrella*—you're on your way. While the trail is well established, you'll encounter plenty of uneven steps, loose rocks, and few signs.

Lighthouse near Anacapri

The lighthouse *(faro)*, at the rocky, arid, and desolate southwestern corner of the island, is a favorite place to enjoy the sunset. This area has a private beach, a pool, small restaurants, and a few fishermen. Reach it by bus from Anacapri (3/hour, departs from Piazza della Pace stop).

CAPRI TOWN AND NEARBY

This cute but extremely clogged and touristy shopping town is worth a brief visit, if only for the window shopping.

Piazza Umberto I

If you arrive by the funicular or walk up, you'll emerge just around the corner from Piazza Umberto I, the town's main square (named after the second king of Italy). With your back to the funicular, the bus stop is 50 yards straight ahead down Via Roma. The **TI** is under the bell tower on Piazza Umberto. The footpath to the port starts just behind the TI (follow *Per Il Porto* signs, a 15-minute walk in either direction: ramp to the left, steps to the right). A WC and baggage storage are down the stairs by the TI.

Imagine the days when, rather than fancy cafés, the square was filled with a public market. Today, Capri town is traffic-free, with only electric service minitrucks scooting here and there. While a coffee costs €2 at any bar, it's €10 at a table on the square.

To the left of City Hall (*Municipio,* lowest corner), a narrow, atmospheric lane leads into the medieval part of town, which has plenty of eateries and is the starting point for the 45-minute hike to Villa Jovis.

Cathedral

Capri town's multidomed Baroque cathedral, which faces the square, is worth a quick look. Its multicolored marble floor at the altar dates from the first century AD—it was scavenged from Emperor Tiberius' villa and laid here in the 19th century.

Ignazio Cerio Museum

Up the stairs immediately across from the cathedral, this four-room old-school museum shows off flora, fauna, and archaeology from the island as it was displayed a century ago (€4, Tue-Sat 11:00-16:00, closed Sun-Mon).

"Rodeo Drive"

The lane to the left of the cathedral (past Bar Tiberio, under the wide arch) is a fashionable shopping strip that's justifiably been dubbed "Rodeo Drive" by residents. Walk a few minutes down the street (past Gelateria Buonocore at #35, with its tempting fresh waffle cones) to Quisisana Hotel, the island's top old-time hotel (formerly a 19th-century sanatorium). From there, head left for fancy shops and villas, and right for gardens and views.

Between the lane and the sea is a huge monastery (Certosa di San Giacomo, described below; access to the left).

To reach the Giardini di Augusto, next, walk to the viewpoint overlooking the garden at Hotel Luna and head downhill (and fragrantly) to the right.

Giardini di Augusto

A five-minute walk leads to this lovely public garden (€2.50, use machines, daily May-Oct 9:00-19:30, Nov-April until 17:30, free to enter off-season, no picnicking). While the garden itself is modest, it boasts great views over the famous Faraglioni Rocks—handy if you don't have the time, money, or interest to access the higher vantage points near Anacapri (Monte Solaro or Villa San Michele).

Monastery of San Giacomo (Certosa di San Giacomo)

While it's one of the most historic buildings on the island, for most visitors the Monastery of San Giacomo is not worth the time or money (€6, Tue-Sun 10:00-16:00, until later in summer, closed Mon, Via Certosa 10, +39 081 837 6218). The stark monastery has an empty church and a sleepy cloister. Perhaps the finest piece of art on Capri, over the church's front entrance, is completely ignored: an exquisite 14th-century fresco of Mary and the Baby Jesus by the Florentine Niccolo di Tommaso. Today, the monastery hosts the **Museo Diefenbach,** a small collection of dark and moody paintings by eccentric German artist Karl Wilhelm Diefenbach, who walked around naked in the gay, avant-garde, politically-liberal Capri of the early 1900s.

Villa Jovis and the Emperor's Capri

Even before becoming emperor, Augustus loved Capri so much that he traded the family-owned Isle of Ischia to the (then-independent) Neapolitans in exchange for making Capri his personal property. Emperor Tiberius spent a decade here, AD 26-37. (Some figure he did so to escape being assassinated in Rome.)

Emperor Tiberius' ruined villa, Villa Jovis, is reachable only by a scenic 45-minute hike from Capri town. You won't find any statues or mosaics here—just an evocative, ruined complex of terraces clinging to a rocky perch over a sheer drop to the sea...and a lovely view. You can make out a large water reservoir for baths, the foundations of servants' quarters, and Tiberius' private apartments (fragments of marble flooring still survive). The ruined lighthouse dates from the Middle Ages.

Cost and Hours: €6, hours unpredictable, generally Tue-Sun 10:00-16:00, closed Mon, closed off-season, confirm info at the Capri TI before setting out.

AMALFI COAST

Amalfi Coast Tour • Positano • Amalfi Town • Ravello • Minori & Maiori

With its stunning scenery, hill- and harbor-hugging towns, and historic ruins, Amalfi is Italy's coast with the most. The breathtaking trip from Sorrento to Salerno is one of the world's great bus or taxi rides. And over the centuries, the spectacular scenery and climate have been a siren call for the rich and famous, luring Roman emperor Tiberius, composer Richard Wagner, actress Sophia Loren, writer Gore Vidal, and others to the Amalfi Coast's special brand of *la dolce vita.*

The Amalfi Coast is one of those places with a "must see" reputation. Staggeringly picturesque and maddeningly touristy, it can be both rewarding and frustrating. As an antidote to intense Naples, it's the perfect place for a romantic break—if done right. The two main Amalfi Coast towns (Gucci-ad Positano and Amalfi town) are pretty, but they're also congested and overpriced. Positano has good overnight options; Amalfi does not. Inland Ravello is fun for that tramp-in-a-palace feeling. And Minori and Maiori are your workaday siblings with a beach but without the intense tourism.

In Paestum, farther south, you can see one of the world's best collections of 2,500-year-old Greek temples, a worthwhile museum with artifacts from the site, and the remains of a Roman town (see the next chapter).

PLANNING YOUR TIME

On a quick visit, use Sorrento (see that chapter) as your home base and do the Amalfi Coast as a day trip. But to slow your pace in some smaller towns, spend a few more days on the coast, sleeping in Positano, Minori, or Maiori.

Trying to decide where to stay? Sorrento is larger, with useful services and the best transportation connections and accommodations. Tiny Positano is more touristy, but also more chic and picturesque, with a decent beach. For a less ritzy home base, many visitors prefer exploring the Amalfi Coast from Minori or Maiori.

Naples can also work as a jumping-off point for an Amalfi Coast day trip, if you get an early start and the timetables align. You have two options by public transport: train to Salerno, then bus (or boat) to Amalfi town; or, Circumvesuviana or Campania Express train to Sorrento, then bus to Positano and/or Amalfi. (You can go out one way and return the other.)

From Rome, high-speed Frecce trains connect to Salerno in just 1.5 hours (6-7/day), making it possible to skip Naples and focus on towns to the south.

GETTING AROUND THE AMALFI COAST

The real thrill here is the **scenic drive** between Sorrento and Salerno. The stretch from Positano to Amalfi is the best. This is treacherous stuff, and parking is a huge challenge. Even if you have a car, you may want to take the bus or hire a driver. Brave (or reckless?) souls enjoy seeing the coast by scooter (rent in Sorrento).

Next, I've outlined your options by bus, boat, and taxi. Many travelers do the Amalfi Coast as a round-trip by bus, but a good strategy is to go one way by land and return by boat. For example, take the bus along the coast to Positano, Amalfi, or Minori/Maiori, then catch the ferry back.

Looking for exercise? Numerous trails connect the main coastal towns with villages on the hills. Get a good map before you venture out (local hiker and orienteer Giovanni Visetti has posted free maps and itineraries at www.giovis.com).

Connections by Bus vs. by Boat: SITA **buses** theoretically run twice hourly, stopping in every town (for schedules, see www.sitasudtrasporti.it or—easier to read—www.positano.com). They're cheap, but keep in mind that in summer, they are reliably jam-packed and slowed to a crawl by traffic.

Boat service (while more expensive) is faster, more comfortable, and reliable (there's no traffic and they can cram in more people). Just a couple of ferry companies serve each coastal town quite well and sell tickets right by the docks (no need to book in advance, though you can check schedules online): **Alilauro** (www.alilauro.it), **Travelmar** (www.travelmar.it), and **NLG** (www.nlg.it)

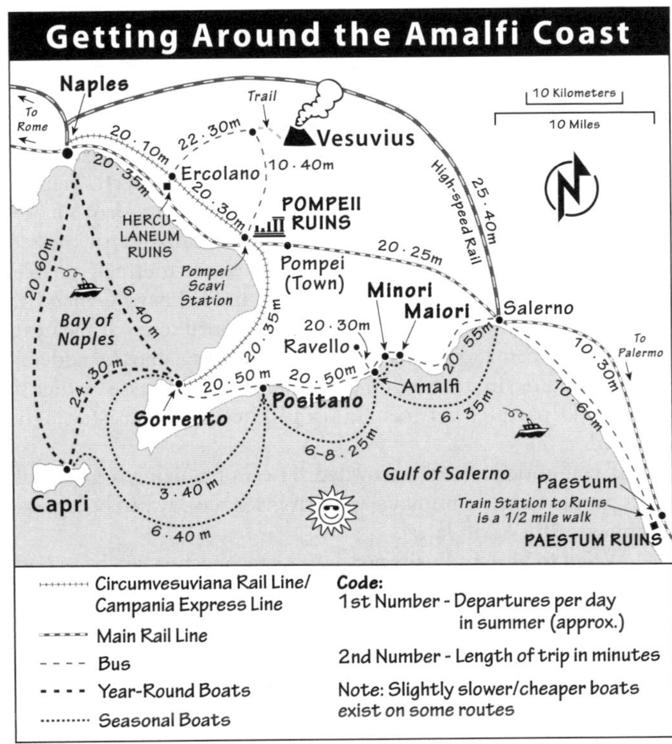

are the main companies, with Travelmar running most of the boats between the Amalfi towns, and Alilauro and NLG filling in with frequent boats to Capri and less frequent boats to Sorrento and Naples. Ferries run less often in spring and fall, and some don't run at all off-season (mid-Oct-mid-April). Boats don't run in stormy weather at any time of year. If you can't find a direct connection, check if you can change boats in Capri.

By Public Bus

SITA buses from Sorrento to Amalfi, via Positano, are the most common, inexpensive way to see the coast. From Sorrento, the first bus leaves at 6:30; from 8:30 they run roughly every half-hour until 17:00, then hourly until 22:00 in summer or until 20:00 in winter (50 minutes to Positano; another 50 minutes to Amalfi). To reach Ravello (the hill town beyond Amalfi), Minori and Maiori, or Salerno (at the far end of the coast), transfer in Amalfi. When checking the schedule, note that *giornaliero* (G) means daily, *scolastico* (S) means school bus, *feriale* (F) denotes Monday-Saturday, and *festivo* (H) is for Sundays and holidays. Individual tickets are inexpensive (€2-4). All rides are covered by the 24-hour Costiera

SITA Sud pass (€10), which may not save you money but does save time buying tickets. Tickets are sold at tobacco shops and newsstands, but usually not by drivers.

In Sorrento, SITA buses leave from the train station (10 steps down, then join the line). Leaving Sorrento, grab a seat on the right for the best views. If you return by bus, it's fun to sit directly behind the driver for a box seat with a view over the twisting hairpin action. Sitting toward the front can also help minimize carsickness.

Avoiding Crowded Buses: SITA buses are routinely unable to handle demand during summer months and holidays. Generally, if you don't get on one bus, you're well positioned to catch the next one. (When demand increases, extra departures may be added.) From Sorrento, aim to leave on the 8:30 bus at the latest—earlier if possible. Departures between 9:00 and 11:00 can be frustratingly crowded.

If you anticipate very crowded buses, organizing a group of eight people to hire a minibus and driver for the day can be a good option (see "By Taxi," later).

When to Stop in Positano: Summer congestion can be so bad that some Amalfi-Sorrento buses don't even stop in Positano (because they fill up in Amalfi). Those trying to get back from Positano to Sorrento are stuck taking an extortionist taxi or hopping a boat. When day-tripping from Sorrento to Amalfi, it's safest to make your Positano stop on the outbound leg, then come straight home from Amalfi, where the bus originates.

By Boat

A few passenger boats per day link Positano and Amalfi with Sorrento, Capri, and Salerno (3-6/day, generally April-Oct only). The last daily departure can be as early as midafternoon and is never much later than 18:00. Check schedules carefully: Frequency varies from month to month, and boats may not run in bad weather (especially at Positano, where there's no real pier). The companies operating each route change frequently, compete for passengers, and usually claim to know nothing about their rivals' services. Go to the dock to confirm times and buy tickets (or check boat company websites for schedules; see earlier). For a summary of sample routes, frequencies, and travel times, see the "Getting Around the Amalfi Coast" map.

If no boats are going directly between Sorrento and Positano/Amalfi, you can usually still connect the two sides of the peninsula via Capri. Here's another useful trick: If you're going to Capri from Positano, and want to see the Blue Grotto, look for a boat that stops at the grotto en route (rather than dropping you at the port in Capri to catch another boat from there).

By Taxi

Given the hairy driving, impossible parking, crowded public buses, and potential fun, you might consider splurging to hire your own car and driver for your Amalfi day. If you can organize a group of seven people to split a €450 minibus, €65 each might be worth it to have your own driver standing by as you explore.

The English-speaking **Monetti family** car-and-driver service—Raffaele, daughter Carolina, son Christian, and cousin Gianpaolo—have taken excellent care of my readers' transit needs for decades. Sample trips and rates: all-day Amalfi Coast (Positano, Amalfi, Ravello, usually with stops in each town and lunch in Ravello), 8 hours, €400; Pompeii, Paestum, and a buffalo farm, 10 hours, €580; transfer between Naples airport or train station and Sorrento, €180). These prices are for up to three people; you'll pay more for a larger eight-seater van. Though based in Sorrento, they can also pick you up from other places. Payment is cash only (as with most of the car services listed). Reserve directly by email (or by phone on short notice—WhatsApp is best; Raffaele's mobile +39 335 602 9158 or +39 338 946 2860, "office" run by his English-speaking Finnish wife, Susanna, www.monettitaxi17.com, monettitaxi17@libero.it). If you get into any kind of serious jam in the area, you can consider Raffaele a friend and call for help. Don't rely on a web search for the name Monetti, as that might lead you to an impersonator trying to siphon off their business.

Francesco del Pizzo is another smooth and honest Sorrento-based driver. A classy man who speaks English well, Francesco enjoys explaining things as he drives (9 hours or so in a vehicle with up to 4 passengers, €360 in sedan, €400 in minibus; up to 7 passengers in a minibus, €450; +39 333 238 4144, francescodelpizzo@yahoo.it).

Wisely Travelling by Carlo Arcucci owner Carlo is an engaging and hardworking driver/guide more excited about today's Italy than archaeological sites. He's good at coming up with creative and customized solutions to your needs and does transfers and driving tours out of Sorrento for up to seven passengers in his minibus (+39 338 597 2676, www.wiselytravelling.com, info@wiselytravelling.com).

Anthony Buonocore, based in Amalfi, is handy for people staying in Minori/Maiori/Amalfi. He specializes in cruise shore excursions, as well as trips anywhere in the region in his eight-person Mercedes van (+39 349 441 0336, www.amalfitransfer.com, buonocoreanthony@yahoo.it).

Rides Only: If you're hiring a cabbie off the street for a ride and not a tour, a one-way trip from Sorrento to Positano might cost about €110 (to Amalfi, €180). All Sorrento taxis are white minivans (taking up to eight passengers), sport a taxi sign on top, and use a meter (fares will vary a bit depending on traffic). If there's no meter, it's not an official taxi.

By Shared Minibus

While hiring your own driver is convenient, it's also expensive. To bring the cost down, split the trip—and the bill—with other travelers using this book. Naples-based **Mondo Guide** offers a nine-hour minibus trip that departs from Sorrento and heads down the Amalfi Coast, with brief stops in Positano, Amalfi, and Ravello, before returning to Sorrento (€70/person). They also offer Rick Steves readers shared tours in Capri, Pompeii, and Naples. For details, see page 32.

Amalfi Coast Tour

The wildly scenic Amalfi Coast drive from Sorrento to Salerno, worth ▲▲▲, is one of the all-time-great white-knuckle rides, whether you tackle it by bus, taxi, or shared minibus. It will leave your mouth open and your camera's memory card full. You'll gain respect for the 19th-century Italian engineers who built the roads—and even more for the 21st-century drivers who squeeze past each other here daily. Cantilevered garages, hotels, and villas cling to the vertical terrain, and beautiful but out-of-reach coves tease from far below. As you hyperventilate, notice how the Mediterranean, a sheer 500-foot drop below, really twinkles. All this beautiful scenery apparently inspires local Romeos and Juliets, with the latex evidence of late-night romantic encounters littering the roadside turnouts.

For the best views, gasp from the right side of the car or bus as you go out from Sorrento and from the left as you return. Traffic is so heavy that private tour buses are only allowed to go in one direction (southbound from Sorrento). Summer traffic is infuriating. Fluorescent-vested police are posted at tough bends during peak hours to help fold in side-view mirrors and keep things moving.

➲ **Self-Guided Tour:** Here's a loose, self-guided tour of what you're seeing as you travel from west to east.

Leaving Sorrento: The road winds up into the hills past lemon groves and hidden houses. The gray-green trees are olives. (Notice the green nets slung around the trunks; these are unfurled in October and November, when the ripe olives drop naturally, for an easy self-harvest.) Dark, green-leafed trees planted in dense groves are the source of the region's lemons (many destined to become *limoncello* liqueur) and big, fat citrons (*cedri,* mostly used for marmalade). The black nets over the orange and lemon groves create a greenhouse effect, trapping warmth and humidity for maximum tastiness, while offering protection from extreme weather (preserving the peels used for *limoncello*).

Atop the ridge outside Sorrento, look to your right: The two small islands are the **Li Galli Islands,** where some say the sirens in Homer's *Odyssey* lived. The largest of these islands was once owned by the famed ballet dancer Rudolf Nureyev; it's now a luxury residence, rented to wealthy visitors for upward of $100,000 per week (bring your own yacht or arrive by helicopter).

When Nureyev bought the island, the only building standing was the stony watchtower—the first of many you'll see all along the coast. These were strategically placed within sight of one another so that a relay of rooftop bonfires could quickly spread word of a pirate attack.

The limestone cliffs that plunge into the sea were traversed by a hand-carved trail that became a modern road in the mid-19th century. Fruit stands sell produce from farms and orchards just over the hill. Limestone absorbs heat and rainwater, making this south-facing coastline a fertile suntrap, with temperatures as much as 10 degrees higher than in nearby Sorrento. The chalky, reflective limestone, which extends below the surface, accounts for the uniquely colorful blues and greens of the water. With the favorable climate, bougainvillea, geraniums, oleander, and wisteria grow like weeds here in the summer. Notice the nets pulled tight against the cliffs—they're designed to catch rocks that often tumble loose after heavy rains.

Positano: The dramatic, exotic-looking town of Positano is the main stop along the coast. The town is built on a series of man-made terraces, which were carefully carved out of the steep rock, then filled with fertile soil carried here from Sorrento on the backs of donkeys. You can read the history of the region in Positano's rooftops—a mix of Roman-style red terra-cotta tiles and white "insulation domes" inspired by the Saracens (see the sidebar).

If you're getting off in Positano, stay on through the first main stop by the round-domed yellow church (Chiesa Nuova), which is a very long walk above town. Instead, get off at the second main stop,

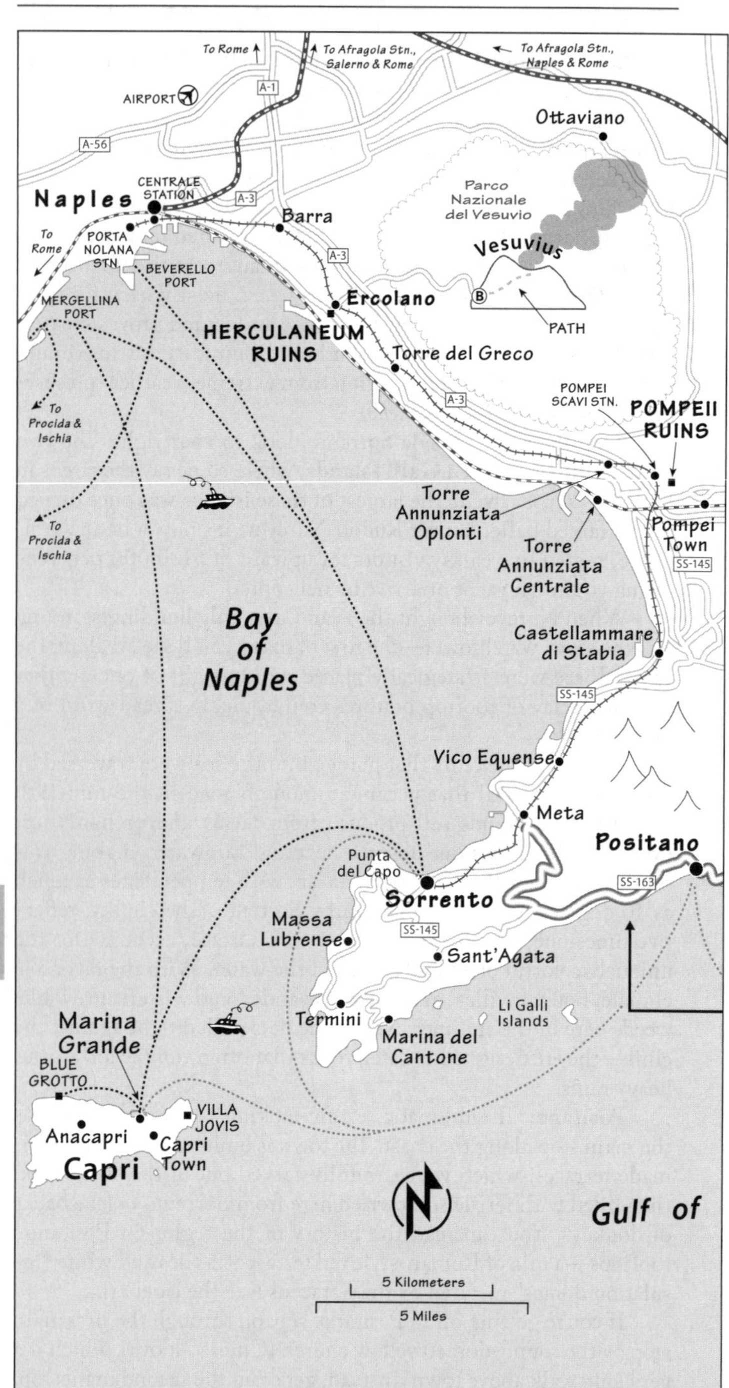
To Rome
To Afragola Stn., Salerno & Rome
To Afragola Stn., Naples & Rome
A-1
AIRPORT
A-56
Ottaviano
Parco Nazionale del Vesuvio
CENTRALE STATION
Naples
A-3
Barra
To Rome
PORTA NOLANA STN.
BEVERELLO PORT
A-3
Vesuvius
MERGELLINA PORT
Ercolano
PATH
HERCULANEUM RUINS
Torre del Greco
A-3
POMPEI SCAVI STN.
POMPEII RUINS
To Procida & Ischia
To Procida & Ischia
Torre Annunziata Oplonti
Pompei Town
Torre Annunziata Centrale
SS-145
Bay of Naples
Castellammare di Stabia
SS-145
Vico Equense
Meta
Positano
Punta del Capo
SS-163
Sorrento
Massa Lubrense
SS-145
Sant'Agata
Li Galli Islands
Termini
Marina del Cantone
Marina Grande
BLUE GROTTO
VILLA JOVIS
Anacapri
Capri Town
Capri
Gulf of
5 Kilometers
5 Miles

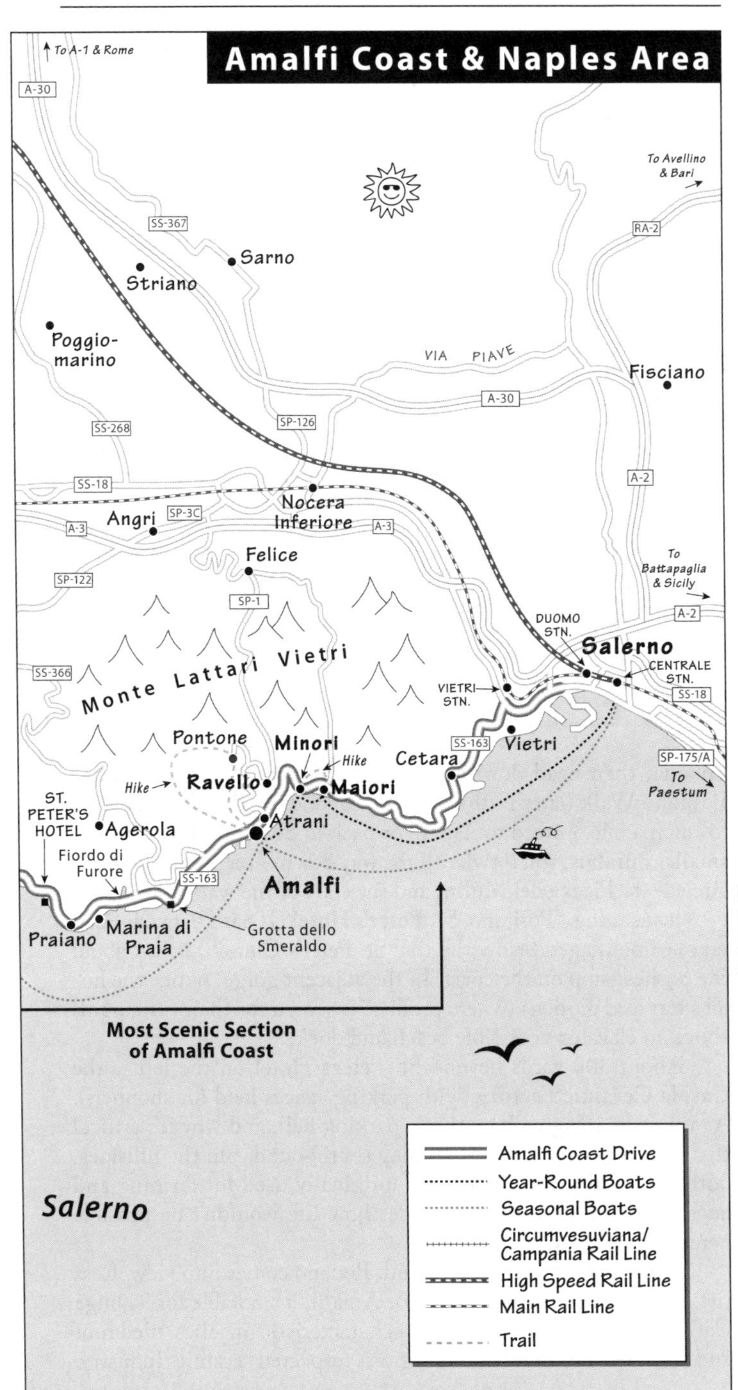

Amalfi Coast & Naples Area
To A-1 & Rome
A-30
To Avellino & Bari
RA-2
SS-367
Sarno
Striano
Poggio-marino
VIA PIAVE
Fisciano
A-30
SS-268
SP-126
A-2
SS-18
Nocera Inferiore
Angri
SP-3C
A-3
A-3
Felice
To Battapaglia & Sicily
SP-122
SP-1
A-2
DUOMO STN.
Salerno
CENTRALE STN.
SS-366
Monte Lattari Vietri
VIETRI STN.
SS-18
Pontone
Minori
SS-163
Vietri
SP-175/A
Hike
Cetara
To Paestum
Hike
Ravello
Maiori
ST. PETER'S HOTEL
Agerola
Atrani
Fiordo di Furore
SS-163
Amalfi
Praiano
Marina di Praia
Grotta dello Smeraldo
Most Scenic Section of Amalfi Coast
Salerno
Amalfi Coast Drive
Year-Round Boats
Seasonal Boats
Circumvesuviana/ Campania Rail Line
High Speed Rail Line
Main Rail Line
Trail

The Saracens

Along Italy's coast, you'll hear about the Saracens. To understand who they were, go back in time and across the sea to Spain in 1492. That's when Ferdinand and Isabel—Spain's foremost Catholic monarchs—defeated the last Moorish stronghold of Granada. The conquered Muslims were allowed to settle in the mountains to the south. But over time, Catholic intolerance forced most Muslims across the Mediterranean to North Africa.

In the 16th century, the North African coast from Tunisia to Morocco was somewhat united and known as the Barbary States. The displaced Moors (chased from Spain), along with indigenous Berber tribes, were often referred to as Saracens, a term perhaps derived from Arabic, meaning "marauder." Saracens raided Christian ships, capturing and reselling cargo and holding crews for ransom. Christian kingdoms paid bribes to keep shipping lanes open. The Barbary Coast Saracens were loosely aligned with the Ottoman Empire, but that wasn't much help when European powers (plus the United States in its first overseas show of strength) had enough of the raids and declared war. Saracen influence came to an end after their defeat in the Barbary War of 1815, but the Saracen legacy lives on along the Italian coast, with everything from watchtowers to restaurants named after them.

Sponda, then head downhill toward the start of my self-guided Positano Walk (later in this chapter). Sponda is also the best place to catch a bus onward to Amalfi or back to Sorrento. If you're on a smaller minibus, you'll twist all the way down—seemingly going in circles—to Piazza dei Mulini and the start of the walk.

Just south of Positano, **St. Peter's Hotel** (Il San Pietro di Positano, camouflaged below the tiny St. Peter's Church) is just about the poshest stop on the coast. In the adjacent gorge, notice the hotel's terraced gardens (where produce is grown for their restaurant) above an elevator-accessible beach and dock.

About 300 yards beyond St. Peter's Hotel on the left is the **Casola Ceramic Factory** (with parking spaces held for shoppers). As you ride, imagine how this is parking hell, and why it's critical that tour buses are limited to going southbound. On the hillsides, notice the centuries-old terraces (originally used for farming and later for building up) and consider how life wouldn't be possible here without them.

Praiano: Just around the bend, Praiano comes into view. Less ritzy or charming than Positano or Amalfi, it's notable for its huge Cathedral of San Gennaro, with a characteristic majolica-tiled roof and dome—a reminder of this region's respected ceramics industry.

In spindly Praiano, most of the homes are accessible only by tiny footpaths and staircases. Near the end of town, just before the big tunnel, watch on the left for the big *presepe* (manger scene) embedded into the cliff face. This Praiano-in-miniature was carved by one local man over several decades. At Christmastime, each house is filled with little figures and twinkle lights.

Just past the tunnel, look below and on the right to see another Saracen watchtower. (Yet another caps the little point on the horizon.)

A bit farther along, look down to see the fishing hamlet of **Marina di Praia** tucked into the gorge *(furore)* between two tunnels. If you're driving—or being driven—consider a detour down here for a coffee break or meal. This serene, tidy nook has its own little pebbly beach with great views of the stout bluffs and watchtower that hem it in. A seafront walkway curls around the bluff all the way to the tower.

Just after going through the next tunnel, watch for a jagged rock formation on its own little pedestal. Locals see the face of the Virgin Mary in this natural feature and say that she's holding a flower (the little pine tree growing out to the right). Also notice several caged, cantilevered parking pads sticking out from the road. This stretch of coastline is popular for long-term villa rentals—Italians who want to really settle into Amalfi life.

Fiordo: Look down and left for the blink-or-you'll-miss-it fishing village that's aptly named Fiordo ("fjord"), filling yet another gorge. You'll see humble homes burrowed into the cliff face, tucked so far into the gorge that they're entirely in shadow for much of the year. Today these are rented out to vacationers; the postage-stamp beach is uncrowded and inviting.

After the next tunnel (and the only gas station on this stretch of the coast), you'll come to a hamlet where, until just a few years ago, you'd see donkeys with big baskets on their backs making heavy deliveries to remote homes high in the rocky hills.

Soon you'll pass the big-for-Amalfi parking lot of the **Grotta dello Smeraldo** ("Emerald Grotto"), a cheesy roadside attraction that wrings the most it can out of a pretty, seawater-filled cave. Passing tourists park here and pay to take an elevator down to sea level, pile into big rowboats, and get paddled around a genuinely impressive cavern while the boatman imparts sparse factoids. (Unless you've got time to kill, skip it.)

Now you're approaching what might be the most dramatic watchtower on the coast, perched atop a near-island. This tower guarded the harbor of the Amalfi navy until the fleet was destroyed in 1343 by a tsunami caused by an earthquake, which also led to Amalfi's decline (back when it was one of Italy's leading powers).

Amalfi Town: Around the next bend you're treated to stunning views of the coastline's namesake town—Amalfi. The white villa sitting on the low point between here and there (with another watchtower at its tip) once belonged to Sophia Loren. Now look up to the very top of the steep, steep cliffs overhead. The hulking former Monastery of Santa Rosa occupies this prime territory. Locals proudly explain that the *sfogliatella* dessert so beloved throughout the Campania region was first created at this monastery. (Today it's a luxury resort, where you can pay a premium to sleep in a tight little former monk's cell.)

Now the bus pulls to a halt—at the end of the line, the waterfront of Amalfi town. Spend some time enjoying this once-powerful, now-pleasant city, with its fine cathedral, fascinating paper museum, and fun-to-explore tangle of lanes (covered later in this chapter).

From Amalfi, you can transfer to another bus to head up to **Ravello,** capping a cliff just beyond Amalfi; or onward to **Minori, Maiori,** or the big city of **Salerno.** Alternatively, buses and boats can take you back to Positano and Sorrento.

If you're continuing the trip southward, look up to the left as you leave Amalfi—the white house that clings to a cliff (Villa Rondinaia) was home for many years to writer Gore Vidal. Soon you'll pass through the low-impact, less touristy town of Atrani. From here, you'll enjoy fine (though slightly less thrilling) scenery all the way to Salerno.

Positano

Specializing in scenery and sand, the easygoing town of Positano hangs halfway between Sorrento and Amalfi town on the most spectacular stretch of the coast.

In the early Middle Ages, Positano was part of the Amalfi Republic, famed for its bold sailors and hearty fleet. But after a big 1343 tsunami and the pirate raids of the Middle Ages, its wealth and power declined. Positano flourished again as a favorite under the Bourbon royal family in the 1700s, when many of its fine mansions were built. Until the late 1800s, the only access was by donkey path or by sea. In the 20th century, Positano became a haven for artists and writers escaping Communist Russia and Nazi Germany. In 1953, Ameri-

can writer John Steinbeck's essay on the town popularized Positano among tourists, and soon after it became a trendy stop. That was when the town gave the world "Moda Positano"—a leisurely *dolce vita* lifestyle of walking barefoot; wearing bright, happy, colorful clothes; and sporting skimpy bikinis.

Today, the village, a breathtaking ▲▲▲ sight from a distance, is a pleasant gathering of cafés and expensive stores draped over an almost comically steep hillside. Terraced gardens and historic houses cascade downhill to the stately Church of Santa Maria Assunta and a broad, pebbly beach. Positano is famous for its fashions—and many of its shops are women's clothing boutiques (linen is a particularly popular item). While many tourists come to Positano hoping to see movie stars, VIPs actually avoid touristy places like this (all you'll find is high prices and women with what locals call "Russian lips"—a popular cosmetic procedure).

Although guests may renovate their faces, for decades, it's been practically impossible to get a building permit in Positano. The "skyline" looks just like it did a century ago. Landowners who want to renovate can't make external changes. Notice the town's white, characteristic Saracen-inspired rooftop domes. Filled with sand, these provide low-tech insulation—to help buildings, in the days before central air, stay cool in summer and warm in winter. Endless staircases are a way of life for the hardy locals. Only one street in Positano allows motorized traffic; the rest are narrow pedestrian lanes.

While Positano has 4,000 residents, an average of 12,000 tourists visit daily from Easter through October. When cruise groups are in town during the day, Positano can be so congested that just walking down the street is a struggle. Until about 17:00, when the tour groups clear out, locals avoid the town's main street altogether. But because hotels don't take large groups (bus access is too difficult), this town—unlike Sorrento—has been spared the worst ravages of big-bus tourism. In winter, hotels shut down and the town once again belongs to the locals.

Consider seeing Positano as a day trip from Sorrento: Take the bus out and the afternoon ferry home, but be sure to check boat schedules when you arrive—the last ferry often leaves before 18:00 and doesn't always run in spring and fall. Or spend the night to enjoy the magic of Positano after dark. The town has a local flavor

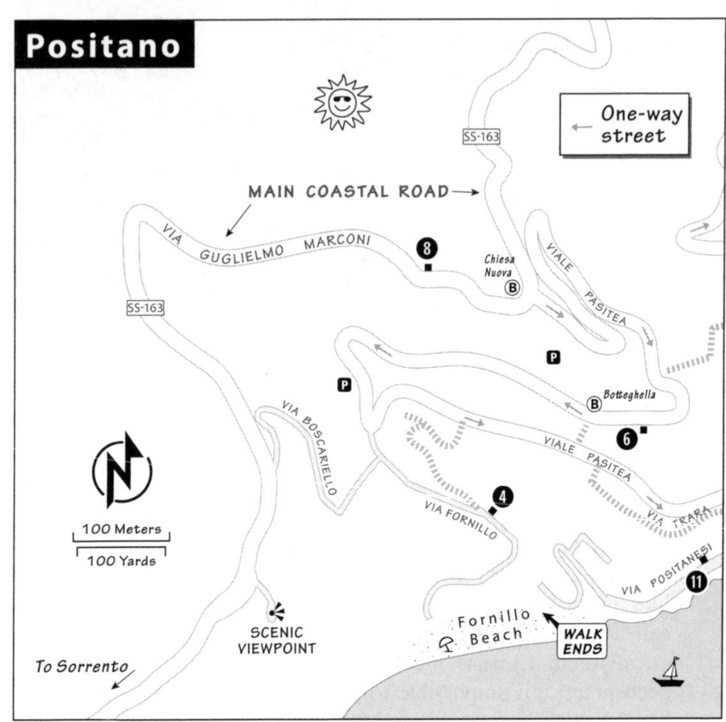

at night, when the grown-ups stroll and the kids play soccer on the church porch.

Orientation to Positano

Squished into a ravine, with narrow alleys that cascade down to the harbor, Positano requires you to stroll, whether you're going up or heading down. The center of town has no main square (unless you count the beach). There's little to do here but eat, window shop, and enjoy the beach and views...hence the town's popularity.

Tourist Information: A small yet helpful TI is tucked away in an alley west of the Church of Santa Maria Assunta. Head down the main set of stairs in front of the church, veering right as the stairs split. At the bottom, jog left and head down the lane to where it dead-ends. The TI is just to the right (daily 9:00-21:00, off-season 10:00-16:00).

Local Guide: Positano native **Lucia Ferrara** (a.k.a. "Zia Lucy") brings substance to this glitzy town. During the day, she leads guided hiking tours, including the "Path of the Gods" high above town (up to 10 people, about 4 miles, 5 hours, €60/person, includes picnic). In the evening, if there's enough demand, she leads a Positano town walking tour (2 hours, departs at 17:00, €30/

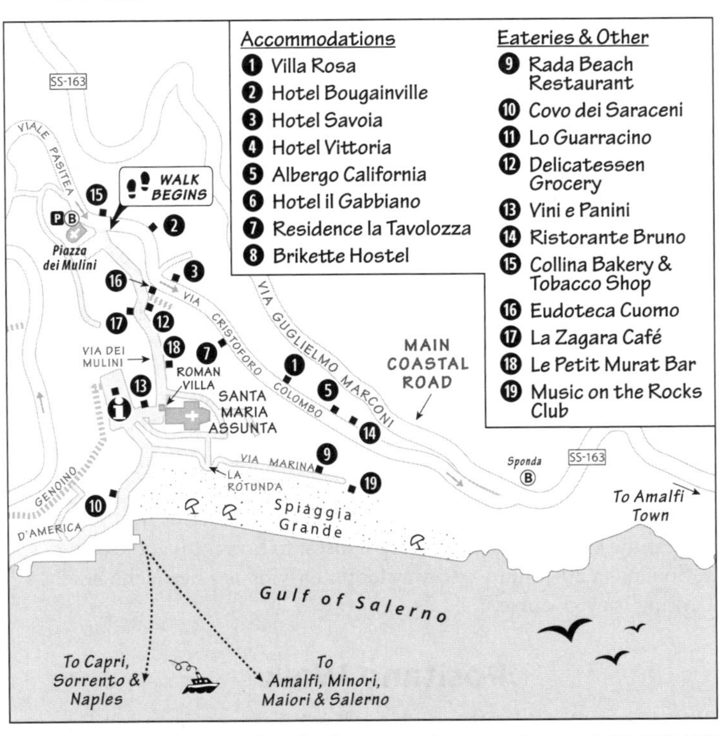

person). She also offers food tours and regional tours (+39 339 272 0971, www.zialucy.com).

ARRIVAL IN POSITANO

The main coastal highway winds above the town. Regional SITA buses stop at two scheduled bus stops at either end of town: **Chiesa Nuova** (at Bar Internazionale, near the Sorrento end of town) and **Sponda** (nearer Amalfi town). Although both stops are near roads leading downhill through the town to the beach, Sponda is closer and less steep; from this stop, it's a scenic 20-minute downhill stroll/shop/munch to the beach.

Neither bus stop has easy **baggage storage.** Positano does have porter services: A porter can meet you at the Sponda bus stop and watch your bags for €10 apiece—but you have to call them in advance (try Positano Porter, +39 089 875 310). A last resort is to get off at the Sponda stop and roll your bags all the way down to Piazza dei Mulini, where the porters tend to hang out. (Their primary base is at the port where they collect bags with the arrival of each ferry.)

If you're catching the SITA bus from Positano, be aware that it may leave from the Sponda stop five minutes before the printed departure time. There's simply no room for the bus to wait, so in case the driver is early, you should be, too. Buy tickets at the tobacco shop on Piazza dei Mulini in the town center. To skip the walk up to the bus stop, catch a shuttle bus from the piazza (see next).

Piazza dei Mulini is as far into town as motor traffic can go. This is the drop spot for Positano's dizzy little **shuttle buses** (marked *Interno Positano*) that constantly loop through town, connecting the lower town with the two bus stops up on the highway (2/hour, €1.50 tickets at tobacco shop, €2 on board). It's also the stop for taxis and other transfer services. Drivers may find parking nearby. If you need cash, legitimate ATMs attached to banks are just downhill from the piazza. And, Piazza dei Mulini is where my self-guided Positano Walk starts (see below).

Coming from the **ferry,** you can give luggage to one of the porter services or lug everything uphill yourself. Follow crowds up wide stairs to the large church, then follow the trellis to Piazza dei Mulini. You'll be doing the reverse of my Positano Walk (described next).

Drivers must go with the one-way flow, entering the town only at the Chiesa Nuova bus stop (closest to Sorrento) and exiting at Sponda (a 20-minute one-way loop). Driving is a headache here. Parking is even worse.

Positano Walk

This short, self-guided downhill stroll will help you get your bearings, from top to bottom.

• *Start at...*

Piazza dei Mulini: This "square" is the town center's main junction—as close to the beach as vehicles can get—and the lower stop for the little shuttle bus. The **Collina bakery** (long hours daily) overlooks the commotion and is a nice place for sandwiches, salads, gelato, or pastries (and late-night pizza). Looking uphill, the street to the left is lined with quality linen shops. The terraces stair-stepping up beyond Positano once provided land for growing flax—the plant that made the linen industry here possible.

Dip into the little yellow **Church of the Holy Rosary** (by the bus stop), with a serene 12th-century interior. Up front, to the right of the main altar, find the delicately carved fragment of a Roman sarcophagus (first century BC). Positano sits upon the site of a sprawling Roman villa, and we'll see a few reminders of that age as we walk.

In summer, look for a popular ***granita* stand** on the square, where the family has been following the same secret lemon slush recipe for generations.

Now continue downhill (past a couple of rare ATMs) into town, passing a variety of **shops**—many selling linen and ceramics. These industries boomed when tourists discovered Positano. The

beach-inspired Moda Positano fashion label was born as a break from the rigid dress code of the 1950s. (For tips on shopping for linen, see "Shopping," under "Sights in Positano," later). Positano also considers itself an artists' colony, and you'll see many **galleries** featuring the work of area artists.

• *Wander downhill to the "fork" in the road (stairs to the left, road to the right). You've reached...*

Midtown: At **Eudoteca Cuomo** (#3), butchers Pasquale and Rosario stock fine local red wines and are happy to explain their virtues. They also make homemade sausages, salami, and panini—good for a quick lunch. The smaller set of stairs leads to the recommended **Delicatessen grocery,** where Emilia can fix you a good picnic.

La Zagara (across the lane from the steps, at #10, with a leafy terrace) is a pricey pastry shop by day and a restaurant by night. Tempting pastries such as the rum-drenched *babà* (a southern Italian favorite) fill the window display. A bit farther downhill, **Brunella** (on the right, at #24) is respected for traditional quality and Positano-made linens.

Across the street, the ritzy **Hotel Palazzo Murat** fills what was once a grand Benedictine monastery. Napoleon, fearing the power of the Church, had many such monasteries closed during his rule here. In the early 1800s, this one became a private palace, named for his brother-in-law, who was briefly the King of Naples. Glance into the plush courtyard to appreciate the scene. Continuing on, under a fragrant wisteria trellis, you'll pass "street merchants' gulch," where artisans display their goodies. This lane can be a bottleneck creating a human traffic jam at peak tourist times.

• *Continue straight down. You'll run into a fork at the big church. For now, turn right and go downstairs to Piazza Flavio Gioia, facing the big...*

Church of Santa Maria Assunta: This church, which sits upon Roman ruins (viewable with a tour, see the "Roman Villa Complex" listing, later), was once the abbey of Positano's 12th-century Benedictine monastery. Originally Romanesque, it got an extreme Baroque makeover in the 18th century, when the town was booming and the coast was clear of pirate attacks. Note that the facade is mostly fascist-style, built in the 1930s. But, at the far left, a bit of the original Baroque front survives (now a chapel with a cute display of manger scenes).

Step **inside** the church and find these items: In the first chapel on the left is a fine manger scene *(presepe)*. Its original 18th-century figurines give you an idea of the folk costumes of the age. Above the main altar is the gilded Black Madonna, an icon-like Byzantine painting likely brought here from Constantinople by monks in the 12th century (and a reminder of the importance of trade here in the Middle Ages). But locals prefer a more romantic origin story for the gilded painting: Saracen pirates had the icon on their ship as plunder. A violent storm hit—sure to sink the evil ship. The painting of Mary spoke, saying, *"Posa, posa"* (lay me down), and the ship glided safely to this harbor. The pirates were so stricken they became Christians. Locals kept the painting, and the town became known as *Posa-tano* (recalling Mary's command).

To the right of the altar in a small side chapel, a freestanding display case holds a silver-and-copper bust of St. Vitus (along with his bones, now holy relics). He's the town patron, who brought Christianity here in about AD 300. In the adjacent niche (on the right) is a rare 1599 painting by Fabrizio Santafede of Baby Jesus being circumcised, considered the finest historic painting in town.

Back outside, you'll see the **bell tower,** dating from 1707. Above the door, it sports a thousand-year-old Romanesque relief scavenged from the original church. The scene—a wolf mermaid with seven little fish—was a reminder to worshippers of how integral the sea was to their livelihood. Nicknamed "our pagan protector," it's a good example of how early Christians incorporated pagan elements into their worship. Notice the characteristic shallow, white "insulation domes" on rooftops in front of the church.

To the Beachfront: Directly in front of the church facade, steps lead down to the tiny Piazzetta del Saracino and Via del Saracino (which dead-ends off to the right). Exploring, you'll find ceramic shops, the TI, linen shops, and sandal makers. Following the lane (Via del Saracino), which ultimately wraps under the church, find a tiny sandal shop (on the right at #18) called Carmine Todisco de l'Antica Positano, where friendly cobbler Carmine is often hard at work. From there a tunnel-like lane leads directly below the church to the **Positano Paradiso Bar,** which has a very simple self-service menu of hot sandwiches, pastries, gelato, and drinks, and amazing seating overlooking the beach (they have a second dining room next door, open long hours daily). Continuing from here, you reach the beachfront terrace between two big restaurants, two Roman columns, and two lions.

La Rotonda: This is the town gathering point in the evening, where local boys try to hustle tourist girls into the nearby nightclub. Step down to beach level. Residents traded their historic baptistery font with Amalfi town for the two iron lions you see facing the beach. Around the staircase, you'll also see some original Roman columns, scavenged from the villa buried by the Mount Vesuvius eruption in AD 79. Look up and admire the colorful majolica tiles so typical of church domes in this region.

Positano's **beach,** called Spiaggia Grande, is atmospherically littered with a commotion of fishing boats and recreational craft. Kiosks on the beach sell excursions to Capri and elsewhere.

Looking out over the beach from this point, you can see three of the **watchtowers** built centuries ago to protect the Amalfi Coast from Saracen pirates: one on the far-left horizon, just below Praiano; a small one on the Li Galli Islands, ahead and right; and the rectangular one far to the right, marking the far end of Fornillo Beach. Defenders used these towers—strategically situated within sight of each other—to relay smoke signals. In more recent times, the tower on the right (near Fornillo Beach) was a hangout for artists, who holed up inside for inspiration. (The people of Positano pride themselves on being artists rather than snazzy jet-setters like those in Capri.)

As you face out to sea, on the far-left side of the beach (below Rada Restaurant) is **Music on the Rocks,** a chic club that's the only remaining piece of the 1970s scene, when Positano really rocked. While it's dead until very late, you're welcome to walk through the cool troglo-disco interior to go upstairs to the Fly Bar for a scenic (if expensive) cocktail.

• *Now turn right and wander across the beach. Behind the kiosks that sell boat tickets, find the steps to the* ***path*** *that climbs up and over, past a 13th-century lookout fort from Saracen pirate days, to the next beach. It's a worthwhile little five-minute walk through a shady ravine to...*

Fornillo Beach: This is where locals go for better swimming and to escape some of the tourist crowds. Via Positanesi d'America is the lane (lit at night) leading to the beach. It's named for the people who emigrated to America between the 1860s and the 1940s (more than 50 percent of Positano's population) and sent money back to build this path. (Some locals remember when priests used to say at Mass, "And now, let's pray for Positanesi d'America.")

• *Our walk is over. Time to relax. When you're ready to return, go back the way you came to the main beach. Although tempting, Via Fornillo continues straight up the cliffside with a whopping 200-plus stairs...not for the faint of heart.*

Sights in Positano

Beaches

Spiaggia Grande, Positano's pebbly and sandy primary beach, is colorful with umbrellas as it stretches wide around the cove. It's mostly private (pay €35-100 to enter, includes lounge chair and umbrella, most expensive near Music on the Rocks). There's a tiny free section near the middle, close to where the boats take off. Look for the pay showers. The nearest WC is beneath the steps to the right (as you face the water).

Fornillo Beach, a less crowded option just around the bend (to the west) of Spiaggia Grande, is favored by residents, with more affordable chair/umbrella rentals (€20-30) and a wider free area. It has a mellow Robinson Crusoe vibe, with a sturdy Saracen tower keeping watch overhead. This beach has a few humble snack bars and lunch eateries. Note that its position, tucked back in the rocks, means it gets shade earlier in the day than the main beach.

Boat Trips

Boats serving Positano pull up to the dock at the west end of Spiaggia Grande (to the right as you face the sea; booths sell tickets). Also consider renting a rowboat, or see whether they can talk you into taking a boat tour. Passenger boats run to Amalfi (with transfers to Minori and Maiori), Capri, Salerno, and Sorrento, plus a couple per day to Naples; see "Getting Around the Amalfi Coast" on page 180.

▲Roman Villa Complex (MAR Positano Villa Romana)

The entire town center of today's Positano—from the church all the way up to Piazza dei Mulini—sits upon the site of a huge Roman villa complex, buried when Mount Vesuvius erupted in AD 79. In 2004, archaeologists started excavating an exciting find under the church crypt: a surviving room from the villa. Now a 45-minute guided tour of the excavated remains (limited to 10 people at a time) will take you down a safe, well-lit stairway to see the walls and floor of what might have been a dining room. The walls are frescoed with decorations not unlike those at Pompeii, though with much more variance in color. Artifacts from the excavation are nicely displayed, and the guide explains the history of the church directly above you, as well as its crypt.

Cost and Hours: €15, tours daily April-Oct 9:00-19:00 on the hour, Nov-March 10:00-16:00, buy in advance at TI as they can sell out, can also book online in advance; Piazza Flavio Gioia 7, +39 331 208 5821, www.marpositano.it.

Visiting the Villa: You're standing in what is believed to be the only Roman-era villa that existed in this area, which predates the town of Positano. The villa was likely only accessible by sea, which originally would have come very close to where you stand now. When Vesuvius erupted, it blew so much ash here (and caused such massive landslides) that it created a new shoreline, as also happened in Herculaneum.

As you enter, peer six feet down through the glass floor to see the most recent excavations from 2021, including some Roman ceiling tiles that collapsed from the weight of the ash and ensuing mudslides when Vesuvius erupted. You'll also see the upper crypt of the previous church (from between the early 17th and late 18th centuries), where you learn about the burial process (which was used until Napoleonic times, when the practice ended for sanitary reasons). Only monks were buried in this area.

Your guide then describes the remarkably preserved frescoes of the villa, which likely belonged to a Roman aristocrat or a politician (evidenced by the "Egyptian" blue paint, which was extremely hard to find—its vibrancy is due to the copper content). After almost 2,000 years the colors are still vibrant, thanks to the ash and pumice, which kept the area protected from humidity. Look down at the tiny mosaics covering the floor.

The next room has some well-preserved cooking instruments from the villa, and lots of artifacts from the crypt, including several jaw bones that show evidence of a poor diet. You'll also see some of the belongings found buried with the monks.

Continuing to the area under today's altar, you'll see the medieval crypt, where anyone who was not a monk was buried. Notice the different column styles—even back then recycling was in vogue. When the church was built, they reused old Roman columns. (You can even see where excavators left an old column partially exposed behind the newer stone.)

As you exit, you'll see where new digs may be taking place by the time you visit, as Italy's Minister of Culture has granted more money to continue excavating the site.

Exploring Back-Lane Positano

Ninety percent of visitors to Positano spend 90 percent of their time on the main drag between the beach and Piazza dei Mulini. But, of course, most of the town is not on that street. Positano's "back lanes" are actually all stepped lanes—everything here is very steep.

For a delightful look at Positano behind the scenes, consider this (downhill and shady) adventure: Catch the shuttle bus marked *Interno Positano* that constantly circles the town from Piazza dei Mulini (details earlier, under "Arrival in Positano"). Enjoy three-quarters of the big scenic circle from the bus. Then (after passing the two big bus stops—Sponda and Chiesa Nuova) hop out at the Botteghella stop (tell the driver ahead of time), and venture off the road into Positano's peaceful parallel world of stepped lanes. Simply keep going downhill following signs marked *to the beach* (not *to the center*).

As you explore, consider that even these remote neighborhoods are being gutted by the "Airbnb effect," as locals can no longer compete with tourists for rooms and are being driven from their hometown by soaring rents charged by opportunistic landlords.

Shopping

Linen: Garments made of **linen** (especially women's dresses) are popular items in Positano. Flax and linen were the big industry here in pretourism days. To find a good-quality piece that will last, look for "Made in Positano" (or at least "Made in Italy") on the label, and check the percentage of linen; 60 percent or more is good quality, and 100 percent is best. Two companies with top reputations and multiple outlets are **Brunella** and **Pepito's** (each has shops on Via Colombo, near the top of town; along Viale Pasitea, a main drag; and along claustrophobic Via del Saracino, near the bottom of town, parallel to the beach).

Ceramics: One of the oldest ceramics stores in Positano, **Ceramica Assunta** carries colorful Solimene dinnerware and more at two locations (Via Cristoforo Colombo 97 and 137).

Custom Sandals: Positano has a tradition of handmade sandals, crafted to your specifications while you wait (prices start at about €70).

Nightlife

For strolling and making the scene, the *passegiata* action is, not surprisingly, along the harborfront. For a drink on the beach, you have plenty of options.

For a more peaceful experience, spend a couple of extra euros for a special memory. **Le Petit Murat Bar,** in the garden of Hotel Murat (non-hotel guests are heartily welcome), is located on the main drag midway between the Church of Santa Maria Assunta and Piazza dei Mulini. It's elegant, away from the rabble (as is fitting for the building's history), and offers chill music nightly, wonderful service, and great cocktails.

The big-time action in the old town center is the impressive club **Music on the Rocks,** literally carved into the rocks on the beach (opens at 23:00 mid-April-Oct, but the party starts even later; there's often a €15-30 cover charge on weekends and in summer, which includes a drink; closed off-season; Via Grotte Dell'Incanto 51, +39 089 875 874, www.musicontherocks.it).

Sleeping in Positano

Most of these hotels are on Via Cristoforo Colombo, which leads from the Sponda bus stop down into the village (ideal for arrival by bus). Most places close in the winter. Drivers can expect to pay at least €30 per day to park.

€€€€ Villa Rosa decorates its 12 spacious rooms plus one apartment with—you guessed it—roses. Most rooms have views plus a large terrace, which is the perfect place to have your breakfast (family rooms with Jacuzzi, no elevator but porters available, Via Cristoforo Colombo 127, +39 089 811 955, www.villarosapositano.it, info@villarosapositano.it).

€€€€ Hotel Bougainville, family-run for over 50 years, rents 16 comfortable rooms, half with balconies. Everything's bright, modern, and tasteful (RS%—must mention this book when you book direct; rooms without views are cheaper, Via Cristoforo Colombo 25, +39 089 875 047, www.bougainville.it, info@bougainville.it).

€€€€ Hotel Savoia, run by the friendly D'Aiello family, has 40 sizeable, breezy, bright, simple, tiled rooms (RS%, most rooms with balcony or terrace, some cheaper nonview rooms, Via Cristoforo Colombo 73, +39 089 875 003, www.savoiapositano.it, info@savoiapositano.it).

€€€€ Hotel Vittoria sits just west of the town center with 20 open, spacious rooms and arched ceilings that feel right out of Positano's 1950s boom era. Sprawling up a cliffside, they offer a free porter service (tips appreciated). Most rooms have balconies, with views overlooking the town (buffet breakfast, uphill from Fornillo Beach on Via Fornillo 19, +39 089 875 049, www.hotelvittoriapositano.com, info@hotelvittoriapostiano.it).

€€€€ Albergo California has 15 spacious rooms (all with lofty views), a grand terrace draped with vines, and full breakfasts (they also offer discounts on lunch and dinner at their restaurant). The Cinque family—including Maria, Bronx-born son John, and grandchildren Giuseppe and Maria—will welcome you (pay parking, Via Cristoforo Colombo 141, +39 089 875 382, www.hotelcaliforniapositano.it, info@hotelcaliforniapositano.it).

€€€€ Hotel il Gabbiano lies west of the busy town center and has 19 simple rooms with dated furnishings, plus one apartment. All have a view terrace. From here you can explore the many eateries downhill (past the curve) along Viale Pasitea without having to trek into the main part of town (Viale Pasitea 310, +39 089 875 306, www.ilgabbianopositano.com, info@ilgabbianopositano.com).

€€€ Residence la Tavolozza is an attractive six-room hotel (doubles only) warmly run by sisters and fourth-generation owners Francesca and Paola, who recently took over the reins from their mother, Celeste (cheh-LEHS-tay). Each cheerily tiled room comes with a view, a terrace, and silence. Paola also leads tours at the Roman villa (lavish à la carte breakfast extra, confirm by phone if arriving late, Via Cristoforo Colombo 10, +39 089 875 040, www.latavolozzapositano.it, info@latavolozzapositano.it).

¢ Brikette Hostel is your best budget option in this ritzy town. Not a party hostel, it has a quiet, mellow, and mature vibe. Its 45 dorm beds are pricey by hostel standards, but you're in Positano. It has a great sun and breakfast terrace and a youthful ambience (breakfast extra, cheap dinners, leave bus at Chiesa Nuova stop and backtrack uphill 500 feet to Via G. Marconi 358, +39 351 980 0821, www.hostel-positano.com, hostelpositano@gmail.com, Cristiana and Peter).

Eating in Positano

Down at the beach, several interchangeable restaurants with view terraces leave people fat and happy, albeit with skinnier wallets (figure €20 pastas and *secondi,* plus pricey drinks and sides, and a cover charge). Little distinguishes one place from the next; all are scenic, convenient, and overpriced.

€€€€ Rada Beach Restaurant (the more casual sister of a fancier rooftop restaurant) has a yacht-clubby vibe with a respected chef and an inviting menu. Their tables literally line the beach at the more peaceful far left end, service is great, and considering the location, the price is right (daily, Località Grotte dell'Incanto 51, +39 089 875 874, www.radapositano.it/rada-beach).

€€€ Covo dei Saraceni offers the best budget value on the beach, with good pizza and salads, tables overlooking the action, and an attached *gelateria* (daily, on the far right as you face the sea, where Via Positanesi d'America starts, +39 089 875 400).

€€€ Lo Guarracino, a local favorite for its great views, is on the path to Fornillo Beach, with good food at prices similar to the beachfront places (daily 12:00-15:30 & 18:30-22:30, closed Nov-March, follow path behind the boat-ticket kiosks 5 minutes to Via Positanesi d'America 12, +39 089 875 794).

Picnics: If a picnic dinner on your balcony or the beach sounds good, sunny Emilia at the **Delicatessen** grocery store can supply the ingredients: *antipasto misto,* pastas, home-cooked dishes, and sandwiches made-to-order. She'll heat it up for you and throw in picnic ware. Come early for the best selection (all sold by weight, daily 7:00-22:00, shorter hours off-season, Via dei Mulini 5, +39 089 875 489). **Vini e Panini** (a.k.a. "The Wine Shop"), another small grocery, is a block from the beach just behind the church steps. Daniela, the fifth-generation owner, speaks English and happily makes sandwiches to order. Choose between the "Caprese" (mozzarella and tomato) and the "Positano" (mozzarella, tomato, and prosciutto), or create your own (also well-priced regional wines, daily 8:00-20:00, until 22:00 in summer, closed mid-Nov-mid-March, +39 089 875 175).

"Uptown": The unassuming, family-run **€€€ Ristorante Bruno** is handy to my listed hotels on Via Cristoforo Colombo. While expensive, it has nice views and is worth considering if you want a meal without hiking down into the town center (daily 12:00-23:00, closed Nov-Feb, near the top of Via Cristoforo Colombo at #157, +39 089 875 179).

Amalfi Town

This tiny town has a big history. After Rome fell, the town of Amalfi was one of the first to trade goods—cloth, spices, carpets, and paper—between Europe and points east. Its heyday was the 10th and 11th centuries, when it was a powerful maritime republic—a trading power with a fleet that controlled this region and rivaled Pisa, Genoa, and Venice. The Republic of Amalfi founded a hospital in Jerusalem and claims to have founded the Knights of Malta order—even giving them the Amalfi cross, which became the famous Maltese cross. Amalfi minted its own coins and established "rules of the sea"—the basics of which survive today.

In 1343, this little powerhouse was suddenly destroyed by a tsunami caused by an undersea earthquake. That disaster, compounded by devastating plagues, left Amalfi a humble backwater. Much of the culture of this entire region was driven by this town—but because it fell from power, Amalfi doesn't always get the credit it deserves. Today its 5,000 residents live off tourism. The coast's namesake is not as picturesque as Positano or as well connected as Sorrento, but you can feel Amalfi's historical gravitas lurking behind its commercial and touristic bustle.

Just as touristy as Positano, Amalfi is packed during the day with big-bus tours (whose drivers pay €60 merely to stop and unload groups). A mix of traffic congestion, chaos, and greed is your first impression. Things that shouldn't be complicated seem impossible. In what must be the wealthiest town in Italy, the tiniest of services are unaffordable. But Amalfi's charms reveal themselves early and late in the day, when the crowds are gone.

Orientation to Amalfi Town

Amalfi's waterfront is a busy transportation hub. Right next to each other at Piazza Flavio Gioia are the bus station, ferry docks, a parking lot, and a place to leave your bags.

Buses: Amalfi is the terminus for SITA buses to Sorrento (via Positano), Ravello, and Salerno (via Minori and Maiori). While there is no actual bus station, you'll see two stops on Piazza Flavio Gioia: One for Ravello (on the left when facing the water) and all other stops (on the right when facing the water, basically in front of the fountain—you'll see the crowds). To buy a ticket, find the person in a brightly colored vest.

Boats: Plenty of boats link Amalfi to and from Positano, Capri, Sorrento, Minori, Maiori, and Salerno. On the same piazza is a line of boat company ticket booths.

Parking: While there is a little parking on Piazza Flavio Gioia, realistically you'll want to go to the huge underground Luna Rossa garage, burrowed into the hillside just past the town (between Amalfi and Atrani).

Bag Check: A small gift shop (look for the sign, a few doors to the right of the city gate at #15 on the coastal road) charges €5 to watch your bag.

Tourist Information: While there is no office, the ticket desk at the Arsenal Museum is essentially a TI (Tue-Sun 9:00-19:00, closed Mon, facing Piazza Flavio Gioia under the big road).

Don't Get Stranded: When day-tripping to Amalfi, check locally to confirm the departure time for the last return bus or boat (in winter this can be as early as 19:00). In peak season, don't plan to leave on the last bus or boat of the day: If it's full, your only way home might be a €100 taxi ride. Get in line early. Ferries are more frequent and carry more people than buses.

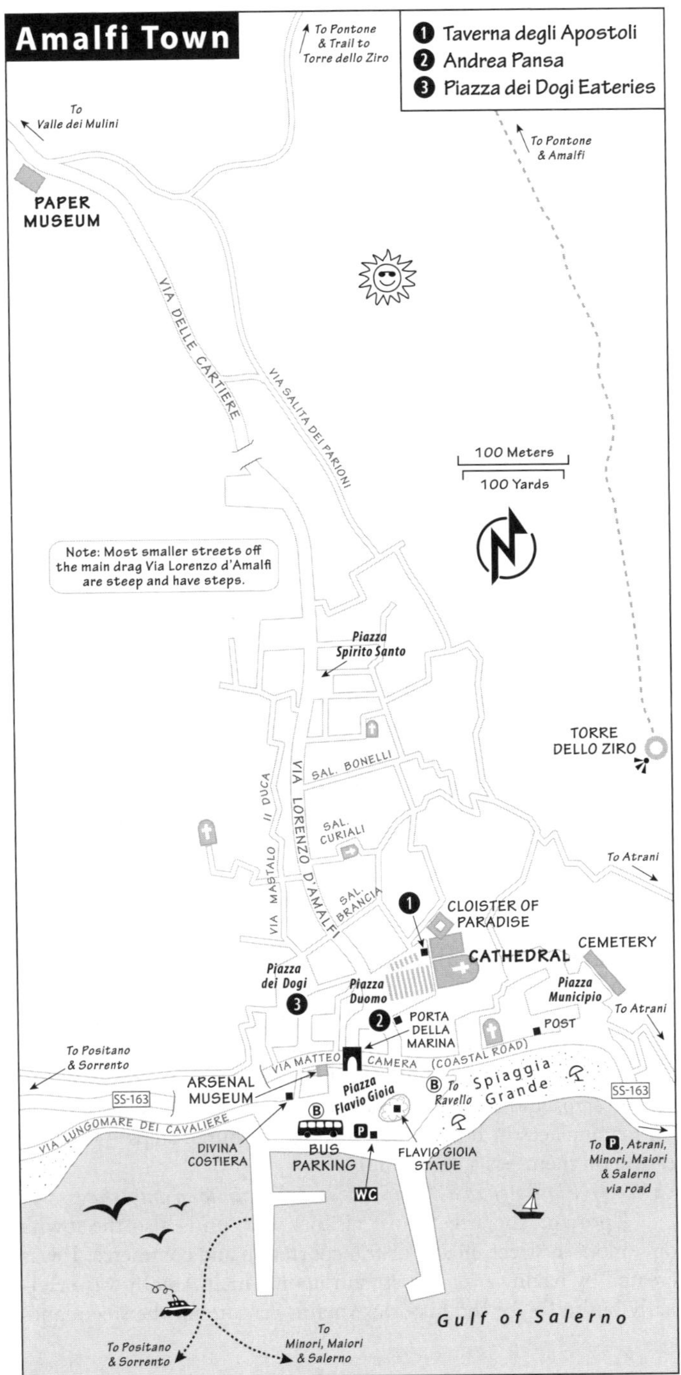
Amalfi Town
1 Taverna degli Apostoli
2 Andrea Pansa
3 Piazza dei Dogi Eateries
To Pontone & Trail to Torre dello Ziro
To Valle dei Mulini
PAPER MUSEUM
To Pontone & Amalfi
VIA DELLE CARTIERE
VIA SALITA DEI PARIONI
100 Meters
100 Yards
Note: Most smaller streets off the main drag Via Lorenzo d'Amalfi are steep and have steps.
Piazza Spirito Santo
TORRE DELLO ZIRO
SAL. BONELLI
VIA LORENZO D'AMALFI
VIA MASTALO II DUCA
SAL. CURIALI
SAL. BRANCIA
To Atrani
CLOISTER OF PARADISE
CATHEDRAL
CEMETERY
Piazza dei Dogi
Piazza Duomo
Piazza Municipio
To Atrani
PORTA DELLA MARINA
POST
To Positano & Sorrento
VIA MATTEO CAMERA (COASTAL ROAD)
ARSENAL MUSEUM
Piazza Flavio Gioia
To Ravello
Spiaggia Grande
SS-163
SS-163
VIA LUNGOMARE DEI CAVALIERE
DIVINA COSTIERA
BUS PARKING
FLAVIO GIOIA STATUE
To P, Atrani, Minori, Maiori & Salerno via road
WC
Gulf of Salerno
To Positano & Sorrento
To Minori, Maiori & Salerno

Sights in Amalfi Town

Amalfi's one main street runs up from the waterfront through a deep valley, with stairways to courtyards and houses on either side. It's worth walking uphill to the workaday upper end of town. Super-atmospheric, narrow, stepped side lanes branch off, squeezing between hulking old buildings. If you hear water under a grate in the main street, it's the creek that runs down the ravine—a reminder that the town originally straddled the stream but later paved it over to create its main drag.

Amalfi Town Walk

This short, self-guided walk takes you from the waterfront's tourist crush uphill to the quieter, more traditional upper town.

• *Start near the beach at...*

Piazza Flavio Gioia: The small square on the waterfront is the transportation hub and a commotion of traffic and people. Stand 20 paces in front of the gate leading into town with the colorful tile map. Before entering, do this counterclockwise spin tour:

The colorful tile above the Porta della Marina gateway shows off the trading domain of the maritime Republic of Amalfi. Just to the left, along the busy road, a series of arches marks the long, narrow, vaulted halls of Amalfi's arsenal—where ships were built in the 11th century. One of these halls is now the little Arsenal Museum (where you can also get tourist info). Spinning farther left, find the line of ferry ticket booths, a bus stop (for Sorrento, Positano, Minori, and Maiori), the statue of Flavio Gioia (the mariner who locals proudly proclaim invented the compass), and another bus stop (for Ravello). Behind that is the public beach and several beach-fronting restaurants.

• *Now walk through the Porta della Marina gate and up to the busy square facing the cathedral.*

Piazza Duomo: This is probably the most touristy piazza on the entire Amalfi Coast. The fountain memorializes St. Andrew (crucified on an X-shaped cross). His relics are inside the cathedral—the most important sight in town—up the long staircase. (The cathedral is described later.) Here you may see people sitting on the steps and licking a gelato—fitting in this hedonistic town (in many places in Italy, simply sitting on church steps—let alone eating on them—is a big no-no).

• *Hike up Via Lorenzo d'Amalfi, the town's main (and only) drag.*

Uptown: The street most visitors walk on is also the town's only modern street, made for transportation and commerce. It was created by paving over the stream upon which Amalfi was originally built. To see the historic Amalfi, venture up the steep lanes and staircases on either side and leave the tourists and their gelato cones behind.

As you get farther away from the water, Amalfi becomes less glitzy and more traditional. As you walk, the main drag changes names to Via Delle Cartiere. Fifteen minutes up is the Paper Museum (see listing, later). On the way up to the museum, don't miss the huge, outdoor *presepi* (Nativity scenes) on your left.

From the museum, the road narrows and you can turn off onto a path leading up a ravine to the shaded Valle dei Mulini (Valley of the Mills); it's full of paper-mill ruins that recall this once proud and prosperous industry.

• *If you didn't do it on the way up, as you return downhill be sure to explore up the winding and narrow lanes and arcaded passages on either side of Via Lorenzo d'Amalfi.*

Arsenal Museum

This small, underground museum just across the road from the bus station tells a bit about Amalfi's maritime glory years. Stepping into the single long room under the dramatic vaulted stone ceiling, you can just tell that 1,000 years ago, they made ships here.

Cost and Hours: €3; Tue-Sun 9:00-19:00, closed Mon; Piazza Flavio Gioia, www.arsenalediamalfi.it.

Cathedral

This church is "Amalfi Romanesque" (a mix of Moorish and Byzantine flavors, built c. 1000-1300), with a fanciful Neo-Byzantine facade from the 19th century. Climb the imposing stairway, which functions as a mini Spanish Steps-style hangout zone and a handy outdoor theater. The 1,000-year-old bronze door at the top was given to Amalfi by a wealthy local merchant who had it made in Constantinople. Visitors are directed on a one-way circuit through the cathedral complex with four stops: the cloister, original basilica, crypt, and cathedral.

Cost and Hours: €4, daily 9:00-19:00, shorter hours off-season, closed Jan-Feb. The cathedral—but not the rest of the complex—can be entered free for prayer or discreet visits daily 7:30-10:00 & 17:00-19:30; it's closed 10:00-17:00 except as part of the paid visit (+39 089 871 324, www.parrocchiaamalfi.com). There's a fine, free WC at the top of the steps (through unmarked green door, just a few steps before ticket booth, ask at booth).

Visiting the Cathedral: You'll follow a self-guided, one-way tour of the complex, beginning in a courtyard of 120 graceful columns—the **"Cloister of Paradise."** This was the cemetery for nobles in the 13th century (note their stone sarcophagi). Don't miss the fine view of the bell tower and its majolica tiles.

The original ninth-century church, known as the **Basilica of the Crucifix,** boasts a fine 13th-century wooden crucifix. Today the basilica is a museum filled with the cathedral's art treasures. The Angevin Mitre (Mitra Angioina), with a "pavement of tiny pearls" setting off its gold and gems, has been worn by bishops since the 14th century. Also on display (waist-high, facing the altar) is a carved wooden decoration from a Saracen pirate ship that wrecked just outside of town in 1544 during a freak storm. The cathedral is dedicated to St. Andrew, who believers credit with causing the storm and saving the town from certain pillage and plunder.

Down the stairs to the right of the basilica's altar is the **Crypt of St. Andrew.** Just as Venice needed St. Mark to get on the pilgrimage map, Amalfi needed St. Andrew—one of the apostles who, along with his brother Peter, left their fishing nets to become the original "fishers of men." Under the huge bronze statue, you'll see a reliquary holding what are believed to be Andrew's remains (kneel at the back of the crypt for a better view). These were brought here from Constantinople in 1206 during the Crusades—an indication of the wealth and importance of Amalfi back then.

Climb the stairs up into the **cathedral** itself. Behind the main altar is a painting of St. Andrew martyred on an X-shaped cross. The altar is flanked by two (brown) Egyptian granite columns supporting a triumphal arch.

Step up to the gated chapel (right of altar) to see the gold and silver **reliquary** showing off one of the most important relics of the Amalfi Coast—the skull of St. Andrew. The room is ringed with other saints and their relics. These are from the 16th century and are in response to the Protestant Reformation, as the Roman Catholic Church dug in with its Counter-Reformation, fighting the message of Luther with more saints and more relics.

Check out the pilasters near the front of the nave and notice that, while stuccoed Baroque, the **pillars** hide ancient columns from the previous church inside. In the rear corner on the right, a purple porphyry monument from ancient Rome was turned into a baptismal font.

Before leaving the church, stand in the center of the **nave** and look up to appreciate the inlaid marble work and the fine baroque décor; on your way out don't miss the delicate mother-of-pearl crucifix (right of door in back).

▲Paper Museum (Museo della Carta)

This excellent little museum in a 13th-century paper mill—worth ▲▲▲ for paper enthusiasts—makes for a good excuse to break free from the crowds and walk up Amalfi's main drag to a quieter, more local part of town. Paper has been an important industry here since Amalfi's glory days in the Middle Ages. Millworkers would pound rags into pulp in a big vat, pull it up using a screen, and air-dry each sheet (the same technique used to make artisan paper today—look for it at shops in town). At this cavernous, cool museum a guide collects groups at the entrance (no particular schedule, about 4/hour) for a 25-minute tour. The guide recounts the history and process of papermaking and turns on the museum's vintage machinery. You'll see how the Amalfi River (which you can still hear rumbling underfoot) powered this important industry, and you'll learn the origins of the term "watermark." Kids can dip a screen into the rag pool and make their own paper. It's amazing to think this factory produced paper through 1969 (when it was replaced by a modern facility up the valley).

Cost and Hours: €7, includes guided tour; daily 10:00-19:00, shorter hours and closed Mon Nov-Jan, closed Feb, last entry 40 minutes before closing; a 15-minute walk up the main street from the cathedral—follow signs to *Museo della Carta* at Via delle Cartiere 23; +39 089 830 4561, www.museodellacarta.it.

NEAR AMALFI TOWN

Hiking Between Amalfi and Atrani

The tiny village of Atrani (described next) is just a 15-minute walk from Amalfi and makes a good target for a hike. Leave Amalfi via the main road heading east and stay on the water side until the promenade ends. Cross the street, continue a few more yards, then go up the whitewashed staircase just past the pizzeria. From here, twist up through old lanes to a paved route that takes you over the hill—with views over town and down the coast—before it drops you into Atrani.

To save time and sweat on the return walk, follow the car ramp angling up from the beach toward Amalfi, looking back for views all the way to Maiori. Then walk up the stairs and through the restaurant terrace, carefully cross the busy street, and enter the big, long tunnel next to the parking garage—this will deposit you in the middle of Amalfi.

From Atrani, you could continue up to Ravello. But unless you're part mountain goat, you'll probably prefer catching the bus to Ravello from Amalfi town instead and then hiking scenically downhill.

Atrani Town

Just a 15-minute walk from Amalfi, tiny **Atrani** has an entirely different vibe, with almost no tourism. This old fishing town, which dates back at least to Roman times, has been a draw for writers and artists over the ages, including graphic artist M. C. Escher, who was smitten by Atrani's evocative setting and featured the town in some of his work.

The Amalfi Coast road cuts across the front of Atrani on an arched viaduct that seems like a dam, keeping the town from spilling onto its photogenic beach. Passageways through the arches allow access from the town to the beach, where there's also a small parking lot. That viaduct also ruins the charm and appeal of the town from a tourism point of view. (So, the hordes pack into Amalfi instead.) Atrani's like a shadowy, ignored cousin of Amalfi.

With few tourists, a delightful town square, and a free, sandy beach, Atrani has none of Amalfi's trendy resort feel. **Piazza Umberto I** is the core of town, with cafés, restaurants, and little grocery stores that can make sandwiches. A whitewashed staircase leads up to the serene and beautiful town church (under the clock face).

Exploring the town, hike up its single main street, **Via dei Dogi,** which runs from the beach through the square to the top of town. Narrow alleys and stairways, surrounded by terraces of lemon trees, invite exploration of hillsides piled with pastel-colored buildings and old churches. In an arcade parallel to the main street, 100 yards above the main square, is a small Escher exhibit. (And across the street is a surprisingly pleasant—and handy—WC; insert a coin and the door slides open.)

Atrani's much-photographed **beach,** known for its wonderfully clear water, is a mix of pebbles and dark sand. It's divided by the outflow of the Dragone River and, in summer, is covered by lounge chairs and umbrellas for rent; a small portion far to the right (when facing the sea) is free. In the afternoon, the rocky promenade along the left side of the beach is a nice place to sit and join the locals enjoying the fading sunlight.

Eating in Amalfi Town

On the Main Square, Piazza Duomo: Several pricey places face the cathedral steps. The best of the bunch is tucked just around the left side of the grand staircase, up a smaller flight of stairs: **€€€€ Taverna degli Apostoli,** with colorful outdoor tables and a cozy upstairs dining room in what was once an art gallery. The menu is brief but thoughtful, going beyond the old standbys, and everything is well executed (closed Wed, cash only, Supportico San Andrea 6, +39 089 872 991).

For dessert, the **Andrea Pansa** pastry shop and café, to the right as you face the cathedral steps, is the most venerable place in town—a good spot to try *sfogliatella* (the delicate pastry invented at a nearby monastery) and other desserts popular in southern Italy (daily 7:30-24:00).

Near the Main Square, on Piazza dei Dogi: If you walk straight ahead from the cathedral stairs, go up the little covered lane (passing an Andrea Pansa gelato shop), and hook right at the fork, you'll pop out in atmospheric little Piazza dei Dogi. Slightly less trampled and more neighborhood-feeling than Piazza Duomo, this has several decent (if forgettable) restaurants aimed squarely at pleasing tourists. The **€ Cuoppo d'Amalfi** fried-fish shop, on the right as you enter the square, fills cardboard cones with all manner of deep-fried sea life. **€€€ Ristorante la Piazzetta** has tables right in the middle of the square, and **€€€ La Taverna di Masaniello**—quiet and quaint and tucked at the corner of the square leading to the port—has good food and big salads. **€ Deli Coast Paninoteca** is a small, bright diner with cheap and cheery sandwiches and salads (Piazza dei Dogi 2). **€ La Tramontina Amalfi** (at #26, across from the pharmacy) is great for made-to-order sandwiches to go (they're big enough for two).

Amalfi Town Connections

Amalfi is connected by bus and boat to all other nearby towns. In season, boats run to Sorrento, Capri, Positano, Minori, Maiori, and Salerno. Amalfi is the terminus for SITA buses to Sorrento (via Positano), Ravello, and Salerno (you must change here for Minori and Maiori). For details, see "Getting Around the Amalfi Coast," on page 180.

Ravello

The Amalfi Coast's version of a hill town, Ravello (a 30-minute bus ride from Amalfi town) sits atop a lofty perch 1,000 feet above the sea. It boasts an interesting church, two villas with stunning gardens, and breathtaking views that have attracted celebrities for generations. Gore Vidal, Richard Wagner, D. H. Lawrence, M. C. Escher, Henry Wadsworth Longfellow, Tennessee Williams, and Greta Garbo all succumbed to Ravello's charms and called it home.

The town is like a lush and peaceful garden floating in a world all its own. It seems to be made entirely of cafés, stonework, old villas-turned-luxury hotels, tourists, and grand views. Ravello feels like a place to convalesce.

GETTING THERE

Ravello and Amalfi town are connected by SITA bus along a very windy road (hourly, 30-minute trip, €1.50). Coming from Amalfi, buy your bus ticket at the bus stop from a ticket-seller wearing a brightly colored vest. Wait for the bus under the big awning by the statue on the waterfront, just to the left of the statue as you face the water. Coming from Positano or Sorrento, you'll change buses in Amalfi. From Naples, you'll change twice (in Salerno and Amalfi).

When returning from Ravello to Amalfi, line up early, since the buses are often crowded (buy ticket in tobacco shop; catch bus 100 yards off main square, by the recommended Ristorante da Salvatore).

Orientation to Ravello

To see the sights listed here, start at the bus stop and walk through the tunnel to the main square, where you'll find Villa Rufolo on the left and the church on the right. Villa Cimbrone is a 10-minute walk from the square (follow the signs).

If you have time for only one villa, consider this: Villa Rufolo is easier to reach (facing the main square) and has a stunning terrace garden. Villa Cimbrone is a 10-minute up-and-down hike from the square, but it's bigger and more rugged and offers even grander views in both directions along the coast.

Tourist Information: From the bus stop, to find the TI, face the church, then walk up the stepped lane to the left and into the Giardino del Vescovo (Bishop's Garden) behind the church (TI open daily 10:00-18:00, closes earlier Nov-April, Viale Richard Wagner 4, +39 089 857 096). The independent website www.ravello.com has helpful information.

Sights in Ravello

Piazza Duomo

Though Ravello is perfectly peaceful today, the weathered watchtower of Villa Rufolo—which once kept an eye out for fires and invasions—is a reminder that it wasn't always postcards and *limoncello.*

The fine umbrella pines on the square provide a shady meeting place for strollers ending up here on the piazza. Opposite the church is a fine view of the terraced hillside and the community of Scala (which means "steps"—historically a way of life there). The terraces—supporting grapevines and lemon trees—mostly date from the 16th century. To the left of the church, Viale Richard Wagner climbs past the TI to the top of town for sea views and ruined villas that are now luxury hotels. The town center is essentially traffic-free.

Duomo

Ravello's cathedral, overlooking the main square, feels stripped-down and Romanesque. The facade of the cathedral is plain because the earlier, fancy west portal was destroyed in a 1364 earthquake. Inside, you'll find tastefully restrained decoration and a floor that slopes upward. The key features of this church are its 12th-century bronze doors (from Constantinople), with 54 biblical scenes; the carved marble pulpit supported by six lions; and the chance to get a close-up look at the relic of holy blood of St. Pantaleone the Healer (in the chapel to the left of the main altar). The geometric designs show Arabic influence. In the afternoon, the church's front doors are locked; to enter, you'll need to pay to visit the museum on Viale Richard Wagner, around the right side. The humble museum is two rooms of well-described carved marble that evoke the historical importance of the town.

Cost and Hours: €3 for the museum—which also gets you into the church, daily 9:00-17:00.

Villa Rufolo

The villa, built in the 13th-century ruins of a noble family's palace, presents wistful gardens among stony walls, with oh-my-God views. The Arabic/Norman gardens seem designed to frame commanding coastline vistas (you can enjoy some of the same view, without the entry fee, from the bus parking lot just below the villa). It's also one of the venues for Ravello's annual arts festival (July-Sept, www.ravellofestival.com) and music society performances (April-June and Sept-Oct, www.ravelloarts.org). Musicians perch on a bandstand on the edge of the cliff for a combination of wonderful music and dizzying views. Wagner visited here and was impressed enough to set the second act of his opera *Parsifal* in the villa's magical gardens. By all accounts, the concert on the cliff is a sublime experience.

Cost and Hours: €8, daily 9:00-20:00, Oct-April until sunset, may close earlier for concerts, +39 089 857 621, www.villarufolo.it.

Visiting the Villa: From Piazza Duomo, enter through the stout watchtower to buy your ticket and pick up the English booklet explaining the sight. Then, walk through part of the sprawling villa ruins. Check out the short video in the tiny theater at the base of the tower and the exhibit upstairs (on the way to the tower's viewpoint). The palace itself has little to show, but the gardens and views are magnificent and invite exploration.

▲Villa Cimbrone

This villa offers another romantic garden, this one built upon the ruins of an old convent. Located at the seaward end of Ravello, it was created in the 20th century by Englishman William Beckett. His mansion is now a five-star hotel. The longish walk out rewards you with dreamy landscaping around a villa set on a bluff over the ocean. At the far end, above a sublime café on the lawn, "the Terrace of Infinity" dangles high above the sea.

Cost and Hours: €10, daily 9:00-sunset, +39 089 857 459, www.hotelvillacimbrone.com.

Getting There: Facing the cathedral on Piazza Duomo, exit the square to the right and follow signs. You'll climb up and down (and up and down) the stepped lanes, enjoying a quieter side of Ravello, before reaching the villa at the point. As it's a long walk, there are far fewer crowds here.

Visiting the Villa: Buy your ticket and pick up the free map/guide of the gardens. Across from the ticket booth, duck into the old monastery. Then pass the rose-garden terrace and head up the "main boulevard," which leads straight to the stunning Terrace of Infinity, with commanding views up and down the coast. If you have the interest and energy, loop back along the more rugged downhill slope (facing the adjacent town of Scala). Tiny lizards scurry underfoot, while mythological statues (Mercury's Seat, Temple of Bacchus, Eve's Grotto) strike their poses before a stunning and serene backdrop.

▲Hike Down to Amalfi Town

Enthusiastic walkers, who have good knees and don't mind lots of uneven stairs, enjoy taking the bus up to Ravello and then making the descent back to Amalfi on foot (there are several ways down). If you plan on this, study your route in advance, get a good map (the free, downloadable one at www.giovis.com will do in a pinch), wear good shoes, and allow extra time to give your knees a break.

The steepest, quickest route starts from Ravello's Villa Cimbrone. From the villa, retrace your steps back toward town. Take the first left, just by the arched entrance gate, onto Via Santa Barbara (this "via" is actually a stairway signposted *Amalfi/Minori*). The stepped path winds its way below the cliff. Pause here to look back up at the rock with a big white mansion—Villa La Rondinaia, where American author Gore Vidal lived for many years. Continue downward, mostly on stone stairs, about 40 minutes to the town of Atrani, where several bars on the main square offer well-deserved refreshments. From here, it's about a 15-minute walk back to Amalfi (see "Hiking Between Amalfi and Atrani" under "Sights in Amalfi," earlier).

Another harder, less scenic route down starts below the Church of Santa Maria a Gradillo (about 200 yards down Via Roma from Piazza Duomo).

Eating in Ravello

Several interchangeable restaurants face Piazza Duomo and line the surrounding streets. To enjoy this fine setting, just take your pick. You can also grab a takeaway lunch at one of the little groceries and sandwich shops that line Via Roma (running off Piazza Duomo). Enjoy your meal at the panoramic benches at the far end of Piazza Duomo (facing the cathedral), or facing even better views just outside of town, near the bus stop and Ristorante da Salvatore. Or try the Giardini Principessa di Piemonte, a peaceful garden that comes with fine views, located not far from the cathedral on Via San Giovanni del Toro. (Picnicking isn't allowed inside the two villas.)

€€€€ Ristorante da Salvatore, near the Ravello bus stop (at the other end of the little tunnel from the Duomo), serves a serious sit-down lunch with great views. Pino, the English-speaking owner of this formal restaurant, serves nicely presented, traditional Amalfi cuisine from a fun, if pricey, menu. Their pasta with potatoes and calamari is a favorite. Be adventurous when ordering and share dishes (closed Mon, Via della Repubblica 2, smart to call ahead for reservations—+39 089 857 227).

€€ Trattoria Cumpà Cosimo, while very touristy, is a classic, indoor family-run restaurant—a good choice for a quicker, less expensive lunch. For a special treat, get their *piatto misto* with five pastas for €20 (daily, Via Roma 44, +39 089 857 156).

Minori and Maiori

By the nature of modern tourism and social media, certain destinations are famous, packed, and expensive...and others are peaceful, overlooked, and almost living in another reality. On the Amalfi Coast, a tiny two-lane road winds scenically along the cliffs, connecting a charm bracelet of beautiful resort towns. But demand in two of those towns, Positano and Amalfi, has exceeded their ability to serve visitors well. I set out to find less touristed alternatives and was very happy with sister towns about a 10-minute drive south of

Amalfi: Minori and Maiori. In either town, for half the price and with half the crowds, you'll enjoy double the Italian-ness.

Although not as exotically situated as Amalfi or Positano, both Minori and Maiori front much better beaches. While they have interesting histories, don't come here for sightseeing. Visit for a slice of traditional Italy that's still shaping the local economy, for practical and affordable hotels, and for welcoming beaches—with plenty of public access, fun beachfront cafés, and convenient bus and boat connections.

Both Minori and Maiori are well served by cheap and frequent SITA buses and more expensive but more reliable (and less crowded) boats to the region's big attractions. The two towns are directly connected to each other (3 minutes by bus and 5 by boat), and to Amalfi and Salerno. To get to Positano and Sorrento, you'll connect in Amalfi.

The towns are less than a mile apart as the crow flies, and also connected up and over the hills by the "Path of Lemons" (Sentiero dei Limoni), an aromatic walk with panoramic views (see "Hiking from Maiori to Minori" on page 225).

Each T-shaped town fills its own ravine, with a long beach promenade and two parallel main boulevards going inland up the center of a ravine, surrounded by terraced lemon groves. (Those boulevards cover streams that the towns were originally built around.)

Minori (think minor) is the smaller, cuter, more historic little sister. Maiori is bigger and more practical, with better transportation connections, less crowded beaches, and more places to eat and sleep affordably. Both are charming but remarkably overlooked by international tourism. Italians enjoy the beach scene, and you'll see only a smattering of Americans. This is the authentic Amalfi.

GETTING THERE

It's all about buses and boats. Either way, if you first arrive in Positano, you'll need to transfer in Amalfi. By **boat,** Travelmar runs the most frequent trips along the coast. While you may see other outfits offering trips to Maiori and Minori from Positano (such as Grassi Junior, www.grassiboatpositano.com), their boats may go all the way to Salerno first before hitting these towns on the way back (about a 2-hour journey). Unless you want a leisurely and scenic boat ride, skip this option.

Leaving by boat, tickets are sold at Travelmar kiosks along the promenades and are easy, practical, and rarely sell out (times are clearly posted, boats are usually branded Alilauro; check www.travelmar.it or www.alilauro.it for schedules).

The SITA **bus** comes through about twice an hour, with stops clearly marked along the beach promenades (either to Salerno to the east or to Amalfi to the west). To continue by bus, you can't buy tickets on board, but kiosks along the promenades in both towns sell them. Validate your ticket when you board.

For more details, see "Getting Around the Amalfi Coast," on page 180.

PLANNING YOUR TIME

Boat-Hopping Day: If you're home-basing here, a fun day plan—which hits four towns—is to take a morning boat to Amalfi town; explore Amalfi, then hike 15 minutes to Atrani (and back); take a short bus or boat ride to Minori; then explore Minori and hike the "Path of Lemons" to Maiori (stopping for a meal/*granita*/*limoncello* along the way; see page 225).

Hiking from Ravello: There's a well-established 90-minute walk steeply downhill from Ravello to Minori. A good activity might be to catch the boat or bus to Amalfi and then a bus to Ravello before returning to Minori, scenically, on foot.

Minori

Minori is (fittingly) the smaller of the two towns. It's known for its historical sights and culinary scene, especially its pasta (try *ndunderi,* a type of gnocchi that dates back to Roman times) and lemon-themed dishes, and particularly its desserts (one of Italy's top pastry chefs is based here). Built upon the site of a Roman villa (buried by the eruption of Vesuvius in AD 79), Minori was an important player when it was part of the Maritime Republic of Amalfi and produced paper, lemons, and the local pasta.

Corso Vittorio Emanuele III, the town's "Main Street," runs up the ravine and is the spine of the town. Long ago, Minori's waterfront was wiped out by a tsunami, so the old town is inland behind newer buildings that face the sea. You'll find the locals friendly and happy to have you here. As one said, "If you walk around three times, people will start to say hi—they'll think you must live here."

ORIENTATION TO MINORI

You'll find a **TI** stocked full of brochures, maps, and books at the far end of Via Roma toward Salerno. The helpful staff can answer questions and sell bus tickets (Via Roma 30, +39 089 877 087, www.prolocominori.it). The **SITA bus** stops right in front of the

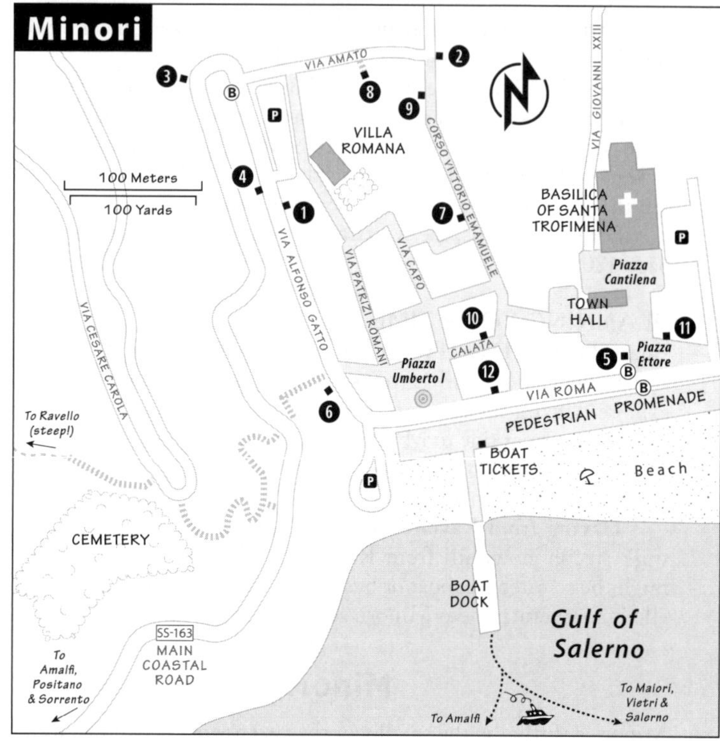

main piazza along Via Roma (waterside stop for Maiori and Salerno, townside for Amalfi).

Buying **boat tickets** is simple—there's just one Travelmar ticket kiosk to the left of the dock as you face the water. To get to Positano or Ravello, you'll change boats in Amalfi.

SIGHTS IN MINORI

Minori Beach

Minori's small but mighty beach has free areas on both sides of the dock (pebbly beach on the right side is all free, where you can also launch a kayak; sandy beach to the left has chairs and umbrellas—about €10).

Basilica of Santa Trofimena

The main church (on Piazza Ettore e Gaetano Cantilena) dates to the seventh century, when it was built to house the relics of St. Trofimena of Sicily. The church was rebuilt in the 18th century, so most of what you see today is in Neoclassical style. Its 11th-century bell tower dominates the town's skyline.

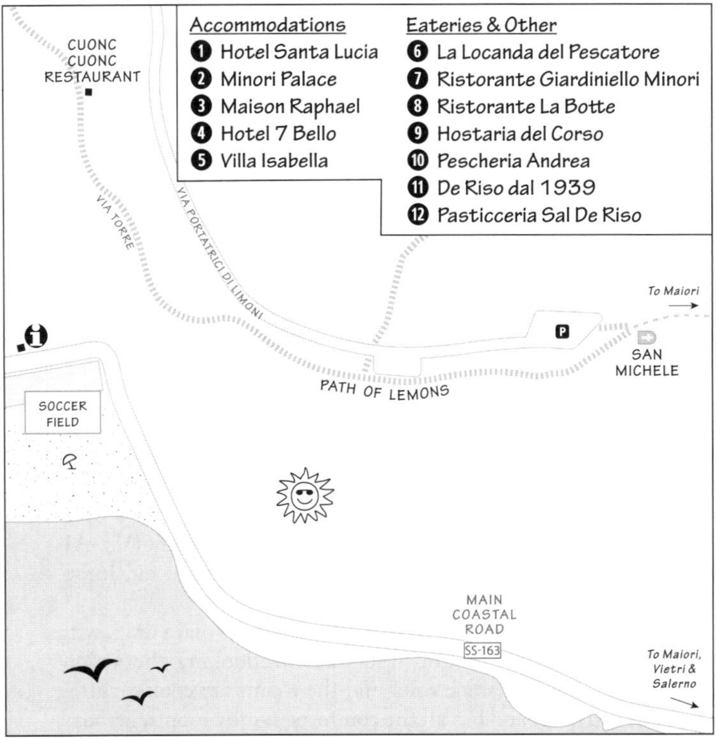

Accommodations

1. Hotel Santa Lucia
2. Minori Palace
3. Maison Raphael
4. Hotel 7 Bello
5. Villa Isabella

Eateries & Other

6. La Locanda del Pescatore
7. Ristorante Giardiniello Minori
8. Ristorante La Botte
9. Hostaria del Corso
10. Pescheria Andrea
11. De Riso dal 1939
12. Pasticceria Sal De Riso

CUONC CUONC RESTAURANT
VIA TORRE
VIA PORTATRICI DI LIMONI
To Maiori
SAN MICHELE
PATH OF LEMONS
SOCCER FIELD
MAIN COASTAL ROAD
SS-163
To Maiori, Vietri & Salerno

Villa Romana

The only sight you'll likely pay to see is the remains of Minori's first-century Roman villa, which is unique for its well-preserved mosaic floor, as well as porticos and a Roman garden. Three sides of its portico and a big pool survive along with Pompeii-style frescoes and mosaics. The villa was buried by the eruption of Mount Vesuvius in 79 AD and excavated in modern times. Discovered by chance in 1932 and excavated starting in 1934, it was buried again by floods in 1954. Excavations restarted the following year, essentially leaving a hole in the middle of the old town center.

After you check out the humble museum, with artifacts found here and at other archaeological sites, wander outside and head to the left. Loop around above the garden, past apartments with locals hanging out their laundry, to the far side (where the seafront once would have been). Here steps lead down into the old Roman garden. Head straight across it to find the preserved mosaic floor of a hunting scene with mythological creatures. Wander through the hallways, with helpful English signage, to see faint frescoes and vaulted ceilings.

Cost and Hours: €6; Tue-Sat 9:00-19:00, Sun until 13:30, closed Mon; good English handouts, Via dei Patrizi Romani 28, +39 089 852 893.

Hiking from Minori to Maiori

A 45-minute hike along the "Path of Lemons" (Sentiero dei Limoni) connects Maiori and Minori, with views and possible stops at the Cuonc Cuonc organic restaurant or Agricola Ruocco's lemon farm. For details, see page 225.

SLEEPING IN MINORI

€€€€ Hotel Santa Lucia is a classy choice. Its lobby lounge and bar have Old World elegance, and the staff is up to the task. Some rooms are a bit old-fashioned, but some come with views overlooking the Roman villa and almost all have a balcony (Via Alfonso Gatto 44, +39 089 877 142, www.hotelsantalucia.it, info@hotelsantalucia.it).

€€€ Minori Palace dominates the top of the main drag, with its big balconies and rooftop restaurant overlooking the action. While you'll long for some color and the rooms are cookie-cutter, it's clean and quiet and has all the comforts (family rooms, laundry, Corso Vittorio Emanuele 70, +39 089 851 506, www.minoripalace.com, reservations@minoripalace.com).

€€ Maison Raphael is lovingly run by Antonio, who took over the family business from his father (and you may see Antonio's grandson behind the desk). Hovering over the end of town where the main coastal road bends west toward Amalfi, the hotel sits picturesquely among lemon and fig trees, with a rooftop terrace topped with kiwi vines. The furniture in the 10 rooms is a bit dated, but the rooms are spacious and crisp with colorful tiles (most rooms with terrace, no elevator—lots of stairs, Via Nazionale 56, +39 089 853 545, www.maisonraphael.it, info@maisonraphael.it).

€€ Hotel 7 Bello is a welcoming, family-run place across from the Roman villa. The rooms are simple but cheery and most have balconies (family rooms, Via Nazionale 39, +39 089 877 619, www.hotel7bellominori.com, info@hotel7belloamalficoast.com).

€€ Villa Isabella, just steps from the beach and the church, is a charming place and as central as can be. Located on the third floor of a historic building, most rooms have a balcony and sea views with high wood-beamed ceilings. You'll also have access to a private beach (family rooms, no elevator, lots of stairs, no breakfast, Via Roma 34, +39 089 877 070, www.villa-isabella.it, info@villa-isabella.it).

EATING IN MINORI

There are plenty of enticing eateries in town, but you'll likely find the best values in the town center, away from the beachfront.

€€ La Locanda del Pescatore, literally the house of the fisherman, is a delightful little place with a few colorful outdoor tables and a dressy yet salty interior usually filled with locals. It's tight and cozy, with the freshest of seafood and good pizza (closed Tue, on the Amalfi end of town a block off the beach at Via Alfonso Gatto 11, +39 089 853 063).

€€€ Ristorante Giardiniello Minori, known for seafood dishes and desserts, is big and dressy on the inside, but casual on the trellis-topped terrace, where they also serve light lunches (closed Tue, reservations recommended for dinner, +39 089 877 050, Corso Vittorio Emanuele 17).

€€ Ristorante la Botte, hiding below street level amid apartment buildings behind the Roman villa, offers charming covered outdoor tables and elegant seating inside. A family-run place, it features fresh ingredients, homemade pasta, wood-fired pizza, and friendly service (daily, Via Santa Maria Vetrana 2, +39 089 877 893).

€€ Hostaria del Corso is smack dab in the historic center, a couple of blocks inland on Corso Vittorio Emanuele, with charming seating on the square, a humble vibe, and a hardworking family (closed Wed, at #39, +39 089 854 1603).

€ Pescheria Andrea serves up paper cones filled with fried fresh fish and vegetables on a little lane off Corso Vittorio Emanuele, just a block up from Via Roma. Look for the crowd of locals, especially around lunch time (long hours daily in summer, likely weekends only rest of the year, Calata Ponte 18).

Dueling Pastry Shops, Dueling Brothers

The Riso brothers seem to help put their town on the map with the town's famous pastries. Each runs an impressive *pasticceria* facing the beach. Alessandro's **De Riso dal 1939** (where Piazza Ettore e Gaetano Cantilena hits Via Roma) is the original shop; it's traditional and quite nice, with outdoor tables serving simple lunches. Step inside for impressive pastries and coffee in a humble little shop. It seems tops...until you visit his brother Sal's place.

At **Pasticceria Sal De Riso** (a block away, also facing the beach), pastry chef Salvatore De Riso serves his signature *torta ricotta e pere,* a hazelnut sponge cake with ricotta cream and pears. He's a bit of a celebrity in Italy, with several cookbooks and awards lining the shelves in the bright, inviting shop. While the tables

out front seem made for a fancy restaurant (and the food is excellent), diners are—it seems—making a meal out of the desserts. Stepping deeper into the establishment you'll find the exquisite counter of various rum-soaked, lavishly iced, and creamy cakes and pies to go (check out the cone-shaped *Dolcezza del Vesuvio,* topped with red jelly and layered inside like the ash of Vesuvius). Beyond that is the gelato room. For takeout pastries, order at the register up front (just tell them how many you want—don't be ashamed; everything is €6), then take your ticket to the counter and make your selection(s) (long hours daily, facing the beach at Via Roma 80, +39 089 877 941, www.salderiso.it).

Maiori

Maiori (my-OH-ree) is bigger, plainer, and more practical than Minori, with the longest beach on the Amalfi Coast and plenty of hotel rooms and transportation connections. It just feels like an Italian town...some tourism, sure, but a real local scene.

In the ninth century, Maiori was an important part of the Maritime Republic of Amalfi, and was the headquarters for several arsenals, customs, and the salt market. A violent tsunami in 1343 and a plague five years later, followed by merciless pirate attacks and terrible floods, resulted in the city's decline. During World War II, Maiori was part of the Allied Operation Avalanche (a.k.a. the "Salerno Landing"), when 1,600 troops landed here in September 1943 to help liberate Italy from the Nazis (a monument facing the beach memorializes the US Rangers who came ashore here). The town feels new: That's because in 1954 it was hit by a disastrous flood that was followed by extensive rebuilding using cheap, modern construction methods.

Today, like its little sister Minori, the town has basically a T-design: a long beachfront road and a single major street, Corso Reginna, running inland up the ravine. That road covers a stream that originally gave the town life. Be sure to hike up that main road far from the beach scene and feel the very real pulse of an Italian town.

ORIENTATION TO MAIORI

Boats arrive in a little harbor at the far west end of town, a short stroll from the center (you'll pass a couple of bus stops and some boat-ticket kiosks along the promenade toward town).

A little **bike-rental kiosk** that also sells bus tickets (cash only) is at the other end of town, one block past Corso Reginna, on the inland side of Lungomare Giovanni Amendola.

SIGHTS IN MAIORI

Maiori Beach

Blessed with the longest stretch of beach on the Amalfi Coast (half public and half private), Maiori's seafront comes with a busy road lined with shops and eateries, but also a wide waterfront promenade that's lovely to stroll. **Lido Villa Hermosa** is a welcoming private beach to settle into for the day (€10/lounge chair). The far-left side of the beach (as you face the water) offers the most free space and quiet from the main road. For some extra water fun, you can rent paddleboats and canoes, or kayak from here to Minori.

Collegiate Church of Santa Maria a Mare

Resting on a rock, with panoramic views overlooking the sea, this church was built in the 13th century on the remains of an old fortress. Its distinctive dome is covered in hand-painted green and yellow ceramic tiles from the 18th century. Inside, the church is adorned with frescoes and fine ceramics. The Sacred Art Museum, in the crypt area, features religious artifacts and hand-painted tiles.

Palazzo Mezzacapo

This former palace, now home to the town's municipal offices, has a few free areas to explore, particularly a peaceful garden with fountains and pools hidden in a courtyard. The pools are believed to be arranged in the shape of the Maltese cross, the order to which several members of the Mezzacapo family belonged. Inside and up one floor, you can view a huge Nativity scene, along with a Rococo room with an elaborate ceiling fresco (free, Corso Reginna, at the top of town).

Castle of San Nicola de Thoro-Plano

This 15th-century fortress built to offer protection from Saracen pirate attacks, while a bit neglected, owns a spectacular location and views overlooking the town, the coastline, and the lush hillsides. The inside can only be seen with a guided tour from the current owner, but hardy hikers will enjoy the workout. The 45-minute hike requires good knees—over 700 steps take you through narrow neighborhood lanes and up to the castle, with panoramic views that make it worthwhile even if you don't tour the inside. If you have a car or a scooter, you could cut some of the steps by driving to its

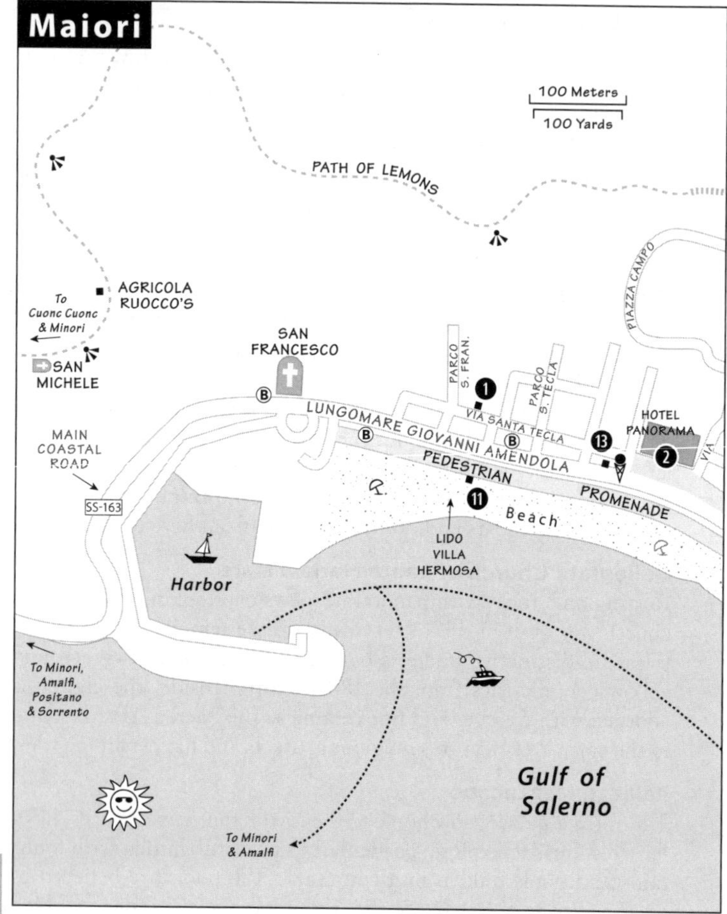

base, but you'll still have almost 300 steps remaining to the castle and viewpoint.

Cost and Hours: €5, daily 8:30-13:30 but call ahead to confirm and schedule a tour, +39 338 940 3552, owner Crescenzo de Martino.

Getting There: The hike starts about 10 minutes outside of the center of town. Walk up Via Nuova Provinciale Chiunzi, getting just a glimpse of the castle above on the right, beyond Hotel San Pietro. When you reach the little intersection with stoplights, look on the right for the path marked *Via Castelo.* From here, the first section up to a little plaza is fairly straightforward, but after you head left and keep climbing, you'll do most of the work. Go as early in the day as you can to beat the heat.

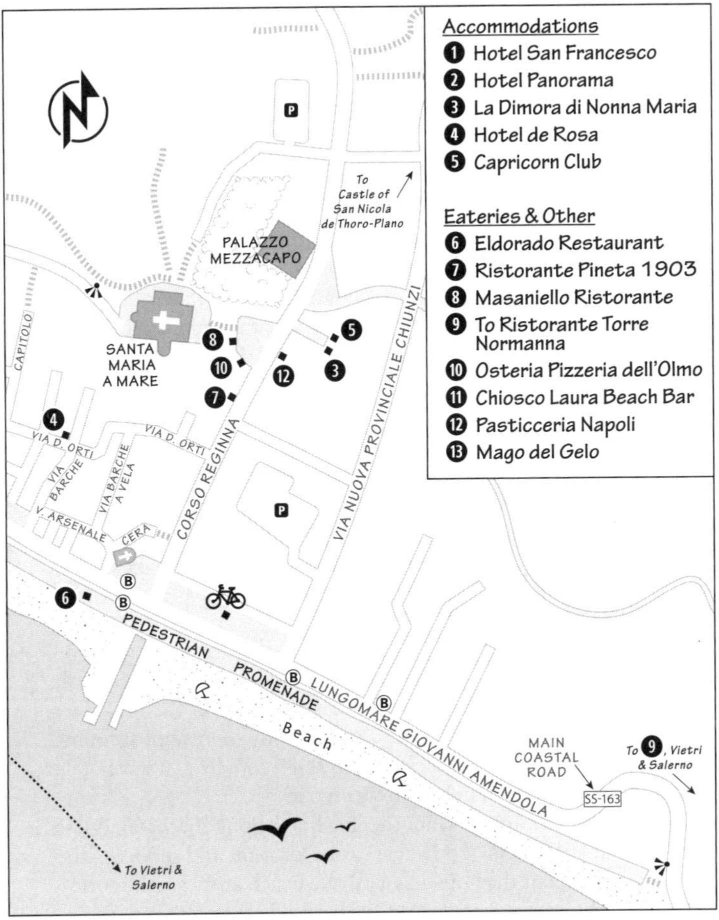

PALAZZO MEZZACAPO
To Castle of San Nicola de Thoro-Plano
SANTA MARIA A MARE
CAPITOLO
VIA D. ORTI
VIA BARCHE
VIA BARCHE A VELA
V. ARSENALE
CERA
CORSO REGINNA
VIA NUOVA PROVINCIALE CHIUNZI
PEDESTRIAN PROMENADE
LUNGOMARE GIOVANNI AMENDOLA
Beach
MAIN COASTAL ROAD
SS-163
To 9, Vietri & Salerno
To Vietri & Salerno

Accommodations

1. Hotel San Francesco
2. Hotel Panorama
3. La Dimora di Nonna Maria
4. Hotel de Rosa
5. Capricorn Club

Eateries & Other

6. Eldorado Restaurant
7. Ristorante Pineta 1903
8. Masaniello Ristorante
9. To Ristorante Torre Normanna
10. Osteria Pizzeria dell'Olmo
11. Chiosco Laura Beach Bar
12. Pasticceria Napoli
13. Mago del Gelo

Hiking from Maiori to Minori

The "Path of Lemons" (Sentiero dei Limoni) connects Maiori and Minori via a 45-minute hike that starts from behind the Santa Maria a Mare church in the center of town, giving you up-close views of the church dome's majolica tiles as you start your climb. (From Minori, it leaves from behind the Basilica of Santa Trofimena on Via Giovanni XXIII.) The popular path is well signed, leads through lemon groves, and comes with great views of the sea and both towns from above.

Once upon a time this was the only overland connection between Maiori and Minori. As you walk, appreciate the unique terraced landscape created by centuries of hardworking farmers. Imagine the workers (including many women) carrying huge loads of lemons to ships for export.

The path has two great places to stop along the way for a rest and a scenic drink or meal. About halfway along the path, **Agricola Ruocco's** overlooks a huge lemon tree farm, and Nadia and Giovanni (whose family has owned the farm for four generations) produce all things lemon. You can sit and sip a *limoncello* or lemon *spritz* as you soak in the scene. They also run tours of the farm that include a *limoncello* tasting (+39 329 203 8449, johnruocco@hotmail.it).

Farther along, just before you drop down to Minori, is **Cuonc Cuonc,** an organic restaurant with homemade pasta and lots of dishes with ingredients straight from their garden, and a spectacular view from their covered terrace (daily, +39 334 128 6193). Now's a good time (especially on a hot day) for a lemon *granita*—you've earned it. From here it's another 10 minutes downhill to Minori.

SLEEPING IN MAIORI

€€€ Hotel San Francesco is the classiest of the big waterfront hotels. It's set back enough from the main road that it feels peaceful. There's ample space to relax in the palatial lobby, on the breakfast terrace, or at their pool across the street (family rooms, most rooms with balconies, Via Santa Tecla 54, +39 089 877 070, www.hotel-sanfrancesco.it, info@hotel-sanfrancesco.it).

€€€ Hotel Panorama, another big hotel along the water, is less personal but still offers good value for its location and services. The rooms are basic, but the hotel has a private beach and a small rooftop pool and restaurant, where breakfast is served. They also rent apartments close by (family rooms, Via Santa Tecla 8, +39 089 877 202, www.hotelpanoramamaiori.com, info@panoramagroup.it).

€ La Dimora di Nonna Maria, overlooking the Capricorn Club, has three fresh rooms, one a two-level apartment nicely set up for families (no breakfast, Corso Reginna 82, +39 379 201 1608, www.ladimoradinonnamaria.com, info@ladimoradinonnamaria.com).

€ Hotel de Rosa, not family-run but with a family-run vibe, is a welcoming, woman-owned place on a side street at the top of town. It has a retro-feeling lobby and 20 fresh rooms all with balconies (family rooms, Via Degli Orti 28, +39 333 887 1657, www.hotelderosamaiori.it, info@hotelderosamaiori.it).

€ Capricorn Club is a peaceful oasis tucked down a small lane and through a courtyard, where you emerge in a lemon grove filled with bungalows. Fabio, Italy's version of "The Dude," welcomes you to this relaxing retreat (he also helps manage the recommended La Dimora di Nonna Maria next door). Each of the 12 bungalows—named after astrological signs—is basic, but well equipped with a kitchen and a veranda. There's also a community barbecue (bike rentals, no breakfast, Corso Reginna 82, +39 334 884 3884, www.capricornioclub.it, fabio@fabiopietroboni.it).

EATING IN MAIORI

€€€ Eldorado Restaurant is the only real restaurant on the beach (others fronting the beach have a noisy road between). It's a big, busy place with a fun menu and is a lovely spot for dining with a Mediterranean view (daily, +39 089 851 266, on the beach in the center of town at the foot of Corso Reginna).

€€€ Ristorante Pineta 1903 doesn't look like much from the outside (or as you walk through the century-old trattoria just inside), but keep going to arrive at a vast, romantic lemon grove that feels a world away. Under the cool of the trees, this "slow-food certified" restaurant—using only organic, seasonal ingredients from local producers—aims to create a dining experience that hits all the senses. They do inventive takes on classic dishes, and even make poke bowls (daily, tasting *menu*s available at dinner, +39 328 881 5393, www.ristorantepineta1903.it).

€€€ Masaniello Ristorante is the classiest restaurant in the town center, with a dressy, elegant atmosphere at dinner but a more relaxed vibe at lunch, with outside tables. Brothers Vincenzo and Pasquale take pride in creating a welcoming environment and offering traditional cuisine that's a notch up in quality (daily, +39 089 877 671, Corso Reginna, Piazza D'Amato 2).

€€€ Ristorante Torre Normanna serves the catch of the day, either in its 13th-century watchtower hugging the side of the cliff or on the 180-degree view terrace. It's run by two brothers, Massimo and Gino, who source ingredients from their family farm. From the far east (Salerno) side of the promenade, take the little stairs up to the main road and carefully walk a few minutes—or you can have a bus take you here—request the stop right out front (daily, Via Diego Taiani 4, +39 089 877 100, www.torrenormanna.ovh).

€€ Osteria Pizzeria dell'Olmo, next to Ristorante Pineta 1903 on the main drag, has good pizza and is a great place to try the area's *ndunderi* pasta. Eat in the cozy, stylish interior or at outside tables ideal for people-watching (closed Mon, Corso Reginna 63, +39 089 854 1594).

€€ Chiosco Laura Beach Bar, right near the boat dock, is a cute little snack shack with tables overlooking the beach. They serve simple food (sandwiches and salads) and cocktails, which you can nurse as you gaze up at the faux French château on the hill. It's friendly and the setting and price are great (long hours daily, +39 334 359 6715).

€ Pasticceria Napoli is a family-run place where locals come to debate sports and politics. Order a coffee and pastry and relax in the classic interior, or at tables out front. In the afternoon, it's a great place for a *limoncello spritz* (closed Tue, Corso Reginna 64, +39 089 853 182).

Mago del Gelo is the local favorite for gelato; line up at the "magician of ice" (facing the beach at Lungomare Giovanni Amendola 18).

PAESTUM

The archaeological park at Paestum (PASTE-oom) includes one of the best collections of Greek temples anywhere—and certainly the most accessible to Western Europe. Serenely situated, Paestum is surrounded by fields and wildflowers. Not quite a village, it also has a train station, a bus stop, a church, a straggle of homes, and a handful of eateries.

The ancient city was founded as Poseidonia by Greeks in the sixth century BC and became a key stop on an important trade route. In the fifth century BC, the Lucanians, a barbarous inland tribe, conquered Poseidonia and tried to adopt the cultured ways of the Greeks. By the time of the Romans, who took over in the third century BC and built a fine town on the site, the name Poseidonia had been simplified to Paestum. The final conquerors of Paestum, malaria-carrying mosquitoes, kept the site wonderfully deserted for nearly a thousand years. The temples were never buried—just ignored. Rediscovered in the 18th century, Paestum today offers the only well-preserved Greek ruins north of Sicily.

While most visitors do Paestum as a day trip (it's 1.5 hours from Naples by convenient direct train), it's not a bad place to overnight. Accommodations offer great value, and you could use Paestum as a base for day trips to Naples or the Amalfi Coast. With more time, there's a beach nearby and local buffalo-milk dairies that you can visit.

GETTING THERE

A dozen slow milk-run trains to Paestum run directly from Naples via the transit-hub city of Salerno; from elsewhere, you'll need to transfer at one of those two points. For those transferring in Salerno, see the "Salerno Connections" map, which shows train, bus, and boat stops as well as some nearby streets with handy eateries. Confirm train schedules at Trenitalia.it and bus schedules at SitaSudTrasporti.it.

From Naples

Direct trains run from Naples' Centrale station to Paestum (12/day, 1.5 hours, direction: Sapri or Reggio; only the more expensive Intercity trains have a first-class section). Buy tickets online or from ticket windows or machines at the station. For a day trip from Naples, it's wise to get an early start—especially in warm weather. Trains typically leave Naples at 6:50, 7:35, 7:50, and 8:50, and then not again until 11:45. In the cooler shoulder season, consider arriving for lunch, visiting the museum, and then exploring the temples as they bask in warm afternoon light. When returning to Salerno or Naples from the Paestum train station, make sure you board the right section of the train—some trains split at Battipaglia.

From Sorrento

For a day trip, the smart (if dull) approach is to go bright and early by Circumvesuviana or Campania Express **train** to Naples (75 minutes), catch a direct Naples-Paestum train, and take the same route back (about 3 hours each way). While it's technically possible to do one leg via an Amalfi Coast SITA **bus,** it makes for a very long day marred by worry about making connections. By **car** from Sorrento, Paestum is 60 miles and at least 3 hours (depending on traffic) via the Amalfi Coast road but a smooth 2 hours by autostrada. To reach Paestum from Sorrento via the autostrada, drive toward Naples, catch the autostrada (direction: Salerno), skirt Salerno (direction: Reggio), exit at Battipaglia, and drive straight through the roundabout. Then continue for about 25 minutes, following *Paestum* signs.

From Maiori, Minori, Amalfi, or Positano via Salerno

First take a **boat** (70 minutes) or SITA **bus** (2 hours, change in Amalfi) to Salerno, where you can catch the **train** on its way from Naples (12/day, infrequent midday, 30 minutes from Salerno to Paestum).

Getting to Salerno: Since boat departures and durations are more reliable (they don't depend on traffic), a boat is a safer bet

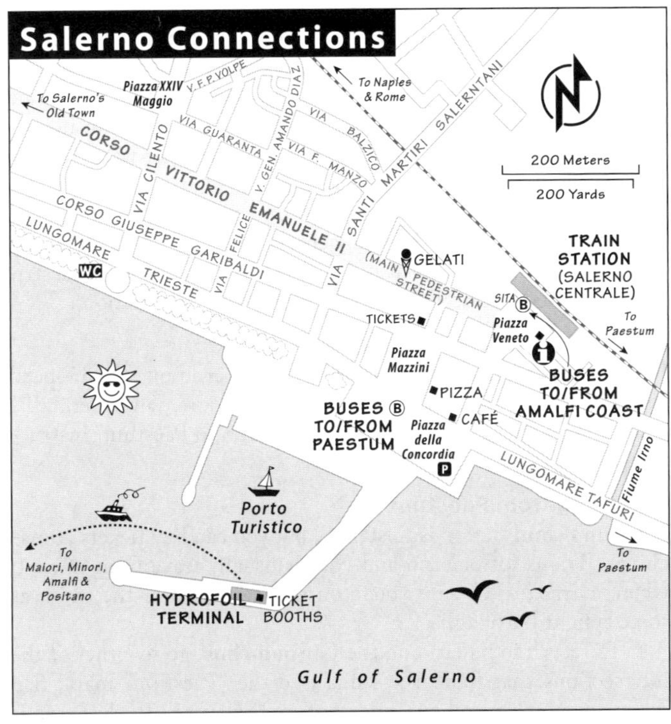

than a bus. Boats arrive at a dock a few short blocks from the train station (about a 10-minute, mostly level walk). Buses from Amalfi to Salerno terminate at the Salerno train station. To start your day trip by bus, you'll need to leave Positano at the crack of dawn—7:00 at the latest—to make the last morning train in Salerno.

Getting from Salerno to Paestum: Once in Salerno, buy your Paestum **train** ticket at ticket machines or the ticket office in the train station. Be sure to check return times; the last possible connection may leave Paestum as early as 16:20 (though in summer it's more likely to be around 21:00).

If you arrive in Salerno during the midday lull in the train schedule, you could take the blue-and-white **Giuliano bus** to Paestum (about hourly, fewer on Sun, 1 hour). It departs from Piazza della Concordia—look for the bus shelter between the big parking lot and the main road just up from the ferry dock, and buy your ticket from the driver (make sure it's going to Paestum; there's also a ticket kiosk one block ahead on the other side of the parking lot). In Paestum, this bus drops you only slightly closer to the ruins than does the train.

If you're staying overnight in Paestum, there's no need to rush.

The ruins are enjoyable in the afternoon, when the crowds thin out and the light is better.

To **drive** from Positano to Paestum, you can either follow the Amalfi Coast road to Salerno or cross back over the peninsula toward Sorrento and then take the expressway. Either way, allow at least 2.5 hours.

Services in Salerno: If you have time to kill in Salerno, there are some eateries along the road across from Piazza della Concordia and more appealing places a couple blocks up on the pedestrianized Corso Vittorio Emanuele (closer to the train station).

From Rome via Salerno

It is possible to go direct from Rome to Salerno on a high-speed Frecce train (1-2 morning departures, 1.5 hours, www.trenitalia.com), then follow the "Getting from Salerno to Paestum" instructions above.

Returning from Paestum

Paestum's **train** station is unstaffed, but you can buy tickets at machines. Trains for Salerno and Naples usually leave from track 1; when you board, be sure you're on the right part of the train, as some split at Battipaglia.

To return to Salerno on the **Giuliano bus,** go to either of the intersections that flank the ruins (see the "Paestum" map), flag down any northbound bus, and confirm "Salerno?" The last stop is the Salerno waterfront; from there you can catch a boat to Maiori, Minori, Amalfi, or Positano or walk up to the train station to catch an Amalfi-bound SITA bus or a train.

Orientation to Paestum

If you arrive by **train,** cross under the tracks, exit the tiny station, and walk through the ancient city gate; the ruins are a half-mile walk straight ahead. When you hit the street with hotels and shops—Via Magna Grecia—turn right to find the museum and north entrance to the archaeological park (where my tour begins). The street is pedestrian-only between the north and south entrances to the ruins.

If you'd rather not walk, English-speaking Patrizia Pecora runs a great team of local **taxi** drivers available to drive you to hotels or to the ruins (€10-15, +39 392 444 9020). **Buses** from Salerno stop near the northeast corner of the ruins (at a little bar/café). **Drivers** park in the large Sosta Camper lot by the museum and La Basilica Pizzeria (€3/up to 2 hours, €5/all day; many shady spots in the back).

Baggage Storage: There's no official baggage storage at the train station or museum. If you're desperate, you can try nicely asking at one of the bars along the main road (they may want a small payment) or at a restaurant you've already patronized.

Local Guide: For an insider's knowledge, **Silvia Braggio** and her team specialize in Paestum and give a fine two-hour walk of the site and museum (RS%—special rate for my readers, arrange in advance, longer tours also available, +39 347 643 2307, www.silviaguide.it, silvia@silviaguide.it). Ask about rounding out the day with a visit to a buffalo farm or another nearby sight. Silvia also offers walking tours of Pompeii and Herculaneum.

Sights in Paestum

PAESTUM ARCHAEOLOGICAL PARK AND MUSEUM

While Paestum is famous for its marvelous Greek temples, most of the structures you see are Roman. Five elements of Greek Paestum survive: three misnamed temples, a memorial tomb (the Heroon), and a circular meeting place (the Ekklesiasterion). The rest, including the wall that defines the site, are the remains of the later Roman town.

Paestum was once a seaport (the ocean is now about a mile away—the wall in the distance, which stretches about three miles, is about halfway to today's coastline). Only about a third of the site has been excavated. The original Greek city, which archaeologists figure had a population of about 7,000, was first conquered by Lucanians (distant relatives of the Romans, who spoke a language related to Latin) and then by the Romans (who completely made it over and built the wall you see today).

The remaining Greek structures survive because the Romans were superstitious—they respected sacred areas and didn't mess with temples and tombs. While most old Christian churches are built on Roman temples (it tends to be what people do when they conquer another culture), no Roman temple is built on a Greek temple. The three Greek temples that you'll see here today have stood for about 2,500 years.

Cost: €15, Dec-Feb-€10, free (and packed) first Sun of each month. Tickets are valid for three days (but only one entry allowed) and also cover a nearby archaeological site at Velia (45 minutes away).

Hours: Daily 8:30-19:30, last entry one hour before closing.

Information: +39 0828 811 023, www.museopaestum.beniculturali.it.

Getting In: While you can visit in any order, I prefer to start at the north end of the archeological site and end back at the museum. The museum is next to the square with the small early Christian basilica, across the street from the ruins. The north entry to the

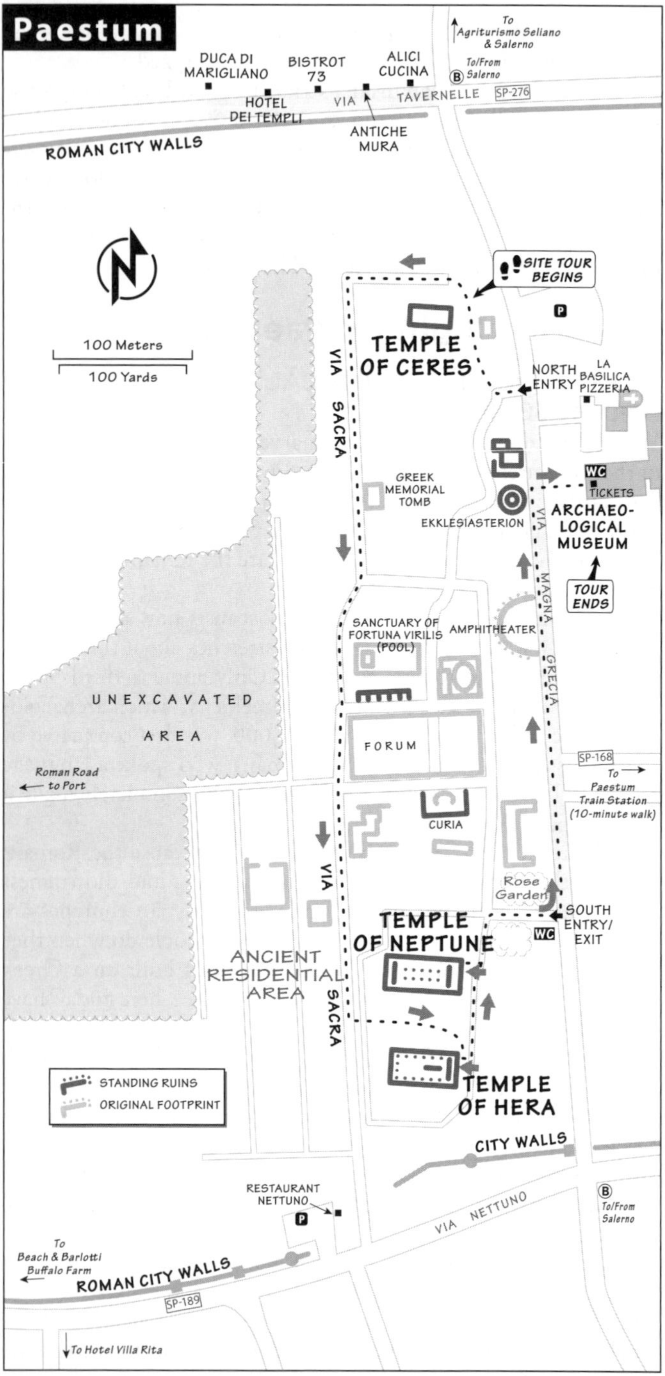

Paestum

To Agriturismo Seliano & Salerno

To/From Salerno

DUCA DI MARIGLIANO

BISTROT 73

ALICI CUCINA

HOTEL DEI TEMPLI

VIA TAVERNELLE

SP-276

ANTICHE MURA

ROMAN CITY WALLS

100 Meters

100 Yards

SITE TOUR BEGINS

TEMPLE OF CERES

VIA SACRA

NORTH ENTRY

LA BASILICA PIZZERIA

GREEK MEMORIAL TOMB

EKKLESIASTERION

WC

TICKETS

ARCHAEOLOGICAL MUSEUM

TOUR ENDS

VIA MAGNA GRECIA

SANCTUARY OF FORTUNA VIRILIS (POOL)

AMPHITHEATER

UNEXCAVATED AREA

FORUM

SP-168

To Paestum Train Station (10-minute walk)

Roman Road to Port

CURIA

Rose Garden

SOUTH ENTRY/ EXIT

TEMPLE OF NEPTUNE

ANCIENT RESIDENTIAL AREA

TEMPLE OF HERA

STANDING RUINS

ORIGINAL FOOTPRINT

CITY WALLS

RESTAURANT NETTUNO

VIA NETTUNO

To/From Salerno

To Beach & Barlotti Buffalo Farm

ROMAN CITY WALLS

SP-189

To Hotel Villa Rita

ruins is a few steps up from the museum, toward the parking lot. The south entry is a few minutes' walk away, past the street from the train station. (If you enter at the south entrance, make your way up to the north entry and Temple of Ceres to begin our tour.)

Visitor Information: The following self-guided tours provide all the information you need for both the site and the museum. Skip the museum's dull audioguide. Renovations are in progress at the museum and ruins; expect changes. You'll enjoy the coolest temperatures in the morning but the best light and smallest crowds late in the day.

Length of This Tour: Allow two hours to see the ruins and the museum (about an hour for each).

▲▲Paestum Archaeological Site

This tour starts at the site's north entry (by the museum), visits the Temple of Ceres, goes through the center of the Roman town past the Greek Memorial Tomb, circles around the other two Greek temples, and then leaves the site through the south entry to walk down the modern road to the Ekklesiasterion (which faces the museum).

Self-Guided Tour

• *Buy your ticket at the museum, then head to the right to find the site's north entry. Stand in front of the...*

Temple of Ceres: All three Paestum temples have inaccurate names, coined by 19th-century archaeologists who based their "discoveries" on wishful thinking. (While the Romans made things easy by leaving lots of inscriptions, the Greeks did not.) Those 1800s archaeologists wanted this temple to be devoted to Ceres, the goddess of agriculture. However, all the little votive statues found later, when modern archaeologists dug here, instead depicted a woman with a big helmet: Athena, goddess of wisdom and war. (The Greeks' female war goddess was also the goddess of wisdom—thinking...strategy...female. The Romans' masculine war god was Mars—just fighting.) Each temple is part of a sanctuary—an open, sacred space around the temple. Because regular people couldn't go into the temple, the altar logically stood outside.

PAESTUM

The Temple of Ceres dates from 500 BC. It's made of locally quarried limestone blocks. Good roads and shipping didn't come along until the Romans, so the Greeks' buildings were limited to local materials. The wooden roof is long gone. Like the other two temples, this one was once painted white, black, and red, and has an east-west orientation—facing the rising sun. This temple's *cella* (interior room) is gone, cleared out when it was used as a Christian church in the sixth century. In medieval times, Normans scavenged stones from here; chunks of these temples can be found in Amalfi's cathedral.

Walk around to the back side of the Temple of Ceres. The capitals broke in a modern earthquake, so a steel bar provides necessary support. Each of the Paestum temples is Doric style—with three stairs, columns without a base, and shafts that narrow at the top to a simple capital of a round, then a square, block. While there were no carved reliefs, colorful frescoes once decorated the pediments.

As you walk away, look back at the temple. Traditionally, Greeks would build a sanctuary of Athena on a city's highest spot (like the Parthenon in Athens, on the Acropolis). Paestum had no hill, so the Greeks created a mound. The hill was more impressive in its time because the level of the Greek city was substantially lower than the Roman pavement stones you'll walk on today.

• *Follow the path down from behind the temple, and turn left to walk on the paving stones of Via Sacra toward the other Greek temples. After about 100 yards, to the left of the road, you'll see a little half-buried house with a tiled roof.*

Greek Memorial Tomb (Heroon): This tomb (from 500 BC) also survived because the Romans respected religious buildings. But the tomb was most inconveniently located, right in the middle of their growing city. So the practical Romans built a perimeter wall around it (visible today), added a fine tiled roof, and then buried the tomb.

There's a mystery here. Greeks generally buried their dead outside the city (as did Romans)—there are over a thousand ancient tombs outside Paestum's walls—yet this tomb was parked smack-dab in the center of town. When it was uncovered in 1952, no bodies were found inside. The tomb instead held nine perfectly preserved vases (now in the museum). Archaeologists aren't sure what the tomb's purpose was. Perhaps it was a memorial dedicated to some great hero (like a city founder). Or perhaps it was a memorial to those lost when a neighboring community had to evacuate and settle as refugees here.

• *Continue walking down Via Sacra, the main drag of...*

Roman Paestum: Roman towns were garrison towns: rectangular with a grid street plan and two main streets cutting north-south and east-west, dividing the town into four equal sections. They were built by military engineers with a no-nonsense standard design. New excavations (on the left) have uncovered Roman-era lead piping. City administration buildings were on the left, and residential buildings were on the right.

Shortly after the road turns into a dirt path, you'll come to the **Sanctuary of Fortuna Virilis** (on the left), a big Roman pool that archaeologists believe was a sanctuary dedicated to goddess of luck and fertility, Fortuna Virilis. The strange stones likely supported a wooden platform for priests and statues of gods. Imagine young women walking down the ramp at the far end and through the pool, hoping to conceive a child.

The next big square on the left was the **Roman forum** and ancient Paestum's main intersection. The road on the right led directly (and very practically) to the port. It made sense to have a direct connection to move freight between the sea and the center of town.

Until 2007, the vast field of ruins on the right (between the forum and the next temple) was covered in vegetation. It's since been cleared and cleaned of harmful lichen, which produce acids that dissolve limestone. Study the rocks: Yellow lichen is alive, black is dead. Even the great temples of Paestum were covered in this destructive lichen until 2000, when a two-year-long project cleaned them for the first time.

• *Ahead on the left are the so-called...*

Temples of Neptune and Hera: The **Temple of Neptune** dates from 450 BC and employs the Greek architectural trick where the base line is curved up just a tad to overcome the illusion of sagging caused by a straight base. The Athenians built their Parthenon (with a similar bowed-up base line) just 30 years after this. Many think this temple could have been the Athenians' inspiration.

The adjacent **Temple of Hera,** dating from 550 BC, is the oldest of Paestum's three temples and one of the oldest Greek temples still standing anywhere. Notice the change 100 years makes in the architectural styles: Archaic Doric in 550 BC versus Classic Doric in 450 BC.

Archaeologists now believe the "Temple of Neptune" was actually devoted to a different god. Votive statues uncovered here suggest that Hera was the focus (perhaps this was a new-and-improved version of the adjacent, simpler, and older Temple of Hera). Or perhaps it was a temple to Zeus, Hera's husband, to honor the couple together.

Together, the two temples formed a single huge sanctuary,

with altars outside the temples on the far (east) side. Walk between the temples, then hook right to get a good look at the front of the Temple of Hera. Notice how overbuilt this temple appears. Its columns and capitals are closer together than necessary, as if the builders lacked confidence in their ability to span the distance between supports. Square pillars mark the corners of the *cella* inside. Temples with an odd number of columns (here, nine) had a single colonnade crossing in the center inside to support the wooden roof. More modern temples (such as the Temple of Neptune) had six columns, with two colonnades passing through the *cella*. This left a line of vision open through the middle so that worshippers could see the big statue of the god.

By the way, in September 1943, Allied paratroopers dropped in near here during the famous Operation Avalanche "Salerno Landings," when the Allies (who had already taken Sicily) invaded mainland Italy. Paestum was part of their first beachhead. The Temple of Hera served as an Allied military tent hospital. From here, the Allies pushed back the Nazis, marching to Naples, Cassino, and finally Rome.

Until recently, you could only walk around these two temples, but it's now possible to walk within them (there's even a wheelchair ramp for access to the Temple of Hera).

• *With the Temple of Hera at your back, turn left then right to leave the site (using the exit straight across from the Temple of Neptune). Now turn left onto the modern road...*

Via Magna Grecia: The king of Naples had this Naples-to-Paestum road built in 1829 to inspire his people with ancient temples. While he was modern in his appreciation of antiquity, his road project destroyed a swath of the ancient city, as you'll see as you pass by half of a small **amphitheater.**

• *Just past the amphitheater, you'll find the...*

Ekklesiasterion: Immediately across the street from the museum is what looks like a sunken circular theater. This rare bit of ancient Greek ruins was the Ekklesiasterion, a meeting place where the Greeks would get together to discuss things and vote. Archaeologists believe that the Greek agora (market) was next to here, where the museum stands today.

• *Across the street is the...*

▲▲Paestum Archaeological Museum

Paestum's museum offers the rare opportunity to see artifacts—dating from prehistoric to Greek to Roman times—at the site where they were discovered. These beautifully crafted works (with good English descriptions throughout) help bring Paestum to life. Not everything you see here is from Paestum, though, as the museum also collects artifacts from other nearby sites.

The museum has been undergoing renovations over the last few years; some items may have shifted.

➲ Self-Guided Tour

Before stepping into the museum, notice the proud fascist architecture meant to imitate the structure of the temples you've just seen. Though the building dates from 1954, it was designed in 1938. It seems to command that you *will* enjoy this history lesson.

The exhibits are on several levels. You find mostly Greek pieces on the ground floor (artifacts from the Temple of Hera in front, frescoes from tombs in the back), with a few more upstairs, and Paleolithic to Iron Age artifacts on the lower level. You may also see Roman art (statues, busts, and inscriptions dating from the time of the Roman occupation). While Roman art is not unique to Paestum, the museum's Greek collection is—so that's what you should focus on.

• *Start on the main floor and look for these highlights.*

Temple Reliefs: The museum's center room is designed like a Greek temple's inner *cella* and only opened for temporary exhibitions. If it's open, look at the large carvings overhead (known as metopes) that wrap around this inner sanctum. They once adorned a sanctuary of the goddess Hera five miles away. This sanctuary, called Heraion del Sele, was discovered and excavated in 1934. Some of the carvings show scenes from the life of Hercules. You'll get a chance to see the details later in this visit.

• *Now continue ahead into the large room (broken up by pillars and interior walls) that holds...*

Relics from the Temples at Paestum: This room displays smaller pieces. Displays tell in which temple each relic was found. The Temple of Ceres is often referred to as the Temple of Athena or as the northern *(settentrionale)* sanctuary. The Temples of Neptune and Hera are spoken of as the southern *(meridionale)* sanctuaries.

Farther into the room, you can't miss the display case of a statue's **torso** emblazoned with swastikas—a reminder that this symbol (carrying completely different meanings) predated Hitler by millennia.

Across the room, look for the short fragment of a **frieze** with lion heads. Paestum's three temples were once adorned with decorations, such as these ornamental spouts that spurted rainwater out of lions' mouths. Notice the bits of surviving black, red, and white paint. Reconstructions on the adjacent wall show archaeologists' best guesses as to how the original decorations might have looked.

• *Head through to the next room and find the two glass cases holding nine perfectly preserved...*

Vases: One ceramic and eight bronze, with artistic handles, these vases were found in Paestum's Greek Memorial Tomb (the Heroon). Greek bronzes are rare because Romans often melted them down to make armor. These were discovered in 1952, filled with still-liquid honey and sealed with beeswax. The honey (as you can see in the display cases below) has since crystallized. Honey was a standard part of funerals because, to ancient Greeks, honey symbolized immortality...it lasts forever.

• *Look out the museum's back window (if it's not covered up for renovations) for a good, if distant...*

View of Paestum's Walls: The walls of ancient Paestum reach halfway to the mountain—a reminder that most of the site is still private property and yet to be excavated. The town up on the mountainside is Capaccio, established in the eighth century when inhabitants of the original city of Paestum were driven out by malaria and the city was abandoned.

• *Walk along the corridor at the back of the museum. This area may be under renovation, or you may see...*

Objects from Tombs: More than 1,000 tombs have been identified outside the ancient city's wall. About 100 were found decorated with frescoes or containing objects such as these.

• *At the far end of the corridor, turn left to see...*

The Tomb of the Diver: This is the museum's treasure and the most precious Paestum find. Dating from 480 BC, it's not only the sole ancient Greek tomb fresco in the museum—it's also the only one ever found in southern Italy. Discovered in 1968, it has five frescoed slabs (four sides and a lid; the bottom wasn't decorated). The Greeks saw death as a passage: diving from mortality into immortality...into an unknown world. Archaeologists believe that the pillars shown on the fresco represent the Pillars of Hercules at Gibraltar, which in ancient times defined the known world. The ocean beyond the Mediterranean was the great unknown...like the afterlife. The Greek banquet makes it clear that this was an aristocratic man.

• *After the Tomb of the Diver, the next room may display...*

Lucanian Tomb Frescoes: The many other painted slabs in the museum date from a later time, around 350 BC, when Paestum fell under Lucanian rule. These frescoes are cruder than their earlier Greek counterpart. The people who conquered the Greeks tried to appropriate their art and style, but they lacked the Greeks' distinctive light touch. Still, these offer fascinating glimpses into ancient life here at Paestum. At the entrance to this room, study the tomb and skeleton of an ancient warrior, who was buried with his armor.

• *Back in the main room, circle around the other side of the replica temple, and then find stairs leading one floor up, where you're greeted by a...*

Seated Statue of Zeus: This painted clay Zeus dates from 520 BC. The king of the gods was so lusty with his antics that he's still smirking.

• *The rest of this room is filled with ancient Greek...*

Votive Offerings: Like the temple reliefs seen earlier, these were dug up at Heraion del Sele (not at Paestum). Such offerings are a huge help to modern archaeologists, since the figures that worshippers brought to a temple are clues as to which god the temple honored. These votives depict a woman with a crown on a throne—clearly Hera. The clay votives were simple, affordable, and accessible to regular people.

• *Before you leave, head downstairs to see a....*

Painted Tomb: This previously unviewable and amazingly preserved third-century BC tomb was opened recently (one person allowed in at a time). The tomb was stolen from a necropolis in Paestum, but the travertine blocks were recovered by Italian police in 1976 and reassembled here after they were carefully restored.

Across the room, you can peek into the storage room, where more painted slabs are being restored and other items from the museum are kept safe.

• *Head back up the stairs. By the time you visit, two additional floors may have reopened. One will be dedicated to Roman times at Paestum, while another will focus on the 1943 "Salerno Landing." (An elevator, near the ticket desk, can take you to these upper floors.)*

MORE SIGHTS IN PAESTUM

Barlotti Caseificio Buffalo Farm

This part of Italy is known for its mozzarella cheese made from buffalo milk. A convenient place to appreciate buffalo mozzarella and other buffalo products is at Barlotti Caseificio, a working buffalo farm about a mile from the Paestum ruins (a 25-minute walk from the museum). Visitors can look around a few areas for free, but it's best to come here for a lunch featuring all things buffalo (buffalo burgers, buffalo-cheese ravioli, and caprese salads), or to buy buffalo gelato and buffalo-based cosmetics in the shop. The farm offers an overpriced tour that's not worthwhile—since production takes place overnight, you won't see much beyond what you can see for free (open daily year-round, shop and gelato counter 8:00-20:00, lunch 12:00-15:00, Via Torre di Paestum 1, +39 0828 811 146, www.barlotti.it, tour@barlotti.it).

Paestum Beach (Lido Cinzia)

Paestum has a yellow-sand beach, a welcome sight if you've come from the pebbly, volcanic-sand beaches around the Amalfi Coast. You'll find plenty of free areas, and the water is shallow for a good distance. Just before you reach the beach, a few decent restaurants cluster together. It's an easy 20-to-25-minute walk from my recommended hotels.

Sleeping in Paestum

Paestum at night, with views of the floodlit ruins, is magic. Accommodations here offer great value. You can sleep in a mansion for the same price you'd pay for a closet in Positano. For locations, see the "Paestum" map, earlier in this chapter.

€€€ Duca di Marigliano is a splurge by Paestum standards. This boutique hotel has artistic touches throughout the property. The recently renovated 19th-century home of a duke now feels modern but with classic touches. Its sprawling garden includes a pool, a spa, and lots of places to lounge with a drink from the bar, and the restaurant serves meals with class to match (some stairs, Via Tavernelle 86, +39 0828 721 297, www.tenutaducamarigliano.it, info@tenutaducamarigliano.it).

€€ Hotel Villa Rita is a family-run country hotel set on two acres of attractive grounds that'll make you want to settle in and stay a while. A half-mile from the ruins (where kind owner Luigi played as a child) and a half-mile from the beach, it has 25 rooms, a kid-friendly swimming pool, beautiful gardens, and an excellent restaurant using only local ingredients (RS%, lunch or dinner available, free parking, closed Nov-March, Via Nettuno 9, +39

0828 811 081, www.hotelvillarita.it, info@hotelvillarita.it, Luigi and his children Rita and Arnaldo).

€€ Hotel dei Templi, with 11 good rooms, is right along the pedestrianized Via Tavernelle, which can be sleepy by day but often comes alive at night (lots of stairs, pay parking, Via Tavernelle 64, +39 0828 811 747, www.hoteldeitempli.it, info@hoteldeitempli.it).

Outside Town: An offbeat option for drivers, **€€ Agriturismo Seliano** has a huge dining room and lounge with a fireplace, a pool, and 14 spacious rooms on a peaceful, once-elegant farm estate that's been in the same family for 300 years (air-con, closed Nov-March; two miles north of ruins—*Azienda Agrituristica Seliano* sign directs you off the main road down a long, potholed dirt driveway; Via Seliano, +39 0828 723 634, www.agriturismoseliano.it, seliano@agriturismoseliano.it). If you stay here, reserve dinner too—it's served at one long table and made with produce fresh from the garden. They can also organize cooking classes. The place is run by Cecilia, an English-speaking baroness, and her family, including a half-dozen nice and friendly dogs.

Eating in Paestum

Picnics in the ruins aren't allowed. Several eateries cluster around the museum and on Via Tavernelle.

€€ La Basilica Pizzeria, on the little square facing the town's church, is the best of the places near the entrance to the ruins. It's reasonably priced, with good pizzas and simple pasta dishes. The seating on the square is pleasant, and they also have a terrace out back facing a pretty little garden (daily, Via Magna Grecia 881, +39 0828 811 301).

At the south end of the ruins, **€€€ Ristorante Nettuno** is elegant, with white tablecloths, a grand piano, and views of the temples; it's built into a surviving tower from the Roman city walls. It has limited hours, though, serving only dinner, and you must make a reservation in advance (mid-June-mid-Sept from 19:30); closed Tue and Nov-Feb; Via Nettuno 2, +39 0828 811 028, www.ristorantenettuno.com).

Just north of the ruins, outside the Roman city wall, Via Tavernelle has been partly blocked off to traffic, creating a fun little restaurant row with casual indoor and outdoor tables (though it can be dead at lunchtime). Consider **€€€ Bistrot 73,** with wonderful pasta dishes (at #48, +39 342 526 1393); **€€€ Antiche Mura,** which accompanies fine grilled meats with an impressive wine list (at #20, +39 0828 199 8535); or **€€€ Alici Cucina** for seafood (at #6, +39 0828 199 6204).

ITALIAN HISTORY

Italy has a lot of history, so let's get started.

ORIGINS OF ROME (c. 753 BC-AD 450)

A she-wolf breastfed two human babies, Romulus and Remus, who grew to build the city of Rome in 753 BC—you buy that? Closer to fact, farmers and shepherds of the Latin tribe settled near the mouth of the Tiber River, a convenient trading location. The crude settlement was sandwiched between two sophisticated civilizations—Greek colonists to the south (Magna Graecia, or "Great Greece"), and to the north (Etruria—present-day Tuscany/Umbria) the Etruscans, whose origins and language have long puzzled historians. Baby Rome was both dominated and nourished by these societies.

According to legend, when the son of an Etruscan king raped a Roman woman (509 BC), her defenders led a revolt, driving out the Etruscans and replacing them with elected Roman senators and (eventually) a code of law (Laws of the Twelve Tables, 450 BC). The Roman Republic was born.

THE ROMAN REPUBLIC EXPANDS (c. 509 BC-AD 1)

Located at the midpoint of the peninsula, Rome was perfectly situated for trading salt and wine. Roman businessmen, backed by a disciplined army, expanded throughout the Italian peninsula, establishing Roman infrastructure as they went. Rome soon swallowed up its northern Etruscan neighbors, conquering them by force and absorbing their culture.

Next came Magna Graecia, with Rome's legions defeating the Greek general Pyrrhus after several costly "Pyrrhic" victories (c. 275 BC). Rome now ruled a united federation stretching from Tuscany to the tip of the Italian peninsula, with a standard currency, a system of roads (including the Via Appia), and a standing army of a half-million soldiers ready for the next challenge: Carthage.

Carthage (modern-day Tunisia) and Rome fought the three bitter Punic Wars for control of the Mediterranean (264-201 BC and 146 BC). The balance of power hung precariously in the Second Punic War (218-201 BC), when Hannibal of Carthage crossed the sea to Spain with a huge army of men and elephants. He marched 1,200 miles overland, crossed the Alps, and forcefully penetrated Italy from the rear. Almost at the gates of the city of Rome, he was finally turned back. The Romans prevailed, and, in the mismatched Third Punic War, they burned the city of Carthage to the ground (146 BC).

The well-tuned Roman legions easily subdued sophisticated Greece in three Macedonian Wars (215-146 BC). Though Rome conquered Greece, Greek culture dominated the Romans. From hairstyles to statues to temples to the evening's entertainment, Rome was forever "Hellenized," becoming the curators of Greek culture, passing it down to future generations.

By the first century BC, Rome was master of the Mediterranean. Booty, cheap grain, and thousands of captured slaves poured in, transforming the economic model from small farmers to unemployed city dwellers living off tribute from conquered lands. The Republic had changed.

CIVIL WARS AND THE TRANSITION TO EMPIRE (First Century BC)

With easy money streaming in and traditional roles obsolete, Romans bickered among themselves over their slice of the pie. Wealthy landowners (patricians, the ruling Senate) wrangled with the middle and working classes (plebeians) and with the growing population of slaves, who demanded greater say-so in government. In 73 BC, Spartacus—a Greek-born soldier-turned-Roman slave who'd been forced to fight as a gladiator—escaped to the slopes of Mount Vesuvius, where he amassed an army of 90,000 angry slaves. After two years of fierce fighting across Italy, the Roman legions crushed the revolt and crucified 6,000 rebels along the Via Appia as a warning.

Amid the chaos of class war and civil war, charismatic generals who could provide wealth and security became dictators—men such as Sulla, Crassus, Pompey...and Caesar. Julius Caesar (100-44 BC) was a cunning politician, riveting speaker, conqueror of Gaul, author of *The Gallic Wars,* and lover of Cleopatra, queen of Egypt. In his four-year reign, he reformed and centralized the government around himself. Disgruntled Republicans feared that he would make himself king. At his peak of power, they surrounded Caesar

Italy Almanac

Official Name: Repubblica Italiana (Italian Republic)

Locals Call It: Italia

Size: 116,000 square miles, including the islands of Sicily, Sardinia, and others. Population is about 61 million.

Geography: Italy is shaped like a boot, 850 miles long and 150 miles wide, jutting into the central Mediterranean. (It's about the same size as California.) The terrain is generally mountainous or hilly, with the Alps in the north and a north-south "spine" of the Apennine Mountains. The highest point is Mont Blanc (15,771 feet), on the border with France. Outside the Alps, the highest point on the peninsula is Corno Grande (9,554 feet). Italy has 5,000 miles of coastline. Major rivers include the Po (the longest at 400 miles), Arno, Adige, and Tiber. Italy has three active volcanoes: Vesuvius, Etna, and Stromboli.

Latitude and Longitude: 43°N and 12°E (similar to Oregon and Maine).

Regions: Italy is divided into 20 regions (including Campania, Tuscany, Veneto, and Lazio). Locally, there are some 8,200 "communes," each with a community council and mayor.

Major Cities: Rome (the capital, 2.8 million), Milan (1.3 million), and Naples (1 million).

Economy: The gross domestic product is $2.3 trillion; the GDP per capita is $52,700. About 74 percent of the economy consists of service jobs (especially tourism), 24 percent is industry (textiles, chemicals), and 2 percent is agriculture (fruit, vegetables, olives, wine, plus fishing). There are over 15,000 miles of train lines (mostly government-run) and 4,300 miles of expressway (autostrada).

Government: Italy is a republic, with three branches of government. The chief executive is Prime Minister Giorgia Meloni. The bicameral legislature is elected by (mostly) direct voting. Since World War II, the fragmented country has had 69 national coalition governments.

Flag: Three vertical bands of green, white, and red.

Italian Inventions: Opera, cologne, thermometer, barometer, pizza, wireless telegraph, espresso machine, typewriter, batteries, nitroglycerin, yo-yos...and the ice-cream cone.

Museums: Over 3,000.

The Average Gio: The average Italian is 46 years old, has 1.4 kids, is nominally Roman Catholic, and will live to the ripe old age of 82 (1 in 5 Italians is older than 65). Every day, he or she consumes two servings of pasta, a half-pound of bread, and two glasses of wine. Despite Italian cuisine, Gio isn't fat—only around 20 percent of Italians are considered obese.

in the Senate on the Ides of March (March 15, 44 BC) and stabbed him to death.

Julius Caesar died, but the concept of one-man rule lived on in his adopted son. Named Octavian at birth, he defeated rival Mark Antony (another lover of Cleopatra, 31 BC) and was proclaimed Emperor Augustus (27 BC). Augustus outwardly followed the traditions of the Republic, while in practice he acted as a dictator with the backing of Rome's legions and the rubber-stamp approval of the Senate. He established his family to succeed him (making the family name "Caesar" a title) and set the pattern of rule by emperors for the next 500 years.

THE ROMAN EMPIRE (c. AD 1-500)

In his 40-year reign, Augustus ended Rome's civil wars and ushered in the Pax Romana: 200 years of prosperity and relative peace. Rome ruled an empire of 54 million people, stretching from Scotland to northern Africa, from Spain to the Euphrates River. Conquered peoples were welcomed into the fold of prosperity, linked by roads, common laws, common gods, education, and the Latin language. The city of Rome, with more than a million inhabitants, was decorated with Greek-style statues and monumental structures faced with marble. It was the marvel of the known world.

The empire prospered on a (false) economy of booty, slaves, and cheap imports. On the Italian peninsula, traditional small farms were swallowed up by large farming and herding estates. In this "global economy," the Italian peninsula became just one province among many in a worldwide Latin-speaking empire, ruled by an emperor who was likely born elsewhere. The empire even survived the often turbulent and naughty behavior of emperors such as Caligula (r. 37-41) and Nero (r. 54-68).

DECLINE AND FALL (AD 200-500)

Rome peaked in the second century AD under the capable emperors Trajan (r. 98-117), Hadrian (r. 117-138), and Marcus Aurelius (r. 161-180). For the next three centuries, the Roman Empire declined, shrinking in size and wealth, a victim of corruption, disease, an overextended army, a false economy, and the constant pressure of "barbarian" tribes pecking away at its borders. By the third century, the army had become the real power, handpicking figurehead emperors to do its bidding: In a 40-year span, 15 emperors were first saluted and then assassinated by fickle generals.

Trying to stall the disintegration, Emperor Diocletian (r. 284-305) split the empire into two administrative halves under two equal emperors. Constantine (r. 306-337) solidified the divide by moving the capital of the empire from decaying Rome to the new city of Constantinople (330, present-day Istanbul). Almost instantly, the once-great city of Rome became a minor player in imperial affairs. (The eastern "Byzantine" half of the empire would thrive and live on for another thousand years.) Constantine also legalized Christianity (313), and the once-persecuted cult soon became virtually the state religion, the backbone of Rome's fading hierarchy.

By 410, "Rome" had shrunk to just the city itself, surrounded by a protective wall. Barbarian tribes from the north and east poured in to loot and plunder. The city was sacked by Visigoths (410) and vandalized by Vandals (455), and the pope had to plead with Attila the Hun for mercy (451). The peninsula's population fell to six million, trade and agriculture were disrupted, schools closed, and the infrastructure collapsed. Peasants huddled near powerful lords for protection from bandits, planting the seeds of medieval feudalism.

In 476, the last emperor sold his title for a comfy pension, and Rome fell like a huge column, kicking up dust that would plunge Europe into a thousand years of darkness. For the next 13 centuries, there would be no "Italy," just a patchwork of rural dukedoms and towns, victimized by foreign powers. Italy lay in shambles, helpless.

INVASIONS (AD 500-1000)

In 500 years, Italy suffered through a full paragraph of invasions: Lombards (568) and Byzantines (under Justinian, 536) occupied the north. In the south, Muslim Saracens (827) and Christian Normans (1061) established thriving kingdoms. Charlemagne, king of the Germanic Franks, defeated the Lombards, and on Christmas Day, AD 800, he knelt before the pope in St. Peter's in Rome to be crowned Holy Roman Emperor, an empty title meant to resurrect the glory of ancient Rome united with medieval Christianity. For the next thousand years, Italians would pledge nominal allegiance to weak, distant German kings as their Holy Roman Emperor.

Through all the invasions and chaos, the glory of ancient Rome was preserved in the pomp, knowledge, hierarchy, and wealth of the Christian Church. Strong popes (Leo I, 440-461, and Gregory the Great, 590-604) ruled like small-time emperors, governing territories in central Italy called the Papal States.

PROSPERITY AND POLITICS (AD 1000-1300)

Italy survived Y1K, and the economy picked up. Sea-trading cities like Venice, Genoa, Pisa, Naples, and Amalfi grew wealthy as middlemen between Europe and the Orient. During the Crusades (e.g., First Crusade, 1097-1130), Italian ships ferried Europe's Christian soldiers eastward, then returned laden with spices and highly marked-up luxury goods from "the Orient." Trade spawned banking, and Italians became capitalists, loaning money at interest to Europe's royalty. Italy pioneered a new phenomenon in Europe—municipalities *(comuni)* that were self-governing commercial centers. The medieval prosperity of the cities laid the foundation of the Renaissance to come.

Politically, the Italian peninsula was dominated by two rulers—the pope in Rome and the German Holy Roman Emperor (with holdings in the north). Italy split into two warring political parties: supporters of the popes (called Guelphs, centered in urban areas) and supporters of the emperors (Ghibellines, popular with the rural nobility).

THE UNLUCKY 1300s

In 1309, enticed by the fast-rising power of France, the pope moved from Rome to Avignon. At one point, two rival popes reigned, one in Avignon and the other in Rome, and they excommunicated each other. The papacy eventually returned to Rome (1377), but the schism created a breakdown in central authority that was exacerbated by an outbreak of bubonic plague (Black Death, 1347-1348), which killed a third of the Italian population.

In the power vacuum, new players emerged in the independent cities. Venice, Florence, Milan, and Naples were under the protection and leadership of local noble families *(signoria)* such as the Medici in Florence. Florence thrived in the wool and dyeing trade, which led to dominance in international banking, with branches in all of Europe's capitals. A positive side effect of the terrible Black Death was that the now-smaller population got a bigger share

1000 Years
Each dashed line = 500 years
Each dashed line =100 years
Each dashed

1000 0 500 1000 1100 1200 1300 1400 1500 1600

THE PAPACY

Jesus
PAPAL STATES
Peter
PAPAL STATES ESTABLISHED
GREAT SCHISM - POPES IN AVIGNON
Julius II
Leo X
Paul III

HISTORY

ORVIETO FOUNDED
ETRUSCAN
Julius Caesar
Constantine
ROMAN
EMPIRE
REPUBLIC
Romulus & Remus
INVASIONS
TREATY OF VERDUN
Charlemagne
PADOVA UNIV.
BLACK DEATH
UNLUCKY 1300s
SACK OF ROME
FOREIGN INVASIONS
PROSPERITY & POLITICS
GUELPHS & GHIBELLINES
RENAISSANCE
QUATTROCENTO (MEDICI RULE)
St. Benedict
St. Anthony of Padova
St. Francis
St. Clare
St. Cath. of Siena
Galileo
REFORMATION & RELIGIOUS WARS
LUTHER'S 95 THESES
COUNCIL OF TRENT
COUNTER-REF.

OTHER EMPIRES & EVENTS

SACK OF ROME
BARBARIANS
Attila
VESUVIUS ERUPTION
NORMANS IN SICILY
CRUSADES
Lorenzo
PEAK
ST. MARK'S BODY TAKEN
FLORENTINE REPUBLIC
Savonarola
Cleopatra
EGYPT
Hagia Sophia
VENETIAN EMPIRE
PEAK
GLORIOUS DECLINE
SACK OF CONST.
BYZANTINE EMPIRE
DA GAMA TO INDIA
BATTLE OF LEPANTO
S. ITALY COLONIZED
ROMAN EMPIRE SPLIT IN TWO
Monreale
FALL OF CONSTANTINOPLE
Polo
GREECE
Justinian

ARTS & ARCHITECTURE

Machiavelli
The Prince
Paestum
Boccaccio
Palladio
BENEDICT FOUNDS 1ST MONASATIC ORDER
Dante
Divine Comedy
Veronese
TOMBS
Petrarch
Titian
ETRUSCAN
Ravenna Mosaics
Pisa Duomo
Orvieto Duomo
Caravaggio
ROMAN
BYZ.
Scrovegni Chapel
David
Sistine Ceiling
Colosseum, Pantheon, etc.
St. Mark's
ROMANESQUE
GOTHIC
Last Judg.
St. Peter's (Old)
Assisi Basilica
Doge's Palace
RENAISSANCE
Duomo Florence
St. Peter's (New) Start
← To Cave Painting
PRE-RENAISSANCE
MANNERISM
Masaccio
Giotto
Michelangelo
Brunelleschi
Leonardo
Duccio
Raphael
Cellini
Donatello
Botticelli

1000 0 500 1000 1100 1200 1300 1400 1500 1600

HISTORY

Italian History & Art Timeline

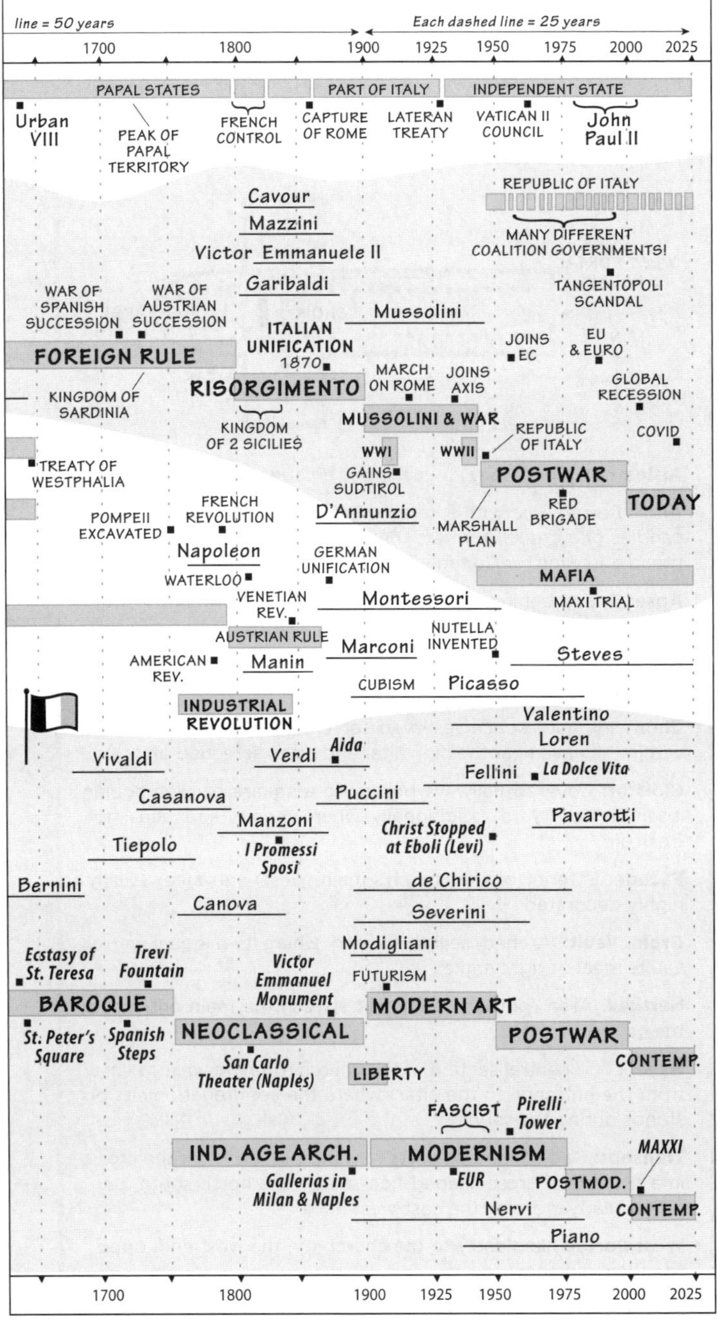

line = 50 years | Each dashed line = 25 years

1700 | 1800 | 1900 | 1925 | 1950 | 1975 | 2000 | 2025

PAPAL STATES | PART OF ITALY | INDEPENDENT STATE

Urban VIII | PEAK OF PAPAL TERRITORY | FRENCH CONTROL | CAPTURE OF ROME | LATERAN TREATY | VATICAN II COUNCIL | John Paul II

REPUBLIC OF ITALY | MANY DIFFERENT COALITION GOVERNMENTS!

Cavour | Mazzini | Victor Emmanuele II | Garibaldi | Mussolini | TANGENTOPOLI SCANDAL

WAR OF SPANISH SUCCESSION | WAR OF AUSTRIAN SUCCESSION | ITALIAN UNIFICATION 1870 | JOINS EC | EU & EURO

FOREIGN RULE | KINGDOM OF SARDINIA | RISORGIMENTO | MARCH ON ROME | JOINS AXIS | GLOBAL RECESSION

KINGDOM OF 2 SICILIES | MUSSOLINI & WAR | REPUBLIC OF ITALY | COVID

TREATY OF WESTPHALIA | WWI | WWII | GAINS SUDTIROL | POSTWAR | TODAY

POMPEII EXCAVATED | FRENCH REVOLUTION | D'Annunzio | MARSHALL PLAN | RED BRIGADE

Napoleon | WATERLOO | GERMAN UNIFICATION | MAFIA | MAXI TRIAL

VENETIAN REV. | Montessori | AUSTRIAN RULE | NUTELLA INVENTED

AMERICAN REV. | Manin | Marconi | Steves

CUBISM | Picasso | INDUSTRIAL REVOLUTION

Valentino | Loren

Vivaldi | Verdi | *Aida* | Fellini | *La Dolce Vita*

Casanova | Puccini | Manzoni | Pavarotti

Tiepolo | *I Promessi Sposi* | *Christ Stopped at Eboli (Levi)*

Bernini | de Chirico | Canova | Severini | Modigliani

Ecstasy of St. Teresa | *Trevi Fountain* | *Victor Emmanuel Monument* | FUTURISM

BAROQUE | MODERN ART | NEOCLASSICAL | POSTWAR | CONTEMP.

St. Peter's Square | *Spanish Steps* | *San Carlo Theater (Naples)* | LIBERTY

FASCIST | *Pirelli Tower* | *MAXXI*

IND. AGE ARCH. | MODERNISM | *Gallerias in Milan & Naples* | *EUR* | POSTMOD. | CONTEMP.

Nervi | Piano

1700 | 1800 | 1900 | 1925 | 1950 | 1975 | 2000 | 2025

HISTORY

Typical Church Architecture

History comes to life when you visit a centuries-old church. Even if you wouldn't know your apse from a hole in the ground, learning a few simple terms will enrich your experience. Note that not every church has every feature, and a "cathedral" isn't a type of church architecture, but rather a designation for a church that's a governing center for a local bishop.

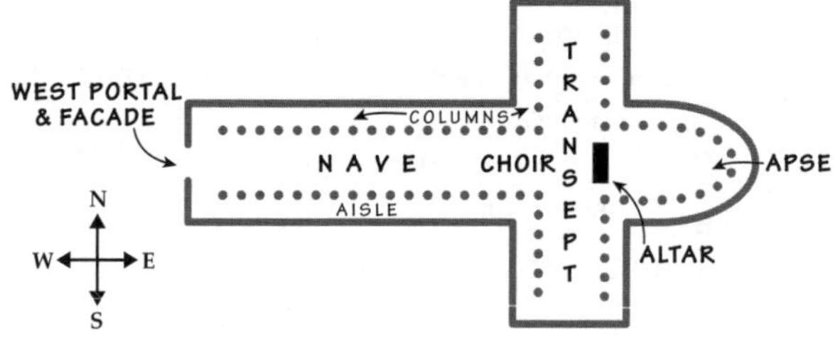

Aisles: Long, generally low-ceilinged arcades that flank the nave

Altar: Raised area with a ceremonial table (often adorned with candles or a crucifix), where the priest prepares and serves the bread and wine for Communion

Apse: Space behind the altar, sometimes bordered with small chapels

Barrel Vault: Continuous round-arched ceiling that resembles an extended upside-down U

Choir: Intimate space reserved for clergy and choir, located within the nave near the high altar and often screened off

Cloister: Covered hallways bordering a square or rectangular open-air courtyard, traditionally where monks and nuns got fresh air

Facade: Exterior of the church's main (west) entrance, usually highly decorated

Groin Vault: Arched ceiling formed where two equal barrel vaults meet at right angles

Narthex: Area (portico or foyer) between the main entry and the nave

Nave: Long central section of the church (running west to east, from the entrance to the altar) where the congregation sits or stands during the service

Transept: One of the two parts forming the "arms" of the cross in a traditional cross-shaped floor plan; runs north-south, perpendicularly crossing the east-west nave

West Portal: Main entry to the church (on the west end, opposite the main altar)

of the land, jobs, and infrastructure. By century's end, Italy was poised to enter its most glorious era since antiquity.

THE RENAISSANCE (1400s-1600s)

The Renaissance (Rinascimento)—the "rebirth" of ancient Greek and Roman art styles, knowledge, and humanism—began in Italy (c. 1400) and spread through Europe over the next two centuries. Many of Europe's most famous painters, sculptors, and thinkers—Michelangelo, Leonardo, Raphael, etc.—were Italian.

It was a cultural boom that changed people's thinking about every aspect of life. In politics, it meant an eventual rebirth of Greek ideas of democracy. In religion, it meant a move away from Church dominance and toward the assertion of man (humanism) and a more personal faith. Science and secular learning were revived after centuries of superstition and ignorance. In architecture, it was a return to the balanced columns and domes of Greece and Rome. In painting, the Renaissance meant 3-D realism.

Italians dotted their cities with publicly financed art that celebrated Greek gods and emulated Roman-style domed buildings. They preached Greek-style democracy and explored the natural world. The cultural boom was financed by thriving trade and lucrative banking. During the Renaissance, the peninsula once again became the trendsetting cultural center of Europe.

FOREIGN INVASIONS (1500s)

In May 1498, Vasco da Gama of Portugal landed in India, having found a sea route around Africa. Italy's monopoly on trade with the East was broken. Portugal, France, Spain, England, and Holland—nation-states under strong central rule—began to overtake decentralized Italy. Italy's once-great maritime cities now traded in an economic backwater, just as Italy's bankers (such as the Medici in Florence) were going bankrupt. While the Italian Renaissance was all the rage throughout Europe, it declined in its birthplace. Italy—culturally sophisticated but weak and decentralized—was ripe for the picking by Europe's rising powers.

Several kings of France invaded (1494, 1495, and 1515)—initially invited by Italian lords to attack their rivals—and began divvying up territory for their noble families. Italy also became a battleground in religious conflicts between Catholics and the new Protestant movement. In the chaos, the city of Rome was brutally sacked by foreign mercenaries (1527).

FOREIGN RULE (1600-1800)

For the next two centuries, most of Italy's states were ruled by foreign nobles, who treated them as prizes in Europe's dynastic wars. Italy ceased to be a major player in Europe, politically or economi-

Top 10 Italians

Romulus: Nursed on wolf milk, this legendary orphan founded the city of Rome (traditionally in 753 BC). Over the next seven centuries, his descendants dominated the Italian peninsula, ruling from Rome as a Republic.

Julius Caesar (100-44 BC): After conquering Gaul (France), subduing Egypt, and winning Cleopatra's heart, Caesar ruled Rome with king-like powers. In an attempt to preserve the Republic, senators stabbed him to death, but the concept of one-man rule lived on.

Augustus (born Octavian, 63 BC-AD 14): Julius' adopted son became the first of the Caesars that ruled Rome during its 500 years as a Europe-wide power. He set the tone for emperors both good (Trajan, Hadrian, Marcus Aurelius) and bad (Caligula, Nero, and dozens of others).

Constantine (c. 280-337 AD): Raised in a Christian home, this emperor legalized Christianity, almost instantly turning a persecuted sect into a Europe-wide religion. With the Fall of Rome, the Church was directed by strong popes and so guided Italians through the next thousand years of invasions, plagues, political decentralization, and darkness.

Lorenzo (the Magnificent) de' Medici (1449-1492): Soldier, poet, lover, and ruler of Florence in the 1400s, this Renaissance Man embodied the "rebirth" of ancient enlightenment. Lorenzo's wealthy Medici family funded Florentine artists who pioneered a new realism in painting and sculpture.

Michelangelo Buonarroti (1475-1564): His statue of David—slayer of an ignorant brute—stands as a monumental symbol of Italian enlightenment. Along with fellow geniuses Leonardo da Vinci and

cally. Italian intellectual life was often cropped short by a conservative Catholic Church trying to fight Protestantism. Galileo, for example, was forced by the Inquisition to renounce his belief that the earth orbited the sun (1633). But Italy did export Baroque art (Bernini) and the budding new medium of opera.

The War of the Spanish Succession (1713)—in which Italy did not participate—gave much of northern Italy to Austria's ruling family, the Habsburgs (who now wore the crown of Holy Roman Emperor). In the south, Spain's Bourbon family ruled the Kingdom of Naples (known after 1816 as the Kingdom of the Two Sicilies), making it a culturally sophisticated but economically backward area, preserving a medieval, feudal caste system.

In 1720, a minor war (the War of Austrian Succession) created a new state at the foot of the Alps, called the Kingdom of Sardinia (a.k.a. the Kingdom of Piedmont, or Savoy). Ruled by the Savoy

Raphael, Michelangelo mastered the visual arts of the Italian Renaissance: painting, sculpture, and architecture. Their innovations spread northward, influencing the rest of Europe.

Giovanni Lorenzo Bernini (1598-1680): The "Michelangelo of Baroque" kept Italy a major exporter of sophisticated trends. Bernini's ornate statues and architectural projects decorated palaces of the rising power brokers in France, even as Italy was reverting to an economically stagnant patchwork of foreign-ruled states.

Victor Emmanuel II (1820-1878): As the only Italian-born ruler on the peninsula, this king of Sardinia played a central role in Italian unification. Aided by the general Garibaldi, writer Mazzini, and politician Cavour (with a soundtrack by Verdi), he became the first ruler of a united, democratic Italy, in September 1870. (The preceding proper nouns have since come to adorn streets and piazzas throughout Italy.)

Benito Mussolini (1883-1945): An inspiration for Hitler, he derailed Italy's fledgling democracy, becoming dictator of a fascist state and leading the country to defeat in World War II. No public places honor Mussolini, but many streets and piazzas throughout Italy bear the name of Giacomo Matteotti (1885-1924), a politician whose outspoken opposition to Mussolini got him killed.

Federico Fellini (1920-1993): Fellini's films *(La Strada, La Dolce Vita, 8½)* chronicle Italy's postwar years in gritty black and white—the poverty, destruction, and disillusionment of the war followed by the optimism, decadence, and materialism of the economic boom. He captured the surreal chaos of Italy's abrupt social change from traditional Catholicism to a secular, urban world presided over by Mafia bosses and weak government.

family, this was the only major state on the peninsula that was actually ruled by Italians. It proved to be a toehold to the future.

ITALY UNITES—THE RISORGIMENTO (1800s)

In 1796, Napoleon Bonaparte swept through Italy and changed everything. He ousted Austrian and Spanish dukes, confiscated Church lands, united scattered states, and crowned himself "King of Italy" (1805). After his defeat (1815), Italy's old ruling order (namely, Austria and Spain) was restored. But Napoleon had planted a seed: What if Italians could unite and rule themselves like Europe's other modern nations?

For the next 50 years, a movement to unite Italy slowly grew. Called the Risorgimento—a word that means "rising again"—the movement promised a revival of Italy's glory. It started as a revolutionary, liberal movement—taking part in it was punishable by death. Members of a secret society called the Carbonari (led by

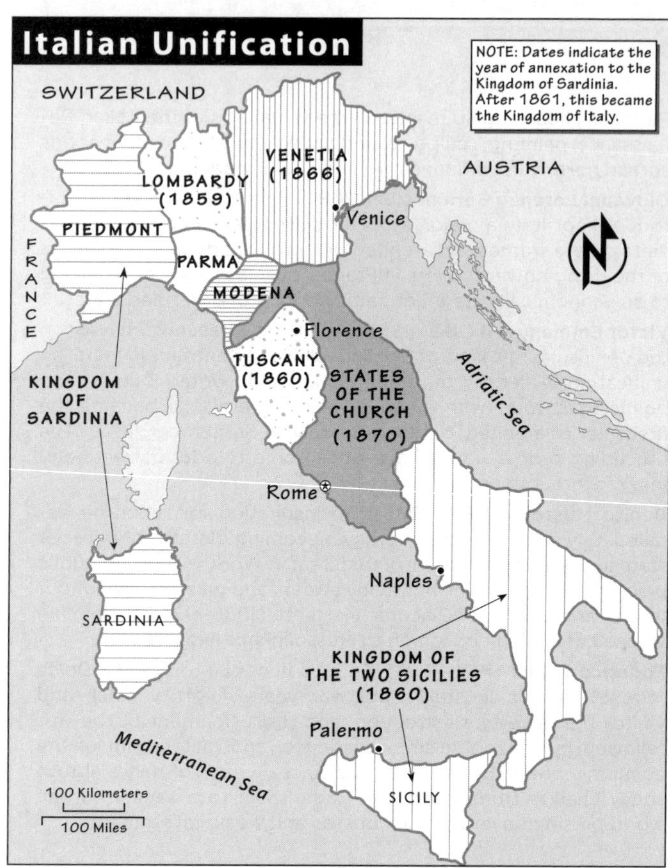

a professional revolutionary named Giuseppe Mazzini) exchanged secret handshakes, printed fliers, planted bombs, and assassinated conservative rulers. Their small revolutions (1820-1821, 1831, 1848) were easily and brutally slapped down, but the cause wouldn't die.

Gradually, Italians of all stripes warmed to the idea of unification. Whether a united dictatorship, a united papal state, a united kingdom, or a united democracy, most Italians could agree that it was time for Spain, Austria, and France to leave.

The movement coalesced around the Italian-ruled Kingdom of Sardinia and its king, Victor Emmanuel II. In 1859, Sardinia's prime minister, Camillo Cavour, cleverly persuaded France to drive Austria out of northern Italy, leaving the region in Italian hands. A vote was held, and several central Italian states (including some of the pope's) rejected their feudal lords and chose to join the growing Sardinian kingdom.

After victory in the north, Italy's most renowned Carbonari

general, Giuseppe Garibaldi (1807-1882), steamed south with a thousand of his best soldiers (I Mille) and marched on Spanish-ruled southern Italy (1860). The old order simply collapsed. In Sicily, in two short months, Garibaldi achieved a seemingly impossible victory against a far superior army. The following year, an assembly of deputies from throughout Italy met in Turin and crowned Victor Emmanuel II "King of Italy." Only the pope in Rome held out, protected by French troops. When the city finally fell—easily—to the unification forces on September 20, 1870, the Risorgimento was complete. Italy went ape.

The Risorgimento was largely the work of four men: Garibaldi (the sword), Mazzini (the spark), Cavour (the diplomat), and Victor Emmanuel II (the rallying point). Today, street signs throughout Italy honor them and the dates of their great victories.

MUSSOLINI AND WAR (1900-1950)

Italy—now an actual nation-state, not just a linguistic region—entered the 20th century with a progressive government (a constitutional monarchy), a collection of colonies, and a flourishing northern half of the country. In the economically backward south (the Mezzogiorno), poverty and lack of opportunity led millions of poor peasants to emigrate to the Americas. World War I (1915-1918) left 650,000 Italians dead, but being on the winning Allied side, Italy was given some former Austrian territory, including the south Tirol and the city of Trieste. In the swirl of postwar cynicism and anarchy, many radical political parties—Communist, Socialist, Popular (Catholic), and Fascist—rose up.

Benito Mussolini (1883-1945), a popular writer for socialist and labor-union newspapers, led the fascists. ("Fascism" comes from Latin *fasci,* the bundles of rods that symbolized unity in ancient Rome.) Though only a minority (6 percent of the parliament in 1921), they intimidated the disorganized majority with organized violence by black-shirted fascist gangs. In 1922, Mussolini seized the government (see "The March on Rome" sidebar) and began his rule as dictator for the next two decades.

Mussolini solidified his reign among Catholics by striking an agreement with the pope (Lateran Treaty, 1929), giving Vatican City to the papacy, while Mussolini ruled Italy with the implied blessing of the Catholic Church. Italy responded to the great worldwide Depression (1930s) with big public works projects (including Rome's subway), government investment in industry, and an expanded army.

Mussolini allied his country with Hitler's Nazi regime, drawing an unprepared Italy into World War II (1940). Italy's lame army was never a factor in the war, and when Allied forces landed in Sicily (1943), Italians welcomed them as liberators. The Italians

The March on Rome

In October 1922, Benito Mussolini, head of the newly formed Fascist Party, boldly proposed a coup d'état, saying, "Either the government will be given to us, or we will take it by marching on Rome." Throughout Italy, black-shirted fascists occupied government buildings in their hometowns. Others grabbed guns, farming hoes, and kitchen knives and set off to converge on the outskirts of Rome. (Estimates of the size of the fascist band range from 300 to the 300,000 of fascist legend.) Mussolini sent the government an ultimatum to surrender. Though the fascists were easily outmanned and outgunned by government forces, the show of force intimidated the king, Victor Emmanuel III, into avoiding a nasty confrontation. He invited Mussolini to Rome. Mussolini arrived the next day (by first-class train), was made prime minister, then marched his black-shirted troops triumphantly through the streets of Rome.

toppled Mussolini's government and surrendered to the Allies, but Nazi Germany sent troops to rescue Mussolini. The war raged on as Allied troops inched their way north against German resistance. Italians were reduced to dire poverty. In the last days of the war (April 1945), Mussolini was captured by the Italian resistance. They shot him and his girlfriend and hung their bodies upside down in a public square in Milan.

POSTWAR ITALY

At war's end, Italy was physically ruined and extremely poor. The nation rebuilt in the 1950s and 1960s with Marshall Plan aid from the United States. Many Italian men moved to northern Europe to find work; many others left farms and flocked to the cities. Over time, Italy regained its standing among nations, joining NATO and what would later become the European Union.

However, the government remained weak, changing on average once a year, shifting from right to left to centrist coalitions. Afraid of another Mussolini, the authors of the postwar constitution created a feeble executive branch; without majorities in both houses of parliament, nothing could get done. All Italians acknowledged that the real power lay in the hands of backroom politicians and organized crime—a phenomenon called *Tangentopoli*, or "Bribe City." The country remained strongly divided between the rich, industrial north and the poor, rural south.

Italian society changed greatly after the liberal reforms of the Catholic Church at the Vatican II conference (1962-1965). The once-conservative Catholic country legalized divorce and contraception, and the birth rate plummeted. In the 1970s, Italy suffered a wave of violence from left- and right-wing domestic terrorists and organized crime, punctuated by the assassination of former Prime Minister Aldo Moro (1978). In the early 1990s, the judiciary undertook a reasonably effective campaign to rid politics of corruption and Mafia ties. The Mafia still exists but is much less powerful.

Italy entered the 21st century buoyed by a growing economy and living standards that were nearly on par with its European neighbors.

ITALY TODAY

That turnaround made Italy a magnet for immigration, especially from Albania, North Africa, and Eastern Europe. The influx brought with it cheap labor but also pressures on social services and cultural norms. Like other European nations, Italy ran up big deficits, and its debt load became the second worst in the euro zone, behind only Greece.

Italy is used to political merry-go-rounds, more recently involving coalition governments; it's had 69 governments since World War II. And while Italy remains the third-largest economy in the eurozone (and the world's ninth-largest exporter), unemployment seems stuck at around 8 percent—with youth unemployment hovering around 22 percent.

As you travel through Italy today, you'll encounter a fascinating country with a rich history and a per-capita income that comes close to its neighbors to the north. Despite its ups and downs, Italy remains committed to Europe...yet it's as wonderfully Italian as ever.

To learn more about Italian history, consider *Europe 101: History and Art for the Traveler,* written by Rick Steves and Gene Openshaw (available at www.ricksteves.com).

PRACTICALITIES

This chapter covers the practical skills of European travel: how to pay for things, sightsee efficiently, find good-value accommodations, eat affordably but well, use technology wisely, and get between destinations smoothly. For more information on these topics, see RickSteves.com/travel-tips.

Travel Tips

Travel Advisories: Before traveling, check updated health and safety conditions, including restrictions for your destination, at Travel.State.gov (US State Department travel pages) and CDC.gov/travel (Centers for Disease Control and Prevention). The US embassy website for Italy is another good source of information (see later).

Entry Requirements: In addition to your **passport,** US and Canadian citizens may be required to register online with the European Travel Info and Authorization System **(ETIAS)** before entering Italy and other Schengen Zone countries (quick and easy process, https://travel-europe.europa.eu/etias). If your travel plans include the United Kingdom (England, Scotland, Wales, Northern

Ireland), you'll need an Electronic Travel Authorization **(ETA).** Apply at least a month before your trip (required for all ages, www.gov.uk/guidance/apply-for-an-electronic-travel-authorisation-eta).

Tourist Information: Before your trip, scan the website of the Italian national tourist office (www.italia.it) for a wealth of travel information. If you have a specific question, try contacting one of their US offices (New York: +1 212 245 5618, newyork@enit.it; Los Angeles: +1 310 820 1898, losangeles@enit.it).

Local tourist information offices (abbreviated TI in this book) are hit or miss. Their advice can be influenced by partnerships with local businesses, but they're still a handy place to pick up a town map, browse brochures, and ask basic questions. If the TI falls short, you can often get local information from your hotelier, or even staff at sights and other businesses.

Be wary of travel agencies or information services that masquerade as TIs but serve fancy hotels and tour companies. They're selling things you don't need, often at a markup.

Holidays and Festivals: For a list of festivals and national holidays observed throughout Italy, see RickSteves.com/festivals. Before planning a trip around a festival, verify the dates with the festival website or the national tourist office.

In Italy, holidays seem to strike without warning, and every town has a festival honoring its patron saint. Hotels get booked up on Easter weekend, Liberation Day (April 25), Labor Day (May 1), All Saints' Day (Nov 1), and on Fridays and Saturdays year-round. Some hotels require you to book the full three-day weekend around a holiday. During the Feast of the Assumption, a.k.a. Ferragosto (mid-Aug), beach destinations are flooded with vacationing Italians. Cities empty out for much of August, and while tourist attractions remain open, shops and restaurants are often closed until September.

Emergency and Medical Help: For any emergency service—ambulance, police, or fire—call **112** (operators typically speak English). If you get sick, do as the locals do and go to a pharmacist for advice. Or ask at your hotel for help—they'll know the nearest medical and emergency services.

Theft or Loss: To replace a passport, you'll need to go in person to an embassy (see next). If your credit and debit cards disappear, cancel and replace them (see "Damage Control for Lost Cards" on page 267). File a police report, either on the spot or within a day or two; you'll need it to submit an insurance claim, and it can help with replacing your passport or credit and debit cards. For help with a lost phone, see "Damage Control for Lost Phones" on page 299. For more information, see RickSteves.com/help.

US Embassies and Consulates: Embassy in **Rome** +39 06 46741, passport and nonemergency consular services, by appoint-

Travel Insurance

Travel insurance can minimize the considerable financial risks of traveling: accidents, illness, missed flights, canceled tours, lost baggage, theft, terrorism, travel-company bankruptcies, natural disasters, emergency evacuation, and getting your body home if you die. The decision to buy travel insurance (and how much) depends on your situation. First determine what coverage you already have; many premium credit cards include generous coverage, and other expenses may be covered through your health, homeowners, or renters insurance. Then consider how likely it is that you'll need to change or cancel (for example, if you or a loved one is in frail health), how much of your prepaid trip costs are nonrefundable, and your risk tolerance.

It costs money to buy away the financial risk of travel. But if insurance costs 10 percent of your total trip cost, that may be a small price to pay—and worth the peace of mind—compared to the potential loss in the event of something catastrophic. You can compare insurance policies and costs at InsureMyTrip.com.

ment only (Via Vittorio Veneto 121). Consulates in **Milan** +39 02 290 351 (Via Principe Amedeo 2/10), **Florence** +39 055 266 951 (Lungarno Vespucci 38), and **Naples** +39 081 583 8111 (Piazza della Repubblica). For all, see http://it.usembassy.gov.

Canadian Embassies: Rome +39 06 854 442 911 (Via Zara 30); **Milan** +39 02 626 94238 (Piazza Cavour 3). For both, see www.italy.gc.ca. After-hours emergency in Ottawa +1 613 996 8885.

Avoiding Theft and Scams: While most travelers visit Italy safely, petty theft is a possibility at popular sights and anywhere there's a crowd. Pickpockets don't want to hurt you—they usually just want your money and gadgets. Consider any jostle or commotion a possible smokescreen for thieves. Wear a money belt, and keep valuables buttoned or zipped up.

Sneaky thieves pretend to be teenagers on holiday, well-dressed businessmen, or tourists wearing fanny packs and even toting Rick Steves guidebooks. Be on guard while boarding and leaving buses and subways, at heavily touristed sights, and while shopping at bustling street markets. In a crowd, hold your bags in front. If you wouldn't walk down a dark and deserted street at home, don't do it in Europe.

Green or sloppy tourists are more likely to fall victim to scams. Be wise to overly kind strangers offering too-good-to-be-true deals. Insist on clear and itemized bills. When paying in cash, know how much you're handing over, and count your change. Be confident and aware, and you'll be fine.

Time Zones: Italy, like most of continental Europe, is generally six/nine hours ahead of the East/West Coasts of the US. If you have cell service, your phone should update to the local time zone when you arrive in Europe (if not, look under "Settings" and "Date and Time" or "Clock" to do it manually). For a handy time converter, use the world clock app on your phone.

Business Hours: "Siesta" hours (with a midday closure) are no longer required by law in Italy, so many shops stay open through lunch or later into the evening, especially larger stores in tourist areas. Stores are usually closed on Sunday, and often on Monday. Throughout Italy, many shops close for a couple of weeks around August 15, when many Italians go on vacation.

Websites: Some Italian websites ending in *.it* only operate while the sight itself is open. This means you may need to stay up late (or get up early) to buy tickets in advance from home.

Watt's Up? Europe's electrical system is 220 volts, instead of North America's 110 volts. All electronics and most appliances convert automatically, so you won't need a converter, but you will need an adapter plug with two round prongs, sold inexpensively at travel stores in the US.

Discounts: Discounts for sights are generally not listed in this book. However, youths under 18 and students and teachers with proper identification cards (obtain from www.isic.org) can get discounts at many sights—always ask. Italy's national museums generally offer free admission to children under 18, but some discounts are available only for citizens of the European Union (EU).

Tobacco Shops: Known as *tabacchi* (often indicated with a big *T* sign), these Italian-style minimarts are ubiquitous across the country. They're handy places to purchase tickets for city buses and subways and sometimes postage. If you aren't sure where to buy something, a *tabacchi* is a good place to start.

Online Translation Tips: Google's Chrome browser instantly translates websites. The Google Translate app converts spoken or typed English into most European languages (and vice versa) and can also translate text it "reads" with your smartphone's camera. Before your trip, it's a good idea to download the Italian dictionary in the app so it can translate even if you're offline.

Going Green: There's plenty you can do to reduce your environmental footprint while traveling. When practical, take a train instead of a flight within Europe, and use public transportation within cities. In hotels, use the "Do Not Disturb" sign to avoid daily linen and towel changes (or hang up your towels to signal you'll reuse them) and turn the air-conditioning off when you leave the room. Bring a reusable shopping tote and refillable water bottle (Italy's tap water is safe to drink). Skip printed materials that you don't plan to keep—get your info online instead. To find out how Rick Steves' Europe is offsetting carbon emissions with a self-imposed carbon tax, see RickSteves.com/about-us/climate-smart.

Money

Here's my basic strategy for using money wisely in Europe. I pack the following:

Credit Card: You'll use your credit card for purchases both big and small. Some European businesses have gone cashless, making a card your only payment option. A "tap-to-pay" or "contactless" card is widely accepted and simple to use.

Debit Card: Use this at ATMs to withdraw a small amount of local cash. Wait until you arrive to get euros (Italian cities have plenty of ATMs); if you buy euros before your trip, you'll likely pay bad stateside exchange rates. While many transactions are by card these days, cash can help you out of a jam if your card randomly doesn't work, and can be useful to pay for things like tips and local guides.

Backup Card: Some travelers carry a third card (debit or credit; ideally from a different bank) in case one gets lost or simply doesn't work.

Stash of Cash: I carry $100-200 in US dollars as a cash backup, which comes in handy in an emergency.

BEFORE YOU GO

Know your cards. In Europe, Visa and Mastercard credit cards are universal, while American Express and Discover are less common. Debit cards with a Visa or Mastercard logo will work in any European ATM.

Go "contactless." Contactless pay options are now standard in much of Europe. Check if you already have—or can get—a tap-to-pay version of your credit card (look on the card for the tap-to-pay symbol—four curvy lines) and consider setting up your smartphone for contactless payment (see next section).

Know your PIN. Make sure you know the numeric PIN for each of your cards, both debit and credit. Request it if you don't have one, as it may be required for some purchases. Allow time to receive the information by mail—it's not always possible to obtain your PIN online or by phone.

Exchange Rate

1 euro (€) = about $1.10

To convert prices in euros to dollars, add about 10 percent: €20 = about $22, €50 = about $55. Like the dollar, one euro is broken into 100 cents. Coins range from €0.01 to €2, and bills from €5 to €200 (bills over €50 are rarely used).

Check XE.com for the latest exchange rates.

Report your travel dates. Some banks want to know that you'll be using your cards overseas, specifically when and where you're headed. Depending on your bank, you can do this either online or over the phone.

Check your ATM withdrawal limit. Find out how much you can withdraw daily and ask for a higher limit if you want to get more cash at once. Note that European ATMs will withdraw funds only from checking accounts, not from savings accounts.

Find out about fees. For any purchase or withdrawal made with a card, you may be charged a foreign transaction fee (1-3 percent). Shop around; you can compare credit cards on Bankrate.com. Some cards offer lower international fees than others—and some don't charge any at all. Most credit unions and some airline loyalty cards have low or no foreign transaction fees.

IN EUROPE

Using Credit Cards and Payment Apps

Tap-to-Pay or Contactless Cards: If your card has a contactless symbol, you can simply tap it against a contactless reader to make a purchase. A PIN or signature is generally required only as a security measure for larger purchases. This is by far the easiest way to pay and is available in much of Europe.

Payment Apps: Just like at home, you can tap-to-pay with your smartphone or smartwatch by linking a credit card to an app such as Apple Pay or Google Pay. If you've arrived in Europe without a tap-to-pay card, you can easily set up your phone with a payment app.

Will my US card work? Usually, yes. Rarely, a vendor or self-service payment machine (such as a transit-ticket kiosk, tollbooth, or fuel pump) may not accept older chip-and-PIN or swipe cards. Have some cash handy or look for a cashier who can process your payment manually. In some countries, gas stations sell prepaid gas cards, which you can purchase with any US card. When approaching a toll plaza or ferry-ticket line, use the "cash" lane.

Always choose to pay in the local currency. During a credit-card transaction, the payment terminal will sometimes ask whether you want to pay in US dollars or in the local currency. Always refuse the conversion and ***choose the local currency.*** While this "service"—called Dynamic Currency Conversion (DCC)—offers the illusion of convenience, it comes with a poor exchange rate and/or higher fees, and you'll wind up losing money.

Using Cash

Cash Machines: European cash machines work just like they do at home—except they spit out local currency instead of dollars. In Europe, the universal term for an ATM is "bankomat"; in Italy, you'll see it as *bancomat.* Look for an ATM operated by a local bank, ideally one just outside a brick-and-mortar bank (in the rare event that you have any issues).

Beware of cash machines run by exchange or money-transfer companies, which have less favorable rates and higher fees than banks. These can be marked Euronet, Travelex, Your Cash, or Cashzone—or simply marked generically as "bankomat" or "ATM." Rip-off exchange ATMs are often the only option at airports and train stations. On arrival, consider using a cashless payment option to get downtown, then find a real bank's ATM near your hotel.

If your debit card doesn't work, try a lower amount—your request may have exceeded your withdrawal limit or the ATM's limit. If you still have a problem, try a different ATM or come back later. When offered the choice to process your transaction in US dollars or the local currency, always choose the local currency.

Exchanging Cash: Minimize exchanging money in Europe; it's expensive (you'll generally lose 5-10 percent). In a pinch you can find exchange desks at major train stations or airports. Banks generally do not exchange money unless you have an account with them.

Security Tips

Pickpockets target tourists. Keep your passport and backup cash and cards secure in your money belt (or your hotel-room safe) and carry only a day's spending money and one card in your wallet.

Before inserting your card into an ATM, inspect the front of the machine. If anything looks crooked, loose, or damaged, it could be a sign of a card-skimming device.

Don't use a debit card for purchases. Because a debit card pulls funds directly from your bank account, potential charges incurred by a thief will stay on your account while your bank investigates.

If accessing your accounts online while traveling, be sure to use a secure connection (see the "Tips on Internet Security" sidebar, later).

Damage Control for Lost Cards

If you lose your credit or debit card, report the loss immediately to your bank (using a secure app) or the following global customer-assistance centers: Visa (+1 303 967 1096), Mastercard (+1 636 722 7111), and American Express (+1 336 393 1111).

You'll need to provide the primary cardholder's identification-verification details (such as birth date, mother's maiden name, or Social Security number). You can generally receive a temporary card within two or three business days in Europe (see RickSteves.com/help for more).

If you report your loss within two days, you typically won't be responsible for unauthorized transactions on your account, although many banks charge a liability fee.

TIPPING

Tipping in Italy isn't as automatic and generous as it is in the US. In general, if someone in the tourism or service industry does a good job for you, a small tip of a euro or two is appropriate...but not required.

Restaurants: In Italy, a service charge *(servizio)* is usually built into your check (look at the menu carefully). If it's not included, you can tip by rounding up the bill (or about 5-10 percent is plenty). European credit card receipts typically do not have a tip line—request to add a tip before they run your card, or leave a tip in cash. For more details on restaurant tipping, see page 282.

Taxis: For a typical ride, round up your fare a bit (for instance, if the fare is €13.50, pay €15). If the cabbie hauls your bags and zips you to the airport to help you catch your flight, you might want to toss in a little more.

Services: For local guides, private drivers, or others who spend several hours with you—and significantly improve the quality of your trip—a healthy tip (of around 10 percent) is not extravagant. In hotel rooms, leaving a tip of €1-3 per night is standard. If you're not sure whether (or how much) to tip, ask a local for advice.

GETTING A VAT REFUND

Wrapped into the purchase price of your Italian souvenirs is a value-added tax (VAT) of about 22 percent. You're entitled to get most of that tax back if you purchase more than €155 worth of goods at a store that participates in the VAT-refund scheme. Typically, you must ring up the minimum at a single retailer—you can't add up your purchases from various shops to reach the required amount. (If the store ships the goods to your US home, VAT is not assessed on your purchase.)

Getting your refund is straightforward...and worthwhile if you spend a significant amount.

At the Merchant: Have the merchant completely fill out the refund document (they'll ask for your passport; a photo of your passport usually works). Keep track of the paperwork and your original sales receipt. Note that you're not supposed to use your purchased goods before you leave Europe.

At the Border or Airport: Process your VAT document at your last stop in the European Union (such as the airport) with the customs agent who deals with VAT refunds (allow plenty of extra time for this process and have your purchased items easily accessible for inspection). At some airports, you'll go to a customs office to get your documents stamped and then to a separate VAT-refund service (such as Forexchange, Global Blue, or Planet) to process the refund. Elsewhere, a single VAT desk handles the whole thing, or you may be able to do it at a self-validation kiosk. (Note that refund services typically extract a 4 percent fee, but you're paying for the convenience of receiving your money in cash immediately or as a credit to your card.) Otherwise, you'll need to mail the stamped refund documents to the address given by the merchant.

CUSTOMS FOR AMERICAN SHOPPERS

You can take home $800 worth of items per person duty-free, once every 31 days. Many processed and packaged foods are allowed, including cheeses, dried herbs, jams, baked goods, candy, chocolate, oil, vinegar, condiments, and honey. Fresh fruits and vegetables and most meats are not allowed, with exceptions for some canned items. As for alcohol, you can bring in one liter duty-free (it can be packed securely in your checked luggage, along with any other liquid-containing items).

To bring alcohol (or liquid-packed foods) in your carry-on bag on your flight home, buy it at a duty-free shop at the airport. You'll increase your odds of getting it onto a connecting flight if it's packaged in a "STEB"—a secure, tamper-evident bag. But stay away from liquids in opaque, ceramic, or metallic containers, which usually cannot be successfully screened (STEB or no STEB).

For details on allowable goods, customs rules, and duty rates, visit Help.cbp.gov.

Sightseeing

Sightseeing can be hard work. Use these tips to make your visits to Naples' and the Amalfi Coast's finest sights meaningful, fun, efficient, and painless.

MAPS AND NAVIGATION TOOLS

Your best navigation tool is on your phone. **Google Maps** (and similar mapping apps) offer turn-by-turn directions for walking and driving, as well as detailed public transit instructions in most big cities. Simply plug in a destination and instantly get detailed directions for reaching it on foot or by subway, bus, or tram—including where to catch it, how long it takes, where to get off, and how far you'll walk at the other end.

To conserve data, most mapping apps let you download maps in advance (do this when you're on strong Wi-Fi). However, offline maps may not include every feature, such as real-time traffic updates (also, most in-city public transit navigation doesn't work offline). For more on using your phone during your trip, see page 297.

The maps in this book are concise and simple, designed to help you locate recommended destinations, sights, hotels, and restaurants. Simple paper maps are generally free at TIs and hotels; maps with more detail are sold at newsstands and bookstores.

PLAN AHEAD

Set up an itinerary that allows you to fit in all your must-see sights. For a one-stop look at opening hours in Naples, see the "At a Glance" sidebar in the Naples chapter.

Don't put off visiting a must-see sight—you never know when a place will close unexpectedly for a holiday, strike, or restoration. Opening days and hours can fluctuate; confirm the latest at the sight's official website (listed throughout this book).

Many museums are closed or have reduced hours at least a few days a year, especially on major holidays (see RickSteves.com/festivals for a list of European holidays). In summer, some sights may stay open late. Off-season hours may be shorter.

Going at the right time helps avoid crowds. This book offers tips on the best times to see specific sights. Try visiting popular sights very early or very late. Evening visits (when possible) are usually more peaceful, with fewer crowds. Late morning is usually the worst time to visit a popular sight.

If you plan to hire a local guide, reserve ahead by email. Popular guides can get booked up.

Study up. To get the most out of the self-guided tours and sight descriptions in this book, read them before you visit.

RESERVATIONS, ADVANCE TICKETS, AND PASSES

Many popular sights in Europe come with long ticket-buying lines. Visitors who buy tickets online in advance (or who have a museum pass covering key sights) can skip the line and waltz right in. Advance tickets are generally timed-entry, meaning you're guaranteed admission on a certain date and time.

For some sights, buying ahead is **required** (tickets aren't sold at the sight and it's the only way to get in). At other sights, buying ahead is **recommended** to skip the line and save time. And for many sights, advance tickets are **available** but unnecessary: At these uncrowded sights you can simply arrive, buy a ticket, and go in.

Don't confuse the reservation options: available, recommended, and required. Use my advice in this book as a guide. Note any must-see sights that sell out long in advance and be prepared to buy tickets early. If you do your research, you'll know the smart strategy.

Given how precious your vacation time is, I'd book in advance both where it's required (as soon as your dates are firm) and where it will save time in a long line (in some cases, you can do this even on the day you plan to visit). In **Naples,** book ahead for the Cappella Sansevero (required) and the underground tours (to avoid lines). A timed-entry ticket booked in advance ensures you get into **Pompeii,** and a timed-entry ticket is required to hike to the summit of **Mount Vesuvius.** Be aware that some websites ending in *.it* only operate while the sight itself is open.

You'll generally be emailed a digital ticket that you'll store on your phone to scan at the entrance (if you prefer, you can print it out). At the sight, look for the ticket-holders line rather than the ticket-buying line; you may still have to wait in a security line.

To avoid surprises, make sure you are using an official site. Many third-party "scalpers"—selling tickets at inflated prices—do a good job of imitating official ones. Use the websites listed in this book.

The **Campania ArteCard regional pass** is handy if you're spending at least 2-3 days in this region, using public transportation, and visiting multiple major sights. It saves the time and hassle of buying tickets (and can save you a few euros). For more details, see the Naples chapter.

Booking a guided tour can help you avoid lines at many popular sights. So can knowing what days to avoid. State museums in Italy are free to enter (and more crowded) on some Sundays—often the first one of the month. In peak season, check museum websites for specifics and avoid free entry days when possible.

AT SIGHTS

Every sight or museum offers more than what is covered in this book. Use the information I provide as an introduction—not the final word. Here's what you can typically expect at sights:

Entering: You may not be allowed to enter if you arrive too close to closing time. And guards start ushering people out well before the actual closing time, so don't save the best for last.

Security Check: Many sights have a security check. You may need to pass through a metal detector and put your bag through a scanner. Allow extra time for these lines. Some sights require you to check day packs and coats. (If you'd rather not check your day pack, try carrying it tucked under your arm as you enter.) Pocketknives may not be allowed.

Photography: If the museum's photo policy isn't clearly posted, ask a guard. Generally, taking photos without a flash or tripod is allowed. Some sights ban selfie sticks; others ban photos altogether.

Audioguides and Apps: I've produced free, downloadable audio tours for my Naples City Walk and Naples' Archaeological Museum tour; look for the 🎧 in this book. For more on my audio tours, see page 22.

Some sights offer audioguides with excellent recorded descriptions in English. Often you'll use free Wi-Fi to scan a QR code and access the tour on your phone (A+ students can check ahead and download audioguides before their trip). Less frequently you'll borrow or rent a device preloaded with the audio content.

Expect Changes: Artwork can be on tour, on loan, out sick, or shifted at the whim of the curator. Pick up a floor plan as you enter and ask the museum staff if you can't find a particular item. Say the title or artist's name, or point to the photograph in this book and ask, *"Dov'è?"* (doh-VEH, meaning "Where is?").

Dates for Artwork: In Italian museums, art is dated with *sec* for *secolo* (century, often indicated with Roman numerals), AC (*avanti Cristo,* or BC), and DC (*dopo Cristo,* or AD). OK?

Services: Important sights usually have a reasonably priced on-site café or cafeteria (handy air-conditioned places to rejuvenate during a long visit). The WCs at sights are free and generally clean.

FIND RELIGION

Churches offer some amazing art (usually free), a cool respite from heat, and a welcome seat.

A modest dress code—no bare shoulders or shorts for anyone, even kids—is enforced at larger churches, but is often overlooked elsewhere. (I wear a super-lightweight pair of long pants rather than shorts for my hot and muggy Italian sightseeing.) If your heart's set on seeing a certain church, err on the side of caution and dress appropriately.

Some churches have coin-operated boxes that trigger lights to illuminate works of art. I pop in a coin whenever I can, to improve my experience (and photos), as a small contribution to that church, and as a courtesy to other visitors enjoying this great art. Whenever possible, let there be light.

Sleeping

One of my joys as a guidebook writer is connecting my readers with the small-hotel owners I've come to know over the years. Even if you're willing to spend more, you'll have a far richer trip if you stay in places with a strong sense of local character.

My best tips for booking rooms: Book direct, and book early. While third-party sites and room-booking services may seem convenient, booking directly with my recommended hotels puts you in contact with your host and can sometimes save you money.

Reserve your accommodations as soon as your itinerary is set, especially if you want to stay at one of my top listings or if you'll be traveling during busy times. See RickSteves.com/festivals for a list of major holidays and festivals in Italy.

Some people make reservations a few days ahead as they travel. This approach fosters spontaneity, and booking sites make it easy to find available rooms, but—especially during busy times—you run the risk of settling for lesser-value accommodations.

FINDING AND RESERVING ROOMS

Curated and opinionated listings of good-value rooms are a major feature of this book's Sleeping sections. Rather than list accommodations scattered throughout a town, I choose hotels in my favorite neighborhoods that are convenient to sights.

My recommendations run the gamut, from dorm beds to luxurious rooms with all the comforts. I like places that are clean, central, relatively quiet at night, reasonably priced, friendly, small enough to have a hands-on owner or manager, and run with a respect for Italian traditions. I'm more impressed by a handy location and fun-loving philosophy than oversized TVs and a fancy gym. Most of my recommendations fall short of perfection. But if I can find a place with most of these features, it's a keeper.

RATES AND DEALS

I've categorized my recommended accommodations based on price, indicated with a euro-sign rating (see sidebar). Room prices can fluctuate significantly with demand and amenities (size, views, and so on), but relative price categories remain constant.

City taxes, which can vary from place to place, are generally insignificant (a few dollars per person, per night).

Booking Direct: Once your dates are set, compare features and prices at several hotels. Start with the recommendations in this book, then use hotel websites, booking sites such as Hotels.com or Booking.com, and user-review sites such as TripAdvisor to narrow down your options.

After you've zeroed in on your choice, **book directly with the**

Sleep Code

Hotels in this book are categorized according to the average price of a standard double room with breakfast in high season. These ranges apply to cities; you may pay less in towns.

€€€€	**Splurge:** Most rooms over €250
€€€	**Pricier:** €175-250
€€	**Moderate:** €125-175
€	**Budget:** €75-125
¢	**Backpacker:** Under €75
RS%	Ask about Rick Steves discount

Unless otherwise noted, credit cards are accepted and hotel staff speak basic English. For the best deal, *book directly with the hotel.*

hotel itself—on the hotel's website or by email or phone. While big booking sites are convenient for travelers, they're both a blessing and a curse for small, independent, family-run hotels. Without a presence on these sites, small hotels become almost invisible. But to be listed, they must pay a big commission...and promise that their own website won't undercut the price on the booking-service site.

When you book directly with the hotel, the price may be the same as via a booking site, but more of your money goes to the hotel, not agency commissions. In exchange, ask if they can give you a nicer room or a free breakfast (if it's not already included). Booking direct also increases the chances that your hotelier will be able to accommodate special needs or requests (such as shifting your reservation).

Getting a Discount: Some hotels extend a discount to those who pay cash or stay longer than three nights. And some accommodations offer a special discount for Rick Steves readers, indicated in this book by the abbreviation **"RS%."** Discounts vary: Ask for details when you reserve. Generally, to qualify for this discount, you must book direct (not through a booking site), mention this book when you reserve and show it upon arrival, and sometimes pay cash or stay a certain number of nights. In some cases, you may need to enter a discount code (which I've provided in the listing) in the booking form on the hotel's website. Understandably, discounts do not apply to promotional rates.

TYPES OF ACCOMMODATIONS

Hotels

While you can snare a spartan, clean, and comfortable double with breakfast and a private bath in Naples for about €150, Sorrento and the Amalfi Coast are pricier: Double rooms range from about €200 (very simple, some with toilet and shower down the hall) to €400

Making Hotel Reservations

Reserve your rooms as soon as you've pinned down your travel dates. For busy national holidays, it's wise to reserve far in advance (see RickSteves.com/festivals).

Requesting a Reservation: Book directly with the hotel (not through a booking website). Even small, family-run places typically have websites that offer online bookings. If not, book your room directly via email or phone.

Here's what the hotelier wants to know:

- Type(s) of room(s) you want and number of guests
- Number of nights you'll stay
- Arrival and departure dates, written European-style as day/month (for example, 18/06 or 18 June)
- Special requests (en suite bathroom, cheapest room, twin beds vs. double bed, quiet room)
- Applicable discounts (such as a Rick Steves discount, cash discount, or promotional rate)

Confirming a Reservation: Most places will request a credit-card number to hold your room. If the hotel's website doesn't have a secure form where you can enter the number directly, share this info by phone.

Canceling a Reservation: If you must cancel, it's courteous—and smart—to do so with as much notice as possible, especially for smaller family-run places. Cancellation policies can be strict; read

and beyond (grand views and maximum plumbing), with most clustered around €250 (with private bathrooms). I've suggested some alternative home bases on the Amalfi Coast where prices are more reasonable.

Some hotels can add an extra bed (for a small charge) to a double; some offer larger rooms for three or more people (I call these "family rooms" in the listings). If there's space for an extra cot, they'll cram it in for you. In general, a family room is cheaper than the cost of a double and a single.

Arrival and Check-In: Hotels and B&Bs are sometimes located on the higher floors of a multipurpose building with a secured door. In that case, look for your hotel's name on the buttons by the main entrance and ring the bell.

Hotel elevators are common, though small, but some older buildings still lack them. If stairs are unavoidable, ask the front desk for help carrying your bags up.

Most European countries require hotels to collect your name, nationality, and passport number. At check-in, the receptionist might ask for your passport and may keep it for a few hours. If

From:	rick@ricksteves.com
Sent:	Today
To:	info@hotelcentral.com
Subject:	Reservation request for 19-22 July

Dear Hotel Central,

I would like to stay at your hotel. Please let me know if you have a room available and the price for:

- 2 people
- Double bed and en suite bathroom in a quiet room
- Arriving 19 July, departing 22 July (3 nights)

Thank you!
Rick Steves

the fine print before you book. Many discount deals require prepayment and can be expensive to change or cancel.

Reconfirming a Reservation: Always call or email to reconfirm your room reservation a few days in advance. For B&Bs or very small hotels, I call again on my arrival day to tell my host what time to expect me (especially important if arriving after 17:00).

Phoning: For tips on calling hotels overseas, see page 298.

you're not comfortable leaving your passport at the desk, bring a copy to hand over instead.

Some hotels now offer self check-in. You'll receive instructions before you arrive with a code for your room (and sometimes for the building's front door).

In Your Room: Pricier hotels usually come with a small fridge stocked with beverages, called a *frigo bar* (FREE-goh bar; pay for what you use).

Nearly all places offer private bathrooms, which have a tub or shower, a toilet, and a bidet (which Italians use for quick sponge baths).

Double beds are called *matrimoniali,* even though hotels aren't interested in your marital status. Twins are *due letti singoli.*

Breakfast and Meals: Italian hotels typically include a satisfying breakfast in their room prices (for details, see page 280). If breakfast is optional, you may want to skip it. While convenient, it's usually pricey for what you get: a simple continental buffet with (at its most generous) bread, croissants, ham, cheese, yogurt, and *caffè latte.* It's cheaper—and much more Italian—to head to the corner café for a light breakfast (see "Eating," later in this chapter).

Keep Cool

If you're visiting Italy in the summer, you'll want an air-conditioned room. Most hotel air-conditioners come with a remote control that generally has similar symbols and features: fan icon (toggle through wind power, from light to gale), temperature (20 degrees Celsius—that's about 68 Fahrenheit—is comfortable), louver icon (steady airflow or waves), snowflake and sunshine icons (cold air or heat), and clock ("O" setting: run X hours before turning off; "I" setting: wait X hours to start). When you leave your room for the day, do as the environmentally conscious Europeans do and turn off the air-conditioning.

If you need a bigger breakfast, have a little picnic in your room before heading out.

Hotels in resort areas may charge you for half-pension, called *mezza pensione,* during peak season. Half-pension means that you pay for one meal per day per person (lunch or dinner). Sometimes half-pension is required; even when optional, it can be worth considering, especially if the per-meal charge is less than you've been paying for an average restaurant meal (and provided the chef is good).

Checking Out: While it's customary to pay for your room upon departure, it's smart to settle your bill the day before, when you're not in a hurry.

Hotelier Help: Hoteliers can be a good source of advice. Most know their city well and can assist you with everything from public transit and airport connections to finding a good restaurant, the nearest launderette, or a late-night pharmacy.

Hotel Hassles: Even at the best places, mechanical breakdowns occur: Sinks leak, hot water turns cold, toilets may gurgle or smell, the Wi-Fi goes out, or the air-conditioning dies when you need it most. Report your concerns clearly and calmly at the front desk.

If you find that night noise is a problem (if, for instance, your room is over a nightclub or facing a busy street), ask for a quieter room in the back or on an upper floor.

To guard against theft in your room, keep valuables out of sight. Some rooms come with a safe, and other hotels have safes at the front desk. I rarely bother to use one and, in a lifetime of travel, I've never had anything stolen from my room.

For more complicated problems, don't expect instant results. Above all, keep a positive attitude. Remember, you're on vacation. If your hotel is a disappointment, spend more time out enjoying the place you came to see.

The Pros and Cons of Short-Term Rentals

Short-term rental services like Airbnb are having a big impact in Europe. With hotels becoming more expensive and less personal post-pandemic—especially in big cities—short-term rentals are filling the gap.

Short-term rentals can provide more space and amenities than a cookie-cutter hotel (and are an especially good value for stays longer than a few days). Having your own kitchen can save on restaurant costs, a washer-dryer can spare you a trip to the launderette, and families who want to spread out get better value renting an apartment rather than multiple hotel rooms. Airbnb fans appreciate feeling part of a neighborhood and getting into a daily routine as "temporary Europeans." Some places are run by thoughtful hosts, allowing you to get to know a local and keep your money in the community. But others are impersonally managed by large, absentee agencies, with self check-in and minimal contact.

Critics of Airbnb see it as a threat to "traditional Europe." Landlords can make more money renting to short-stay travelers, driving rents up—and local residents out. Traditional businesses are replaced by ones that cater to tourists. And the character and charm that made those neighborhoods desirable to tourists in the first place goes too. Some cities have cracked down, requiring owners to obtain a license and to occupy rental properties part of the year (and staging disruptive "inspections" that inconvenience guests).

As a lover of Europe, I share the worry of those who see residents nudged aside by tourists. I've witnessed some of my favorite charming old neighborhoods sell out to the tourist dollar. Locals are left feeling like strangers, no longer able to identify with their temporary neighbors.

As an advocate for travelers, I appreciate the value short-term rentals provide in offering the chance to stay in a local building or neighborhood with potentially fewer tourists, and the convenience for families. But before searching on a short-term rental site, consider staying in a small, family-run hotel, to help preserve the culture you are traveling so far to see.

Bed-and-Breakfasts

B&Bs can offer good-value accommodations in excellent locations. Usually converted family homes or apartments, they can range from humble rooms with communal kitchens to high-end boutique accommodations with extra amenities. Boutique B&Bs can be an especially good option, as they are typically less expensive than a big hotel, but often newer and nicer, with more personal service.

Short-Term Rentals

Short-term vacation rentals offered through Airbnb and other services can be cost-effective, especially if you plan to settle in one location for several nights or are traveling as a group. Keep in mind that European apartments, like hotel rooms, tend to be small by US standards. But they often come with laundry facilities and small, equipped kitchens, making it easier and cheaper to dine in.

Many places require a minimum stay and have strict cancellation policies. And you're generally on your own: There's no reception desk, breakfast, or daily cleaning service.

Finding Accommodations: Websites such as Airbnb, FlipKey, Booking.com, and Vrbo let you browse a wide range of properties. Alternatively, rental agencies such as InterhomeUSA.com or RentaVilla.com can provide a more personalized service (their curated listings are also more expensive).

Before you commit, be clear on the location. I like to virtually "explore" the neighborhood using Google Street View. Consider the proximity to public transportation, and amenities that are important to you (elevator, air-con, laundry, Wi-Fi, parking, etc.). Reviews from previous guests can help identify trouble spots.

Think about the kind of experience you want: just a key and an affordable bed...or a chance to get to know a local? Some hosts offer self check-in and minimal contact; others enjoy interacting with you. Read the description and reviews to help shape your decision.

Confirming and Paying: Many places require payment in full before your trip, usually through the listing site. Be wary of owners who want to take your transaction offline; this gives you no recourse if things go awry. Never agree to wire money (a key indicator of a fraudulent transaction).

Other Options: Swapping homes with a local works for people with an appealing place to offer (don't assume where you live is not interesting to Europeans). A good place to start is HomeExchange.com.

Hostels

A hostel provides cheap beds in dorms where you sleep alongside strangers for usually under €40 per night. Travelers of any age are welcome, and family and private rooms are often available. Most hostels offer kitchen facilities, guest computers, Wi-Fi, and a self-service laundry. Hostels almost always provide bedding, but the towel's up to you (though you can usually rent one).

Independent hostels tend to be easygoing, colorful, and informal (no membership required; www.hostelworld.com). You may pay slightly less by booking directly with the hostel. **Official hostels** are part of Hostelling International (HI) and share a booking

Crowd-Sourcing vs. Guidebooks

User-generated reviews on platforms such as TripAdvisor, Yelp, and Booking.com can give you a consensus of opinions about everything from hotels and restaurants to sights and nightlife.

I find online reviews more reliable for accommodations and sightseeing experiences than for restaurants (which tend to favor touristy options over local gems). When scanning reviews, I look for patterns: repeated complaints about bad service, a problematic location, or nighttime noise. I take one-off complaints with a grain of salt: Even the most expertly run business can have a bad day...or a cranky guest.

As a guidebook writer, my sense is that there is a big difference between the uncurated information on a review site and the vetted listings in a guidebook. A user review is based on the limited experience of one person, who stayed at just one hotel in a given city and ate at a few restaurants there. A guidebook is the work of a trained researcher who forms a well-developed basis for comparison by visiting many restaurants and hotels year after year.

Both types of information have their place, and in many ways, they're complementary. If something is recommended in a guidebook and also gets good online reviews, it's likely a winner.

site (www.hihostels.com). HI hostels typically require that you be a member or else pay a bit more per night.

Eating

The Italians are masters of the art of fine living. That means eating long and well. Lengthy, multicourse meals and endless hours sitting in outdoor cafés are the norm. Americans eat on their way to an evening event and complain if the check is slow in coming. For Italians, the meal is an end in itself, and only rude servers rush you.

I've written an entire book (with co-author Fred Plotkin) on the subject: *Rick Steves Italy for Food Lovers,* a region-by-region handbook on how to appreciate Italian cuisine like an Italian. This section condenses that book's most valuable tips and insights.

A highlight of your Italian adventure will be this country's cafés, cuisine, and wines. Trust me: This is sightseeing for your palate. Even if you liked dorm food and are sleeping in cheap hotels, your taste buds will relish an occasional first-class splurge. You can eat well without going broke. But be careful: You're just as likely to blow a small fortune on a disappointing meal as you are to dine wonderfully for €25. Rely on my recommendations in the various Eating sections throughout this book.

Traditionally, lunch *(pranzo)* was the largest meal of the Italian day, eaten at home between 13:00 and 14:30 (earlier in northern Italy, later in the south). Dinner *(cena)* was a lighter affair, often just soup with cold cuts, eaten around 20:00 or 21:00 (maybe earlier in winter).

However, as times have changed, so have eating habits. So, while some Italian families still have a big lunch and a small dinner, others do the reverse. Many Italian urbanites grab a quick lunch in a *tavola calda* bar (cafeteria) or buy a *panino* or *tramezzino* (sandwich). To bridge the gap until dinner, people drop into a bar in the late afternoon for a cocktail *(aperitivo),* often served with snacks.

RESTAURANT PRICING AND HOURS

I've categorized my recommended eateries based on the average price of a typical main course, indicated with a euro-sign rating (see sidebar). Obviously, expensive specialties, fine wine, appetizers, and dessert can significantly increase your final bill.

The categories also indicate the personality of a place: **Budget** eateries include street food, takeaway, order-at-the-counter shops, basic cafeterias, and bakeries selling sandwiches. **Moderate** eateries are nice (but not fancy) sit-down restaurants, ideal for a pleasant meal with good-quality food. Listings that fall in this category are great for a taste of the local cuisine at a reasonable price.

Pricier eateries are a notch up, with more attention paid to the setting, presentation, and (often inventive) cuisine. **Splurge** eateries are dress-up-for-a-special-occasion swanky—typically with an elegant setting, polished service, and pricey and refined cuisine.

Most of my recommended restaurants are open daily for lunch and dinner; I've noted exceptions in the listings.

BREAKFAST

Italian breakfasts, like Italian bath towels, used to be small. But many Italian hotels now offer generous buffet breakfasts. The basic, traditional version is coffee and bread with butter and marmalade, and often pastries. Many places have yogurt and juice (in season, look for *spremuta d'arancia rossa*—fresh-squeezed juice from Sicilian blood oranges), and possibly also cereal, cold cuts and sliced cheese, and eggs (typically hard-boiled; scrambled or fried eggs are less common). Small budget hotels may leave a basic breakfast in your room (stale croissant, roll, jam, yogurt, coffee).

If you want to skip your hotel breakfast (or if it's not included with your room), consider browsing for a morning picnic at a local open-air market. Or do as the Italians do: Step into a bar or café to

Restaurant Code

Eateries in this book are categorized according to the average cost of a higher-end pasta or typical main course. Drinks, desserts, and splurge items can raise the price considerably.

€€€€	**Splurge:** Most main courses over €25
€€€	**Pricier:** €20-25
€€	**Moderate:** €15-20
€	**Budget:** Under €15

Pizza by the slice and other takeaway food is **€,** a basic trattoria or sit-down pizzeria is **€€,** a casual but more upscale restaurant is **€€€,** and a swanky splurge is **€€€€.**

drink a cappuccino and munch a *cornetto* (croissant) while standing at the counter. While the *cornetto* is the most common pastry, you'll find a range of *pasticcini* (pastries, sometimes called *dolci*). Look for *otto* (an 8-shaped pastry, often filled with custard, jam, or chocolate), *sfoglia* (filo-dough crust that's fruit-filled, like a turnover), or *ciambella* (doughnut filled with custard or chocolate).

ITALIAN RESTAURANTS

In Italy, a ***ristorante*** typically means a high-end, sit-down restaurant. A ***trattoria*** is a notch below a *ristorante* in price, but the food is often just as good, if not better. An ***osteria,*** which originated as a place to drink wine accompanied by food, is similar. *Trattorie* and *osterie* are generally family-owned and serve home-cooked meals at moderate prices. A *locanda* is an inn, a *cantina* is a wine cellar, and a *birreria* is a brewpub. *Pizzerie, rosticcerie* (delis), *tavola calda* ("hot table") bars, *enoteche* (wine bars), and other alternatives are explained later.

I look for restaurants that are convenient to your hotel and sightseeing. When restaurant hunting, choose a spot filled with locals, not tourists. Restaurants parked on famous squares generally serve bad food at high prices to tourists. Venturing even a block or two off the main drag leads to higher-quality food for a better price. Locals eat better at lower-rent locales. Family-run places operate without hired help and can offer cheaper meals.

Most restaurant kitchens close between their lunch and dinner service. Good restaurants don't reopen for dinner before 19:00. If you arrive at opening time, most restaurants will be empty and available—the main push of customers arrives later. Small restaurants with a full slate of reservations for 20:30 or 21:00 often will accommodate walk-in diners willing to eat a quick, early meal, but you aren't expected to linger.

When you want the bill, mime-scribble on your raised palm or request it: *"Il conto, per favore."* You may have to ask more than once. If you're in a hurry, request the check when you receive the last item you order. At more casual places, you can usually skip asking for *il conto,* and just walk up to the register and pay.

Cover and Tipping

Avoid surprises when eating out by familiarizing yourself with two common Italian restaurant charges: *coperto* and *servizio.* You won't encounter them in all restaurants, but both charges, if assessed, by law must be listed on the menu.

The ***coperto*** (cover) is a minor fee (€1.50-3/person) covering the cost of the linens, cutlery, and typical basket of bread found on your table. (It's sometimes called *pane e coperto*—"bread and cover.") It's not negotiable, even if you don't eat the bread. And it's not a tip. Think of it as a fee paid to the owner entitling you to use the table for as long as you like.

The ***servizio*** is a 10-15 percent "service" charge that goes to the server (similar to the mandatory gratuity that American restaurants often add for groups of six or more). These days, most Italian restaurants don't charge this separately; rather, they include service in their prices—you'll see *servizio compreso* or *servizio incluso* on the menu. (At places that do levy a separate *servizio* charge, you don't need to leave an additional tip.)

Italian servers are well paid and are not as reliant on additional **tips** as servers are back home. Even so, if you're pleased with the service, it's polite to add a small tip *(una mancia).* At a simple restaurant or pizzeria, figure on €1 per person (or simply round up the bill); at a finer restaurant, figure a few euros per person. If paying with a credit card, ask to add the tip before they run your card, or tip separately with cash or coins. (Credit card receipts don't come with a "tip line" to fill in.) If paying with cash, it's classy to simply round up the bill when paying. (For instance, if the bill is €46, hand the server €50 and tell them to keep the change.)

Italian Menu Courses

A full Italian meal consists of multiple courses. On some menus, you'll see a few numbers—such as 1, 3, 7—listed after each dish (not the price); these correspond to allergens (ask the restaurant for a decoder list if it's not at the bottom of the menu).

Antipasto: An appetizer such as *salumi* (cured meats, including salami and prosciutto), cheeses, bruschetta, grilled veggies, or deep-fried tasties. To get a sampler plate of *salumi* and cheeses, look for *affettato misto* (mixed *salumi*), *antipasto misto* (*salumi,* cheeses, and marinated vegetables), or *tagliere* (a sampler "board").

Primo piatto: A "first dish" generally consisting of pasta, soup, rice (usually risotto), or polenta

Secondo piatto: A "second dish" of meat or fish/seafood

Contorno: A vegetable side dish may come with the *secondo* but more often must be ordered separately. Typical *contorni* are *insalata mista* (mixed salad), spinach, roasted potatoes, or grilled veggies. Vegetarians can skip the *secondo* and order several *contorni* to make a meal.

Dolce: No meal is complete without a sweet. On most menus, you'll find typical Italian desserts such as tiramisu and *panna cotta,* or other local favorites (such as the shell-shaped, ricotta-filled pastry called *sfogliatella*). Servers are accustomed to diners splitting a single dessert—just ask for extra forks. Fruit *(frutta)* is often eaten as a dessert, often in the form of *macedonia* (a mixed-fruit salad). A shot of espresso *(un caffè)* is typically served after dessert. (Or skip the restaurant dessert and wander around licking a cone of gelato.)

Ordering Tips

For most travelers, a complete, multicourse meal is simply too much food—and the euros can add up in a hurry. To avoid overeating (and to stretch your budget), share dishes. A good rule of thumb is for each person to order two courses. For example, a couple can order and share one *antipasto,* one *primo,* one *secondo,* and one dessert; or two *antipasti* and two *primi;* or whatever combination appeals. Small groups can mix *antipasti* and *primi* family-style (skipping *secondi*).

It can be worth paying a little more for an inventive fixed-price meal that shows off the chef's creativity. A *menù turistico* is a made-for-tourists plate of Italian food clichés for one fixed price. But locals have their own, typically more interesting version, usually called a *prezzo fisso* or sometimes *menù del giorno* (menu of the day). For a smaller appetite, some restaurants serve a *piatto unico,* with smaller portions of each course on one plate (for instance, a meat, starch, and vegetable).

Seafood and steak may be sold by weight and priced by the *etto* (100 grams, 3.5 ounces) or the kilo (1,000 grams, 2.2 pounds). The abbreviation *s.q. (secondo quantità)* indicates an item is priced by weight (often used at antipasto buffets). Unless the menu indicates a fillet *(filetto),* fish is usually served whole with the head and tail. You can always ask your server to select a small fish and fillet it for you. Sometimes, especially for steak, restaurants require a minimum order of four or five *etti* (which diners can share). Make sure you're clear on the price before ordering.

Some dishes come in larger quantities meant to be shared by two people. The shorthand way of showing this on a menu is "X2" (for two), but the price listed could indicate the cost per person.

If you order only a pasta and a salad, the server may bring them in that order, which is the opposite of what you might expect; astute severs ask if you want it *insieme* (een-see-EH-meh; together).

Because pasta and bread are both starches, Italians consider them redundant. If you order only a pasta dish, bread may not come with it; you can request it, but you may be charged extra. On the other hand, if you order a vegetable antipasto or a meat *secondo,* bread is often provided to balance the ingredients.

At places with counter service—such as at a bar or a freeway rest-stop diner—you'll first order and pay at the *cassa* (cashier). Then take your receipt to the counter to claim your food.

When going to an especially good restaurant with an approachable staff, I like to find out what they're eager to serve. Sometimes I'll simply say, "Make me happy"...and set a price limit.

BUDGET EATING

Italy offers many budget options for hungry travelers. Self-service cafeterias offer the basics without add-on charges. Travelers on a hard-core budget equip their room with a pantry stocked at the market (fruits and veggies are remarkably cheap), or pick up a sandwich or a kebab, then dine in at picnic prices. Bars and cafés are also good places to grab a meal on the go.

Pizzerias

Italians head to a pizzeria at dinnertime to order a one-person pie. Some shops sell *pizza rustica* (also called *pizza al taglio* or *pizza al trancio*)—thick pizza baked in a large rectangular pan and sold by weight. If you simply ask for a piece, you may wind up with a gigantic slab. Instead, clearly indicate how much you want: *un etto*—100 grams—is a hot and cheap snack; *due etti*—200 grams—makes a light meal. Or show the size with your hands: *tanto così* (TAHN-toh koh-ZEE; this much). They may ask if you want it *riscaldata* (ree-skahl-DAH-tah; heated up). The correct answer is *sì.* For a rundown of common types of pizza, see that section, later. Pizzerias also sell *cecina,* a savory crêpe-like garbanzo-

bean flatbread—a cheap snack that pairs well with a glass of red wine.

Bars/Cafés

An Italian bar isn't so much a tavern as an inexpensive café. These neighborhood hangouts serve coffee, light food, and drinks from the cooler. This is where locals go for a breakfast of cappuccino and *cornetto* (croissant). Throughout the day, bars are the place to drop in for a coffee or another drink.

Many bars are small—if you can't find a table, you'll need to stand or find a ledge to sit on outside. Most charge extra for table service. To get food to go, say, *"da portar via"* (for the road). Most bars have a WC *(toilette, bagno)* in the back, available to customers...and the discreet public.

Food: To save time for sightseeing, stop by a bar for a light lunch. For quick meals, bars usually have trays of cheap, premade sandwiches (panini, on a baguette; *piadine,* on flatbread; *tramezzini,* on crustless white bread; or *toasts,* on, well, toast)—some are delightfully grilled. They'll sometimes have a variety of salads ready to serve up from under the glass counter.

Ordering: If the bar isn't busy, you can probably just order and pay when you leave. Otherwise, there's a particular procedure: First look around to decide what you want, then go to the cashier *(la cassa)* to order and pay. Often, a list with two sets of prices is posted near the cashier: *al banco* (standing at the bar) or *al tavolo* (seated). Unless you really plan to settle in and watch the world go by, have your drink at the bar. If you're not sure, you can ask, "Same price if I sit or stand?": *"Costa uguale al tavolo o al banco?"* (KOH-stah oo-GWAH-lay ahl TAH-voh-loh oh ahl BAHN-koh).

Upon paying, you're handed a receipt *(scontrino)*. Take that to the bartender (whose clean fingers handle no dirty euros) and say what you want. It's customary to set a small coin or two on the bar, as a tip, when you place your order. Throughout Italy, you can get cheap coffee at the bar of any establishment, no matter how fancy, and pay the same low, government-regulated price (generally about a euro if you stand).

Tavola Calda Bars and *Rosticcerie*

For a fast and cheap lunch, find an Italian variation on the corner deli: a *rosticceria* ("roasting place," specializing in roasted meats and accompanying sides, such as roasted potatoes or sautéed greens) or a *tavola calda* bar (a "hot table" point-and-shoot cafeteria with a buffet spread of meat and vegetables; sometimes called *tavola fredda*). For a healthy light meal, ask for a mixed plate of vegetables with a hunk of mozzarella (*piatto misto di verdure con mozzarella;* pee-AH-toh MEE-stoh dee vehr-DOO-ray). Don't be limited by what's displayed. If you'd like a salad with a slice of cantaloupe and some cheese, they'll whip that up for you. With a pointing finger, you can assemble a fine meal. If something's a mystery, ask for *un assaggio* (oon ah-SAH-joh) to get a little taste. To have your choices warmed up, ask for them to be heated (*riscaldata;* ree-skahl-DAH-tah).

Wine Bars

Wine bars *(enoteche)* are a popular, fast, and generally inexpensive option for lunch. Meaning "wine library," an *enoteca* is usually a bar highlighting local wines, accompanied with well-paired light food (such as *salumi* and cheese, a salad, or simple seasonal dishes). A good *enoteca* aims to impress visitors with its wine—look for a blackboard listing today's selection and price per glass. The food prices can add up—be careful with your ordering to keep this a budget choice). For more on Italian cocktails and wines, see page 294.

Aperitivo Snacks ("*Apericena*")

The Italian term *aperitivo* means a predinner drink, but it's also used to describe their version of what we might call happy hour: a few light snacks served with the order of a drink during the predinner hours (typically around 18:00 or 19:00 until 21:00). Some places offer a buffet of light bites (though these are becoming less common). The drink itself may not be cheap (typically around €8-12), but some bars offer an enticing array of *salumi,* cheeses, grilled vegetables, and other *antipasti*-type dishes.

Really good spreads earn the nickname *"apericena"*—a pun combining *aperitivo* and *cena,* dinner. It's intended as an appetizer course before heading out for dinner. For light eaters who've had a too-big lunch, this could wind up being enough to skip dinner. Drop by a few bars to scope out their *apericena* before choosing. Or opt for a place with a big view and simpler snacks—either way, you'll get your money's worth.

Markets, Groceries, and Delis: Assembling a Picnic

Picnicking saves lots of euros and is a great way to sample regional specialties. Try the fresh ricotta, *presto* pesto, shriveled olives, and anything else locals are excited about.

Markets: For the most colorful experience, gather your ingredients in the morning at a produce market. Towns big and small have markets selling everything imaginable for a fantastic picnic, including cheese, meat, bread, sweets, and prepared foods. You'll often find street-food stalls tucked into the marketplace as well (note that many markets close in the early afternoon).

Groceries and Delis: Another budget option is to visit a supermarket (look for the Conad, Carrefour, Esselunga, and Co-op chains), *alimentari* (neighborhood grocery), or *salumeria* (delicatessen) to pick up *salumi,* cheeses, and other picnic supplies. Some grocery stores, *salumerie,* and any *paninoteca* or *focacceria* (sandwich shop) can make a sandwich to order. Just point to what you want, and they'll stuff it into a *panino.* Almost every grocery store has a deli case with prepared items like stuffed peppers, marinated olives, lasagna, and chicken, all usually sold by weight; if you want it reheated, remember the word *riscaldata.* And *rosticcerie* sell cheap food to go—you'll find options such as lasagna, rotisserie chicken, and sides, including roasted potatoes and spinach. For more on *salumi* and cheeses, see those sections, later.

Ordering: A typical picnic for two might be fresh rolls, *un etto* (3.5 ounces) of cheese, and *un etto* of meat (sometimes ordered by the slice—*fetta*—or piece—*pezzo*). For two people, I might get *un etto* of prosciutto and *due pezzi* of bread. Add some fruit and veggies, yogurt, and juice. Total: about €10.

If ordering *antipasti* (such as grilled or marinated veggies) at a deli counter, you can ask for *una porzione* in a takeaway container *(contenitore).* Use gestures to show exactly how much you want. To set a price limit of €5 or €10 on what you order, say *"Da [cinque/dieci] euro, per favore."* The word *basta* (BAH-stah; enough) works as a question or as a statement.

Shopkeepers are happy to sell small quantities of produce, but it's customary to let the merchant choose for you. Say *"per oggi"* (pehr OH-jee; for today) and he or she will grab you something ready to eat. To avoid being overcharged, know the cost per kilo, study the weighing procedure, and do the math. Remember that a kilo is 2.2 pounds.

ITALIAN CUISINE STAPLES

Much of your Italian eating experience will likely involve the big five: pizza, pasta, *salumi,* cheese, and gelato. Here's a rundown on what you might find on menus and in stores. For more food help, consider *Rick Steves Italy for Food Lovers* or the *Rick Steves Italian*

Phrase Book & Dictionary, both of which have menu decoders and plenty of useful phrases for navigating the culinary scene.

Pizza

Naples is rightfully proud of its heritage as the birthplace of pizza. Here are some of the pizzas you might see at restaurants or at a pizzeria. Note that if you ask for pepperoni on your pizza, you'll get *peperoni* (green or red peppers); instead, try requesting *salsiccia piccante* (spicy sausage) or *salame piccante* (spicy salami).

Bianca: White pizza with no tomatoes

Capricciosa: Prosciutto, mushrooms, olives, and artichokes—literally the chef's "caprice"

Carciofi: Artichokes

Diavola: Spicy hot

Funghi: Mushrooms

Margherita: Tomato sauce, mozzarella, and basil—the red, white, and green of the Italian flag

Marinara: Tomato sauce, oregano, garlic, no cheese

Napoletana: "Naples style"—mozzarella, anchovies, and tomato sauce

Ortolana or ***vegetariana:*** "Greengrocer-style," with vegetables

Quattro formaggi: Four different cheeses

Quattro stagioni: "Four seasons," with tomato, mozzarella, and usually one-quarter each of ham, mushrooms, artichokes, and olives

Salsiccia: Sausage

Siciliana: Capers, olives, and often anchovies

Pasta

In Italy, pasta is considered a *primo piatto*—a first course. There are hundreds of varieties of Italian pasta, each used to highlight a certain sauce, meat, or regional ingredient. *Pastasciutta* is dry-stored pasta, which is boiled until *al dente* (chewy, "to the tooth") and tossed with a sauce. *Pasta fresca* is fresh pasta cut into noodles and served with sauce, or cut into sheets *(sfoglie),* filled with different ingredients, folded, cooked, and then covered lightly with butter, cream, or broth.

Don't assume that dry pasta is inferior to fresh. If prepared well, it can be just as satisfying. There are two general types of dry pasta. *Pasta lunga* (long pasta) is long enough to twist around a fork: think spaghetti, linguine, and fettuccine. The noodles can be round, such as *capellini* (thin "little hairs"), *vermicelli* ("little worms"), and *bucatini* (long and hollow); or flat, such as *tagliatelle* (flat and wide) and *pappardelle* (very wide, best with meat sauces).

Pasta corta (short pasta) is smaller and in shapes that can be scooped or speared with a fork, such as penne or macaroni. It goes

Eating with the Seasons Across Italy

Italian cooks love to serve fresh produce and seafood at its tastiest. Each region in Italy has its seasonal specialties, which you'll see displayed in open-air markets. To get a plate of the freshest veggies at a fine restaurant, request *"Un piatto di verdure della stagione, per favore."* ("A plate of seasonal vegetables, please.") Italians take fresh, seasonal ingredients so seriously that a restaurant cooking with frozen ingredients *(congelato)* must note it on the menu. Here are a few examples of what's fresh when:

April-May: Romanesco (similar to cauliflower), green beans, artichokes

April-May and Sept-Oct: Black truffles

April-June: Asparagus, zucchini flowers, zucchini

May-June: Mussels, cantaloupe, loquats, strawberries

May-Aug: Eggplant, clams

July-Sept: Figs, cherries, peaches, apricots, plums

Oct-Nov: Mushrooms, white truffles, persimmons, chestnuts

Nov-Feb: Cardoon (wild artichoke)

well with creamy sauces and chunkier meat sauces. Tubular pastas come either *lisce* (smooth) or *rigate* (grooved—so sauce clings better). Many short pastas are named for their shapes, such as *conchiglie* (shells), *farfalle* (butterflies), or *cavatappi* (corkscrews).

Here's a list of common pasta toppings and sauces. On a menu, these terms are usually preceded by *alla* (in the style of) or *in* (in):

Aglio e olio: Garlic and olive oil

Alfredo: Sweet butter and heaps of Parmigiano-Reggiano cheese

Amatriciana: *Guanciale* (pork cheek), tomatoes, *pecorino romano* cheese, and chili peppers

Arrabbiata: "Angry," spicy tomato sauce with chili peppers

Bolognese: "Bologna-style" meat-and-tomato sauce

Boscaiola: "Woodsman-style," with mushrooms and sausage or ham

Brodo: Broth (typical for filled pastas)

Burro e salvia: Butter and sage

Cacio e pepe: *Pecorino romano* cheese and fresh-ground pepper

Carbonara: Raw egg, *guanciale* (pork cheek), *pecorino romano* cheese, and fresh-ground pepper

Carrettiera: Spicy and garlicky, with olive oil and little tomatoes

Diavola: "Devil-style," spicy hot

Frutti di mare: Seafood
Genovese: Basil ground with Parmigiano-Reggiano cheese, garlic, pine nuts, and olive oil; a.k.a. pesto
Gricia: Cured pork cheek and *pecorino romano* cheese
Marinara: Usually tomato, often with garlic and onions, but can also be a seafood sauce ("sailor's style")
Mollicata: Simple sauce of tomato, onion, red wine, breadcrumbs, and sometimes anchovy
Norma: Tomato, eggplant, basil, and *ricotta salata* (Sicily)
Pescatora: Seafood ("fisherman style")
Pomodoro: Tomato only
Puttanesca: Tomato sauce with anchovies and/or tuna, olives, capers, and garlic
Scoglio: Mussels, clams, and tomatoes
Sorrentina: "Sorrento-style," with tomatoes, basil, and mozzarella (usually over gnocchi)
Sugo di lepre: Rich sauce made of wild hare
Tartufi: Truffles (also called *tartufate*)
Vongole: Clams and spices

Salumi

Salumi (cured meats)—sometimes called *affettati*—are an Italian staple. While most American cold cuts are cooked, in Italy they're far more commonly cured by air-drying, salting, and smoking. While called "raw"—*crudo*—these are perfectly safe to eat.

The two most familiar types of *salumi* are *salame* and *prosciutto. Salame* is an air-dried, sometimes-spicy sausage that comes in many varieties. When Italians say *"prosciutto,"* they usually mean *prosciutto crudo*—the raw ham that air-cures on the hock and is then thinly sliced. Produced mainly in northern Italy, *prosciutto* can be either *dolce* (sweet) or *salato* (salty). Purists say the best is *prosciutto di Parma.* Squeamish eaters should avoid *testa in cassetta* (headcheese—organs in aspic) and *lampredotto* (cow stomach).

Other *salumi* may be less familiar, but no less worth trying:

Bresaola: Air-cured beef
Capocollo: Peppery pork shoulder (also called *coppa*)
Culatello: High-quality, slow-cured prosciutto
Finocchiona: *Salame* with fennel seeds
Guanciale (or ***quanciale***): Tender pork cheek
Lardo: Pork lard made fragrant with herbs and spices; the best is *lardo di Colonnata*
Lonzino: Cured pork loin
Mortadella: A finely ground pork loaf, similar to our bologna
'Nduja: Super-spicy, smoky, soft, spreadable pork sausage that's bright red and with a texture like pâté
Pancetta: Salt-cured, peppery pork-belly meat, similar to bacon

Salame di Sant'Olcese: What we'd call "Genoa salami"
Salame piccante: Spicy hot, similar to pepperoni
Soppressata: A simple dry *salame* that has some kick, common in the south
Speck: Smoked pork shoulder

Cheese

When it comes to cheese (*formaggio* or *cacio*), you're probably already familiar with most of these Italian favorites:

Asiago: Hard cow cheese that comes either *mezzano* (young and firm) or *stravecchio* (aged and pungent)
Burrata: Ball of mozzarella wrapped around a buttery center
Caciocavallo: Depending on its age, a mild to sharp cow's-milk cheese shaped like a pear
Fontina and ***Montasio:*** Semihard, nutty, Gruyère-style mountain cheeses
Gorgonzola: Pungent, blue-veined cheese, either *dolce* (creamy) or *piccante* (aged and sharp)
Grana or ***Grana padano:*** Hard, nutty cheese used for grating; a less expensive alternative to Parmigiano-Reggiano
Mascarpone: Sweet, buttery, spreadable dessert cheese
Mozzarella di bufala: Made from the milk of water buffaloes
Parmigiano-Reggiano: Hard and nutty cow cheese, ideal for grating over pasta
Pecorino: Sheep's cheese, either *fresco* (fresh and soft) or *stagionato* (aged, sometimes called *pecorino romano* and popular for grating)
Provolone: Rich, firm, aged cow cheese
Ricotta: Soft and creamy, made by "recooking" cheese curds a second time; ***ricotta salata*** ("salted") is hard and used for grating
Scamorza: Similar to mozzarella, but often smoked

Gelato

American and Italian ice cream are similar but decidedly not the same. Italy's gelato is denser and creamier (even though it has less butterfat than ice cream) than American versions, and connoisseurs swear it's more flavorful.

A key to gelato appreciation is sampling liberally and choosing flavors that go well together. At a *gelateria,* ask, as Italians do, for a taste: *"Un assaggio, per favore?"* (oon ah-SAH-joh pehr fah-VOH-ray).

Most *gelaterie* clearly display prices and sizes. Point to the price or say what you want—for instance, for a €3 cup, say: *"Una coppetta da tre euro"* (OO-nah koh-PEH-tah dah tray EH-oo-roh).

The best *gelaterie* display signs reading *artigianale, nostra produzione,* or *produzione propria,* indicating that the gelato is made on the premises. Seasonal flavors are also a good sign, as are mellow hues (avoid colors that don't appear in nature). Gelato stored in covered metal tins (rather than white plastic) is more likely to be homemade. The chain called Grom is the Starbucks of Italian gelato: It's an acceptable choice, but try to find something more local.

Other Italian frozen treats include *sorbetto* (sorbet—made with fruit, but no milk or eggs), *granita* or *grattachecca* (a cup of slushy ice with flavored syrup), and *cremolata* (a gelato-*granita* float). *Caffè affogato* is a scoop of gelato "drowned" in a shot of hot espresso.

Classic gelato flavors include:

Bacio: Chocolate hazelnut, named for Italy's popular "kiss" candies
Caffè: Coffee
Cassata: With dried fruits
Ciliegia: Cherry
Cioccolato: Chocolate
Crema: Plain (similar to vanilla)
Croccantino: "Crunchy," with toasted nut bits
Fior di latte: Creamy milk
Fragola: Strawberry
Frutti di bosco: Mixed berries
Gianduia (or ***gianduja***): Chocolate-hazelnut
Lampone: Raspberry
Limone: Lemon
Macedonia: Mixed fruits
Malaga: Similar to rum raisin
Menta (or ***cioccomenta***): mint or mint-chocolate
Nocciola: Hazelnut
Noce: Walnut
Pistacchio: Pistachio
Riso: With actual bits of rice mixed in
Stracciatella: Vanilla with chocolate shreds
Tartufo: Super chocolate
Zabaione: Named for the dessert of egg yolk and Marsala wine
Zuppa inglese: Sponge cake, custard, chocolate, and cream

BEVERAGES

Italian bars serve great drinks—hot, cold, sweet, caffeinated, or alcoholic.

Water, Juice, and Other Drinks

Italians are notorious water snobs. At restaurants, it's customary and never expensive to order a *litro* or *mezzo litro* (half-liter) of bottled water. Ask for *con gas* if you want fizzy water and *senza gas* if you prefer still water. You can try asking for *acqua del rubinetto* (tap water), but your server may give you a funny look—they just can't understand why you wouldn't want good water to go with your good food. Water is rarely served with ice; Italians are adamant that ice-cold drinks are bad for digestion. If you request ice, you'll likely be given a few cubes on a little saucer.

Chilled bottled water—still *(naturale)* or carbonated *(frizzante)*—is sold cheaply in stores. Half-liter bottles of mineral water are available everywhere for about €1.

Juice is *succo,* and *spremuta* means freshly squeezed. Order *una spremuta* (don't confuse it with *spumante,* sparkling wine)—it's usually orange juice *(arancia),* and from February through April it can be made from Sicilian blood oranges *(arance rosse).*

In grocery stores, you can get a liter of O.J. for the price of a Coke or coffee. Look for *100% succo* or *senza zucchero* (without sugar) on the label—or be surprised by something diluted and sugary sweet.

Tè freddo (iced tea) is usually from a can—sweetened and flavored with lemon or peach. Lemonade is *limonata.*

If you want a hot drink other than coffee, *cioccolato* is hot chocolate, and *tè* is hot tea.

Coffee

The espresso-based style of coffee so popular in the US was born in Italy. If you ask for *"un caffè,"* you'll get a shot of espresso in a little cup. Most Italian coffee drinks begin with espresso, to which varying amounts of hot water and/or steamed or foamed milk are added. The closest thing to American-style drip coffee is a *caffè americano*—a shot of espresso diluted with hot water. Milky drinks, like cappuccino or *caffè latte,* are served to locals before noon and to tourists any time of day. To an Italian, cappuccino is a morning drink; they believe having milk after a big meal impairs digestion. If they add any milk after lunch, it's just a splash, in a *caffè macchiato.*

Italians like their coffee only warm—to get it very hot, request *"Molto caldo, per favore"* (MOHL-toh KAHL-doh pehr fah-VOH-ray). Any coffee drink is available decaffeinated—ask for it *decaffeinato* (deh-kah-feh-NAH-toh).

Cappuccino: Espresso with foamed milk on top (*cappuccino freddo* is an iced cappuccino)

Caffè latte: Espresso to which heated milk is added (ordering just a "latte" gets you only milk)

Caffè macchiato: Espresso "stained" with a splash of milk, in a small cup

Latte macchiato: Layers of hot milk and foam, "stained" with an espresso shot, in a tall glass. Note that if you order simply a *"macchiato,"* you'll probably get a *caffè macchiato* (see above).

Caffè corto/lungo: Concentrated espresso diluted with a tiny bit of hot water, in a small cup. Get a ***caffè lungo*** if you want more water added.

Caffè americano: Espresso diluted with even more hot water, in a larger cup

Caffè corretto: Espresso "corrected" with a shot of grappa or brandy

Marocchino: "Moroccan" coffee with espresso, foamed milk, and cocoa powder; the similar *mocaccino* has chocolate instead of cocoa

Caffè freddo: Sweet and iced espresso

Caffè hag: Instant decaf

Alcoholic Beverages

Beer: While Italy is traditionally considered wine country, the production of craft beer *(birra artigianale)* has seen a recent and passionate growth. Even in small towns, you'll see microbreweries slinging their own brews. What's on tap is often inspired by the same trends you'll find stateside—IPAs, ambers, stouts, saisons, sours, seasonal beers, and so on. You'll also find local brews (Peroni and Moretti), as well as imports such as Heineken. Italians drink mainly lager beers. Beer on tap is *alla spina.* Get it *piccola* (33 cl, 11 oz), *media* (50 cl, about a pint), or *grande* (a liter). A *lattina* (lah-TEE-nah) is a can and a *bottiglia* (boh-TEEL-yah) is a bottle.

Cocktails and Spirits: Italians appreciate both *aperitivi* (palate-stimulating cocktails) and *digestivi* (after-dinner drinks designed to aid digestion).

The classic ***aperitivo*** is the *spritz:* prosecco (or white wine) and soda livened up with either Campari (carmine red bitters with a secret blend of herbs and orange peel) or Aperol (sweeter, softer, bright orange bitters with herbal, citrusy undertones). Vermouths (both red and white) from Carpano, Cinzano, Martini, or Riccadonna can be served straight, on the rocks, with a splash of soda, or as part of drinks like Punt e Mes (sweet red vermouth and red wine). Other choices include Americano (vermouth with bitters, brandy, and lemon peel), Garibaldi (also known as Campari-Orange, a mixture of Campari and orange juice), and Cynar (bitters flavored with artichoke).

Digestivo choices fall into three categories. First is the bittersweet, syrupy herbal drink called *amaro* (many restaurants have their own brew; popular commercial brands are Fernet Branca and Montenegro). For something sweeter, try *limoncello* (lemon), *amaretto* (almond), Frangelico (hazelnut), *sambuca* (anise), or Marsala wine. Grappa is a brandy distilled from grape skins and stems; *stravecchio* is an aged, mellower variation. *Acquavite* ("water of life") is similar to grappa, but distilled from fruit such as apples, berries, or plums.

Wine: The ancient Greeks who colonized Italy more than

Ordering Wine

To order a glass of red or white wine, say, *"Un bicchiere di vino rosso/bianco."* House wine comes in a carafe; choose from a quarter-liter pitcher (8.5 oz, *un quarto*), half-liter pitcher (17 oz, *un mezzo*), or one-liter pitcher (34 oz, *un litro*). When ordering, have some fun, gesture like a local, and you'll have no problems speaking the language of the *enoteca. Salute!*

English	Italian
wine	*vino* (VEE-noh)
house wine	*vino della casa* (VEE-noh DEH-lah KAH-zah)
glass	*bicchiere/calice* (bee-kee-EH-ray/KAH-lee-chay)
bottle	*bottiglia* (boh-TEEL-yah)
carafe	*caraffa* (kah-RAH-fah)
red	*rosso* (ROH-soh)
white	*bianco* (bee-AHN-koh)
rosé	*rosato* (roh-ZAH-toh)
sparkling	*spumante/frizzante* (spoo-MAHN-tay/freed-ZAHN-tay)
dry	*secco* (SEH-koh)
fruity	*fruttato* (froo-TAH-toh)
full-bodied	*corposo/pieno* (kor-POH-zoh/pee-EH-noh)
sweet	*dolce* (DOHL-chay)

2,000 years ago called it Oenotria—land of the grape. Centuries later, Galileo wrote, "Wine is light held together by water." Wine *(vino)* is certainly a part of the Italian culinary trinity—grape, olive, and wheat. (I'd add gelato.) Ideal conditions for grapes (warm climate, well-draining soil, and an abundance of hillsides) make the Italian peninsula a paradise for grape growers, winemakers, and wine drinkers.

In most years, Italian winemakers produce more wine than any other country—more than 4 million liters annually. Production is mainly red *(rosso)* and white *(bianco)* wines. Rosé *(rosato)* is less traditional—though as it's become trendy stateside and elsewhere, more Italian vintners are experimenting with it. A sparkling wine is *frizzante* or *spumante;* prosecco is a bubbly white wine from northeastern Italy.

Wines of Campania

In almost every part of Italy, you'll find wine varieties designed to go with the regional cuisine. In Campania, which includes Naples, Sorrento, and nearby, plentiful sun and volcanic soils provide great wine-growing conditions. The wine tradition here goes back 2,000 years to the Greeks, and Campania is famous for producing two of Italy's most ancient whites: the mineral Greco di Tufo and the flavorful Fiano di Avellino. Among the more modern wines, Taurasi is an excellent ruby-colored, full-bodied red. And Lacryma Christi ("tears of Christ") comes in both a medium-bodied red and a dry and fruity white.

Even if you're clueless about wine, the information on an Italian wine label can help you choose something decent. Terms you may see on the bottle include *classico* (from a defined, select area), *annata* (year of harvest), *vendemmia* (harvest), and *imbottigliato dal produttore all'origine* (bottled by producers).

In general, Italy designates its wines by one of four official categories:

Vino da Tavola (VDT) is table wine made from grapes grown anywhere in Italy. It's often inexpensive, but Italy's wines are so good that, for many people, a basic *vino da tavola* is just fine with a meal. Many restaurants, even modest ones, take pride in their house wine *(vino della casa),* bottling their own or working with wineries. These days a *vino da tavola* can also be a high-end niche wine—the price will tell you.

Denominazione di Origine Controllata (DOC) meets national standards for high-quality wine. Made from grapes in a defined area, these are usually quite affordable and good.

Denominazione di Origine Controllata e Guarantita (DOCG), the highest grade, meets national standards for the highest-quality wine (made with grapes from a defined area whose quality is "controlled and guaranteed"). These wines can be identified by the pink or green label on the neck...and the high price. (*Riserva* indicates a DOC or DOCG wine that's been aged for even longer than required.)

Indicazione Geografica Tipica (IGT) is a broad group of wines that don't meet the standard for DOC or DOCG status but have been designated as "typical" of a particular region.

If you're on a tight budget, try looking for a more affordable alternative. For example, in Tuscany, the world-famous Brunello di Montalcino (a DOCG) can break the bank, but Rosso di Montalcino (a DOC)—made in the same zone with similar grapes, in

Hurdling the Language Barrier

Many Italians—especially those in the tourist trade and in big cities—speak English. Still, you'll get better treatment if you learn and use Italian pleasantries. In smaller, nontouristy towns, English is less common. Italians have an endearing habit of talking to you even if they know you don't speak their language—and yet, thanks to gestures and thoughtfully simplified words, it somehow works. Don't stop them to tell them you don't understand every word—just go along for the ride. For a list of survival phrases, see the appendix.

Note that Italian is pronounced much like English, with a few exceptions, such as: *c* followed by *e* or *i* is pronounced ch (to ask, *"Per centro?"* "To the center?" you say, pehr CHEHN-troh). In Italian, *ch* followed by *e* or *i* is pronounced like the hard c in Chianti (*chiesa*—church—is pronounced kee-AY-zah). Adding a vowel to the English word often gets you close to the Italian one. Give it your best shot. Italians appreciate your efforts.

For more tips on hurdling the language barrier, consider the *Rick Steves Italian Phrase Book* (available at RickSteves.com).

a similar way, but aged for a shorter period of time—costs half as much.

Staying Connected

Your mobile phone is an indispensable tool for efficient travel. Fortunately, staying connected in Europe gets easier (and less expensive) each year. You can use your devices much like you do at home, either by getting an international plan or connecting to free Wi-Fi whenever possible. Another option is to buy a European SIM card for your phone. More details are at RickSteves.com/phoning.

USING YOUR PHONE IN EUROPE

Here are some budget tips and options.

Prepare your phone. Before your trip, stock your device with any content or apps you'll want on the road. Helpful tools include Google Translate, Google Maps, your airline's app, public transit apps for your destinations, and sight-specific apps (such as museum audioguides). Also download maps if you plan to use offline navigation, and TV shows or movies to watch on the plane or during downtime.

Sign up for an international plan. To stay connected at an affordable cost, sign up for an international service plan through your carrier. Most providers offer a simple bundle that includes calling,

How to Dial

Here's how to dial from anywhere in the US or Europe, using the phone number of one of my recommended Florence hotels as an example (055 213 154). If a non-Italian number starts with 0, drop it when dialing internationally.

From a US Mobile Phone

Phone numbers in this book are presented exactly as you would dial them from a US mobile phone. For international access, press and hold 0 (zero) to get a + sign, then dial the country code (39 for Italy) and phone number.

▸ To call the Florence hotel from any location, dial +39 055 213 154.

From a US Landline

Replace + with 011 (US/Canada access code), then dial the country code (39 for Italy) and phone number.

▸ To call the Florence hotel from your home landline, dial 011 39 055 213 154.

From a European Landline

Replace + with 00 (Europe access code), then dial the country code (39 for Italy, 1 for the US) and phone number.

▸ To call the Florence hotel from a Spanish landline, dial 00 39 055 213 154.

▸ To call my US office from an Italian landline, dial 00 1 425 771 8303.

From One Italian Phone to Another

To place a domestic call (from an Italian landline or mobile), drop +39 and dial the phone number.

▸ To call the Florence hotel from Rome, dial 055 213 154.

More Dialing Tips

Local Numbers: European phone numbers and area codes can vary in length and spacing, even within the same country. Mobile phones use separate prefixes (for instance, in Italy, landlines begin with 0, and mobile numbers begin with 3).

Toll and Toll-Free Calls: It's generally not possible to dial European toll or toll-free numbers from a US mobile or landline. Look for a direct-dial number instead.

Calling the US from a US Mobile Phone, While Abroad: Dial +1, area code, and number.

More Phoning Help: See howtocallabroad.com.

messaging, and data. Your normal plan may already include international coverage (for example, T-Mobile's covers unlimited text and low-speed data, plus reasonable per-minute voice calls).

Use free Wi-Fi whenever possible. In Europe, look for and use Wi-Fi for most online tasks. Most accommodations in Europe offer free Wi-Fi. Many cafés offer hotspots for customers; ask for the password when you buy something. You may also find Wi-Fi at TIs, city squares, major museums, public transit hubs, and airports, and aboard trains and buses.

Tips on Internet Security

Whether using a laptop or phone on the road, make sure it's running the latest versions of its operating system, security software, and apps. Ensure that your device and apps are password-protected (enable facial recognition where possible). If two-factor authentication is an option, activate it.

Use only secure, password-protected Wi-Fi. Ask the hotel or café staff for the specific name of their network, and make sure you log on to that exact one.

To access sensitive information (such as bank accounts), use a dedicated app, and ideally a cellular connection, which is more secure than a shared Wi-Fi network. Or consider subscribing to a VPN (virtual private network). If you're using the Safari browser on an Apple device, an encryption feature called "Private Relay" works in a similar way.

Minimize the use of your cellular network. The best way to make sure you're not accidentally burning through data is to put your device in "airplane" mode (which also disables phone calls and texts) and connect to Wi-Fi as needed. Turn on your cellular network (or turn off airplane mode) only when you can't find Wi-Fi.

Save large-data tasks for Wi-Fi. If your included data is slow or metered, wait until you're on Wi-Fi to make video calls, download audio tours or apps, stream videos, or do other megabyte-greedy tasks. Navigation apps such as Google Maps require lots of data; download maps when you're on Wi-Fi, then use the app offline.

Limit automatic updates. By default, your device constantly checks for a data connection and updates app content. Check your device's menu for ways to turn this off.

Use Wi-Fi calling and messaging apps. WhatsApp, FaceTime, and Google Meet are great for making free or low-cost calls or sending texts over Wi-Fi worldwide. WhatsApp is especially popular throughout Europe and is often the easiest way to communicate with guides, drivers, or other local contacts.

Consider buying a European SIM or eSIM card. Both give you a European phone number and access to local calling and data rates; if you're traveling to other countries within the EU, there are no additional roaming fees. Physical SIM cards can be purchased at mobile-phone shops and inserted into your (unlocked) phone; electronic SIM cards (or eSIMs) can be purchased online and downloaded. In Italy, you'll be required to register the SIM card with your passport as an antiterrorism measure.

Damage Control for Lost Phones: Losing your phone can be a significant inconvenience. Before you leave home, make sure your device is set up for automatic cloud backups, and enable the "find my phone" feature (make sure you have access to it from another device, like your travel partner's phone or a laptop). Familiarize yourself with your phone's "lost and lock" mode, which you can enable from another device if your phone goes missing. Report the loss to your mobile carrier; if your phone remains lost, use the "wipe" feature to erase its data.

MAIL

For details on sending packages to your own home or to others, visit CBP.gov, then select "Travel" and "Know Before You Go." The Italian postal service works fine, but for quick transatlantic delivery (in either direction), consider services such as DHL (www.dhl.com).

Transportation

If your trip will cover more of Italy than just Naples and the Amalfi Coast, you may need to take a long-distance train or bus, rent a car, or fly. Buses are an alternative to trains (and may be your only option for reaching some small Italian towns), but they are generally slower and less efficient. Renting a car is great for touring the countryside elsewhere in Italy, but not in this region. I give some specifics on trains, buses, and flights here. For more detailed information on transportation throughout Europe, including car rental and driving tips, see RickSteves.com/transportation.

TRAINS

To travel by train affordably within Italy, you can simply buy tickets as you go. For travelers ready to lock in dates and times weeks or months in advance for longer trips, buying nonrefundable tickets online can cut costs in half. Note that the Italy rail pass is generally not a good value, but if your travel extends beyond Italy, then a Eurail Global Pass might be worth looking into. For advice on figuring out the smartest train-ticket or rail-pass options for your trip, visit the Trains & Rail Passes section of my website at RickSteves.com/rail.

Types of Trains

Most trains in Italy are operated by the state-run **Trenitalia** company (www.trenitalia.com, a.k.a. Ferrovie dello Stato Italiane, abbreviated FS). Ticket prices depend on the speed of the train, so it helps to know the different types of trains: pokey Regionale (R or REG), medium-speed Regionale Veloce (RV), fast InterCity (IC) and EuroCity (EC), and super-fast Frecce trains.

Regional trains offer only open seating (no assigned seats for love nor money). All other trains have assigned seats, which are built into your ticket for a specific date and time. If you're traveling with a rail pass, you'll need to buy a separate seat reservation if riding a fast train (see "Rail Passes," later).

The private train company Italo (www.italotreno.it) runs fast trains on major routes serving large cities on the mainland but few small towns. Italo has fewer departures than Trenitalia but its service is comparable to Trenitalia's Frecce service, with similar prices and advance purchase discounts. In Naples, Milan, and Rome, a few departures use secondary stations. Italo does not accept rail passes but is a worthy alternative for point-to-point tickets.

Both train companies have call centers for answering general questions (Trenitalia: daily 7:00-24:00, +39 06 5210 550, option 1 for English; Italo: daily 6:00-23:00, +39 06 8937 1892). Trenitalia and Italo don't cooperate. If you buy a ticket for one train line, it's not valid on the other. Both companies tend to ignore the other's schedules.

Schedules

Check schedules at Trenitalia.it and ItaloTreno.it (domestic journeys only) or use their apps; for international trips, use Bahn.com (Germany's excellent all-Europe schedule website, which reflects national railways but not private companies like Italo). At the train station, the easiest way to check schedules is at a ticket machine. Enter the desired date, time, and destination to see all your options. Printed schedules are also posted at the station (yellow posters show departures—*partenze;* white posters show arrivals).

Schedules list the time of departure *(ora)*, the type of train *(treni)*, and service classes offered *(classi servizi)*—first- and second-class cars, dining car, *cuccetta* berths, and whether you need reservations (usually denoted by an R in a box). The train's destination *(principali fermate destinazioni)* is shown, along with intermediate stops, and notes such as "also stops in..." *(ferma anche a...)*, "doesn't stop in..." *(non ferma a...)*, "stops in every station" *(ferma in tutte le stazioni)*, "delayed..." *(ritardo...)*, and so on.

At the station, look at the electronic display to find your train's track *(binario)* number. Remember that your destination may be listed as an intermediate (not final) stop. For example, if you're going from Naples to Rome, you'll notice that virtually all northbound Frecciarossa trains stop in Rome, regardless of their final

Italy's Public Transportation
SWITZERLAND
To Innsbruck
San Candido
Brennero
St. Moritz
Locarno
DOLO- MITES
Kast.
Geneva
Lugano
Men.
Bolzano
Domodossola
Tirano
Mtn. Lift
Varenna
Trento
Chamonix
Pré-Saint-Didier
Stresa
Como
Riva
La Palud
Gallarate
Aosta
Bergamo
Vicenza
Malpensa
To Lyon & Paris
Milan
Desezano
Verona
Modane
Cremona
Mantova
Torino
Parma
Genoa
Santa Margherita Ligure
Modena
FRANCE
Bologna
Vernazza
Florence
To Paris
Finale
CINQUE TERRE
La Spezia
Lucca
Marseille
Ventimiglia
Pisa
Livorno
To Barcelona
Nice
San Gim.
Ligurian Sea
Volterra
Poggi.
Siena
Bastia
ELBA
Piombino
Civitavecchia
Mediterranean Sea
CORSICA (FRANCE)
Porto Torres
Olbia
SARDINIA
100 Kilometers
100 Miles
Chilivani
To Cagliari
To Naples
To Aeolian Islands
To Naples & Rome
To Tunis
Palermo
Milazzo
Messina
Villa San Giovanni
Trapani
Cefalù
Reggio Calabria
Marsala
SICILY
Enna
Taormina
To Cagliari
Castelvetrano
Catania
Ionian Sea
See detail map
Agrigento
Mediterranean Sea
Piazza Armerina
Ragusa
Siracusa
To Tunis
Same scale as main map

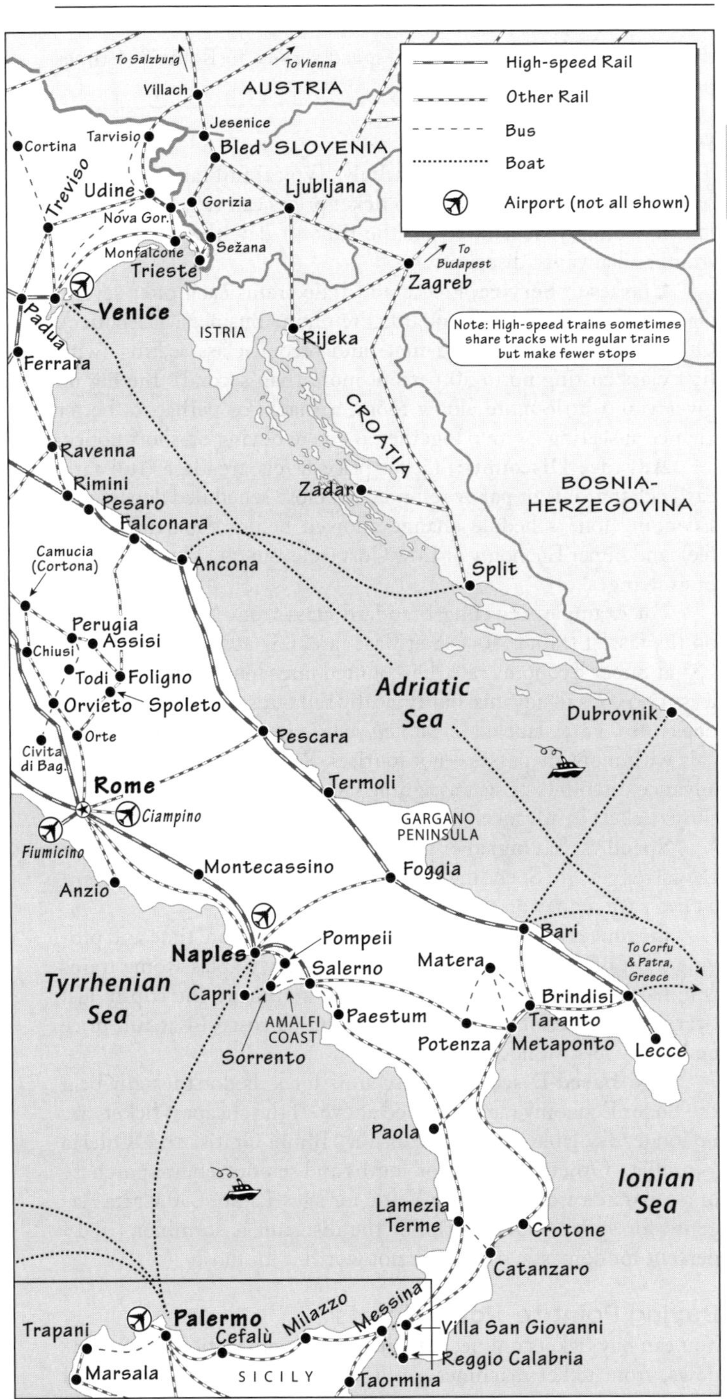
High-speed Rail
Other Rail
Bus
Boat
Airport (not all shown)
Note: High-speed trains sometimes share tracks with regular trains but make fewer stops
To Salzburg
To Vienna
AUSTRIA
Villach
Jesenice
Bled
SLOVENIA
Tarvisio
Cortina
Treviso
Udine
Gorizia
Ljubljana
Nova Gor.
Monfalcone
Sežana
Trieste
To Budapest
Zagreb
Venice
Padua
ISTRIA
Rijeka
Ferrara
CROATIA
Ravenna
Rimini
Pesaro
Falconara
Zadar
BOSNIA-HERZEGOVINA
Camucia (Cortona)
Ancona
Split
Perugia
Assisi
Chiusi
Todi
Foligno
Spoleto
Orvieto
Orte
Adriatic Sea
Dubrovnik
Civita di Bag.
Pescara
Rome
Termoli
Ciampino
Fiumicino
GARGANO PENINSULA
Montecassino
Foggia
Anzio
Bari
Pompeii
Naples
Salerno
Matera
To Corfu & Patra, Greece
Tyrrhenian Sea
Capri
Brindisi
AMALFI COAST
Paestum
Taranto
Potenza
Metaponto
Lecce
Sorrento
Paola
Ionian Sea
Lamezia Terme
Crotone
Catanzaro
Trapani
Palermo
Cefalù
Milazzo
Messina
Villa San Giovanni
Reggio Calabria
Marsala
SICILY
Taormina

destination. This results in high-speed service to Rome 3-4 times per hour through most of the day.

Point-to-Point Tickets

Train tickets are a good value in Italy. Typical full fares are shown on the map on page 306, though ticket prices can vary for the same journey, mainly depending on the time of day, the speed of the train, and advance discounts.

Classes of Service: Frecce and Italo trains each offer several classes of service (e.g., Standard, Premium, Business, Executive). Other trains offer standard first- and second-class seating (with first class costing up to 50 percent more than second). Buying up gives you a little more elbow room, a snack, or perhaps a better chance at seating a group together, if you're buying on short notice.

Advance Discounts: Ticket price levels are Base (full fare, easily changeable or partly refundable before scheduled departure), Economy (one schedule change allowed before departure, for a fee), and Super Economy or Low Cost (sells out quickly, no refunds or exchanges).

For example, traveling Standard class from Naples to Rome on the fastest train costs €48 at Base fare, €37 at Economy fare, or €35 at Super Economy rate. Discounted fares must be purchased at least two days in advance but typically sell out several weeks before departure. Fares labeled *servizi abbonati* are available only for locals with monthly passes—not tourists. Regional trains don't offer advance discounts or seat assignments, so there's little need to buy those tickets in advance.

Speed vs. Savings: For point-to-point tickets, you'll pay more the faster you go. Spending a modest amount of extra time in transit can save money on shorter trips.

On longer mainline routes, fast trains save more time and provide most of the service. For example, speedy Naples-Rome trains run 3-4/hour, cost €35 in second class, and make the trip in just over an hour; less frequent InterCity trains cost €14 at full price and take over two hours.

Age-Based Discounts: Discounts for kids don't usually beat the Super Economy rate described above. If the cheapest tickets are no longer available, look for deals like "Bimbi Gratis" and "Offerta Famiglia." Other discounts for youths and seniors require purchase of a separate card (€40 Carta Verde for ages 12-26, €30 Carta Argento for ages 60 and over), but the discount is so minor (10-15 percent for domestic travel), it's not worth it for most.

Buying Point-to-Point Tickets

You can buy tickets online, with an app, at train station ticket windows, from ticket machines, or at travel agencies. For long-haul runs or travel on a busy weekend or holiday, it can be cheaper to buy tickets in advance and lock in a seat assignment. But because most Italian trains run frequently and there's no deadline to buy tickets, for the most part I prefer to keep my travel plans flexible by purchasing tickets as I go.

It's easy to buy tickets **online** at Trenitalia.com or ItaloTreno.it. On either website, choose English and be sure to read the pricing info, as many of the cheaper tickets are not refundable or changeable. You can keep the ticket on your mobile device (either as a PDF or with a QR code), or you can print it out. Or download the Trenitalia or Italo **app** to your phone—both have English versions that make ticket-buying a breeze.

At the train station, avoid lines by using the **ticket machines** in station halls. You'll be able to easily purchase tickets for travel within Italy, make seat reservations, and even book a *cuccetta* (koo-CHEH-tah; overnight berth). If you do use the **ticket windows,** be sure you're in the correct line: *biglietti* (general tickets), *prenotazioni* (reservations), *nazionali* (domestic), and *internazionali.* Some big stations have counters (close to the tracks) marked "Last Minute," which let you jump the line if your train is departing soon.

Trenitalia's ticket machines are user-friendly and found in all but the tiniest stations in Italy. You can pay with cash (change given when indicated) or by debit or credit card (even for small amounts, but you may need to enter your PIN—even when using "tap-to-pay"). Select English, then your destination. If you don't immediately see the city you're traveling to, keep keying in the spelling until it's listed. You can choose from first- and second-class seats, request tickets for more than one traveler, and pick seats, when applicable. Don't select a discount rate without being sure that you meet the criteria (for example, Americans are not eligible for certain EU or resident discounts).

To buy tickets at the station for **Italo** trains, look for a dedicated service counter (in most major stations) or a red ticket machine labeled *Italo.*

Some **international tickets** can't be bought online or from machines; for these tickets and anything else that requires a real person, you must go to a ticket window at the station. A good alternative, though, is to drop by a local travel agency. Agencies sell domestic and international tickets and make reservations. They charge a small fee, but the language barrier (and the lines) can be smaller than at the station's ticket windows.

Rail Passes

The single-country Eurail Italy Pass may save you money if you take several long train rides or prefer first-class travel, but for most people it's not a good value. Most train travelers in Italy take rela-

Rail Pass or Point-to-Point Tickets?

Will you be better off buying a rail pass or point-to-point tickets? It pays to know your options and choose what's best for your itinerary.

Rail Passes

A Eurail Italy Pass lets you travel by train in Italy for three to eight days (consecutively or not) within a one-month period. Italy is also covered (along with most of Europe) by the classic Eurail Global Pass.

Discounted rates are offered for seniors (age 60 and up) and youths (ages 12-27). Up to two kids (ages 4-11) can travel free with each adult-rate pass (but not with senior rates). All rail passes offer a choice of first or second class for all ages.

While most rail passes are delivered electronically, it's smart to get your pass sorted before leaving home. For more on rail passes, including current prices and purchasing, visit RickSteves.com/rail.

Point-to-Point Tickets

Italian train tickets are relatively cheap, and most include seat reservations, making them the best deal for most travelers. Use this map to add up approximate pay-as-you-go fares for your itinerary, and compare that to the price of a rail pass plus reservations. Keep in mind that significant discounts on point-to-point tickets may be available with advance purchase.

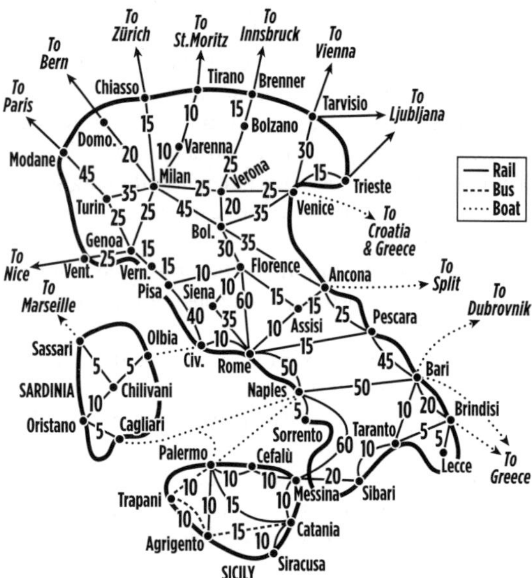

Map shows approximate costs, in US dollars, for one-way, second-class tickets on faster trains.

tively short rides on the Milan-Venice-Florence-Rome circuit. For these trips, it can be cheaper to buy point-to-point tickets. Remember that rail passes are valid on Trenitalia trains but not on Italo trains.

Furthermore, a rail pass doesn't offer much hop-on convenience in Italy, since even with a rail pass, seat reservations are required for InterCity, EuroCity, and Frecce trains (€5-15 each; make seat reservations at station ticket windows or at Eurail.com for €2 more). Most regional trains (such as Florence-Pisa-Cinque Terre service) don't require (or offer) reservations. Reservations for berths on overnight trains cost extra and aren't covered by rail passes.

If you're also traveling by train in other countries, consider a Eurail Global Pass. Although it covers most of Europe, prices can work for trips as short as three travel days or as long as three months.

Train Tips

Validating Tickets: An open ticket (generally for a *regionale* train) bought from a ticket desk or machine must be validated (date-stamped) before you board (the ticket may say *da convalidare* or *convalida*). To validate it, before getting on the train, stamp your ticket in the machine near the platform (usually marked *convalida biglietti* or *vidimazione*). An open *regionale* ticket bought online must be validated online before boarding the train. Once you validate a ticket, you must complete your trip within the stamped timeframe (usually about four hours). If you forget to validate your ticket, go right away to the train conductor—or you'll pay a fine.

In big-city stations, you may need to show your ticket to a staff member to access the tracks. Tickets for fast trains, which include a reserved seat *(biglietto con prenotazione)*, don't need validation; you can just get on board.

Getting a Seat: If you're taking an unreserved *regionale* train that originates at your departure point (e.g., you're catching the Naples-Rome train in Naples), arriving at least 15 minutes before the departure time will help you snare a seat.

Baggage Storage: Many Italian stations have *deposito bagagli* where you can safely leave your bag for a standardized but steep price (double-check closing hours; they may ask to photocopy your passport). Due to security concerns, no Italian stations have lockers.

Theft: In big cities, exercise caution and prudence at train stations to avoid thieves and con artists. If someone helps you to find your train or carry your bags, be aware that they are not an official porter; they are simply hoping for some cash. And if someone other than a uniformed railway employee tries to help you use the ticket machines, politely refuse. Italian trains are famous for their thieves. Never leave a bag unattended. Police do ride the trains, cutting down on theft. Still, for an overnight trip, I'd feel safe only in a *cuccetta* (a bunk in a special sleeping car with an attendant who keeps track of who comes and goes while you sleep—an additional €40 or more).

Strikes: Strikes, which are common, generally last a day (often a Friday). Train employees will simply explain, *"Sciopero"* (SHOH-peh-roh, strike). But in actuality, a minimum amount of "essential" or "guaranteed" *(garantito)* main-line service is maintained (by law) during strikes. When a strike is pending, travel agencies, savvy hoteliers, and station personnel can check to see when the strike will go into effect and which trains will continue to run. Revised schedules may be posted online and in Italian at stations. Visit Trenitalia.com, choose English, then "Information and Contacts" and "In Case of Strike" (but detailed info will be in Italian).

If your train is canceled, your reserved-seat ticket will likely be accepted on any similar train running that day (either earlier or later than the original departure time) but you won't have a seat assignment. Tickets for canceled trains should also be exchangeable without penalty ahead of the original departure time, or can be refunded (have an agent mark it "unused," and check refund deadlines). A rail pass works on any train still operating, but partially used rail passes can't be refunded—so make full use of any pass you have to continue your trip.

BUSES

You can usually get anywhere you want in Italy by bus, as long as you're not in a hurry and you plan ahead (pick up bus schedules online or at local TIs or bus stations). For reaching small towns, buses are sometimes the only option if you don't have a car.

Long-distance buses are a cheaper alternative to the train, using modern coaches, often with free Wi-Fi. They're especially useful on routes poorly served by train, or to allow a direct connection instead of having to change trains. Some of the operators you'll see are FlixBus (www.flixbus.com) and Marozzi (www.marozzivt.it). In general, orange buses are local city buses, and blue buses are for long distances.

Larger towns have a (usually chaotic) long-distance bus station *(stazione degli autobus* or *autostazione),* with ticket windows and several stalls (usually labeled *corsia, stallo,* or *binario*)—but to save time, buy your ticket at a travel agent or online; many companies use etickets (they'll scan your emailed QR code as you board). Smaller towns—where buses are more useful—often have a central bus stop *(fermata),* likely along the main road or on the main square, and maybe several more scattered around town. In small towns, buy bus tickets at newsstands or tobacco shops (with the big *T* signs). When buying your ticket, confirm the departure point *("Dov'è la fermata?")*.

Before boarding, confirm the destination with the driver. You are expected to stow big bags underneath the bus (if the compartment is closed, ask the driver for help; which compartment you use may depend on your destination). If you'll be continuing on later by bus, upon arrival, double-check that the posted schedule lists your next destination and departure time.

Traveling by bus on Sundays and holidays can be problematic; even from large cities, schedules are sparse, departing buses are jam-packed, and ticket offices are often closed. Plan ahead and buy your ticket in advance. Most travel agencies book bus (and train) tickets for a small fee.

TAXIS AND RIDE-BOOKING SERVICES

Most Italian taxis are reliable and cheap. Often, two people can travel short distances by cab for little more than the cost of bus or subway tickets.

In many cities, you can use an app called **Free Now** to hail a taxi. This can be a convenient alternative to calling a dispatcher or finding a taxi stand; prices are fixed up front, and you can pay with a credit card (through the app).

Uber and other ride-booking apps operate in some parts of Europe, and rides can be cheaper than taxis. However, the details may differ from location to location. In some places, Uber works just like back home; in others, the app looks the same, but it hails a regular taxi rather than a private car. Uber is banned in some cities and countries, though sometimes similar companies operate where Uber cannot. In Italy, Uber faces legal challenges, and may not be consistently available.

FLIGHTS

To compare flights, begin with a search engine: Easy-to-use Google Flights is the top site for flights to and within Europe, Kayak has price alerts, and Skyscanner includes many inexpensive flights within Europe. Before you book, be sure to read the small print about change or cancellation policies, and the costs for "extras" such as reserving a seat, checking a bag, or printing a boarding pass.

Flights to Europe: Start looking for international flights about four to six months before your trip, especially for peak-season travel. Depending on your itinerary, it can be efficient and no more expensive to fly into one city and out of another.

Flights Within Europe: Flying between European cities is surprisingly affordable, though it leaves a larger carbon footprint than a train or bus. Before buying a long-distance train or bus ticket, check the cost of a flight on one of Europe's airlines, whether a major carrier or a no-frills outfit like Easyjet or Ryanair. Be aware that flying with a discount airline can have drawbacks, such as minimal customer service, strict carry-on size or weight limits, hidden fees (read the fine print carefully), and time-consuming treks to secondary airports.

EU Air Passenger Rights: Tourists are covered by Europe's generous consumer protections for airline passengers. For any flight within the EU—and for flights into and out of the EU operated by European airlines—you're entitled to compensation for delays of three or more hours (or if your flight is canceled or rescheduled, or a connection is missed). The service FlightRight.com walks you through the steps to apply for compensation.

Resources from Rick Steves

Begin Your Trip at RickSteves.com

My expansive **website** is *the* place to explore Europe in preparation for your trip. You'll find thousands of fun articles, beautiful photos, videos, and radio interviews; a wealth of money-saving tips for planning your dream trip; travel news dispatches; a video library of travel talks; our latest guidebook updates (RickSteves.com/update); and the free Rick Steves Audio Europe app. You can also follow me on Facebook, Instagram, and other social media channels.

To add context to your trip, we've compiled a list of recommended books, films, and TV shows that feature Italy. See RickSteves.com/travelreading.

Our **Travel Forum** is a well-groomed collection of message boards where our travel-savvy community answers questions and shares their personal travel experiences—and our well-traveled staff chimes in when they can be helpful (RickSteves.com/forums).

Our **online Travel Store** offers bags and accessories that I've designed to help you travel smarter and lighter. These include my popular carry-on bags (which I live out of four months a year), money belts, totes, toiletries kits, adapters, guidebooks, and planning maps (RickSteves.com/shop).

Our website can also help you find the perfect **rail pass** for your itinerary and your budget, with easy, one-stop shopping for rail passes, seat reservations, and point-to-point tickets (RickSteves.com/rail).

Rick Steves' Tours, Guidebooks, TV Shows, and More

Small-Group Tours: Want to travel with greater efficiency and less stress? We offer more than 40 itineraries reaching the best destinations in this book...and beyond. Each year more than 30,000 travelers join us on about 1,000 Rick Steves bus tours. You'll enjoy great guides and a fun bunch of travel partners (with small groups of 24 to 28 travelers). You'll find European adventures to fit every vacation length. For all the details, and to book a tour, visit RickSteves.com/tours or call us at +1 425 771 8303.

Books: This book is just one of many in my series on European travel, which includes country and city guidebooks, Snapshots (excerpted chapters from bigger guides), Pocket guides (full-color little books on big cities), "Best Of" guidebooks (condensed, full-color country guides), and my budget-travel skills handbook, *Rick Steves Europe Through the Back Door.* A complete list of my titles—including phrase books, cruising guides, and travelogues on European art, history, and culture—appears near the end of this book.

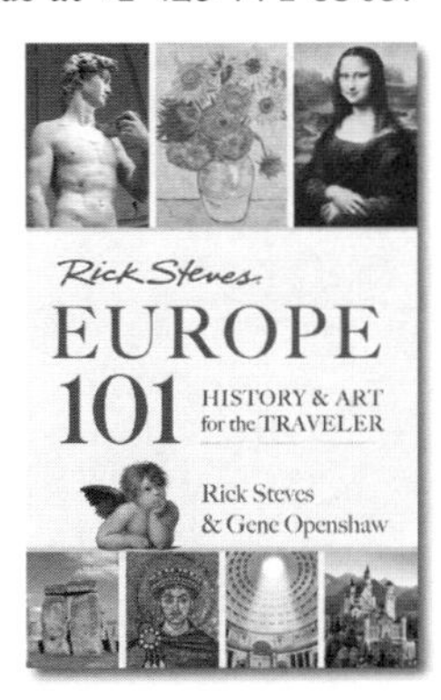

TV Shows and Video Library: My public television series, *Rick Steves' Europe,* covers Europe from top to bottom with more than 100 half-hour episodes—and we're working on new shows every year. Watch full episodes for free (RickSteves.com/tv). My free online video library, Rick Steves Classroom Europe, offers a searchable database of short video clips on European history, culture, and geography (Classroom.RickSteves.com).

Monday Night Travel Talks: To raise your travel I.Q., join our virtual travel party every Monday, featuring travel experts discussing European destinations, art, culture, food, travel tips, and more. Stream the live events or check out the video recordings (RickSteves.com/mnt).

Audio Tours on My Free App: I've produced more than 60 free, self-guided audio tours of the top sights in Europe. For those tours and other audio content, get my free **Rick Steves Audio Europe app,** an extensive online library organized by destination. For more on my app, visit RickSteves.com/audioeurope.

Radio: My weekly public radio show, *Travel with Rick Steves,* features interviews with travel experts from around the world. It airs on 500 public radio stations across the US. An archive of programs is available at RickSteves.com/radio.

Podcasts: You can enjoy my travel content via several free podcasts. The podcast version of my radio show brings you a weekly, hour-long travel conversation. My other podcasts include a selection of video clips from my public television show and video recordings of my travel classes (RickSteves.com/podcasts).

APPENDIX

Conversions

Numbers and Stumblers

- Europeans write a few of their numbers differently than we do. 1 =1, 4 =4, 7 =7.
- In Europe, dates appear as day/month, so Christmas is 25/12.
- Commas are decimal points and decimals commas. A dollar and a half is 1,50, one thousand is 1.000, and there are 5.280 feet in a mile.
- When counting with fingers, start with your thumb. If you hold up your first finger to request one item, you'll probably get two.
- What Americans call the second floor of a building is the first floor in Europe.
- On escalators and moving sidewalks, Europeans keep the left "lane" open for passing. Keep to the right.

Metric Conversions

A **kilogram** equals 1,000 grams (about 2.2 pounds). One hundred **grams** (a common unit at markets) is about a quarter-pound. One **liter** is about a quart, or almost four to a gallon.

A **kilometer** is six-tenths of a mile. To convert kilometers to miles, cut the kilometers in half and add back 10 percent of the original (120 km: 60 + 12 = 72 miles). One **meter** is 39 inches—just over a yard.

1 foot = 0.3 meter	1 square yard = 0.8 square meter
1 yard = 0.9 meter	1 square mile = 2.6 square kilometers
1 mile = 1.6 kilometers	1 ounce = 28 grams
1 centimeter = 0.4 inch	1 quart = 0.95 liter
1 meter = 39.4 inches	1 kilogram = 2.2 pounds
1 kilometer = 0.62 mile	32°F = 0°C

Roman Numerals

In the US, you'll see Roman numerals—which originated in ancient Rome—used for copyright dates, clocks, and the Super Bowl. In Italy, you're likely to observe these numbers chiseled on statues and buildings. If you want to do some numeric detective work, here's how: In Roman numerals, as in ours, the highest numbers (thousands, hundreds) come first, followed by smaller numbers. Many numbers are made by combining numerals into sets: V = 5, so VIII = 8 (5 plus 3). Roman numerals follow a subtraction principle for multiples of fours (4, 40, 400, etc.) and nines (9, 90, 900, etc.); the number four, for example, is written as IV (1 subtracted from 5), rather than IIII. The number nine is IX (1 subtracted from 10).

Big numbers such as dates can look daunting at first. The easiest way to handle them is to read the numbers in discrete chunks. For example, Michelangelo was born in MCDLXXV: M (1,000) + CD (100 subtracted from 500, or 400) + LXX (50 + 10 + 10, or 70) + V (5) = 1475. It was a very good year.

M = 1000	XC = 90	IX = 9
CM = 900	L = 50	V = 5
D = 500	XL = 40	IV = 4
CD = 400	X = 10	I = duh
C = 100		

Clothing Sizes

When shopping for clothing, use these US-to-European comparisons as general guidelines (but note that no conversion is perfect).

Women: For pants and dresses, add 36 in Italy (US 10 = Italian 46). For blouses and sweaters, add 32 for most of Europe (US 8 = European 40). For shoes, add 30-31 (US 7 = European 37/38).

Men: For dress shirts, multiply by 2 and add about 8 (US 15 = European 38). For jackets and suits, add 10. For shoes, add 32-34.

Children: Clothing is sized by height—in centimeters (2.5 cm = 1 inch), so a US size 8 roughly equates to 132-140. For shoes up to size 13, add 16-18, and for sizes 1 and up, add 30-32.

Packing Checklist

Whether you're traveling for five days or five weeks, you won't need more than this. Pack light to enjoy the sweet freedom of true mobility.

Clothing

- ❑ 5 shirts: long- & short-sleeve
- ❑ 2 pairs pants (or skirts/capris)
- ❑ 1 pair shorts
- ❑ 5 pairs underwear & socks
- ❑ 1 pair walking shoes
- ❑ Sweater or warm layer
- ❑ Rainproof jacket with hood
- ❑ Tie, scarf, belt, and/or hat
- ❑ Swimsuit
- ❑ Sleepwear/loungewear

Toiletries

- ❑ Basics: soap, shampoo, toothbrush, toothpaste, floss, deodorant, sunscreen, brush/comb, etc.
- ❑ Medicines & vitamins
- ❑ First-aid kit
- ❑ Glasses/contacts/sunglasses
- ❑ Face masks & hand sanitizer
- ❑ Sewing kit
- ❑ Packet of tissues (for WC)
- ❑ Earplugs

Money

- ❑ Debit & credit cards
- ❑ Hard cash (US $100-200)
- ❑ Money belt

Electronics

- ❑ Mobile phone
- ❑ Camera & related gear
- ❑ Tablet/ebook reader/laptop
- ❑ Headphones/earbuds
- ❑ Chargers & batteries
- ❑ Plug adapters

Documents

- ❑ Passport (with ETIAS/ETA if required)
- ❑ Driver's license, International Driving Permit (if required), student ID, etc.
- ❑ Tickets & confirmations: flights, hotels, trains, rail pass, car rental, sight entries
- ❑ Copies of important documents
- ❑ Insurance details
- ❑ Guidebooks & maps

Miscellaneous

- ❑ Laundry supplies
- ❑ Small umbrella
- ❑ Travel alarm/watch
- ❑ Water bottle

Optional Extras

- ❑ Second pair of shoes
- ❑ Travel hairdryer
- ❑ Picnic supplies
- ❑ Disinfecting wipes
- ❑ Fold-up tote bag
- ❑ Small flashlight
- ❑ Small towel or washcloth
- ❑ Inflatable pillow/neck rest
- ❑ Tiny lock
- ❑ Extra passport photos

Italian Survival Phrases

Hello. (informal)	Ciao.	chow
Good day.	Buongiorno.	bwohn-**jor**-noh
Do you speak English?	Parla inglese?	**par**-lah een-**gleh**-zay
Yes. / No.	Si. / No.	see / noh
I (don't) understand.	(Non) capisco.	(nohn) kah-**pees**-koh
Please.	Per favore.	pehr fah-**voh**-ray
Thank you.	Grazie.	**graht**-see-ay
You're welcome.	Prego.	**preh**-go
I'm sorry.	Mi dispiace.	mee dee-spee-**ah**-chay
Excuse me.	Mi scusi.	mee **skoo**-zee
No problem.	Non c'è problema.	nohn cheh proh-**bleh**-mah
Goodbye.	Arrivederci.	ah-ree-veh-**dehr**-chee
one / two / three	uno / due / tre	**oo**-noh / **doo**-ay / tray
four / five / six	quattro / cinque / sei	**kwah**-troh / **cheeng**-kway / **seh**-ee
seven / eight	sette / otto	**seh**-tay / **oh**-toh
nine / ten	nove / dieci	**noh**-vay / dee-**ay**-chee
How much is it?	Quanto costa?	**kwahn**-toh **koh**-stah
Write it?	Me lo scrive?	may loh **skree**-vay
Is it free?	È gratis?	eh **grah**-tees
Is it included?	È incluso?	eh een-**kloo**-zoh
Where can I buy / find...?	Dove posso comprare / trovare...?	**doh**-vay **poh**-soh kohm-**prah**-ray / troh-**vah**-ray
I'd like / We'd like...	Vorrei / Vorremmo...	voh-**reh**-ee / voh-**reh**-moh
...a room.	...una camera.	**oo**-nah **kah**-meh-rah
...a ticket to ___.	...un biglietto per ___.	oon beel-**yeh**-toh pehr ___
Is it possible?	È possibile?	eh poh-**see**-bee-lay
Where is...?	Dov'è...?	doh-**veh**
...the train station	...la stazione	lah staht-see-**oh**-nay
...tourist information	...informazioni turisti	een-for-maht-see-**oh**-nee too-**ree**-stee
...the bathroom	...il bagno	eel **bahn**-yoh
men / women	uomini, signori / donne, signore	**woh**-mee-nee, seen-**yoh**-ree / **doh**-nay, seen-**yoh**-ray
left / right / straight	sinistra / destra / sempre dritto	see-**nee**-strah / **deh**-strah / **sehm**-pray **dree**-toh
What time does this open / close?	A che ora apre / chiude?	ah kay **oh**-rah **ah**-pray / kee-**oo**-day
At what time?	A che ora?	ah kay **oh**-rah
Just a moment.	Un momento.	oon moh-**mehn**-toh
now / soon / later	adesso / presto / tardi	ah-**deh**-soh / **preh**-stoh / **tar**-dee
today / tomorrow	oggi / domani	**oh**-jee / doh-**mah**-nee

In an Italian Restaurant

I'd like / We'd like...	Vorrei / Vorremmo...	voh-**reh**-ee / voh-**reh**-moh
...to reserve a table for one / two.	...prenotare un tavolo per uno / due.	preh-noh-**tah**-ray oon **tah**-voh-loh pehr **oo**-noh / **doo**-ay
...the menu (in English).	...il menù (in inglese).	eel meh-**noo** (een een-**gleh**-zay)
Is this seat free?	È libero questo posto?	eh **lee**-beh-roh **kweh**-stoh **poh**-stoh
service (not) included	servizio (non) compreso	sehr-**veet**-see-oh (nohn) kohm-**pray**-zoh
cover charge	(pane e) coperto	(**pah**-nay ay) koh-**pehr**-toh
to go	da portar via	dah **por**-tar **vee**-ah
with / without	con / senza	kohn / **sehnt**-sah
and / or	e / o	ay / oh
breakfast / lunch / dinner	(prima) colazione / pranzo / cena	(**pree**-mah) koh-laht-zee-**oh**-nay / **prahn**-zoh / **chay**-nah
fixed-price meal (of the day)	menù (del giorno)	meh-**noo** (dehl **jor**-noh)
specialty of the house	specialità della casa	speh-chah-lee-**tah** **deh**-lah **kah**-zah
appetizer	antipasto	ahn-tee-**pah**-stoh
first course	primo (piatto)	**pree**-moh (pee-**ah**-toh)
main course	secondo (piatto)	seh-**kohn**-doh (pee-**ah**-toh)
side dishes	contorni	kohn-**tor**-nee
cold cuts / bread / cheese	salumi / pane / formaggio	sah-**loo**-mee / **pah**-nay / for-**mah**-joh
sandwich	panino	pah-**nee**-noh
soup / salad	zuppa / insalata	**tsoo**-pah / een-sah-**lah**-tah
meat / chicken	carne / pollo	**kar**-nay / **poh**-loh
fish / seafood	pesce / frutti di mare	**peh**-shay / **froo**-tee dee **mah**-ray
fruit / vegetables	frutta / verdure	**froo**-tah / vehr-**doo**-ray
dessert	dolce	**dohl**-chay
tap water	acqua del rubinetto	**ah**-kwah dehl roo-bee-**neh**-toh
mineral water	acqua minerale	**ah**-kwah mee-neh-**rah**-lay
still / sparkling	naturale / frizzante	nah-too-**rah**-lay / freet-**zahn**-tay
(orange) juice	succo (d'arancia)	**soo**-koh (dah-**rahn**-chah)
coffee / tea / milk	caffè / tè / latte	kah-**feh** / teh / **lah**-tay
wine / beer	vino / birra	**vee**-noh / **bee**-rah
red / white	rosso / bianco	**roh**-soh / bee-**ahn**-koh
glass / bottle	bicchiere / bottiglia	bee-kee-**eh**-ray / boh-**teel**-yah
Cheers!	Salute! / Cin cin!	sah-**loo**-tay / cheen cheen
The bill, please.	Il conto, per favore.	eel **kohn**-toh pehr fah-**voh**-ray
Do you accept credit cards?	Accettate carte di credito?	ah-cheh-**tah**-tay **kar**-tay dee **kreh**-dee-toh
Delicious!	Delizioso!	day-leet-see-**oh**-zoh

For more user-friendly Italian phrases, check out *Rick Steves Italian Phrase Book* or *Rick Steves French, Italian, & German Phrase Book.*

INDEX

C

INDEX

W

INDEX

MAP INDEX

Start your trip at

Our website enhances this book and turns

Explore Europe

At ricksteves.com you can browse through thousands of articles, videos, photos and radio interviews, plus find a wealth of money-saving travel tips for planning your dream trip. And with our mobile-friendly website, you can easily access all this great travel information anywhere you go.

TV Shows

Preview the places you'll visit by watching entire half-hour episodes of *Rick Steves' Europe* (choose from all 100 shows) on-demand, for free.

ricksteves.com

your travel dreams into affordable reality

Radio Interviews

Enjoy ready access to Rick's vast library of radio interviews covering travel tips and cultural insights that relate specifically to your Europe travel plans.

Travel Forums

Learn, ask, share! Our online community of savvy travelers is a great resource for first-time travelers to Europe, as well as seasoned pros.

Travel News

Subscribe to our free Travel News e-newsletter, and get monthly updates from Rick on what's happening in Europe.

Classroom Europe®

Check out our free resource for educators with 500 short video clips from the *Rick Steves' Europe* TV show.

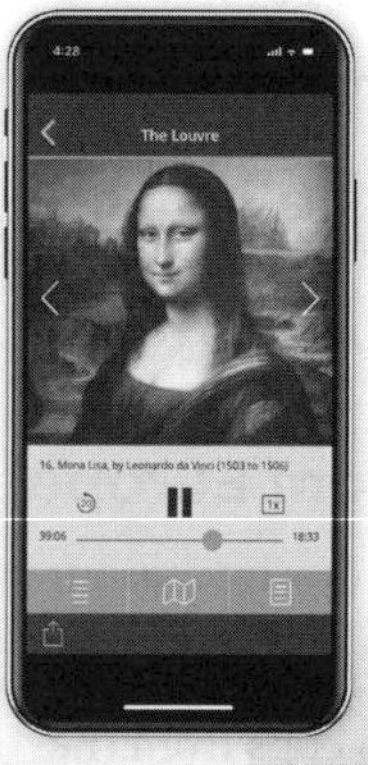

Rick Steves has

Experience maximum Europe

Save time and energy

This guidebook is your independent-travel toolkit. But for all it delivers, it's still up to you to devote the time and energy it takes to manage the preparation and logistics that are essential for a happy trip. If that's a hassle, there's a solution.

Rick Steves Tours

A Rick Steves tour takes you to Europe's most interesting places with great

A Guide for Every Trip

BEST OF GUIDES

Full-color guides in an easy-to-scan format. Focused on top sights and experiences in the most popular European destinations

Best of England
Best of Europe
Best of France
Best of Germany
Best of Ireland
Best of Italy
Best of Portugal (coming in 2026)
Best of Scotland
Best of Spain

HE BEST OF ROME

ne, Italy's capital, is studded with an remnants and floodlit-fountain res. From the Vatican to the Colos- , with crazy traffic in between, Rome derful, huge, and exhausting. The s, the heat, and the weighty history of the Eternal City where Caesars walked can make tourists wilt. Recharge by taking siestas, gelato breaks, and after-dark walks, strolling from one atmospheric square to another in the refreshing evening air.

*d **Pantheon**—which st dome until the ly 2,000 years old y over 1,500).*

*f Athens in the **Vat**- lies the humanistic e.*

ladiators fought nother, entertaining

COMPREHENSIVE GUIDES

City, country, and regional guides printed on Bible-thin paper. Packed with detailed coverage for exploring iconic sights and venturing off the beaten path

Amsterdam & the Netherlands
Barcelona
Belgium: Bruges, Brussels, Antwerp & Ghent
Berlin
Budapest
Central Europe
Croatia & Slovenia
England
Florence & Tuscany
France
Germany
Great Britain
Greece
Iceland
Ireland
Istanbul
Italy
London
Naples & the Amalfi Coast
Paris
Portugal
Prague & the Czech Republic
Provence & the French Riviera
Rome
Rome, Florence & Venice
Scandinavia
Scotland
Sicily
Spain
Switzerland
Venice
Vienna, Salzburg & Tirol

Rick Steves books are available from your favorite bookseller. Most guides are available as ebooks.

POCKET GUIDES

Compact color guides for shorter trips

Amsterdam
Athens
Barcelona
Florence
Italy's Cinque Terre
London
Munich & Salzburg
Paris
Prague
Rome
Venice
Vienna

SNAPSHOT GUIDES

Focused single-destination coverage

Basque Country: Spain & France
Copenhagen & the Best of Denmark
Dublin
Edinburgh
Krakow, Warsaw & Gdansk
Lisbon
Madrid & Toledo
Milan & the Italian Lakes District
Nice & the French Riviera
Normandy
Norway
Sevilla, Granada & Andalucía

TRAVEL SKILLS & SPECIALTY GUIDES

References for smart travel, eating well in Italy, and cruise ports of call

Europe Through the Back Door
Italy for Food Lovers
Mediterranean Cruise Ports

Complete your library with...

CULTURE & TRAVELOGUES

Gain insight on history and culture

Europe 101
Europe's Top 100 Masterpieces
European Christmas
European Easter
European Festivals
For the Love of Europe
On the Hippie Trail
Travel as a Political Act

PHRASE BOOKS & DICTIONARIES

Print alternative to online translators

French
French, Italian & German
German
Italian
Portuguese
Spanish

PLANNING MAPS

Uncluttered and round-trip tough

Britain & Ireland with London
Europe
France with Paris
Germany, Austria & Switzerland
Iceland
Ireland
Italy
Portugal
Scotland
Spain & Portugal

Credits

RESEARCHERS

For help with this edition, Rick relied on...

Rosie Leutzinger

Rosie's love of travel was ingrained at an early age, thanks to vacations to visit her British mother's family. Opportunities to play softball for Great Britain's national team, and professionally in Austria and Japan, turned that love of travel into an obsession. An editor and researcher at Rick Steves' Europe, she spends her free time exploring the Puget Sound region and watching women's sports.

CONTRIBUTOR

Gene Openshaw

Gene has co-authored more than a dozen books with Rick, specializing in Europe's art, history, and culture. In particular, their *Europe 101: History and Art for the Traveler* and *Europe's Top 100 Masterpieces* have helped bring European art to life. Gene also writes for Rick's television shows, produces the audio tours, and is a regular guest on Rick's radio show. For public TV, Gene has co-authored two television specials with Rick: *Fascism in Europe* and the ambitious six-hour series *Art of Europe.* Outside of the travel world, Gene has composed an opera called *Matter,* a violin sonata, and dozens of songs. Gene lives near Seattle, where he roots for the Mariners in good times and bad. Check out his latest book on art, travel, and love: *Michelangelo at Midlife.*

ACKNOWLEDGMENTS

Thanks to Risa Laib for her 25-plus years of dedication to the Rick Steves guidebook series.

PHOTO CREDITS

Front Cover: Positano © johnwaddell, Getty Images

Back Cover (Dreamstime.com, left to right): Villa Rufolo, Ravello © Janoka82; Neapolitan pizza © Konstantin Malkov; Temple of Hera, Paestum © minnystock

Dreamstime.com: 2 (bottom) © Dzianis Rabtsevich; 15 (top) © Mdfotori; 15 (bottom) © Dmitrii Moroz; 61 © Marcobrivio6; 189 © Gigavisual; 265 © Areg43

Additional Photography: Dominic Arizona Bonuccelli, Ben Cameron, Claire Conway, Orin Dubrow, Cameron Hewitt, Suzanne Kotz, Rosie Leutzinger, Addie Mannan, Gene Openshaw, Rick Steves, Gretchen Strauch, Ian Watson. Photos are used by permission and are the property of the original copyright owners.

Avalon Travel
Hachette Book Group
555 12th Street, Suite 1850
Oakland, CA 94607 USA

Printed in China by RR Donnelley
First Edition. First printing November 2025.

ISBN 978-1-64171-665-9

For the latest on Rick's talks, guidebooks, tours, public television series, and public radio show, contact Rick Steves' Europe, 130 Fourth Avenue North, Edmonds, WA 98020, +1 425 771 8303, RickSteves.com, rick@ricksteves.com.

Rick Steves' Europe
Managing Editor: Jennifer Madison Davis
Editorial Group Manager: Cathy Lu
Editors: Kim Eckart, Glenn Eriksen, Ellen Hurst, Suzanne Kotz, Rosie Leutzinger, Teresa Nemeth, Jessica Shaw, Carrie Shepherd, Chelsea Wing
Researcher: Rosie Leutzinger
Contributor: Gene Openshaw
Creative Director: Sandra Hundacker
Maps & Graphics: Claire Conway, Orin Dubrow, David C. Hoerlein, Lauren Mills, Mary Rostad

Avalon Travel
Senior Managing Editor: Madhu Prasher
Managing Editors: Jamie Andrade, Sierra Machado
Copy Editor: Maggie Ryan
Proofreader: Elizabeth Jang
Indexer: Stephen Callahan
Production and Typesetting: Lisi Baldwin, Rue Flaherty, Jane Musser, Ravina Schneider
Cover Design: Kimberly Glyder Design
Maps & Graphics: Kat Bennett

COLOR MAPS

Naples • Naples Transportation • Amalfi Coast & Naples Area

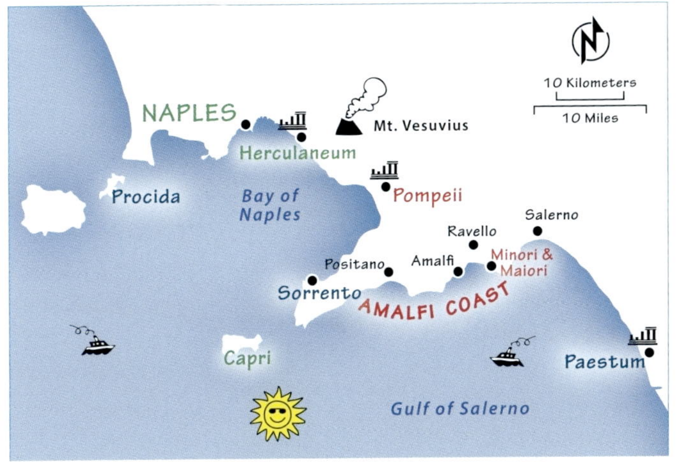

Naples

To Capodimonte
SANITÀ
JAGO MUS.
VIA FORIA
VIA MATERDEI
To Materdei
SANTA TERESA
Cavour (Line 2)
Piazza Cavour
PORTA SAN GENNARO
MADRE ART MUSEUM
VIA SETTEMBRINI
ARCHAEOLOGICAL MUSEUM
VIA STA. TERESA
VIA SALVATOR ROSA
Museo (Line 1)
VIA M. LONGO
VIA DUOMO
VIA DONNAREGINA
DUOMO
GALLERIA PRINCIPE
VIA S. M. COST.
VIA CONTE DI RUVO
NAPOLI SOTTERRANEA
S. PAOLO
PIO MONTE MIS.
VIA SAPIENZA
VIA PESSINA
BELLINI THEATER
VIA BELLINI
Piazza Bellini
VIA O SOLE MIO
V. ATRI
S. GREG. ARMENO
S. LORENZO MAGGIORE
SALITA PONCORVO
V. PORT' ALBA
VIA DEI TRIBUNALI
CAPPELLA SANSEVERO
Dante (Line 1)
Piazza Dante
PORT' ALBA
SAN DOM.
Piazza San Dom. Maggiore
NILE STATUE
V. NILO
BAR NILO
VIA S. BIAGIO
D'AURIA SHOP
"SPACCA NAPOLI"
TARSIA
SAN SEB.
GESÙ NUOVO
VIA B. CROCE
VIA PALADINO
VIA GRAN ARCHIVIO
Montesanto (Line 2)
MONTESANTO FUNICULAR
Piazza Sette Settembre
Piazza Gesù Nuovo
SANTA CHIARA
To San Martino/ Vomero District
VIA MADDALONI
CLOISTER
VIA S.G. PIGNA.
V. CAND.
VIA MEZZO
S. CHIARA
VIA P. SCURA
VIA PIGNASECCA
Piazza Monte.
CALATA TRINITÀ MAGGIORE
VIA MONTEOLIVETO
STREET MARKET
Piazza Carità
VIA TOLEDO
FASCIST BLDG.
POST
V. DONNALBINA
VIA SEDILE DI PORTO
CORSO UMBERTO I
VIA PORTA DI MASSA
MARADONA
VIA BATT.
Pompeii Shuttle
Università (Line 1)
Piazza Bovio
VIA S. MARIA
BNL BANK
Piazza Matteotti
VIA S. FELICE
V. CAMPO
CALATA PORTA DI MASSA (CAR FERRY TERMINAL)
VIA A. DIAZ
Toledo (Line 1)
VIA MEDINA
VIA A. DEPRETIS
VIA A. D. GASPERI
VIA PORTA. E MONTE.
VIA SPER.
VICO LUNGO
Piazza Immacolatella
SPANISH QUARTER
VIA PORTA DI TAPPIA
VIA COLOMBO
V. S. GIACOMO
BANCO DI NAPOLI
Piazza Municipio
VICO TOFA
V. IMBRIANI
Municipio (Line 1)
PEDESTRIAN UNDERPASS
PINTAURO
BANCA INTESA SANPAOLO
V. D'AFF.
Piazza Municipio
Alibus (to Airport)
CENTRALE FUNICULAR
V. S. BRIG.
GALLERIA UMBERTO I
CASTEL NUOVO
BERIO
V. MAD.
VIA SAN CARLO
TEATRO SAN CARLO
VIA AM. FERD. ACTON
STAZIONE MARITTIMA (CRUISE TERMINAL)
To Chiaia District & Lungomare Promenade
VIA CHIAIA
GRAN CAFFÈ GAMBRINUS
ROYAL PALACE
MOLO BEVERELLO DOCK (HYDROFOIL & FAST FERRY)
V. SERRA
TUNNEL TO LUNGOMARE
Piazza del Plebiscito
GALLERIA BORBONICA
SAN FRANCESCO DI PAOLA
V. CONSOLE
VIA ACTON
To Castel dell'Ovo, Chiaia District, Lungomare Harborside Promenade & Posillipo Hill

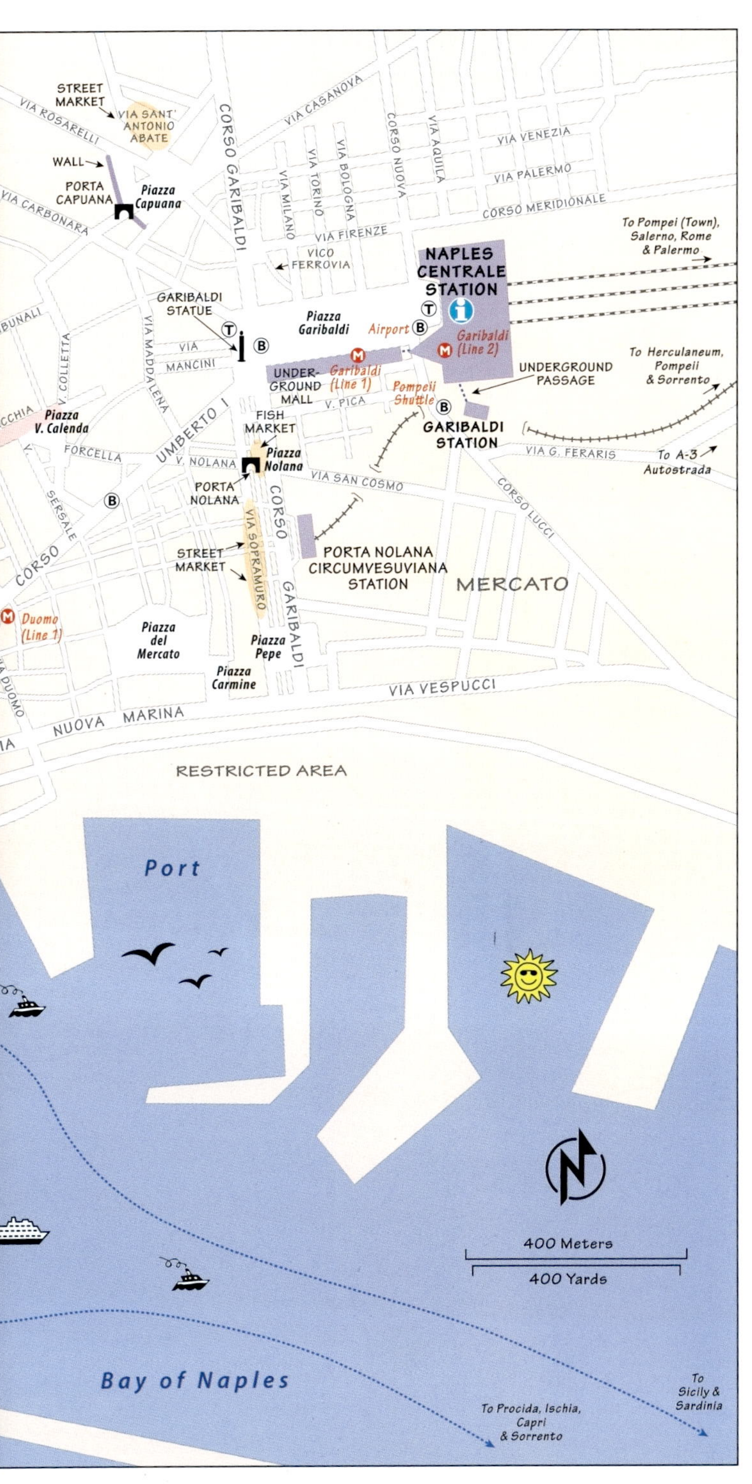
STREET MARKET
VIA SANT' ANTONIO ABATE
VIA ROSARELLI
WALL
PORTA CAPUANA
Piazza Capuana
VIA CARBONARA
CORSO GARIBALDI
VIA CASANOVA
VIA MILANO
VIA TORINO
VIA BOLOGNA
CORSO NUOVA
VIA AQUILA
VIA VENEZIA
VIA PALERMO
CORSO MERIDIONALE
VIA FIRENZE
VICO FERROVIA
NAPLES CENTRALE STATION
To Pompei (Town), Salerno, Rome & Palermo
GARIBALDI STATUE
Piazza Garibaldi
Airport
Garibaldi (Line 2)
VIA MANCINI
VIA MADDALENA
UNDER-GROUND MALL
Garibaldi (Line 1)
UNDERGROUND PASSAGE
To Herculaneum, Pompeii & Sorrento
Pompeii Shuttle
V. PICA
GARIBALDI STATION
V. COLLETTA
Piazza V. Calenda
UMBERTO I
FISH MARKET
Piazza Nolana
V. NOLANA
FORCELLA
VIA G. FERARIS
To A-3 Autostrada
VIA SAN COSMO
CORSO LUCCI
PORTA NOLANA
SERSALE
CORSO
VIA SOPRAMURO
STREET MARKET
PORTA NOLANA CIRCUMVESUVIANA STATION
MERCATO
CORSO GARIBALDI
Duomo (Line 1)
Piazza del Mercato
Piazza Pepe
Piazza Carmine
VIA VESPUCCI
NUOVA MARINA
RESTRICTED AREA
Port
400 Meters
400 Yards
Bay of Naples
To Procida, Ischia, Capri & Sorrento
To Sicily & Sardinia

Naples Transportation
To Piscinola/ Scampia
CAPODIMONTE MUSEUM
Policlinico
Line 1
CAPODIMONTE
Rione Alto
Not to Scale
SANITÁ
ARCHAEOLOGICAL MUSEUM
Montedonzelli
Museo
Line 1
Materdei
Salvator Rosa
Medaglie d'Oro
Dante
Montesanto
Line 1
Quattro Giornate
Montesanto
MONTESANTO
Morghen
Vanitelli
Piazza Fuga
SAN MARTINO
Toledo
Cimarosa
SPANISH QUARTER
CHIAIA
CENTRALE
VOMERO
Parco Margherita
Amedeo
SAN CARLO
CHIAIA
Chiaia
Arco Mirelli
San Pasquale
Piazza del Plebiscito
Line 2
Piazza della Vittoria
Bus #140
To Pozzuoli
SANTA LUCIA
LUNGOMARE HARBORSIDE PROMENADE
Manzoni
BORGO MARINERO
MERGELLINA
Mergellina
CASTEL DELL'OVO
MERGELLINA DOCK
To Posillipo
Bay of